Ode to My Mother's Voice and Other Poems

Ode to My Mother's Voice and Other Poems

Loretta Diane Walker

LITERARY PRESS
LAMAR UNIVERSITY

ISBN: 978-1-942956-71-6
Library of Congress Control Number:2019944576

Cover art: Chris Rodgers

Lamar University Literary Press
Beaumont, Texas

In Loving Memory of Mary Agatha Walker

Recent Poetry from Lamar University Literary Press

Bobby Aldridge, *An Affair of the Stilled Heart*
Walter Bargen, *My Other Mother's Red Mercedes*
Mark Busby, *Through Our Times*
Julie Chappell, *Mad Habits of a Life*
Stan Crawford, *Resisting Gravity*
Chip Dameron, *Waiting for an Etcher*
Glover Davis, *My Cap of Darkness*
William Virgil Davis, *The Bones Poems*
Jeffrey DeLotto, *Voices Writ in Sand*
Chris Ellery, *Elder Tree*
Alan Gann, *That's Entertainment*
Larry Griffin, *Cedar Plums*
Michelle Hartman, *Irony and Irrelevance*
Katherine Hoerth, *Goddess Wears Cowboy Boots*
Michael Jennings, *Crossings: A Record of Travel*
Gretchen Johnson, *A Trip Through Downer, Minnesota*
Ulf Kirchdorfer, *Chewing Green Leaves*
Jim McGarrah, *A Balancing Act*
J. Pittman McGehee, *Nod of Knowing*
Laurence Musgrove, *One Kind of Recording*
Godspower Oboido, *Wandering Feet on Pebbled Shores*
Carol Coffee Reposa, *Underground Musicians*
Jan Seale, *The Parkinson Poems*
Steven Schroeder, *the moon, not the finger, pointing*
Glen Sorestad, *Hazards of Eden*
Vincent Spina, *The Sumptuous Hills of Gulfport*
W.K. Stratton, *Ranchero Ford/ Dying in Red Dirt Country*
Wally Swist, *Invocation*
Loretta Diane Walker, *Desert Light*
Dan Williams, *Past Purgatory, a Distant Paradise*
Jonas Zdanys, *Three White Horses*

For information on these and other Lamar University Literary Press books go to www.Lamar.edu/literarypress

Gratitude

Thank you, Raymond and Glenda Walker, James Walker, Chris and Lisa Walker, Vincent and Earnestine Walker, Mark and Kimberley Schiff for your encouragement.

Thank you, to my Reagan Magnet School family and all of my friends for your support.

Thank you, Diane Frank, for your continual gentle pushes and belief in my work.

Thank you, Barbara Blanks and Cindy Huyser, for your input and insight and the time you spent with my words.

Thank you, Christine Vovakes, for sharing your beautiful butterfly photograph.

Thank you, Jax, for your continued words of encouragement and inspiration.

Thank you, Chris Rogers, for channeling your mother's voice, for gifting your painting.

Acknowledgments

I would also like to thank the editors of the following publications where some of these poems have previously appeared:

A Book of the Year: Poetry Society of Texas
Amarillo Bay
BaylorLine Magazine
Beautiful Cadaver Project Pittsburgh Dreamers Anthology
Boundless Anthology of Rio Grande Valley International Poetry Festival
Chaos Texas Mountain Trail Writers
Concho River Review
Connecticut River Review
di-verse-city: Anthology of Austin International Poetry Festival
Encore: Prize Poems of the National Federation of Poetry Societies
The Enighmatist
A Galaxy of Verse
Haight-Ashbury
Hocus Pocus
Homestead Review
Ilya's Honey
InSpirity: Anthology Sewing a Seed of Hope
The James Dickey Review
Langdon Review of the Arts in Texas Volume 15
Nomad's Choir
Pennsylvania Prize Poems Anthology
Pennessence
Poetica Magazine: Mizmor L'David Anthology Volume I: The Shoah
Poetry at Round Top Anthology
Re-Creating Our Common Chord: Wising Up Anthology
Red River Review
River Poets Journal
Sandstorm Literary Journal
San Pedro River Review
Universal Oneness: An Anthology of Opus Magnus
The Texas Observer
Texas Poetry Calendar

Unlocking the Word: An Anthology of Found Poetry
Voices de la Luna
Weaving the Terrain:100-Word Southwestern Poems
Wordfest Anthology
Words in Concert Music Anthology
Writing Texas 6

CONTENTS

Mixes Seasons

I

20 Descending the Stairs of Day
22 Variations on Glory
24 Of Falling Leaves
25 Invitation
26 Urban Dweller
28 Of Long and Longing
29 On the Return Home, the Sun Boycotted the Sky
30 About Nothing
31 Waiting in Line at Starbucks
32 Trilogy on Seasons

II

35 Canvas
37 Two Police Officers and the Rest of Us Patrons
39 Stargazer
40 Photograph of a Thirteenth Century Church
41 Gray Rocker
42 Lack of Manners
43 Shopping for Flowers at Lowe's Saturday Afternoon
44 Living History
45 When Friendship Becomes a Shadow
46 Of Hot Cheetos
47 After Hearing Javier Zamora
48 Why I Am Not a Foster Mother
49 Thoughts of You
50 The Proposal
52 Gull Watching at Ocean Beach
54 Un-Loving
55 Us

56   What the Heavy Rain Makes Me Remember

57   Breakfast, Brahms, and Beethoven

58   Gardening While Listening to Music

59   Six Harps

60   Day Stars

62   Strangers on the San Antonio Riverwalk

64   Portrait of an Aging Poet #1

65   Portrait of an Aging Poet #2

66   To Get Beyond Writer's Block

67   Autumn and Poets

68   Music Lessons

69   Read the Door

71   Afternoon Assembly

III

74   Warrior

75   Charity

77   Generosity

78   Chronicle of Muath's Eyes

80   Big Penny

81   Lost

82   Bullying's New Face

83   Something about Billy

84   Beauty

85   Two Thinkers

86   Caught

87   Sleepy

88   Regret

89   Diary of a Chameleon Soccer Player

90   On the Pages of His Memories

91   Teacher Dreaming

93   Class Discussion after Singing Variations of Little Bunny Foo Foo with My 5th Graders

IV

96   Five Ways of Looking at America

100   My America

102   The First Juneteenth

103   Daisy

104   Staying Put

106   At the Holocaust Memorial Museum in Washington D.C.

107   The Sound of Peace

109   Three Seeds and Hope

110   Snapdragons, Passion Flowers, and Cabbage

Revelation

I

112   Tonight

113   Sacrifice

114   Lessons From Night's Visit

116   In My Old Neighborhood

117   Two Birds Break the Dam

119   Behind My Eyes One Night

120   Pond

121   Ode to a Skinny Wandering Muse

122   Throughout the Day

123   The Fly on My Window Sill

124   Eddie

126   Before the Light

128   At the Last Garage Sale

II

130   Ode to My Mother's Voice

132   Drawing with Mama

135   Letting Go

136   Never Went to Kindergarten
137   The Hospital Shuffle is Not a Dance
138   Aftermath
139   The Last Christmas Gathering
140   Bartering with Death
142   When Writing Your Mother's Obituary
143   Watching Mother Dance
144   Cleaning Your Closet

III

147   After the Little Girl Says You're Too Old . . .
148   Words as Inheritance
149   Shredded Evidence
151   Two Months after Mother's Day
153   Ant
154   Witnessing My First Hockey Game at the Local Coliseum
156   Top Shelf
158   Conversation with a Furr's Cafeteria Employee
160   Before My Birth
161   On Our Thirtieth Anniversary
162   The Last Photo
163   What Mama Taught Me in High School About Love, Breakups
        and Other Such Things
165   Last Instructions

IV

168   Lust
169   In This Town That Never Ages
171   Finding You after the Storm
173   Portrait of a Summer's Day
174   Squirrel and Red Balloon
175   Of Children and Bees
176   Birth of Autumn
177   Autumn in West Texas
178   Drinking Poetry

179   Breathless
180   Winter
181   Christmas Day
182   After the Rain Stops
183   Ode to a Cactus
184   Interpretations
185   Dawn in the Spring
186   Celebration
187   Self-Portrait with Athena
188   Still Becoming
190   Into the New Year

Mixed Seasons

I embrace emerging experience. I participate in discovery.
I am a butterfly. I am not a butterfly collector.
I want the experience of the butterfly.

—William Stafford

I.

Four Seasons fill the measure of the year;
There are four seasons in the mind of man . . .
His lusty Spring, when fancy clear . . .
His Summer nearest unto heaven . . .
His soul has in its Autumn wings . . .
His Winter of pale misfeature . . .

—John Keats, "The Human Seasons"

Descending the Stairs of Day

Amidst the sorrows and sufferings of human strife
and pain, the hope and solace of nature.
I am thankful for the swans and butterflies.

—Kayleen Asbo

Odessa is a deep pond of light, a chrysalis of flat open land.
Who are the swans? Butterflies? The beautiful and sacred
creatures living in the geometry of this distant city?

The grocery store cashier with telescopic eyes?
She exams coupons, double checks
as if proving her answers for an algebra problem.
When numbers and products align,
a smile flashes across her face like a correct answer.

The postman who ignores the gazing eye of this day?
The way it mounts the soft blue socket of sky.
The way it does not apologize for staring at our vulnerabilities.
He stuffs mailboxes with desire, surprise, expectations,
and those unwanted things the world forces on us.

The homeless man who wears a dirty red hat?
His skin lives in an asylum of tattoos.
The hard lines of his life soften when he feeds
a mutt whose appearance is more desperate than his.

The street sweeper who leans against a monstrous wooden broom?
Sensible black-soled shoes are the yin,
a mount of Styrofoam snow, the yang
in her restful moment. She closes her eyes
as she wipes trickles of sweat from her long neck.
Curious how her hair remains unsullied in the ruffling wind.

The weatherman stretched taller than the six-foot yellow ruler
stenciled on the 7-Eleven door frame?
His head bald as a snow globe, smile a concealed weapon.
Skin flavor mocha chocolate.
Age—slide the scale between upper forties,
lower fifties—handsome.
His baritone voice is rich with confidence
when he sweeps his arms across maps
and predict highs and lows.

The musician who licks and buzzes his lips
before he plays *Salt Peanuts* on a trumpet
older than his grandfather?
The complex rhythms of his solo cues
for his wife's applause.
Her hands sound like mallets pounding
against a bass drum.

The veteran who wears his wounds on a bumper sticker?
The veteran who pins a tiny metal flag on the beak of his cap?
The veteran who stuffs his memory in a Jim Beam's bottle,
wakes and sleeps with the color of dawn's faded crimson face
in his eyes?

The daughter sleeping in a cocoon of grief
in a night bloated with darkness, wrinkled with stars?
She dreams of ink-stained palms,
wakes to wash her hands, finds the newspaper
opened to the obituary page
where she last searched for her mother.

On the horizon, orange spreads across the morning sky
like a fluttering monarch.
Night, painted the color of air, watches
as the moon tumbles slowly down the stairs of day.

Variations on Glory

For Cassy Burleson

I
A tired wind rests in the clear lap of day.
In the gentle arms of evening, *Old Glory's*
stars and stripes still above the courthouse,
its colors becoming shadows in the escaping light,
its meaning radiant, even in the growing darkness.
How do we hang it from the poles of our hearts
when the battle is not with steel or blade,
rather with the struggle to reach for someone
or something when turmoil is enemy?

II
How does earth, with all of its credentials,
decide which plaque to hang on its boundless walls?
Isn't this glory?
The throaty composition of hummingbirds,
delicate art of a field of wildflowers,
dissonant chords of crowing roosters,
the dew soaked lining in the translucent purse of morning?

III
What of the seasons' revolving door—
the way flames of autumn leaves scorch the horizon,
how winter's cold scalps the maple, the oak
and weeping mulberry? In their bare beauty,
they exalt themselves with stiff raised branches.
See the delight of the embarrassed grass
when spring restores its yellowed blades with green dignity.
Isn't that glory?

IV

For those born of woman, how do we rejoice
in the frailty of our flesh?
How do we meld our voices to amplify the volume of unity?
What wild passion will make us blow the horn of revelry?
Isn't this glory, to fill the deep pond of our days with amazement—
to feel the feathered breath of God in a handshake?

Of Falling Leaves

"and the sky can't hold color anymore."
From *Winter Chickens and Other Poems*
— Wendy Barker

Yesterday, in a warm cloth of evening,
I raked and bagged a multitude of aged
conspirators, stowed them on the backyard porch.
Fatigued, I flooded my body with a long shower
as the sky scrubbed away its orange blush
with a bland dark paste.

Morning wears her water-colored blouse.
More leaves than before coat the ground.
I wear a mask of disbelief.
Was I so wrapped in a cocoon of dreams
I could not hear the wind chimes tinkling alarm,
feel the fist of a rising storm?

How beautiful the way green clings
to its needled flared skirt.
Even in the dying flames of autumn.
Even in the quibbling air of winter.
Should I forgive the mulberry's brawny limbs
for their inability to hold leaves,
the mulberry itself for not being
the spruce in my front yard?

Is this how we mark our days, collecting
and discarding burdensome things?

Invitation

For Lisa Salinas

Come with me on this limb where grief is withering
and the day is fresh with its lemon-colored eye.
Under the mantle of morning, a robin whistling,
a Golden Retriever scratching
his signature in the dew-blotted dirt.
A skirt of wind sails the tiny smile of a Calvin Kline model
across the backyard fence; this is how healing comes—
in tiny constant swirls.

This is how bad news comes—
a message of terror is stuffed in the ears.
Today, someone was told sickness is rowing
in the veins of their blood-river.
Who is left holding sadness?

This is how joy climbs: up into the heart
of one man and out the mouth of another.
I leave the door open so happiness can run in and out.
When it is gone, I sit by the window, waiting
for its return.

Urban Dweller

For Diane Frank and Barbara Saxton

With your long wings, white rump, purple breast,
you are such a gregarious fellow.
Where is the rest of your clan this lazy afternoon?
Did you abandon them or did they abandon you?
I am not complaining of your presence.
I have no bread, only the grain of light to give you;
it's truly not mine to offer.

Loneliness does not bring me to this bench,
neither does sadness;
I desire the simplicity of this pond and garden.
Look how beautiful these bushy-head marigolds!
They alone are an invitation to sit.
And you—what's your desire?
Do you miss the soft *coo-cuk-cuk-cuk-cooo*
of your wild ancestors?
Do you wonder if they ever envy your life?
You get to carry lovers' messages and forage
from the goodness others drop on the ground.
I know goodness; two friends gave me gifts yesterday;
from one, two snowy egrets, from the other, a beret.
Now you are my gift.

Do you secretly dream of nesting on high cliffs,
far away from this chattering city?
Are you so happy dwelling on window ledges
and rain gutters you do not dream?
I know a secret about you, Mr. Dweller!
When you want a mate, you strut around, spread your tail,
puff up your chest, constantly bow and coo.
When she succumbs to your antics, she's yours for life.

Oh, to witness such a courtship—but this is not the time.
Soon you will fly away and I will beg
for a waterfall of mercy to pour down from a sky
into a day already queasy with heat.

Of Long and Longing

For Barbara Blanks

I can't remember the last time I woke
in the bright hand of morning
with joy curled around my mouth.
Today joy unwound, stretched
all the way through my cheeks
and back to my sleepy eyes.

Dressed in melancholy's heavy dark gown,
I started my day with a ritual of sadness.
How long can a heart begin the day
with a longing for death,
end the same day longing because of it?

Words! Those wonderful creatures
have no preference to station,
will open themselves to anyone.
Will dine with kings, sleep with peasants,
make a dull mind sharp
enough to cut through any wall of pain.
Maybe this smile isn't an expression,
rather a word to remind me to live.

On the Return Home, the Sun Boycotted the Sky

For Margie McIlroy

Dark shape-shifting clouds cap the sky.
For three hundred miles rain modulates
from hard drops crashing against the pane,
to a drizzle like a slow running faucet,
then drops softly as salt crystals.

I shuffle back and forth between
an audio book on CD and music from my iPhone.
The rhythmic swoosh of windshield wipers
the only constant for four and a half hours.

Even with complaints from my bladder and occasional cramps
in my limbs, I drive on, escorted by a quartet of eighteen-wheelers.

Is this perseverance? Lunacy? Or a futile attempt
at raging against *that* butterfly flooding me with fear?

About Nothing

Not because the sky is congested
with heavy gray clouds.
Not because I follow a caravan of raindrops
for several miles, rejoice
when a spit of blue drips through the gray.
Not because of the unending crops
of mammoth white windmills slowly spinning
in wide fields five miles before Roscoe, Texas.

Because it's Wednesday,
the day before my birth date.
Change is a stubborn backseat driver.
I invite it to ride shotgun.
It will not budge, forces me to look in my review mirror
at all the Tuesdays trailing behind.
There is a Tuesday I return to as if it's on a loop.
Each time it plays, the cavern of regret deepens.
Each time I say, *If I could just go back before …*

Today Change shakes its head in the negative, tells me
There is nothing you can do about it.
Absolutely nothing.

Waiting in Line at Starbucks

Linda Miller

Now that it is half over,
November stops bantering with temperatures,
decides to wear chilly air.
In my backyard, more leaves fall
from the balding fruitless mulberry
coloring the yard shades of mustard and mocha.
The sun no longer meanders,
skips out on the sky before 7:00 p.m.

Curious how one decision can change
the face of a day.
I decide to use a Starbucks gift card,
spend fifty minutes in line, washing the rear bumper
of a dark gray Toyota Tundra with my headlights,
and listening to a chorus of cars hum with exhaust.
Why do I sit beneath this roof of clouds
on this cold Saturday night?
Spend much of the time staring
into carved-out darkness left
by bouquets of artificial light
hung on long stalks of metal poles?
Because I can.

Like the fallen leaves piled in my backyard,
I am filled with gratitude for the many leaves
of kindness that have fallen into my life
from so many kind people. For this and other
things, I give thanks.

Trilogy on Seasons

i.
Fall is
an event:
a gorgeous movie,
a salute to
art,
a gift
like the wings of a bird. [1]

ii.
The year is racing towards
winter.
Where does it want to be? It raged its way through
autumn
without stopping for breath.
Blackbirds
stopped singing. [2]

iii.
There is indecision before winter. Plants die.

Relieved of hot summers and terrified of the
long winter ahead,
we celebrate and mourn the green times
behind us.
Seasons split into
words.

Splintered, winter comes,
littered with scraps of
autumn. [3]

II

Why should citizenship depend on one exclusive form of a relationship?
What about love between friends, community, love of work?

—Chelsey Johnson, *Stray City*

Canvas

For Shelia Denton, Kayli Eakin and all the ladies at Southern
Charm Beauty Salon and Julian Gold

We are not framed by what invaded our bodies,
rather how we live our lives.

Cancer whispered its way into my right breast;
its quiet cruelty changed the fabric of my body.
Five years later, it still remembers
the surgeon's scalpeled signature,
nausea's assault, chemo's chemical castration,
the itch and burn of radiation.

On this warm October day, temperatures debate,
have yet to side with a season.
I am dawning new memories in a space crowded
with survivors, cosmetologists and hair stylists.
The astute wings of compassion whisk me up,
spill me into Kayli's chair.
My anxiety's stretched taut beneath her hands
armed with a pallet of eye shadows, powder
and blush. This is trust for me—
to shutter my eyes in the hands of a stranger.

You all are the miracle workers? I ask.
You all are our canvases, Kayli responds.
The tender strokes of brush across my lids
feel foreign. It's been years since I've worn
makeup. Lipstick is the only cosmetic I use
to alter the plainness of myself.

After the application of lashes, I hear my name
from across the room, *You look beautiful.*

35

Kayli gives me a mirror; how can I not fall
in love with the gift smiling back at me?
I look around at the other beautiful survivors
in this tiny room congested with kindness.
In our shyness, we are like stars on a clear night
that cannot bury themselves in the darkness.
Dressed in elegance, we lineup at the foot
of the catwalk, waiting for our turn to shine.

Time clips away minutes; anticipation is giddy
in the quarry of my stomach. I carry the fear
of stumbling onto the runway, but smile when a
spotlight swallows me in its wide throat of light.

Two Police Officers and the Rest of Us Patrons

stand in a crowded lunch line at Bush's Chicken.
Belted, the officers' black revolvers
and handcuffs sit low on their waists.
A motorcycle's length is the distance between them
and the next patron.

The breath of a man in a Grande uniform
is one exhale away from the neck of two teenage girls
going on and on about which sorority they will rush
in the fall; it's April.

In line behind the teenage girls,
a cluster of mechanics from the Ford dealership.
Behind them, two men clad in khaki pants
and short-sleeve pale polo shirts, then us—
educators, shifting feet as if this will accelerate time.

We avert our eyes from the rear, from the desire
of those wanting our station in this universe
of sizzling grease.
Snippets of conversations, wafts of too much perfume
and not enough deodorant cram our space

as we wait for the officers to finish scanning the menus.
What grants them the comfort of this gap?
Uniform? Gun? Cuffs? Power we have given them?

They step aside, smile self-consciously as they wait.
How can they not feel the emptiness,
the isolation imparted upon on them?
After their number is called, they find a booth.

The tallest cop nods a greeting as she walks past the line.
The two of them sit across from each other; no words are spoken.
Their eyes are filled with the longing of many young women—
notice me, not the body I am draped in.

Squeaks from their red plastic seats occasionally scale
a high wall of silence.

—For Danielle Rudolph

Stargazer

For Sonya Wilson

He sweeps his garden with the lens;
a Stargazer lily claims his focus.
How wonderful the way it receives
the full press of day.

At night, when a light craved sky unwraps stars,
its crimson blossom enchants the darkness.
What if this lily were happiness?
What if we could open ourselves like this lily?

We could hang joy from the long hook of morning—
walk into it no matter how brief our days.

Photograph of a Thirteenth Century Church

13th Century Church Photograph
—Fran J. Scott

A Sunday afternoon, the sun clutters
the azure manicured sky with light.
Still, there is clarity in the blue,

unlike the sky over this centuries old church,
littered with rumpled white clouds and eight black birds.
In the cloudiness, there is mystery,
a turning of the mind to seek beauty in other things.

A diaspora of green grass and bushes
settles peacefully around aged bricks.
A panda-red spackles the shingled roof
and a small cluster of roses.

Behind the polygon windows, parishioners seek absolution.
Men in black robes collect their prayers
then fill their nostrils with burning incense.
All is forgiven, I suppose.

On the other side of the wooden fence
a bushy-headed ecclesiastical tree does not bow
when it gives thanks for the sweet fruit of air
and handprints smeared on the church's doorknob.
Those handprints are stains
the slipstream of history cannot cleanse.

Gray Rocker

He drinks whisky to remain upright,
to rinse his tongue of the sins he cannot confess.
But who is guilty?
The innocent who pulls the trigger,
pushes the button when the command is given?
He used to pray until he found his prayers
scattered in the drawer with his discharge papers.
He is home, warmed by whisky
while bombs, bullets, and young men who look like boys
are cold on the page, reduced to two columns
in Monday's newspaper.

One day I will get a gray rocker,
invite him and all things dark
and sorrowful to sit on my lap,
rock until they are sleepy with light
and *war* is a cracked *raw* egg
with its yoke dripping yellow peace.

Lack of Manners

"If I don't eat you quickly,
you'll melt in my palm."
—Rita Dove

A half-eaten Honey Bun falls
onto the sullied floor.
A small hand sweeps it up.
She swallows dirt, discard, and secrets
veiled in the soles of shoes.

Hunger has no etiquette,
requires no superstitious cleansing.
Means to quiet a complaining stomach
is the only blessing she desires.
The sticky sweet starch
is a gift from the food gods,
a delicacy on the plate of tongue.

Shopping for Flowers at Lowe's Saturday Afternoon

For Robin Gutierrez

There is no parable for this obsession,
the desire to buy puny and colorless plants,
to resurrect their crumbling limbs.

She does not see herself as a garden goddess.
Her small plot is intensive care for the dying
begonias, dusty millers, Mexican heather.

Her hands wobble with pleasure
when she uses them as shovels to dig in the wet red dirt.
Soil roots underneath her fingernails.

In the bed near the tall wooden fence,
rain-polished morning glories smile
across the pointed pickets. The backyard looks happy!

How planting joy restores withering stems of sadness.
How it roots through darkness so light may grow.

Living History

"the earth will continue to spend merrily
and revolve in a timely manner
around the sun."
—Billy Collins

My bond with Arthur, since age six—
we make a pact on the playground, pinkie swears make
us siblings. I enter the temple of memory where I am out
for recess with Arthur, regurgitating the rules of offense
and defense. I know football, how it can bond boys and men,
make girls spectators. Curious how I train myself to listen
to him, tuck knowing beneath my tongue; this is honor.

Curious how my mind drifts to our high school reunions.
At our tenth, Arthur brags on his wife and two children.
When we speak at our twentieth, his throat is clogged
with despair. Divorce ripped the seams of his happiness.
Thirtieth, we gather in July at St. James Baptist Church.
I listen to classmates talk about Arthur's pranks,
charity, talent—him; he is gray with silence.
The minister consoles, "We must all travel this path
and one day we will be reunited with Arthur." Not now
I think to myself; it's too hot. As if heat wears a Timex.

Outside, my face is watered with sweat; I fold the obituary,
press his frozen smile in my hand, feel our ten-year-old
selves tossing a football in the stuttering sadness.

When Friendship Becomes a Shadow

In the moonlight, silhouettes of two mulberries
appear to embrace, their black shadowy leaves still
in the quiet air of this weak darkness.
How can you be a memory when just yesterday,
on a steaming summer's night like this,
we are learning to be teenagers.
You are headed for seventh grade, I lag a year behind.
We are inseparable until you go away to college.

We lean against your brother's car, hair curled,
no more braids; we are too old.
You eat a strawberry sno-cone, I eat coconut;
we watch other neighborhood girls chase the boys
in a game of tag. We do not play; we are too mature.
You say, "When I grow up, I am going to have a big house
and lots of children." "Me, too," I chime in.
When we grow up, I am barren and you do not live
to see your only child grow into a man. You know
there are not many moons left for you, ask me
to love your son like my own; I promise to do so.
I have not seen him since he was seven.
The one who used to be your husband took him away.
I searched for them then stopped.
Tonight this desert night sky sings with stars;
my vow is broken and your voice has faded.

Of Hot Cheetos

*For Elsa Fernandez because I wrote it with you in mind, and for
Shirley Richardson, Marsha Dry, Gay Crawford, Carol and Barbara
Hall because it is your absolute favorite poem*

This flame on our stained tongues
is a new friendship.
We laugh beyond our differences.
Orange dye dirties our fingers.
They are messy just as love can be.

We laugh beyond our differences.
My lips know the cruel punch of the desert's heat,
yours the soft kiss of the Pacific's fog—
both are consuming just as love can be.
We watch gray eat up the horizon.

Even though my lips know the cruel punch of the desert's heat,
and yours the soft kiss of the Pacific's fog,
Hot Cheetos compel us both to purse our mouths with urgency
as we watch darkness cloak the horizon.
We do not wash our hands.

Hot Cheetos compel us both
to purse our mouths with urgency
as the heat lingers,
the orange dye that dirties our fingers is history.
Before we wash our hands, we make certain
this flame on our stained tongues continues
to burn with friendship.

After Hearing Javier Zamora

"When you can't understand the language, the syllables
 sound like birds."
—Diane Frank, *Swan Light*

I wanted to be his mother,
to swaddle him
in my Hershey-colored arms,
to comfort him with my clumsy tongue.

Ahora, mi valiente muchacho.
Me asegurar, que la obscuridad no viaje a través de ti.

 (Now, my brave boy;
I will make sure that darkness does not travel through you.)

I wanted my body to be the water
to carry a child my womb could never hold.

Why I Am Not a Foster Mother

"Yesterday, when it was tomorrow,
It was too much day."
—Winnie the Pooh

1
"It's life and death for you. Life and death for you."
The doctor says it twice as if I am going deaf,
as though his words need a hearing aid.
Grief mutes me, not deafness.
My voice is vacuumed into his office walls.
Two weeks later I am barren.

2
Silence fills every hole of light and space,
our conversation weighted with heart language only.
Her three-year-old eyes blaze with anticipation
as the last pouch of Kraft's microwavable
macaroni and cheese is emptied into a bowl.

3
For six months I explore life with her:
fill her stomach with comfort, security, love;
chauffeur her through confusion, displacement;
watch her chest ascend, descend with sleep;
explode with laughter as she impersonates
Picasso, Cinderella, movie critics.

4
Last night when I read *One Fish, Two Fish
Red Fish, Blue Fish* to her, these word slipped
from her mouth, "Mama read it again."
She did not retract; I did not correct.
I let them soak in my pillow—tomorrow she will leave

and that well of barrenness will grow deeper.
This is how motherhood becomes my shadow.

Thoughts of You

"Love is a waltz
 starving death for a moment."
—Lisha Adela Garcia

You said, "I like your eyes on Sundays."
They are drained of worry, yes;
rested—yes, also filled with longing;
I want to be near you,
not to hear your voice clogged
with the memories of last night,
not to feel your hands gentle on my shoulders,
not to taste coffee from your lips.
I want to see you when I look up
from wondering, thinking, dreaming
of us and our tomorrows.
Earlier I was reading a book of poetry
with thoughts of you enmeshed
between each word. I'm returning to the pages
now, your picture a deep breath away.
Silence framed itself around us.
When we ran out of words,
we ran out of love.

The Proposal

"As you placed your gauntlet of love at my feet,
 you spoke these words:"
—George E. James

While waiting for a verdict, he listens
to the cicadas' humming abdomens.
Their buzzing melodies are as musical
as ringing phones.

How he wishes now for Sinatra, Davis, Crosby,
or any crooner. They could make a love song
from the wet leaves shaking water from their flat fingers.

The sky spent half the day pouting,
puffed its cloudy cheeks to charcoal gray.
The fear brooding inside of him is darker
than the sky was then as he kneels
in the mahogany evening—waiting.

Did he speak too soon? Make proclamations
she was unable to acknowledge? Did he misjudge
the way she smiled when he walked in a room?

How life can take a turn like the tornado's tail,
sweep one in a direction thought only others would go.
Just last year he needled his best friend
about being *one of their prisoners.*

He is one of them, arms cuffed with anxiety's irons.
The possibility of no is like a prison guard and the silence
stronger than any barred windows. Maybe telling her
"I want to be your prisoner for life" was too barbaric?

He does not want a bouquet of words, just one.
When surprise releases her vocal chords, she says, "Yes."

Gull Watching at Ocean Beach

"We find out the heart only by dismantling what
the heart knows. By redefining the morning"
—Jack Gilbert

I stand at the edge of my heart,
a shabby pier, watching seagulls
take flight, land on the wet part of the beach,
dip their heads in sweeping water.
What is it to lift wings,
carry the self from shore to shore?

When I speak into the air
chipping into the chill of late morning,
a flock of my words flap
over the Pacific's wide hand.
A cold blue wave catches the remnants of my voice.
Another tosses children's laughter
as they bake mud pies, build castles from soft sand
and salty water, fiddle with seaweed, shells,
broken branches.

I throw pebbles in its wet mitt,
sulk when it catches lovers' moans
as they gulp down each other's kisses
as though they are warm liquid.
Will they have this desire when life,
that shape-shifter, wrinkles their skin?
Gulls pair for life, co-incubate their eggs.
I crave this type of pairing as I watch
ships sail from mystery to mystery.
Is it vulgar to be jealous of the gulls' love?
Covet their simple rituals,
swayed by neither a prim sun nor shy moon?

I walk an hour in the beach's soft mouth,
let the sand swallow my feet
as picnickers pack up their baskets,
surfers turn their backs, tote their boards
away from the seagulls' brash song.
When the day dies, darkness drapes, like a mantilla
over the widowed edge of the ocean.

Un-Loving

Don't say I love you, you tell me.
If you keep saying it, then it becomes truth.

My heart is this pencil, the eraser a drum;
I tap at the memory of that day you said,
*Don't say I love you. If you keep saying
it, then it becomes truth.*

I tap until my thoughts are a mouth and you a toothpick,
flat, sharp, scraping particles of love
trapped between tiny teeth.
After seven years, how can you say,
*Don't say I love you. If you keep saying it,
then it becomes truth?*

My teeth are termites now, your words rotted wood;
they gnaw your brood of broken promises
until my heart collapses like an old house.

I pack my things, you turn your back to me;
it is a *no trespassing* sign.

I understand the power of repetition,
how sameness breeds familiarity.
I tell myself on the way out,
*Don't say I love you. Don't say I love you.
Don't say I love you.*

Silence escorts me to my car.
On the long ramp of road,
broken white lines extend to the horizon,
affirmations of a truth neither one of us will say.

Us

"Love yourself. Then forget it.
Then, love the world."
—Mary Oliver,

In this web we once called us,
you tell me twice you are unhappy.
After we snip the strings,
I see your face on a distant page.
Happiness runs all the way to your eyes
and I dance in a circle of joy
I would have not known
had I tried to keep you bound to me
with one thin filament.

What the Heavy Rain Makes Me Remember

"What will help us live these years
marked by tests?"
—Mary Kay Rummel

Dear, the severe pouring reminds me
how we once equated a hard rain to baseball,

the pitch and catch
between the swift hand of sky
and concrete mitt of street.
Curious, neither of us cares for this game.

As we watched the falling,
you said, *It will not last long.*
I said, *It's not enough.*
We were not speaking about the rain.

We were talking about a word
we stopped saying, writing,
carrying with us
into the temple of our small talk.

Hours pass, the dark caravan of clouds
drift into the distance.
Years pass; you are a fleeting memory.
A monarch, your wings flutter with happiness.

You fly from flower to flower
in the bright arc of morning.
I am a moonflower, the full white bloom
of joy opening in the dark garden of night.

Love is a rain puddle that fills both
of our mouths with the name of someone new.

Breakfast, Brahms, and Beethoven

For Stacey Nash

My stomach is full with hunger; I don't know how.
A multiverse of melodies—Brahms and Beethoven,
Mendelssohn and Mozart, Handel and Haydn—
exist inside of me.

How can emptiness thrive when the slow river
of music flows and fills each cavity of my body?
Why is longing unending?

Balancing a cup of chai tea, fried eggs,
turkey bacon, a toasted bagel,
and an unfinished manuscript,
I slide into a royal-blue mesh chair,
stretch my legs across the warming concrete.

A soft wind moves about,
flipping the mulberry's leaves like pages.
Brahms' Lullaby and the chorus of leaves
accompany me as I read aloud,
feed words to a noisy sparrow.

I ask myself, "How would Beethoven compose
this morning?"
A Sonata for the Waking Orange Cat?
Symphony #10, Trek of the Blue Morning Glories?
A Concerto for Car Horn and Drifting Lean Clouds?

Gardening While Listening to Music

For Pat Harper

A milk-colored moonflower droops its face;
day has aged its beauty.
No orator will tell its story,
rehearse how it opened with abandon
in a night blooming with heat—
the same darkness that gave it birth.

I search for a spade to free a clump of knotweed
trapped in dry desperate dirt.
Curious, how even the earth struggles to hold
onto what can be carried in the hand.
Curious, how music's long breath is stilled,
how time filled every measure with rests—
until I feel the stinging silence.

Six Harps

For Catherine Alred

If there were no music,
the world would spin in a silent yearning.

Six ebony-garbed ladies file from the yawn
of a side stage door. Their wide smiles aimed

at parents. The tap of her feet on the hardwood
floor stalls the audience in their seats.

Each lady claims an instrument of angels,
caresses it against their chest even as King David.

How divine the way their spidery fingers crawl
through strings. Bach, Mozart, Handel melodies

are untangled from a nest of notes.
From the tall wide tree of music, beauty falls like leaves.

In the back of the auditorium—a butterfly
escapes the room trembling in silence.

Day Stars

"I feel above me the day-blind stars waiting for their light."
—Wendell Berry

The wind with its burly hands is a harsh butler,
yanks my car door open, and cold minces my body.
A commotion of leaves, plastic bags, flyers,
and an assortment of other debris twirls
in the drunken air.
Beneath the refrigerator of sky,
I walk through Walmart's parking lot shivering,
fill my eyes with stars
that were blinded by day's deep volume of blue.

Kat from Jaguar's Gentleman's Club has been lost
in the grocery basket I claim from the cart garage.
Her perky silhouette is covered in lust.
She is to perform Friday at 8:30; it's Tuesday.
Maybe someone will get her to the club by Friday.
For now I am her ward;
she comes with me to grocery shop.

When we reach the aisle where dairy products converge,
I have a conference with her, ask, "Yogurt, too?"
An alarm goes off in the chamber of my mind
when a dark- haired woman flashes a look of paranoia at me.
A smile teases across my mouth; my head is a searchlight
as I hunt for my phantom companion.

Kat and I push onward to the canned vegetables.
I put yams on her feet.
Is this the way we conceal our vulnerabilities,
barreling forward, collecting things we neither need
nor desire—sweet things to mask the bitter taste
of embarrassment, make it bearable?

What of Kat?
How many failed launches landed her
in the cage of this basket?
How many little girls dream of revealing their sacred selves
one beat, one garment, one compromise at a time
before groping eyes?

I hope Friday night's firmament is minted with brash stars
that scream *Look up! Look up!*
So Kat can see the reflection
of her younger self in their lively light.
The moon, a silent mystic, stalks me back to my car
as a sigh of wind tickles my ear.

What if this is her dream?
I crumble the flyer, throw it in the trash,
pray this is the only crushing hand she has known.

Strangers on the San Antonio Riverwalk

I.

At the Omni La Mansi¢n del Rio Hotel,
a blue-suited man with an artless face
and arms spread like wings
shoves his way through open stainless steel doors.

Two maids and I hunch in a corner.
With a voice chirpier than a whistling robin,
he pins his eyes to mine, "I know you!
You were on my plane from Tennessee this morning!"
When I was in Tennessee, the sun was licking the air
with sticky heat.

After the electric motor halts on floor three,
Mr. Smiley steps into a narrow welcoming hallway.
I tell the maids, "I've never seen him before.
I flew in yesterday."
The elevator's gravity of joy is inexplicable;
our laughter is continuous combustion.
Lifted to floor seven, the three of us spill out,
leave smudges of delight on sad beige walls.

II.

At the end of a day rambled with light,
a friend and I walk into the first whisper of darkness
and become strangers among a throng of strangers.
Curious how I never see myself as foreigner
when I look at unfamiliar people with nervous glances.
Crammed on *The American Venice* long narrow sidewalks,
we all jockey for places to pose for photos—
in front of restaurant doors, man-made waterfalls,
arched bridges, and foliage with undetermined origins.

Tiers of beauty stalk us as if we are aristocrats.
I, who seek such exquisiteness, long to find a blank space,
a refuge from the crowd.
Curious how the universe knows our needs;
a gentle nudge of wind prods me to look up.
A sparse patch of cream-colored clouds drifts
across this night filled with gossiping stars.
The sky looks like an Oreo; how delicious for the eyes!
How charming is a trio of sight-seeing boats
with their bottoms flashing
like disco lights as they paddle the San Antonio River.
We walk on, listen to a Mariachi band perform
for two young lovers
whose fingers are roped together like liquorice sticks.

Portrait of an Aging Poet #1

I come from a lineage of ink and paper.
Age six, I compose in a Big Chief Tablet,
in high school, the typewriter.

I am an immigrant in a technological society,
writing poems with a computer now.
I grow fluent in computer language—
red line warns misspelled words,
green questions grammar.

Out of nostalgia, I reach for a pen,
clutch my fingers around its bony body
the way newborns hold the first air of light;
my hand sings home again.

Portrait of an Aging Poet #2

"The Poet is like this monarch of the clouds
riding the storm above the marksman's range"
—Charles Baudelaire

Arthritis moves like water
streaming through my body,
my fingers slowly curving paddles.

I wade through its existence,
try to net comfort with pills
as my knuckles swell.

My knee pokes
through a black brace,
looks like an injured Cyclops.

At night I sleep with a wrist brace,
a rolled towel for extra neck support,
and a CPAP machine to breathe.

Maybe this day will drown in goodness,
gentleness will float in the breath of time.
Maybe my bones will sing without pain.

My body is an epigraph for helplessness.
Alas, like yesterday,
I spend one hour jerking, jumping,
pumping, grinding my hips
with the Latin rhythms of Zumba.

I wave my hands in the air, move my body
like I don't care, my breath finally landing
like a deflated hot-air balloon.

To Get Beyond Writer's Block

Pamper the page with words like
map, pacify, escape.

The breaking open
of body, of lust.

To consume whatever
makes you not want.

But you will want because the body is
an organism of want.

Isn't the page one part brain, one part heart,
one part that part of us no hand can touch?

The lover who lives in us
after death carries away their flesh.

Every commodity in the commissary
of sky and earth.

The jaw of a dried riverbed
where stones are pilled like broken teeth?

Isn't it the all-in-all?
Feed the paper what you need

and somewhere in a distant room
a mouth will swallow your words,
carry you into a history
you can't make for yourself.

Autumn and Poets[4]

For Suzanne Dudley

Poets have reflected on
mysterious qualities,
the need to balance light
and darkness within us,
the slow, steady
growth of
a wonderful story.

We are answers
drinking tea
until deep into the night.

We watch leaves fluttering,
mirrored in our lives. Autumn is a time for
releasing,
to pay tribute to
our lives,
come fully out—
the writer and the painter.

Letting go,
we open to all   carry
profound knowing, freedom.

Autumn reminds us
we have experienced the budding of life
          and bare branches
the fleeting nature of all things.

We grow appreciative of beauties that surround us:
the beauty of a sunrise, a child's hug, this world.

Music Lessons

For Cindy Benbow and Trenton Davis

My ego is a welcome mat for students.
Bar lines, meter, and measures—
topics of analysis this morning.
We sing *bickle bockle blue bottle fishes in the sea,*
if you want a partner just choose me.

Their arms are branches, reaching, trembling
in the air with want. "Can we play the game?"
I write the song on the board, prepare it for dissection.

Their thoughts are olive shoots,
mouths baskets filled with too much fruit.
Music terms fall from their lips.

I know what words they remember
by the wrong answers they give.
We review the responses: "Beat! Rhythm! Tempo!"

I instruct them to march, chant, "Keep the beat in your feet."
I toss out commands, "Faster. Slower. Really fast."

Conspiratorial giggles fill the air as they march backward.
With the craftiness of an evening sky, they change my lesson,
steer learning towards their desires, remind me a plan is theory.

The clock flashes 10:10 a.m., end of class.
"Next week we will review bar lines . . ."
Gabriel's voice is a medium in the middle of my sentence,
"And the game."

They exit, carrying the beat into a tottering winter,
their destinations like miles of blinding snow.

Read the Door

A long yellow scroll.
Chunky red apple.
Big blocky black letters.
DEAR STUDENTS:
I LOVE YOU AND THERE IS NOTHING
YOU CAN DO ABOUT IT.

Their eyes sweep across the door then back to me.
Silence is a thick reed,
my tongue the only one sharp enough to slice it.

I say my name, call roll,
tick off a litany of class expectations,
then ask, *Are there any questions?*
Dora raises her hand, *What if we make you mad?*
Will you love us then?

I tell her to read the door again but aloud.
She refuses; embarrassment is a mural across her face.
I explain, *Just like there is variety in music,*
there are different types of love.

The first day mellowness wanes after ten minutes.
A barrage of what ifs fills the air
as they search their sixth grade psyches
for condemnable offenses.

Jack raises his hands, a smile of triumph
marches across his mouth, *What if we don't like you?*
I shrug, my smile matching his,
There is nothing I can do about it.

Afternoon Assembly

"Rejection sits in the far corner of a library,
reading . . ."
—Rustin Larson

I am in the fall of my life,
letting go of the dark leaves of insults
that once cluttered the garden of my mind.

Maybe the earth's my advocate.
Not the assistant coach for the Jackalopes.
He confiscates a stack of papers
from the stage where students
are lined arrow-straight—asks me,
How many kids do you have?
When I tell him, *I teach music,*
he takes the papers back.
I want only real teachers.

Does the long-haired willow tree tell
the smooth-tongued white oak it's not a tree?

Do the Pacific's playful waves tease
skinny runnels, proclaim they are not water?

Does the eagle say to the house sparrow
you are not a real bird?

Am I an imitation because I fill children with melody, help
them feel the rhythm of math and science in their bodies?

I received a card from Becky today:
THANKS FOR BEING A WISE TEACHER
Happy Valentine's Day!

I am the owl in her life, the one who sits on the bench waiting, watching for a mother we both know forgot her again.

III

A person's a person, no matter how small.
—Dr. Seuss

Adults are just outdated children.
—Dr. Seuss

Warrior

For McCray Gann

McCray sits silently, posed like a warrior.
When dribbles of sweat bead my brows,
he edges forward in the paisley print chair.
With elbows on knees and a severe gaze, he
scans the classroom, his ten-year old eyes
challenging any hints of ridicule.
He wants to protect my dignity
against the heat of other mocking ten-year olds.
Is this act of chivalry an inherent gene?
Or the way his father is teaching him
to become a noble man?

Chemo has made me a bald emotional contortionist.
Out of shame, maybe fear, I wear beautiful scarves
to hide my hairless head.
I swipe my wet face with a paper towel;
my blouse is soaked with perspiration.
Cray orphans his silence, tells me to,
"Take that thing off of your head! You're hot!"
In obedience, I unveil my head,
now a bare tree where students nest their eyes.
Snug in my vulnerability, I wait for laughter
that never comes.
Cray leans gingerly, back
against the chair. I tremble with the urge to cry.

If I succumb, his kind hands might cup the tears.

Charity

"It is easier to build strong children than to repair broken men."
—Frederick Douglass

An assembly line of little hands
passes Goldfish Crackers down the lunch table,
offers them to me.

I look at the tiny school of fish seasoned with sweat,
licked fingers, and other food crumbs.
"No thank you. We are not allowed to share food."

Disappointment ripples their pond of goodness,
"But they're your favorite and the jar
on your desk is empty."

The jar is empty, but this day is stuffed with joy–
the sun in its pale canary dress,
the cardinal in its crimson coat,
the squirrel in the pantry of a tall pine.

Even they refuse charity.
See how the wind tickles that elm
until the old tree raises its arms in submission?

Once, on a cheerful day like today,
the sun squeezed inside the lungs of clouds,
the red-bird left an ink of feather on a skinned branch,
the squirrel abandoned a pinecone for a road in the grass

when the wind tried to gather the whole earth of this city—
suddenly, with swift strong wobbly hands,
it deracinated trees, toppled cinder block fences,
scalped roofs of their shingles. But that's history.

I want to fill this cup of morning
with one scoop of its soft breath, pour it into little
salty hands. Their generous desire to feed me love
is stuffed inside the tiny fins of Goldfish Crackers.

Generosity

Tyler

Port-au-Prince wakes with a nervous stomach.
The earth of her bowels splits, swallows
body and beast, fear and faith, death and dung.
Morning assembly, sixth graders solicit support
to "Help Haiti."

Lunch duty, I am an empty measuring cup.
I can't calculate how much light to pour
into a bottle of darkness,
or explain to a watery brown-eyed boy
his coins of generosity are not enough
to repair a rubbled city.

Liquid cheese, a yellow river,
flows over tortilla chips.
He stirs the current with a finger.
His voice the pleading of a broken-wing bird—
"Don't we have enough money for Haiti
from the sticker machines?"

In his seven-year-old world, puppies, smiley-faces,
superheroes live in the glass head of a vending machine.
He covers his arms in their sticky comfort
when pain squeezes them.

Chronicle of Muath's Eyes

"What flag can we wave? I wave the flag of stone and seed,
table mat stitched in blue."
—Naomi Shihab Nye

September 6

Muath's arms are invisible when joy propels him
across the threshold of my classroom.
His *Happy Birthday to you* is a proclamation, not song.
In one hand, half dozen roses, in the other,
a giant KitKat bar.

I go to Granbury where my roses drink
from a Sonic Drive-In cup and the memory
of Muath's smile crawls from my suitcase.

December 16

The end of day, fatigue is trapped on my face.
I meet Muath, his mother, in the checkered hall
where thousands of small feet scuff the floor
with the heels of their mischief.

His pride hangs in the air; "This is my mom."
I smile at the origin of his eyes
shrouded in the cocoon of a gold hijab.

"Here. Take. They're for Christmas."
I eat a hoskia; the sweet bread is happiness
on my tongue. They smile, walk away—
their eyes a pair of luggage
carrying a language I do not understand.

January 11

We sing the *Star-Spangled Banner*.
He is a ten-year-old boat drifting between two countries.

"Now let's sing Palestine's national anthem," he asks.
"I don't know it. We can look for it."
The class crowds around the computer, we search.

The flag of his native tongue is stuffed
in the long arm of a rifle, pointed at a fearful boy
who could be his cousin, curled like a snail.
Tears float around the harbor of his eyes.
He hides shame that does not belong to him.
Silence. We begin to drown in the cold deep
river of shock. When my voice returns, I tell them,
"This is not Palestine."

The lungs of the classroom fill with air.
Sorrow tears through the cuff of my heart
when Muath's head brushes my shoulder.

My words, soft against his ear.
"Go get water. Take a friend."
I watch healing escort two countries out the door.

Big Penny

For Katie Russell

I am an empty carton, speak with gestures and nods.
A drop of smile falls from somewhere inside of me
when I hear Miss Walker.

"I like this lunch. It's good!"
Leah's eyes shine like the greasy chili.
Chocolate milk trickles down the fall of her mouth.
Between bites, she makes me an offer.
"Look what I got. This is from Guadalajara.
It's bigger than a quarter. You can have it."

"No thank you. Keep it and put it in your pocket
where it's safe."

Her coin buys my memories; I'm seven.
Navy polka dots cover my orange dress like splitting cells.
On the playground, I collect broken marbles,
battered pennies, dried peach seeds
the way Rosa de la Cruz collects art.

Maybe this is the role of offerings,
to dig up those pearls from the mussels of the past
that make us tender, pliable in the hands of kindness.

Lost

Maggie

When God unlocks the caged night sky,
stars grow like tiny teeth,
bite through torrential darkness.
How joyful! The *Great Bear's* bright tail,
the *Dog Star's* brilliant nose,
Leo the Lion's majestic mane.

She stretches her jaw with one finger,
unlocks the planetarium of her mouth—
small teeth a constellation of innocence.

"Look! I lost another tooth!"
Maggie's missing teeth glimmer
like tiny galaxies.

Bullying's New Face

"We worry about what a child will become tomorrow,
 yet we forget that he is someone today."
—Stacia Tauscher

Beautiful! Heartlessly beautiful. The depth of her
Untamed contempt, intolerance
Loveless demeanor towards "those" is daunting. She
Lashes out with furious indignation at young girls
Yearning her presence. She rejects their
Imperfections—Too fat, too tall, too different.
Nothing about anyone like "them"
Good enough to cross her tracks of friendship.
She shreds them apart for

Not being her
Equal, for not donning the right
Wardrobe, twist of hair. Only seven—

Filled with an adult-sized sense of self,
Arrogance soils the innocence of her
Countenance with indifference at the tears of others. An
Empty life growls at her
           as loneliness sharpens its claws.

Something about Billy

"Every child you encounter is a divine appointment."
—Wess Stafford

Billy blankets his face with half of his lunch—
uses the long blue broom of his sleeve to sweep
potato chip crumbs from his mouth when he is finished.

Satisfied with the spotless transformation, he squints
with his left eye at the clock glaring down
from its tower on the wall.

As I watch him rapidly spin his hands up, down
the ladder of air then dialogue with the light,
my question is a gentle intrusion, "What are you doing?"
He does not look at me or discontinue his charade;
"I have an imaginary friend. We play like this."

His table mate's eyes roll in disbelief.
I see the cruel name dubbed for Billy
shaping on his lips, ready to leap from his tongue.
My voice is a wall between them.
"I had an imaginary friend until I was in the fifth grade."

Billy hears *friend,* wants to play with him.
The small flock of second grade eavesdroppers
wants to know his name.
My answer is a cliffhanger; I walk away,
leave them wondering and Billy playing
tag with light and air.

Asperger's Syndrome is serious impairment in social
interaction skills . . . and repetitive behaviors. Others usually
consider them "strange" or "weird" (Atwood, 1998).

Beauty

Isaiah

Perhaps it's the way morning slowly creeps
towards noon,
my stomach fueled with only yesterday's supper,
or the way my head throbs that makes my face a do-not-disturb sign.

With a surly demeanor and frustration heavy in my feet,
I take slow deliberate steps toward a hand waving
from across the room.

When I reach the table, Isaiah bursts into a smile,
pride pushes through the space where his two front teeth
used to hang.

His summons is to inform, *I am going to marry a model.*
My expression questions him before my words;
A model? Why not a super model?

His eyes, like this turtle-paced morning, slowly widen
with animated light, *I'm gonna marry one of them, too!*

This is the beauty I want him to see:
the high wide target of sky where
fields of New York skyscrapers snag at its blue hem.
On the High Road to Taos, green ramps of mountains
tilt so far upwards the breath is caught in awe.
In Muir Woods, the redwoods' old arms are so long
they appear to hold up the sun.

The Thinker

Nolan

After Rodin

He dips his face
in the cup of his hands. They are smooth,
not like the muscled-bronzed veins of *Le Penseur*.

He is energy and smiles.
His sudden granite-like stillness alarms me.
"What's the matter?"
"My head hurts."
"Did you bump it?"
"No. I just think I lost my imagination."

What terror to have the lampshade
of loss drape your mind.
How do I help him search through air and light,
the buzz of a classroom, to reclaim the dreams
seven-year-old boys carry in the bags of their bodies?

But like Dante, he is determined
to *transcend his suffering*.
He moves his body
with the convincing skill of a sculptor,
works his face until it is chiseled
with an image of a smile.

Caught

Taylor

Curious about Taylor's silence and bowed head,
I walk to the table where he is seated.

Standing behind him, I watch him use his eyes
like search lights as he scans the page of a magazine.

"What are you reading?"
My voice heaps fear into him.

He holds the magazine to his bony chest.
His words are random like falling leaves.

"Cornbread and stew are on the menu today
but I like the chicken fries better."

I take the magazine with glossy rifles aimed at something.
"Is this your father's?"

He answers with the softest volume of fear, a fawn
in his own woods of interest. "We hunt."

What must the forest see when two pairs of brown eyes
peer through its hingeless door,
in the blind, love is a thirst for blood, the large rack of a buck
their intended glory?

Father and son walk along graveled road—
reticent, as they crush the silence
beneath their heavy heels.

Sleepy

Jessica

Her drooping brown eyes are highlighted with hints of crimson.
It's Monday morning; both of us are too tired to feign enthusiasm.

"We visited my grandparents in Missouri.
Ugh, it took us eighteen hours. We drove straight through!"

I ask, voice flat as earth's former history, "When did you get home?"
Her face is a deep scene of struggle, "Yesternight."

I try to envision her family gathering—children smearing memories
on the dinner table, grandparents uncurling history in their
storytelling.

I only imagine road signs and the tired eyes of a ten-year-old
blinking back miles of lost sleep.

Regret

Alyssa

For years I turn my head away from apathy's trap.
This pre-noon moment my face is a desolate land
of compassion.

Balancing a tray of tea, beans, rice, enchiladas,
I stuff a white napkin like an envelope through slits
of fingers.

My pupils, aimed at the door, ignore my other pupils'
cafeteria chatter, their voices rattling
like empty pots.

A few steps away from the door, my name echoes
in my ears. I turn to an invitation,
"Would you like to join us?"

My answer shadows the sun of joy in her eyes.
She listens to trees falling from my voice, "Not today.
Maybe tomorrow?"

Curious how loudly a crushed withered leaf sounds
beneath a heavy foot. "That's okay. It's almost time
to go."

After noon, I return my tray, glance at the vacant table,
remember how my words died—her invitation a small
voiceless ghost.

Diary of a Chameleon Soccer Player

For MaKayla Lewis

"A mode of conduct, a standard of courage, discipline,
fortitude and integrity can do a great deal to make a woman
beautiful."
—Jacqueline Bisset

From January to December, she wears Nike running shoes.
Passion is her everyday wardrobe.

Her soft voice and quiet demeanor are a ruse.
A whistle shrills; guttural cries rise

from the cave of her competitiveness and split the air.
She is a lioness charging the field.

She carries the trophies of her body into the matches,
a broken nose, thumb; deep bruised ribs; two surgeries.

Injuries do not tame this hurricane of toughness.
Her mind is stronger, swifter than her legs.

She reads opponents like CliffsNotes;
her cleats are highlighters of intimidation.

For her, the frontier of soccer is obsession and love;
tirelessness, resilience have no edge.

Sweat knows no season—neither does she.
Bathed in the dim darkness of her bedroom,

she sleeps, a soccer ball near her dreams
instead of a teddy bear.

On the Pages of His Memories

On the pages of his memories,
small framed pictures on a Viewmaster toy.
With one click, anyone can fly
to foreign places like Sesame Street
or see Clifford the Big Red Dog
sitting in the school nurse's office
with a bandage on his head.
Caption reads, *It doesn't hurt.*

She lashes her son's soul
with a razor-sharp tongue
because he saw her nakedness
drape the cold wooden floor.
She forgets to close the closet door;
her son forgets to close his mind.
He sees mom's sixth husband for the night.

That little boy tells the teacher his secret,
and asks if he can sing for the class
what he learned at the Baptist church.
His strong voice of seven years bellows
Jesus loves the little children.
Applause.
When she makes the call
and CPS takes him away,
Teacher prays these ovations will echo
in the closet where he lost his innocence
and he will never know the loneliness of shame.

Teacher Dreaming

"I am not a teacher, but an awakener."
—Robert Frost

During the dusk of my sleep, the classroom lit
with learning. The state test hobbled on crutches
because creativity broke its leg.
Children painted bouquets of bluebonnets,
butterfly weeds, and baby's breath on its cast;
one child painted an emerald sky.

Sheets of shredded status quo drooped from the ceiling.
Stress disappeared like dinosaurs, the teacher's smile
like confetti. Lesson plans littered with anticipation
as children hovered hungrily around the desk.
Books were served like appetizers; students hung out
at the library the way children hang out at malls.
They sampled Carson, Cleary and Blume.

At recess, children screamed to an audience of crows
on the chain link fence around the playground.
The crows flapped their black wings,
applauded the children's melodies of freedom.

Pencils were little teeth biting ideas onto the page.
The teacher said, *It's time for math.*
The children cut snowflakes out of white unlined paper,
counted them. The teacher asked, *If you give away one
snowflake how many snowflakes will you have left?*

A redhead in the back of the room answered,
You can't count snowflakes.
A little girl, with a withered hand, gave the
redhead the only snowflake she crafted with her good hand.

The teacher asked him, *How many snowflakes do you have?* He answered,
Enough to heal a country.

Class Discussion after Singing Variations of Little Bunny Foo Foo with My 5th Graders

"Little Bunny Foo Foo hopping through the forest
Scooping up the field mice and bopping them on the head . . .
Little Bunny Foo Foo if you don't behave
I will turn you into a goon."
—The Good Fairy

Easter will arrive soon.
We sing about Little Bunny Foo Foo, a rabbit of ruff
character and brutality towards other animals.
Students laugh when Foo bops field mice
on the head and throws mud pies at woodchucks.

Why does the pain of "the other" bring laughter?
How can I, older than a half century, facilitate
this bloodless celebration of violence
disguised in an upbeat and playful melody?
Years of Foo Foo's cruelty stain my conscious.
Maybe there is absolution when I suggest,
"Little Bunny Foo Foo is a boy in our class;
his name is Bob. If he exhibited this behavior
here, what would you call him?" Jackson: *A bully*.
"Were the consequences from the Fairy Godmother
too harsh?" Camden, *No*. Calista, *Yes. Little Bunny
Foo Foo's actions were temporary. What the Fairy
Godmother did is permanent.* Camden, *He was given
three chances. He turned himself into a goon.*
Jackson: *If she hadn't, he would have kept on
doing it.* Mo-Mo, *She saved humanity. She kept him
from hurting other animals or people.*
Dirty clouds drift into the sky, unify
like a tribe of elders preparing to pass judgment.
Guilt, old as the beginning, has seized me;

maybe that's why I rejoice when it finally rains.
Is it sacrilegious to think the drops as holy?
I have no desire to be God; I want sky water
to fill my hands as if they are a cistern.
Maybe then I can cleanse that bruise on the heart
of each child I allowed Foo Foo to club.
Maybe then I can carry the true weight of forgiveness.

IV

And that is just the point how the world, moist and beautiful,
calls to each of us to make a new and serious response.
That's the question, the one the world throws at you every morning.
Here you are, alive. Would you like to make a comment?
—Mary Oliver

Five Ways of Looking at America

For William Wright

After reading Stevens' "Thirteen Ways of Looking at a Blackbird"

I.
Around the world, fists punch through darkness.
Change is what we search for in weather reports.
An old man sits in America's belly,
the shine on his teeth brushed with hope.
He hums the *Blues* into restless waves.
Across the oceans, voices hum back;
their melodies harmonize with the wind.

II.
A sweet loaf of bread hummingbirds cannot eat.
They swallow the light, the fire, and broken wishes
spilled from a dismantled heart.

III.
There is no landscape like loneliness,
no branch heavier than dreams,
no tree like America.
The claws of her roots scratch
at the lonely spaces stuffed between stars.

IV.
The sun ties a handkerchief
around all things invisible.
In the open vest of day,
promises shimmer like silver wedding invitations.

V.
Broken ribs, an apple, a sanctuary for wounded sparrows.
In the night air where silence prays,
the moon is the only way faith can show itself.

My America

"Let America be the dream the dreamers dreamed."
—Langston Hughes

I am eating dinner at the Cracker Barrel Restaurant—
meatloaf, mashed potatoes, broccoli casserole—
in Midland, Texas where a print of assorted oil wells
gawks at me from one of the walls.
The caption reads: *Our America: From Oil Well to Refinery.*

It's June; temperatures of one hundred
degrees or more volley back and forth.
Perspiration oozes from the pores
of my cornbread and dinner rolls.
I eat a forkful of casserole, read the caption again,
think to myself; my America is more than oil wells.

It is violets for Easter, disabled veterans selling
miniature flags to help support the local VFW,
a black man jack-hammering the presidency's white wall
for the first time since the birth of America.

I was birthed from the womb of a black woman,
never used it as an excuse to keep from going forward.
At times it held me back—not by my own doing.

I finish my mashed potatoes, drain my tea,
drive towards home, scan the scenery
of half-naked tumbleweeds and yellowed dried grass.
I spot two tailless steel horses grazing,
heads pumping up and down like gigantic yo-yos
before boredom directs my attention towards the sky.
I watch the sun descend at the pace of eternity—
setting as if its wilting blaze brought on a migraine.

Night's brewing in the distance;
after nine p.m., darkness will shower the city,
street lights will become umbrellas,
and I will sleep with fertile, oil-less dreams
in my corner of my America.

The First Juneteenth

After hearing they were free, some former slaves
tossed their ragged garments into creeks and rivers.

Oh, to eavesdrop on gossiping gar
overshadowed by cotton.
Tossing those rags into the Gulf of Mexico,
they paced the banks, witnessed their past
sink into the swamp of the unknown.
Did anyone salvage a cuff, a pocket, a yoke?
Even the unsolved cradles a period
somewhere in its mystery.

Maybe this is freedom—
to shoulder the pain of others,
to gather remnants together.
Maybe freedom is a river
each of us can step into daily,
rid ourselves of what no longer fits.
Maybe water is to sacrifice what silence is
to dignity—
so the vulnerable walk without shame.

Daisy

Like you, my ancestors come from Africa—
skin diverse shades of night.
Look how we have grown
in the derelict fields of conflict:
You in wild carpets of grass,
Me in the garden of suspicion.
Oh, Day's Eye, you, too, know the crushing hand
of myth.
Your colors, beautiful sister, bring cheer!
Mine, too often, fear.
We rise like a hesitant moon
and from the dark skies of our mouth
hope is shooting stars.
Somewhere the drum
beats the rhythm of our names
in the palm of acceptance.

Staying Put

"The newspapers would arrive with their careless stories,
the news would pour out of various devices."
—Muriel Rukeyser

After the internet inundates us with the *bad*,
after the disgruntled burn symbols of freedom,
after generous measures of meanness
cloaked as humor fill the day, I want to give up.

Maybe my compassion is crippled.
Sometimes I don't like being responsible
for the well-being of others.
Call me selfish if you like.
I'd rather listen to these garrulous grackles,
than listen to this litany of heavy news.

There is no escape
from marriages in Massachusetts
to divorces in Delaware,
soiled earth to immigration,
taxation to global warming,
social security to drug lords,
political loops to payoffs.

I want to turn my head, sit on Sunday's back porch.
Watch the sun settle over peace's blue mountain,
wake up to ripples of morning pooling over wet blades.
Pretend my presence does not make a difference.
Pretend if I close my eyes the intimidating darkness
will go away.
There are no exempt boxes on the applications
for living, thinking souls.

If asked to leave, my claws would bleed
from hanging on to the borders
of this home I call America.

At the Holocaust Memorial Museum in Washington D.C.

"Do I want to remember, my fearful return?
Families vanished in the midst of the day.
The mass grave steaming with vapor of blood.
Mothers searching for children in vain."
—Alexander Kimel, Holocaust Survivor

Hitler's smooth tongue convinces fathers, sons,
(good men) to stamp expiration dates on flesh.

I watch documentary reels spin a sundry of shoe
sizes into mountains of desolate soles—
stacked as if never worn by life.

Death powders the slopes with such sorrow
words are impotent; groans claw at my marrow.
Countless souls climb the peak of eternity
with hatred anchored around their ankles.

The silent tongues of leather and graves of bones
make me mourn until I taste bile in the back of my throat.

In the wooly light of this November morning,
the softness of my house slippers hugs my heels.
History's reels continue to spin as I cart shackled ghosts
of my ancestors on my night-colored back,
and those desolate soles keep climbing
as if they see the morning light of justice.

The Sound of Peace

"Folded up wishes, back into air.
This is how it happens."
—Terry Ehret

I.
This desert city is a broken sewing machine.
Long threads of heat wrap a bobbin of sun.

II.
Rain clouds dye the city an angry shade of gray.
The sky, an assault rifle, unleashes rounds
of rapid drops on vulnerable civilians.
Cools the streets with its wet bullets.

Why is comfort so dark? Need so loud?
Waking so painful?

III.
At Sonic Drive-In, I listen to rain ping
against cars, feel the city's pulse
change from placid to frenzied;
watch neighbors vacate their lawns.
Idle conversations drown in urgency,
empty spaces fill with water.

IV.
What will fill our footprints
if war tramples them?
Streets of wishes?
Wishes, those cardboard replicas of ourselves,
folded and carried with us.

My voice grows vines.
I wish fear was not a strong whip.
I hear it cracked in the air
until pigmentation becomes enemy.

I wish for a place where bodies can lean
against borders, exchange differences
like Valentine cards.

I wish peace were a wolf.
I wish old men would send young men
to unmuzzle her, let her howl
until her screams pull darkness
from a silence-stuffed moon.

Three Seeds and Hope

For Anne McCrady

A haze of happiness hangs over
the playground. The sweet fruit of sun
is ripe near the Jungle Gym and slide.
I am a signal light at the school doors
this aged morning. Green with encouragement,
I tell students, "Have fun" as they sprint
to lunch recess. Abby stops, opens her hand.
"Look! I saved my apple seeds.
I'm going to plant them."
"Good for you," I tell her.
She runs towards the sandpit,
her six-year-old hair bouncing with pride.

It is not my station to bruise her joy, tell her
an apple orchard requires more than seeds
and hope. Maybe she carries in her small palm
answers for this bruised universe.
Isn't kindness a sweeter language,
benevolence a better book,
acceptance a greater light than hate?

Fear is a weapon, a strong whip to lash
our differences.
Why is disdain the salve rubbed into wounds?
Who is fear's benefactor?

If we till our hearts, plant seeds
of empathy, mercy, and generosity,
we can harvest a crop of peace
large enough to feed the world.

Snapdragons, Passion Flowers, and Cabbage

Silence crosses its legs, listens
to the sunrise through the cello's "f" hole.
Beyond a wide windowpane, the Pacific
rolls shamelessly in her gray bonnet.
Isn't this peace?

And isn't this peace, the way a gentle wind lifts
the white skirt of a "fried egg plant?"
The way its flamboyant yellow center invites a bee
to dine from its bountiful table?

And isn't this peace, the way a snapdragon
with its ancient face and chirpy colors, offers grace
to a lounging butterfly?

And isn't this grace, the way passion flowers proffer
their tendril vines across a high wooden fence—
how they reach for something greater than themselves,
perhaps a neighbor?

And isn't this peace, the way water drips
from the leafy head of a cabbage
down the palm's skinny streams?
The drops soft landing in the sink make history clear.
And if we sow the smallest of goodness in ourselves,
scatter it like mustard seeds, maybe we can change
a fractious moment peace by peace by peace.

Revelation

Each one of us has lived through some devastation,
some loneliness, some weather superstorm
or spiritual superstorm, when we look at each other
we must say, I understand.
I understand how you feel
because I have been there myself.
—Maya Angelou

I.

I understand pain. I have had plenty of it.
No matter how dark life gets, keep your head up.
Change will come. Night always comes before morning.
—Mother

Tonight

"I keep having this dream that there is a garden
growing inside my chest, under the bones."
—Melissa Studdard

The honeysuckle climbs
over pickets in a long chain-link fence,
the soft swirl of wind teases
the topmost branches of a mulberry,
dusk dyes a blue-headed Friday
a deep shade of ebony.

How crafty this summer's eve!
Shadows make this dilapidated barn beautiful.
A family of tumbleweeds sit in the middle
of its cracked concrete floor and rock.
The aged slats look like a rib cage;
fortitude engraved its initials in rotting wood.

At *Freedom Park*, a jittery frog leaps
from the moon-stamped pond then disappears.
Who can resist such gifts, or hold happiness hostage
when this West Texas desert offers such splendor?
Look at this sky's buffet of delicious stars!
Their champagne-light drips from a flute of darkness
into the yawn of the scalped pasture.

Sacrifice

Night is a single mother
who shyly disrobes in the sky's corner boudoir.
Behind its high doors, she unswaddles the stars,
sweeps them from the hem of her seal-black rebozo.

When she senses their light drifting down
the length of her wide ancient thighs, then scattering
across velvet heaven, she rocks.

Perhaps this is faith—
watching your hard labor fall,
un-netted, into the unknown.
Maybe this is prayer—
that spangled swallowtail,
newly released from a mason jar.

Each beating wing soaring toward the matins of sky,
breath caught, then released behind the sun's glaring eye.

Lessons From Night's Visit[5]

For Cindy Huyser and Debra Winegarten

night
walked and
jumped

moved with
an unexpected yearning to
sit at a table with my family

on the table's surface
a freshly
cooked meal

night gathered around me
our hands folded on top of our heads
a vocabulary for friendship

I've learned
what it
means to be
family

a year
contains a lot of contradictions
strengthens
in new ways

climbing
is a confrontation of morality and an
adventure that makes me feel

I've learned
that grass
smells great and wind feels
amazing and rain is a miracle

earth,
a swirl of chaos and conflict,
is beautiful

In My Old Neighborhood

For Sandi Horton

Little boys bounce basketballs
between the stretched shadows of evening
and make funny faces at their flat selves
dancing on the sidewalk.

Trees, those flimsy umbrellas,
soak with a setting sun;
quiet rains of light drizzle on the grass
around their long wooded shafts.

Soft shingles of darkness
cover the roof of a new night sky;
a cluster of blushing stars graffiti
the horizon's high wall.

The boys cover their eyes with cotton t-shirts
and stretch haggard bodies across a bed of grass.
Sleep curls on their bony bare chests and around
the corner of their mouths.

In the distance, a mockingbird trills
a soft benediction.

Two Birds Break the Dam

"If the day was not your friend, she was your teacher."
—Kimberly Nyogi

of my eyes; trickles of tears flow at first
when I stumble past the lifeless robin
fate leaves at my front doorstep.

Work requires a seven-thirty a.m. sign in;
it's seven-fifteen.
My darkened porch light delivers hours long eulogy
before I shovel the sealed beak and stilled wings
into a bucket,
the only way I know to honor the fallen soprano.

When I take my evening walk,
find an orphaned baby sparrow
flitting on the sidewalk, tiny wings too weak
to lift itself,
a waterfall of tears covers my face.

The sparrow is a dot in the distance now.

Somewhere between the first and second laps,
I wear guilt like a pair of shoes.
I backtrack, scoop up the fearful orphan
put it in the grass, convince myself
the ruffle of branches is its mother
beating gratitude against oak leaves.

What if the heart could grow morning glories?
What if we were morning glories growing
in each other's hearts?
What is this day trying to teach me?

On the walk home, yards of orange rickrack
baste the long skirt of evening.
Night is armless, cannot cover what I try to conceal;
I am an open wound in the palms of the universe.

Behind My Eyes One Night

The stairs in my eyes are how I climb
from the terror of my dream.
I start to run; the grass moves like a treadmill.
A single bulb in the middle of a field
rains down wild light.
Every unkind word
I spat into the world rolls back toward me.

I run behind an elm.
A brute wind charges from the south, yanks it up.
The emptiness pounds in my chest.
When the elm's roots become my fingers,
I shake my hands until each shackled fear
becomes a bead of water.

They drop into a blue chalice.
The chalice becomes a street of doors.
I walk through each one looking back.
My tongue is clumsy; tears are my only speech.

I scratch the word *forgiveness*
on a dirty window pane. A voice
from the corner of the sky says,
"Clean the house of your heart."

I scrub, try to erase all things restraining
and wounding.
Olive cotton sheets noose my neck
as I kick hard against the warm morning
trying to pour a cup of mercy into the wells of my eyes.

Pond

"The pond has dreams too deep to be spoken,
deeper than the sky."
—Diane Porter

Why do you hover as a hummingbird
over yesterday, feeding off the nectar of nostalgia?

What is so sweet back there?
Can you find no solace in the now?

Is the past a transpicuous telescope?
Isn't the aim as important as the eye?

You continue the safari of *what was*
with its roads of dead ends.

Are dreams too dangerous
because their widths cannot be measured?

Luminous wings can fly them
beyond a cobalt canopy of sky.

Zealous voices are like a stalking wind,
can slip through a needle's slender mouth.

You are cluttered with longing,
yet wallow in the safety of bygones.

Visions are not for harnessing;
they are floating celestial beacons.

Fear soiled your scope; how quickly you forget; your
memories are a black hole in an ancient galaxy of dreams.

Ode to a Skinny Wandering Muse

How can such a scrawny gypsy
fill the white emptiness of the page,
feed the hungry margins a poem?

Oh wandering sister, you are not *Polymnia*.
There is elegance in the way you trap
stars in your tangled tresses,
grace when you balance your gaunt feet
on Saturn's moons,
loveliness in your night-colored eyes.

Free the tattered clothes from your shoulders;
dip yourself in the sky's milky river.
Let the earth feed you the unknown, the unseen,
the unspoken words she swallowed in the beginning.

Throughout the Day

Dawn comes riding bareback on this cold day.
A homeless man noses the front wheel
of his overburdened grocery basket
against the side of a 7-Eleven.
Like a turtle, his head and hands disappear
in the dirty shell of his thin shabby coat.

Midday heat arrives like the cavalry.
The sky fills with clouds that look like mashed potatoes.
Grackles perch on telephone lines—
beads in a rosary.
Then as a sudden wisp of wind,
their wings disappear
behind the dark line of a pine tree.

How can hunger can find its way to the sky?
A pine tree full enough to eat the shadows of birds.
A desolate mulberry's only fodder is air.
Life's feast or famine the turn of the head?
When the earth swivels where stars pump
in her breastbone,
night attempts to anchor their light.

The Fly on My Window Sill

"Tell the truth the first time. You won't have
to try and remember what you said. The truth
stands still. Lies keep on running."
—Mother

A horsefly beats the bedroom window
with its morning-colored wings.
This constant rhythmic annoyance
against the pane makes me want to peel
a wide lace of light from the screen,
silence the droning.

I drive into the day with a sour mood.
At a light, I shift my gaze from a homeless
man's sign: *Will work for food.*
His eyes seem to flutter with need.
Perhaps hunger beats in his belly.

The signal light lingers on red,
my wallet lingers in my purse.
Compassion tries to stretch her soft arms
into my body, breach the routine of my day.
When the green arrow gives me permission
to turn left, I drive on, lying to myself
about the time I didn't have.

Eddie

"For in his morning orisons he loves the sun and
the sun loves him. For he is of the tribe of Tiger."
—Christopher Smart, "Jublilate Agno"

In the Morning

Sunday morning continues its ritual of sliding light
underneath the skirt of lilac curtains.
Eddie wakes me with persistent purrs of want.
I slip from underneath the covers;
my body brushes against the soft cheek of day
as Eddie brushes against my leg.

This is our ceremony.

I scrape his wet food into a bowl,
stroke his back as he eats.
Is it fingers against fur that makes him twitch his tail?
Bones against bones that make him point it
towards the ceiling like an exclamation mark?
My touch a conversation he understands?

At Night

I rest my feet beneath the coffee table.
Eddie crawls in my lap, curls his body.
The soft pulse of his breathing feels like a drum
in his belly; the slow rhythm taps me to sleep.

I dream Eddie and I are two birds in a nest of clouds.
When we lift our wings, I feel emptiness, open my eyes.
Through the bare window I see him near the huge oak,

124

his small back arched like a doorway.
This is how we keep trust open.
My hand rests where he unspooled himself,
remembering, waiting for his return.

Before the Light

"the shores of morning loom up lined with little shadows."
—Naomi Shihab Nye

The morning smells of cinnamon
and Odessa continues to rip the seams of her borders.

Muscled weight of spring heat wins the seasonal
wrestling match, pins the cold to the mat.

My will, a shell of its former self as I drive half-heartedly
into the day, squinting at the unthinkable—traffic.

I blink as if taking notes with my vision, recording
billboard signs and the flow of new found wealth.

My pupils are dilated with impatience
and my knee is an angry red mistress

as I mow through the overgrown fields
of a once friendly city.

My mind leapfrogs between past and present
as I hunch over the wheel ten car-lengths away

from the traffic light and its patient blinking.
Five car-lengths away from freedom, my cornea drills

a hole back to the time when I was a teenager;
love was over six feet tall, drove a '72 Cougar.

Going through the light, I put the frogs of my past
and future back in the pond of the present,

as I drive in a crowded white lane towards home.
On my car seat, the newspaper headline reads,

A Boom In Oil Jobs Has Meant A Rise In Fatal Auto
Accidents. I drive through the shadows of metal ants

with large eyes crawling down Forty-Second Street—
statistics slowly wearing down the tread in my new tires.

At the Last Garage Sale

August glares with its primitive orange eye.
Early morning light glitters in the heat.
A cluster of dedicated garage-sale hoppers sift
through goods displayed on a five-dollar table.

I pick up a painting of withering roses slumped
over the lip of a vase ornamented with parrots.
What hands painted these colorful feathers?
How crafty the illusion of them dancing.

Twin pears rest at the base.
A stream of questions flow through my fingers
as I search for the artist's name. Why
not cucumbers, watermelons, or pomegranates?

Why not lively tulips, lilies, or daisies?
Why is there no pedestal, table, counter, crate?
Heavy white strokes on the canvas anchor the vase,
keep it from falling into the future.

I place it back in the box behind a house painted
with watercolors. Outside a tiny window, blackbirds
hover over a withering field. Is this the totem
of the owner's life? Birds and withering?

I walk past a sleeping corgi—back into morning's
unbending will of heat and a faded print of wind.

II

When dementia took up residency in Mother's mind, the first precious things we lost were our names coming from her lips.

My brother, Vince—

"My mother was the most caring person I can think of, but I knew when I was in trouble when she would utter these words, Vincent Todd! It was something about the way she would call out your name, our names, and command respect! To this day I can still hear her, chastising, correcting, directing us ever onward to live right and be right with something as simple as Vincent Todd! Thank you, Mama!"

Ode to My Mother's Voice

For Jeffery and Tobi Alfier

"Another gift is a child's face in a dark room."
—Robert Bly

Each of our faces is a dark room
in the house of her eyes.
Her strangled whispers a gift,
even if she calls us by the wrong name.
Her memory, a dissonant chord;
my memory in a pew
at St. James Baptist Church.
Mama's singing "Amazing Grace."
The congregation's crying—
the lilt of her soprano voice a key
to unlatch the cage of their tears.

I fidget in my seat,
feet streaked with boredom.
In my twelve-year-old narcissism,
I want the Jackson 5 to burn the mike
with "ABC" or "I Want You Back"—
melodies that can dry tears,
make the hymnals' stiff hands clap.
Mama's voice is common as dawn's
blooming hues.
She's the radio we listen to before
she cleans enough houses to buy a Motorola.

She packs Aretha Franklin tunes in her handbag,
carries them to work,
brings them home in the evenings.
"Bridge Over Troubled Waters" is her anthem

for tuna casserole.
Now—I'm the one who works hard.
I beg, open your eyes, Mama.
Hold my hand. Speak to me!
An ambulance's emergency lights split the darkness.
I inhale, walk into the night
where luminous stars hang from the gallery of sky.
A nurse tells me to breathe.
I can't exhale until hospital instruments
stop improvising her heartbeat—
until her voice is an ostinato of life.

Drawing with Mama

I.

I am trying to draw your name in my mind,
Mama tells me when I walk into her room
at Madison Medical Resort.

She looks at me; her memory is like cold hands
warming in a pair of tattered gloves.
I say my name as if it is a bird flying
toward the nest of her mouth.

We watch a reality show neither one of us will remember.
I hear recognition in her voice
when she uses the sing-song syllables
of who I am to ask for a cup of water.
I watch her drink as if seeing her for the first time.

II.

My sister Kim and I sit in the oncologist's office
with Mama, waiting to hear what we don't want to receive.
We are steel cisterns as a downpour of words fills us:
The cancer is in the liver and the bones.
In the ribs right here. We can't do chemo . . .
Come back in three months.

Kim pushes Mama's wheelchair,
tears stored where we can't find them.
Mama draws circles of silence with her eyes.

III.

The oncology center is two hours behind me.
I sag in the beautician's chair, a white porcelain sink
hard against the back of my head.
Tears drain from my eyes, stop-up the wells of my ears.
Outside, thin strips of maize boomerang
off the roof of Music City Mall.
A stream of pink scuds over a windmill's busy blades.
Dodge Durango and Toyota Camry horns
blast obscenities at each other as the fading day tries
to draw out the sadness clogged in my throat.

IV.

At home, my mind insists I draw up the memory
of talking to Mama after Hurricane Ike.

Ike raced in at 110 miles, splintering lives
and all things fragile.
Her heart was four hundred miles south;
her compassion a tugboat,
rage floating on Galveston's flooded beach.
She trembled with fury. I listened,
window cracked, the radio's volume above a whisper.

I glanced at the review mirror; Mama trained
her eyes, told me:

I feel sorry for the rescue workers. It's not fair
to those guys. Their lives are in danger
because people refused to evacuate.

Somewhere between Murphy and Eighth Street,
calm filled the basket of her voice.

You are not going to believe this.
A squirrel walked down my sidewalk this morning.
He didn't run when he saw me.

Mama's words dipped in and out of my silence
when I flipped my blinker to turn left on Autumn Street.
I felt her panic when she said,

Your brother told me don't go outside after dark.
A coyote's prowling in the neighborhood.
Cats are disappearing.

Maybe this memory is a coyote of fear
roaming through the dark neighborhood of my heart
as I watch Mama silently disappearing.

Letting Go

Under the stoop of Mama's tongue,
a clutter of words, a hull of memory,
small dented canisters of secrets.

Her fists open and close
as she searches for my palms to press
against the splintered lines in her hands.

From the twilight of her eyes, she begs the universe
to collect withered petals of pain dropping
from the flower of her body.

She waves her arms over a bridge of air,
embracing the mother who held her
for only nine months before death lifted its skirt.

She reaches up; *I want to go in the yard*
to wipe the tiny froth of sweat seeping
from the brim of her daddy's straw hat.

How can I, a love letter from her womb,
release her to return to the belly of her beginning—
suckle stars from the Milky Way—

wait for dawn to retract the text of darkness?
Then whisper *Run, Mama, leap up the stairs of light.*
Let her dew-soaked ankles slip
through the broken chains of my fingers.

Never Went to Kindergarten

When I was a little girl, my mother's voice was round
as the earth; I lived inside her mouth.
Her words were the air I breathed.
For months she prepared me for big school
and told me, "School gives legs to dreams."
I wanted to keep my dreams; I didn't want them
running away with other children
into those shiny hallways of the unknown.

The first day of first grade she packed a Gala apple,
fried bologna sandwich, and chocolate chip cookie—
their aromas heavy in a brown paper bag.
I wanted to smell her talcum powder,
Big Mama's greens with bacon fat, cornbread,
and the sweet flesh of apricots chasing each other
up and down the street of my tongue.

At the intersection of Lindy and Murphy streets,
the crossing guard who held a red STOP sign
and wore thick black sole shoes told me, "Good morning."
I could not give those words back to him, reached
for my brother's hand and he would not hold it.

When the teacher called my name, asked me to share
something I liked, fear was the horizon
I could not see beyond.
I only saw the landscape of other children's faces.
I wanted the crossing guard's red STOP sign
to make them turn away.
I wanted my big brother's shadow next to me.
I wanted to run home to Mama,
crawl back inside of her, all the way back
to the place where I could only feel words.

The Hospital Shuffle is Not a Dance

"When you were born, you cried all night and slept
all day. Not much has changed."
—Mother

A telephone call unhinges the door of my day.
Can you meet me at Madison Medical Resort
and bring Mama's stuff?
Darkness collects like dust in my home
as I collect her belongings
from Room 950 of Medical Center Hospital.
I stuff clothes she never wore, toiletries, a cup
into a K &G shopping bag.

After rummaging through the closet,
I sling her cosmetic bag across my shoulder,
heft her prosthetic legs. The uneven pedals of feet
and hard plastic make my right side sag.

I hobble from the elevator, cross the grass
to the parking lot, my emotions, a crowded factory.
At Madison, nurses examine a stage-two bed sore
eating towards the bone of mother's already festering life.

When the nurses turn her, she reaches for me, my sister,
with desperate tears in her eyes. We cry.
The nurses reprimand, *Stop crying or leave.*
We turn our backs, their voices tourists in our grief.

Aftermath

"But it is the doing of old things, small acts
that are just and right; And the doing of them
over and over again."
—Ella Wheeler Wilcox

Light drizzles through the open blinds
onto the silvery window ledge of mother's hospital room.

Handmade get-well cards from other people's children
are displayed like art in a museum.

Mother can't read them.
There's more moon than sun in her eyes.

We read the cards to her, slice her meat, scoop
her vegetables, sweeten her coffee for weeks

after the stroke. I tap the yellow limb of a pencil
against the spine of Diane Frank's *Canon for Bears*

and Ponderosa Pines. My sister sits on the edge
of the bed. We watch mama hold a plastic fork

with an unsteady tilt of hand. When rice falls
through the prongs, we do not disturb

the sticky grains beached like white sand
on her hospital gown.

We take deep grateful breaths as autumn's
red fiery leaves burn another day off the calendar.

The Last Christmas Gathering

"We are a three strand chord not easily broken."
—Vonnie Walker

My quartet of brothers sits at the dinner table
paired by birth order.
Mom and I are spectators on opposite ends.
Once, in the shuffle of age, we were tumblers
on a combination lock.
Now their fingers do not touch.
Many times I watch them bump
knuckles that bruised other boys
under the shield of protection.

I, the one with alto voice,
desire to unlock the mystery of this space.
Is it a fissure in the bond of childhood—
a collage of trust gathered through the years?

Maybe their palms are heavy
from holding this fat-bellied moon we call life
or staving off that large charging ship of death
aimed towards the one we love.
Maybe they need space to exhale.

At the door my brothers hug;
their hearts crowd the space where the rhythms
of brother-to-brother beat against their chest—
a rhythm I can never play.

Bartering with Death

"Honey, everybody dies. I just pray God
will never let me look down at one of my
children in the grave."
—Mother

Death comes to the neighborhood lean and cocky,
takes Mrs. Norris in ER room #4.
Hungry still, it skips over, takes Mrs. Mitchell,
the neighborhood reporter,
Mrs. Deaver, the fifth grade elementary teacher,
Mr. Richmond the high school principal,
and Roger McNeil the Baptist minister.

Death leans on the cheap nursing home dresser,
slips mother's hand from mine,
slowly drags her beyond my reach.
How do you barter with something so confident?
I beg, tears clogging my throat, "Hold my hand, Mama!"
Ambulance drivers with their miracle machines
bring her back.

With a hunch of shoulders and revenge on its tongue,
Death takes Mrs. Lily, mother-in-law,
Donna, longtime friend
and neighborhood record keeper.
It ravishes time, chews until months dwindle down
to hours. Where is the mercy? There is no reprieve
from this procession of funerals.
I am still bleeding with sorrow when it takes
Bobbi, older sister, and Leslie, childhood friend.

There is no forgiveness in Death.
It stares at my family rooted together

like aspen trees and taunts us.
It makes us beg for it to embrace Mother
after her body fails, pain contorts her face,
and she screams but her voice forgets to make a sound.

After a hospice nurse barters kindness,
Death is a quiet river, Mother a canoe.
She drifts softly across its tender currents,
her mouth opened in gratitude.
My siblings and I are six fish, caught-released, to swim
through this day with gaping holes in our hearts—
torn open by sorrow's hook.

When Writing Your Mother's Obituary

Rehearse the funeral in your mind.
Let the church walls
drink each drop of sorrow
mourners bring in the cup of their eyes.

Wear her favorite shade of pink.
Swap the vase of lilies for thorny roses.
When you prick your thumb, remember
the joyous pain that gave you life.

Dab your wrist with *Shea Cashmere*
to breathe the memory of her.
When you type the last period, cry
for what you cannot make breathe on the page.

Watching Mother Dance

"The last full sentence I remember Mother saying is,
  I want to go home. I want to go home."

Mother, you are
a pink rose, monarch butterfly, elegant hat,
bowl of fresh cherry tomatoes, domino diva,
needle, thread, silk, cotton, denim, gingham,
cedar chest of fabrics, dream reviser.
If fate had let you be the dealer,
you would have been a pediatric nurse.
Instead, you nurtured six children.
Here we are wondering
if the air where you are is sweet
like apple pie or pineapples slopping
atop a heap of vanilla ice cream.

You are
a psychologist, philosopher, referee,
the beam of a tennis racket, socket of a golf club,
the star on a Dallas Cowboy football helmet,
moon watcher, cloud interpreter, sun navigator.
This is how you get us to hold the sky,
carry the wind in the pockets of our skin, lift our heads,
and make the tears fall backward into our ears
as if they are soft words like your voice.
Our hearts hear you say,
Shush. Shush. Look at Mama!

Your eyes laugh as you tap dance your way
to a shiny heaven, your ruby red slippers clicking in joy
as angels follow, flapping their wings like happy birds.

Cleaning Your Closet

For Lynn Lewis

The clothes are still grieving you, will not let go
of your *Moonwind* and *True Blue Shea Cashmere* scents.
While packing up your clothes, Kim holds your head cover,
sniffs and says, "This smells like Mama."
I take the soft black cloth, do the same.
"I'll keep this one," she tells me.

When I hand it back, your smell leaves my hand.
How come your scent lingers on these clothes
but will not remain in my palms?
How many times will you leave me?

I do not dream your face, rather your fragrance.
Do you know security smells like talcum powder?
When I was six, and afraid of shadows in the dark,
you let me sit in your lap, my head against your chest.
Your warmth and the aroma of processed roses
soothed me to sleep.

Now Kim and I sort everything you've touched
and has touched you—boxed for others
to wash forgetfulness into your clothes.

I keep some blouses, gloves, a couple of coats,
and your favorite shabby sweater,
fit them in a clear plastic container, load it in the car.
Before leaving, I dab *Shea Cashmere* on my finger.
I can smell you returning.

III.

*Before my retirement as a fireman, my fellow firemen
complimented Mama on what a wonderful son she has,
how I was a nice and polite man. Based on their assessments
of me, she encouraged me to take the captain's test.
Three times I passed; three times I was overlooked.
I knew politics were involved the second time I took it.
The test took at least an hour or an hour and a half
to complete. My beliefs were confirmed when a man we know
walked in to take the test. The time it took him to write
his name and fill out the form took less than fifteen
minutes. I watched him walk out the door. I knew then
I would not get the position. Sure enough, his name
was posted the next day. When I asked to see the scores,
I was told with colorful language there was no way
that was going to happen. After the third rejection, I felt
dejected and made up my mind I would not try again. Still,
Mama wanted me to try again. When I told her, she said,
"Don't judge who you are based on someone else's choices."*
—My brother, Raymond

*Gosh, when I was young, I blew so much money!
I didn't think about it. If I wanted it, I would buy it.
This really bothered Mama. She was so frugal. Now
that I am older, I understand, after I spent large sums
of money, why she would say, "If I had a dime for
every dollar you spend, I could retire."*
—My brother, James

*Mama has said so many things that shaped my life.
One saying that has stuck with me the most is,
"If and when someone tells you no, no means no,
maybe means no, and sometimes even yes means no!"*
—My Brother, Chris

I worked at the daycare with Mama for a couple of years. Over the course of my life, I have worked other jobs where I was directly in charge of children. Now that I have a child of my own, other people make suggestions on how I should raise him. Mama overheard one of the conversations and said, "Don't let anyone tell you how to raise your child. There is no book that can tell you how to raise J.J."
—My Sister, Kim

After the Little Girl Says You're Too Old . . .

"That's just the way it is. You don't have to do anything.
Somebody somewhere will find something wrong with you.
Just don't pay them any attention."
—Mother

Sixty decades clap their hands.
Rejoice in the misty dawns of these wrinkling years.
Aging is no clean matter.
When youth slowly drains from the tub of your body,
wisdom settles like rust on aged pipes.
Tell the little girl: you remember
the frisson of your first kiss,
the way your volcanic self erupted with pleasure
and confusion, how lava of the unknown
spewed into the slope of your tongue,
how rapturous that innocent memory.
Do not judge the order of things. For life to transpire,
the one who once suckled becomes a suckling mother;
her daughters become the same. How beautiful
the way the body stretches into generations.
Look at the commodious sky with its different coifs,
maize-colored mornings, ocean-hued days,
orange-striped evenings, how they fold into themselves
when time changes its mind.
Stars do not attempt to shame
the ancient gazing eye of moon
for the way it mounts the soft black night,
for the way it does not apologize for staring down
at winter's naked trees.

Words as Inheritance

"Don't make promises you can't keep. When you break them,
 someone gets hurt."
—Mother

Begging is no foothold.
Her *No* is a large stone lodged in the cleft
of a high mountain.
We scale the cliff with *I won't ask again if you*
Chisel that boulder with a barrage of *p-l-e-a-s-e*.
Her answer remains.

It's not her authority we try to plea bargain—
rather her word, the thing she values most
next to her children.
We don't know to rejoice, celebrate her words
as a ledge we can stand on.

Maybe this is the inheritance she wants us to have—
to know the invaluable price of your word,
a promise is mightier than currency,
do not break oaths then furnish frivolous excuses,
nor have a swift and nimble tongue when making a pledge.

Too many broken promises are sharp teeth,
will maul the trust others have given you.
Vows, when written down, trot through history.
When spoken aloud, they are like air,
can fill spaces you cannot see.

Shredded Evidence

"Not all women can have children. Not all women
want children. It's okay one way or the other."
—Mother

The paper shredder is clogged, constipated
with ripped numbers, life's information, secrets.
I pull them out of the filing cabinet one by one:
bank and credit card statements,
old medical bills, canceled checks, uncanceled dreams,
and feed them to the gray mouth.

Tax season provides a catalyst for cleaning,
with the ripping of outdated importance,
the emptying of paper snow,
the purging of yesterday.

I rummage through files, find a folder
labeled *Hysterectomy*. It's been ten years.
I hold the folder in my hand, the barrenness
of my womb fresh in my mind—so is the conversation.

Tears crowd my face as I tell the doctor,
"You're taking away my hope of having children."
"You can get pregnant," he says, "but you can't have children."

I put the shredder in reverse with hopes of unclogging it,
but the blades are damaged, twisted, turned inwards.
With a pair of tweezers, I pull at the trapped ripped
pieces; I cannot free them.

The conversation continues in my head;
I feel the seriousness in his voice,
"You have a number of cysts."

"How many," I ask.
"A few," he answers without giving numbers.
"You might need a transfusion. Do you have
anyone that will donate blood?
This does not make you less of a woman."

His words fall away; I put the *Hysterectomy*
folder back in the filing cabinet and the
tweezers back in the drawer, after I fail to pick
away the shredded evidence of my life.

Two Months after Mother's Day

"You do know some people make up stories about themselves
because they don't like who they are."
—Mother

Heat and light dance across my window
this July morning.
Too tired to sleep, too tired to wake fully,
I sink my head deeper into the pillow,
wish caffeine would drip from the ceiling into my veins.
I morning dream my body is a canoe floating
in a sapphire stream.
The sudden drubbing against the bedroom door shakes me.
Two pair of excited eyes remind there's a promise
to keep.
All week the kids speak of hippopotamuses, rhinoceroses,
dolphins, tigers, and "a sweet soccer kick"
their friends dub *legitness*.
Two weeks ago, the obsession was football, beehives,
wolf pups, and purple hair.
Is motherhood an animal, too?

Morning shrinks into the broad embrace of a day
that feels like the inside of a microwave.
I pack lunches—hotdogs, bananas, pineapples,
corn on the cob, and dinosaur cookies,
before the kids and I pile into the car.
A kilometer from the zoo, our favorite song
shuffles to track three, we sing, our voices
riotous as a field of bluebonnets.
At the zoo's entrance, we smile, take selfies,
text them to Dad.

This is desire, my dream of a fictitious family.
This is truth: hugs live inside my stomach.

Ant

"Sometimes when you get what you want,
you find out later you didn't want it all."
—Mother

Ant, you remind me how Nell and I chase
neighborhood boys through a sun-infested day
when we are ten.
Heat grows around our joy like overgrown weeds.
I do not figure age into the equation of being,
believe I will be as a gazelle all my days—
young, lean, swift, fruitful
like lemon trees.

We shout to each other in our secret language
across one backyard and two wire fences.
We conspire how to catch the boys—tomorrow.
They are safe; the words of our conspiracy float
across rough grass, leave syllables in the sharp blades.

Night, stars sprawl like pimples
across the dark face of sky.
Nell rocks her grandchild;
Her words muted, voice soft,
in the sleeping child's ear.
I rock with an empty womb.

Ant, this moment is no accident.
I find a withered lemon beneath the kitchen cabinet.
A company of your cousins leads me to it.
Does the collection of the small direct
us to the withered and aged?
I spray life out of them the way barrenness sprays me.
Now their bodies are wet, still, purpose fulfilled.

They have made me a god.
I do not like it.

Witnessing My First Hockey Game at the Local Coliseum

"Let me get this straight. You're not going because you've never been?
Do you hear yourself? What sense does that make?"
—Mother

After fans stream into the arena
with anticipation stuffed in their limbs
and their favorite warrior's number
stitched on their backs, they stop
at the concession stand, sweep their eyes
across the menu board, purchase snacks and drinks.
After balancing food in one hand,
program in the other, they drift to their seats,
listen to pregame announcements,
chatter with fans two rows back.
Gladiators spill out
from behind ice-colored Plexiglass
with their razored skates clacking
and their sword-stick blades scraping ice.
The whistle's unpledged shrill,
the drop of the puck propels gladiators forward.
Battle cries from the crowd echo
across the rink, unleash victory lust,
cement the bond between players and fans.

For three periods, fans witness:
the hive of bodies thronging, clashing
against each other's wills,
the repeated sweeping, slashing, gliding
of the puck. Is this combat, too—
the black hard disk crashing against glass,
the swish of cloth against flesh,
the smell of sweat and energy trapped in the air

after a goal?
There is beauty in this ballet of brutality,
coordination in this chaos of violence,
and grace in the cut and charge through ice.
Beneath the heavy shield of uniforms,
there are faces of men too young to buy beer.

After time retires from the scoreboard's clock,
the final score is frozen in neon triumph.
After bruised gladiators shed their armor,
return their swords to sheaths of bags,
fans stream into the parking lot,
leaving the ice ravaged in silence.

Top Shelf

"For one minute, child, for just one minute,
put yourself in other people's shoes. Then you can moan
about what you don't have."
—Mother

1.
Darkness is a shoddy doorman,
allows fatigue to walk through
its knobless frame.

Surprise is a loose chain on the gate of memory,
its slack a wide opening when I touch
the emptiness my Asics filled earlier.

"Someone took my shoes!" I
remember the suddenness of loss,
how shifty hands can whisk a ball away

from a little girl playing soccer in the street,
how she runs through night's air chasing it,
fear smudged on her brow.

2.
Jeffry's eyes are blurred with desire for home;
he skips his brown Coleman's,
slips on my gray Asics.

I wonder if he can feel:
the imbalance of my stride,
the swollen left foot, the twisted left knee,

my desideratum to run again,
the poems written in my ankles.
Here is my life stretched between his heel and toes.

Maybe this is forgiveness—
to confuse the soles, oblivious
of others transgressions, differences.

Maybe this is compassion—
to feel the shape of someone else's chi and
mistake that quivering heart as your own.

Conversation with a Furr's Cafeteria Employee

"I don't know what else to tell you. There's not much more
you can do. Sometimes people just want you to listen to them.
Sometimes that's the only way you can help."
—Mother

Perhaps it's the way I shift my book
in the fledgling silence,
after the waitress sweeps dishes into a plastic tub,
that make my eyes a net for hers.
"I am getting hungry now. My blood sugar is low."
She tells me this as if winged-silence makes us friends.
My turn to sweep—
as if this is my purpose: to notice *Joann* engraved
on the faux platinum-plated tag.
She is grief in a red shirt, lotus tattooed right arm,
fuchsia painted lips. "Are you diabetic?"
Her broken English sounds mended,
heritage a whisper on her tongue.
"No. I don't eat much. I don't sleep much.
I live mostly on coffee."

Her body is a haggard testament, my hand
a podium for my chin. I bookmark pages
78 &79 with a clean white paper napkin;
Baldacci's Will Robie can wait. I will read
of his absolution later.

Silence, the only syllable in the language
of my body when she says,
"I am grieving; my mother is, too."
Is grief a clairvoyant? The reason she pours
more sadness into me?

"My father and brother got killed in an accident.
Last July. There were five people involved."

My mind flinches with recognition. I ask, "The one
with the lady and two children?"
My heart wants a new calendar.

Maybe Joann needs someone to remember, says
"Yes, that's the one . . ."
"She was driving the wrong way
because she was drunk?"
"My brother son come from China 4 July.
But his daddy dead. Sorry, Honey. More customers.
I have to go."

There is no room in my gullet
for cucumbers or cabbage.
A lone wolf, I get a to-go box,
pick up my book, pay the cashier.
Joann pushes a cart, back slumped.
The Guilty and I walk outside into a forest of light.

Before My Birth

"Think long and hard about it. You won't get a second
chance with this one."
—Mother

I want to return to a sticky September afternoon,
back before my umbilical cord was snipped
and tied. Even further still, back before I was a seed
in the garden of my mother's life.
There are a few things I want to negotiate
with the Creator, "do overs" for squandered opportunities.

This time I would fly a yellow dragon kite with red wings,
watch its long paper tail whip at thin clouds.
Straddle the faux-jeweled saddle of a carousel's
fiberglass horse, ride without clinging to the pole.
Play tag with the fair-skinned boy who made me cry
when he said, "You're too dark to be beautiful."
But only after I make each of us the color of stars.
I would play hide-and-go-seek at dusk
with neighborhood children.
I want to run swiftly beyond the sun's shuttering eye,
down a dirt ridden path and hide so far behind
a safe door of darkness I would hear the wind's
contented sigh as it watches tree branches wave at nothing.

On Our Thirtieth Anniversary

"Today you think you can't live without him.
Tomorrow you will be thanking God he's gone."
—Mother

The flame of a cinnamon-scented candle burns,
stowing its memory in heavy red curtains.
This small room is where I feel the music
of your arms when you ask, *Will you choose me, too?*
A voyeuristic moon pokes a partial eye
through the window.
In the lean darkness, I lean my head
closer to the drumming sound of your chest.
Our embrace is a tiny hall of breaths and desire.
This halcyon night is our thirtieth anniversary
that never happens.
Age twenty-three, rejection was a hammer against my teeth.
Now it's a banjo strumming joyful melodies under an elm,

its leaves shaking like maracas
in the hands of an excited wind.

The Last Photo

of my mother, Mary Walker, and her sister, Katie Arnold

Because I was
born to a mother without a mother,
a father who withheld me from his mother,
I have no stories of their beginnings.
Shadows fill the empty branches of my origin.

I do have a picture of my mother and her sister,
four years mark the distance between their births.
Decades shaped their faces almost identical.
Warm light feathers across the frame of a red screen door.
With mirrored bodies, they sit,

and sit.

And sit.

They do not fill the empty
silence with words.
The diction of their eyes
is a contiguous knowing,
the emptiness my inheritance.

What Mama Taught Me in High School about Love, Breakups, Choices, and Other Such Things

1.
Don't confuse love with control. Control tries
to hold you back. Love pushes you forward.

2.
If a man ever raises his hand to strike you, don't let
there be a second chance. Love doesn't hit!

3.
It doesn't matter what he looks like.
He can have a square head and peg leg;
somebody will want him because you are with him.

4.
I told you before not to get a boyfriend with a new car.
Get one with a clunker. At least he can take you out.
The other one can't. He's too busy paying for that car.

5.
I'm not changing my mind; you're too young to date
and he's too old for you. Besides, by the time you're old
enough he will have forgotten you.

6.
Break up with him if you want to.
Just know as soon as you say "shoo, shoo"
someone else is on the other side of the street
saying "here chickie, chickie."

7.
Don't tell me what someone else is doing wrong;
I don't want to hear it. The only difference between them
and you is you haven't gotten caught yet and they have.

8.
I don't care if you tried it a hundred times. Try it again.
Maybe you will get it right after one hundred one.

9.
I spent time matching bows and socks with your dresses.
You would look so cute when I sent you to school.
I never knew what I was going to get when you got home.

Last Instructions

Whatever you do,
I don't want y'all fighting when I'm gone.

Mother instructs as if on her way to work,
will return before the far west corner of sky
wrings orange into a big bucket of evening.

We sit around the table of our loss,
spar with the tears raging to punch through our eyes.
We call a truce for now, plan her life's celebration.

There's no birth order in grief. We're all born
June 15 at 10:36 p.m. into this new world without her.
Tomorrow I will ask, "What do you remember about this day?"

I'll tell them I focus on her river of clothes
hanging in the polished light of her closet.
The hangers' plastic shoulders fail to hold her shape.

My eyes swim left then right; I shut the door.
A fresh stream of darkness flows into the tiny room.

> white teardrop of moon
> drifting clouds carry sorrow
> even the blue-black mourns

IV

*I knew when my mother was about to make a revelation
or share some part of her history. Inevitably, she would
look up, make a reference to something in the sky or
comment on the weather or the season.*
"That's a harvest moon. I used to pick cotton under it."
"Boy! Those are some puny clouds; I feel the same way."
*I have inherited the same nuances. My poems are filled
with her voice; I can feel her singing in the scratching
of my pen.*
—LDW

Lust

How many June days will this greedy canyon eat?
All day this summer sky pours pitchers of light,
stuffs bowls of hot air into a wide gully.
Maybe this is the curse of beauty, an endless longing.
Maybe this is the fate of a desert dweller
to live with an unsatisfied appetite.
After witnessing a roadrunner streak
beneath a high white-collared moon
into a rumpled pasture
populated with tumbleweed and cacti,
after a white butterfly ascends like a dove
from an ocean of bluebonnets,
after a serenade of wind stops the heart,
when breath returns, eyes greedily beg for more.

In This Town That Never Ages

"The question is not what you look at, but what you see."
—Thoreau

The air, a synthesis of scents—horse dung and goats,
lilac and roses, mint and lima beans.
Chickens outnumber citizens, yards touch as lovers,
and summer, a broken metronome, hovers
over charcoal roofs in this tiny town of Eden.
Its borders are bloodless.

At the end of a graveled road, gray stones
piled like a monument to kindness are welcome mats.
A rooster Edgar Hunt might envy, prances, pecks
corn where there are no sidewalks.
His tail feathers are motionless as a tight wig.

A constant tarp of light
covers two white stucco cottages,
their red doors closed as cautious lips.
Who lives behind these walls
where windows are framed with Christless crucifixes?
Adam, the potter, who does not concern himself
with the grass?
For days, he spins the afternoon with mud, fire,
makes a flowerpot.
His small child traces her handprints on the pot's belly,
stows flowers from the garden in its clay mouth.

She takes her cheerful totem next door
where despair lives in the form
of grandmother's broken bruised body—
a fall after the cancer and demented mind.

Granny smiles, reaches for the gift
as she opens then shuts the doors.
Her eyes fatigued. Red.

She tries to hush the stay, stay, stay
of her son's begging voice
disguised as flowers.

She clenches, unclenches her fists,
tries to pick cotton under a harvest moon
in a town where night has forgotten
how to write its name.

Finding You after the Storm

The E-Z Rider van driver wheels you
into a speechless house.
Those thrust through the canal of your thighs
are too far away to shoo the swarming emptiness.

Suddenly the sky recants its kindness—
in the hard gray of its madness, a storm.
Fear strikes your body with loud fists
of hail walloping windows, stucco, roof.

Frenzy shakes the bruise in your back
when I find you in the muggy dark,
hands clawed to your wheelchair.
I cradle you with night creeping into my arms.

So much darkness surrounds this house—
the television, your eyes
filmed with an early dusk-color.

On the way to you, Mother,
my friend Melanie drives.
My hands wobble with dread.
My armpits gully with anxiety.
My mouth fills with dry stories.

We follow behind cars with hail-punched windshields,
roll down streets where shingles, broken glass, and bricks
are lakes of debris. We coast through neighborhoods
where splintered fences, tree limbs, leaves, litter lawns.
Walls of homes resemble colanders;
streetlamps are fireless torches.

On Esmond Drive, an oak is
uprooted like the foundation of this day.
A mature maple with its severed trunk
blocks traffic on Forty-Second Street.
Mama, I feel like those trees—
until I touch your back,
until I see the sky force a blush of rainbows.

Portrait of a Summer's Day

For Dr. Tracie Gibson

Untamed creatures shuffle
through the forest of morning—
unimpressed with its sprays of beginnings.

Light puddles, floods wild grass.
In a steeple of trees, a chorus of robins
croons a flirting melody.

In a far field, a ladybug rests
her wings in the hollow of a dried log,
her polka dot dress invisible

to the squirrel busying its cheeks with breakfast
of acorns. It's curious how it ignores searching arms
of an unkempt purple sage.

This is how a summer day wakes
before the sun unveils its full face.
Its heat is no humanitarian.

Unshielded by its greatness,
the heavy panting of a stray dog
sounds like a breathless alarm.

This is where kindness sprouts hands, fills a
bowl with water, leaves the back gate open.
Its wide back is a pleading invitation.

Squirrel and Red Balloon

Light fits over his body like a muscle shirt.
Squirrel flexes his forearms, deadlifts a pinecone
marooned at the foot of a tall thirsty pine.

He scurries up the rough runway of tree,
disappears in a cushion of pine needles.

I use my eyes like search lights,
sweep them through limbs and leaves.
At the fork of two fat branches,
a deflated red balloon hangs from a twig.

It's amazing how life snags the smallest of things,
tucks them away in its unpredictable hands—
the dark silhouettes of memory,
day blooming in the middle of June,
a squirrel's busy hunger.

Of Children and Bees

This is how you walk inside of a smile,
listen to a small swarm of children buzz with laughter.
Joy thick as honey clogs their throats
as they thread their bodies
through the windows of a Jungle Gym,
swing toward the blue umbrella of a summer's day.

They are like the honey bee with its language of dance,
circling to the music of sun inside her nest—
body too large for its gauzy wings.
She defies aerodynamics, flutters, flirts, kisses
white-faced, stout-nosed wildflowers with her long tongue.
Is it promiscuous the way she swaps their seeds,
infects them with beauty?

Scientists say the bees are disappearing.
So is the laughter of children
clutching, threading fingers through small windows
of chain link fences.
Their bodies are silhouettes caught in the wire netting.
They press faces against wire, willing tears to fly
over the long valley of terror,
into the flowers of their mothers' hands.
But their mothers are wounded bees
trapped in rolling steel hives—
walls aching from the constant buzz of sorrow.
The sky clogs its ears with stars to silence the lamenting
as the masses sing hallelujah to a promise.

Birth of Autumn

For Ann Howells

This is an ultrasound of my city.
Summer heat is so primal it screams.
Imitation skyscrapers stretch
their square necks toward a sadistic sky.

Boarded windows in front
of a flaking orange building
swallow light and darkness
with the same tight-lipped bite.

The pavement knows the language of feet,
the incessant medley of need,
how I use sunrises and sunsets to tick off
rumbling urgency in the calendar of my stomach.

This afternoon wind is packed
in an attic of clouds.
Gray drizzle hoods the city for days.
Silence is trapped in a mulberry's wet fallen leaves.

Next month that tree will be a naked effigy.
There is no sleight of hand; this is how fall arrives.
September with its powerful cold arms
wrestles to fit into the same skin of space

as summer's screaming heat
in the birth canal of a fire-colored season.

Autumn in West Texas

For Terri L. Anthony

Strong winds fill morning's lungs.
Trees wake with an unsteady sway,
the future of their leaves trembling.
Is this how fear violates our joy—
with shuddering and shouting?
A wren watches as day draws change,
outlines light with orange.
Oh, to be a denizen of the sky!
Freedom is lifted by air,
and wings are for the longing.
Is this beating against my breastbone envy,
thickening in the tunnel of my throat desire?
The answer is in the crisping leaves.

Drinking Poetry

For Patrick and Andrea Marshall

It's fall; Odessa's desert heat doesn't know
the difference, keeps temperatures turned up
to high nineties.
Our fifth grade classroom smells like spoiled sun.
We sit in class, ignore each other's sweaty odors.
A dissonance of sounds fills the room—
a whirring pencil sharpener, a fan's aged hum,
fingers thumping on desks.

Our teacher's voice is the soprano
we're trained to listen for; she stands
in front of the room, reads "If."
After she tells us, *You'll be a Man, my son*!
she passes out blue mimeographed copies
of the poem, says, "Write what Kipling means."

I lean my head against the window, wait
for a revelation from the baking fall day.
What does a ten-year-old know of *twisted knaves,
nerve and sinew, the unforgiving minute?*
In the back of the room, I hear my best friend's
noisy slurps at the drinking fountain. My paper
is still a white question mark when he sits down.

Maybe this is what Kipling meant: drink life
noisily! When your thirst is slaked, answers will
open like a lotus garden in the sudden silence.

Breathless

Tonight's full moon is a canvas
behind the fluttering American flag
in the parking lot of Music City Mall.
A few generous stars drop the
light of their memories onto Old Glory—
each white replica a high note
in the chorus of unity.
I drive, window down,
listen to the timid wind hum
O beautiful for spacious skies.

Winter

For Michelle Hartman

Winter toys with shadows
whispering shocks of cold.
A bare oak like fingers of lightning
is silhouetted on a canvas of snow.

Tonight's sky is glassy.
The language of impish stars is visible.
Their dialogue of laughter circles the moon,
that aspirin-colored belle of darkness.

In the distance, a car horn intrudes silence.
A pigeon sits on the porch of a blue row house.
Maybe change happens with a sudden blow
or in the privacy of continuous unwinding.

Christmas Day

It's Christmas.
After day sheds its woolly layers of light,
the moon slips out of the dark closet
of sky robed in a full white mantle.
My sister pours broth as I crumble
cornbread and mix other ingredients
for dressing.
Christmas lunch—
there's not an empty chair at the table.
The branches of my family tree
crowd the place
where Mama once sat with stories
and memories of her.

In the cloudless mature night,
I drive through Starlight Village
where decorations
are as colorful and bright
as a Las Vegas skyline.
In the empty seat next to me,
Mama's metal snowflake
rattles in a small glass heart.

After the Rain Stops

In 2017, identical twin sisters died within six
months of each other from breast cancer.

In the eye of the feeble rainbow
browed overhead, we are two raindrops
puddled together.

We embrace in winter's twilight;
the smell of rain clings to this desert air
as we cling to each other.

Our time-illiterate hearts cannot decipher
beginnings from endings; this moment feels
like we are in the dark cloud of our mother's womb.

Fifty-five years are stacked in our histories.
Here we are, still reaching for the other's hand
even as we step away from our embrace.

Why is separation such a steep wall,
death a border we must all cross,
illness a shape shifter?

Now our hearts are bags of tangled yarn.
Cancer, like a pair of sharp scissors, snips the knots
of your life; loose twine falls into my hands,

and for six months cancer reties those clipped strings
until they are a long thick rope. Until the rope is a harness
to drag me across the border where you are—

in that place where the rain will no longer fall.

Ode to a Cactus

On Mother's Day, my younger brother gives Mom a cactus.
It's a a green prickly leg rooted in clay and stone,
its veins juicy with fortitude.
The bulb of an orange flower struggles to open
in the hesitant space of ribbed skin.
This plant refuses to abort beauty; time is its servant.
Is this how my brother sees my mother,
as a lone bloom rooted in resilience?
Mom smiles, sits the pot on her lap,
traces the lip as though her finger is telling a secret.
Both are sunlight eaters, she from a wheeled chair,
the cactus from a thimble of desert.

Interpretations

"The ultimate goal is not to understand the dream,
however, but to understand the dreamer."
—Calvin S. Hall

I am a sycamore tree
levitating over a deep hole
where I was once planted.
With roots intact, fanned like wild hair,
I stare down
at the gaping wound.
No thing or thought can fill its yawning.
No longing is large enough
to fit inside or cork it.
The bark on my aged wide trunk
is smooth and slippery.
Light slides up and down my chest
with its quick fingers grasping
for purchase around my neck.
My fleshy branches are hundreds of arms
reaching in all directions, searching
for something to hold
or give my life to.

Dawn in the Spring

Oh, fluttering bird,
spring is a seductive foe;
the lure of dawn's budding seeds
weakens the resolve.
This garden of growing light
demands tending.
This plump sprouted air is a tease
against the face.
How can you not walk in the wilderness
of the unknown without holding your breath?
How can you not splatter your voice
into the canvas of this day without expecting?

Celebration

How do I celebrate your leaving
when I am a paper boat navigating life without you?
You are my anchor, my compass; I float aimlessly.
My desire is your hat-wearing self.
Where is the relief of your laughter?
I am listening.
When autumn was skipping across the calendar,
and we were watching the orange fire of leaves
burn, you were the spine holding us up.

Summer is hot and happy with a kaleidoscope of colors.
I am wobbly with sadness.

Now you live in that city where mothers gather
before they are mothers.
Before you leave, you forget
you loved peppered cherry tomatoes,
the scaly wings of butterflies,
that I am your daughter.

Self-Portrait with Athena

Age marches through your body,
your ruler-straight back slowly curving.
So many years you use it as a canoe
to paddle across the river of motherhood.
Pity you did not grow with the sound
of your mother's voice.
Your blood carries her memory.
Crimson nail polish cannot disguise injuries
or mend broken oars.
Dock your beautiful battered boat.
Drag your strong hands across the river.
Let healing waves salve bruised places.
Rest your head on the collected decades.
Shroud yourself in the stillness of this breezeless night.
Close your eyes;
the living will learn to swallow grief.

Still Becoming

"Live into what you already say you are."
—Dawn Weaks

You look like your father
people tell me before he makes his exodus
from this life to the next.
Since his departure, I wear my mother's face.

Curious how I am a reflection of both the dead
and the living, a tree in the forest—
their oxygen & carbon, hydrogen & nitrogen,
calcium & phosphorus.
Who then am I if I have my mother's mother's hands,
my father's father's eyes?
What is the origin of this voice that cannot sing soprano?
Who in this lineage beat the drum in the Congo's
protective arms, left rhythm in my feet?

When will my image become my own forest—
where the lust for more than my mouth can utter
is an organism I can't name,
where the bountiful secrets of my limbs
will buffer the ageless walls of this earth,
the animal of my mind roam through the long
path of undergrowth on an undefined journey?
To find my way beneath a map of stars
my grandmother, who did not live long enough to wean
her youngest child, and my grandfather, who did not live
long enough to teach my father to become a man,
in the deep night of their skin?

Maybe I am not a forest, rather a compass
whose needle is made of pulse, blood, and flaws.

Or maybe I am that one word needed
to continue their stories.

Into the New Year

We are a band of stars
in a sky orchestrated with grief.
Each tuned to a different loss—
a father, mother, sister,
brother, lover, cousin,
husband, wife, niece,
nephew, uncle, friend,
those generations of grand.
We improvise in the key of sadness.
For who can truly compose
the melody of longing
for someone else's heart?
Say hold this note of desire
for this duration of time?
Place dynamics over tears?
We each have our measures of missing . . .

A baby was born today.

That second before midnight
is the conductor that will lead
us into a new year.
Another child will be born.
Yet another, and another, and . . .
when they are caressed
by the light of this world,
they will fill this large earth
with their small cries.
In celebration, loving hands
will hold them, cease their tears.

What if we open our hands,
release into the deep darkness
beautiful memories of the ones
we hold in our hearts?

What if we made those memories
our planets, stars, clouds of jubilation
held together by the gravity of love?
Together, even as light streaks our tears,
maybe, even for a moment, we can create
a small galaxy of joy.
On the clear staff of morning,
the sky will compose a new song.

Notes

[1] Pg. 32: Found poem.

Eckert, Amy S. and Ianzito, Christina. "Heartland Getaways." AARP October/November 2017: 44-46, 50-51. Print.

[2] Pg. 32: Found poem.

"Early signs of autumn already appearing in natural world." The Guardian. Web. Tuesday 1 July 2014 01.00 EDT.

[3] Pg. 32: Found poem.

Nosowitz, Dan. "Why Does the Season Before Winter Have Two Names? A Look at the History of Fall and Autumn." Atlas Obscura. Web. Tuesday 3 November 2017.

[4] Pg. 68: Found poem.

Frederic and Mary Ann Brussat, "Autumn: Reflections on the Season, Naming the Days Feature," Spirituality Practice, September 23, 2017.

[5] Pg. 113: Found poem.

Kelly, Scott. "What I Learned in Space." AARP October/November 2017: 41-43. Print.

CPSIA information can be obtained
at www.ICGtesting.com
Printed in the USA
BVHW072041080919
557876BV00002B/483/P

MR MARTIN &
MRS MIDDLETON
MAKE MUSIC

MR MARTIN &
MRS MIDDLETON
MAKE MUSIC

L H SMITH

Yoell Books

ISBN 978-1-912892-78-5

Also available as an ebook
ISBN 978-1-912892-79-2

Typeset by Jill Sawyer
Project management by whitefox

For Peter, without whose unstinting patience and encouragement Mr Martin & Mrs Middleton would never have made it through to the printed page, and for Paul.

Verily, men do foolish things thoughtlessly, knowing not why; but no woman doeth aught without reason.

Gelett Burgess, *The Maxims of Methuselah* (1907)

PART ONE

SHADOWED BY THE PAST

Prague, October 2016

Henni Horbach was excited. As a belated ninth-birthday treat, she had asked her parents to take her, and friend, Anna, to the National Marionette Theatre. They were on their way to the box office now, to get tickets.

Henni's mother Linda, went to the desk, "Two adults and two children for the next performance of The Magic Flute please."

"Oh no, Máma," squeaked Henni. "I want to see 'Dong-Gee-Vany' please."

"Don Giovanni? But whatever for, that's grown-up opera."

"I am nine now and that's really grown-up. Frieda at school has seen them both, and she says 'Dong-Gee-Vany' is best, because it's much funnier and," she continued, "it's an evening performance, so much more sorry-fish-ticated than going in the afternoon. Please, Máma, it's still alright, isn't it?"

Mrs Horbach looked at the assistant, who was trying hard to suppress a smile.

"Really, madame, it is a much-bowdlerised version, not quite as Mr Mozart wrote, and is quite suitable for a nine-year-old sorry-fish-ticate." Mrs Horbach didn't look convinced, but it was Henni's treat, the choice was hers, so she bought the tickets.

The marionette opera turned out to be every bit as funny as Henni and Anna had hoped. The whole audience, adults and

3

children alike, roared with laughter and approval as Prague's own monster, Golem, appeared instead of the conventional statue of the Commodore, to punish the Don for his sins. Golem, huge and fearsome, shook the Don by the strings from side to side, and threw him about the stage with gusto. Henni and Anna clapped their hands in delight.

When the time came for the final bows, Henni turned and said, "Poor Dong-Gee-Vany, he really was very naughty, wasn't he?... I don't think I'd like Golem to do that to me!"

After they'd taken her home, Anna very properly shook hands, thanked, and said goodnight to Henni's mother and stepfather. Later, putting a still excited, chattering Henni to bed, Linda's smile faded from her lips and she said, "Franz, I've punished him enough. He's got to know."

Her husband nodded and kissed her cheek softly. She took out pen and paper and began writing a letter which she addressed to Mrs M. Martin, Gamekeepers Cottage, Manor Farm, Dovedale, Derbyshire, England.

CHAPTER ONE

Ripon North Yorkshire, January 2017

Having boarded her cat, Bob, out to a neighbour the previous evening, Sara Middleton, at an eye-watering 3.00am, perched on her seat in the rear of a rather grubby taxi, bound for Tees Valley airport. Unbelievably, at the age of forty-eight she had never flown before. Her parents had taken her on a ferry trip to Calais once, when she was twelve, other than that she had never been out of the UK. It wasn't a life-style choice, she'd always longed to travel, but…

She closed her eyes and thought of her husband George. He'd travelled a lot, after leaving school he'd joined the merchant navy. They'd spend hours talking about how when he was captain of his own ship, he would take her everywhere she dreamed of, in a style fit for a queen. But it wasn't meant to be. The first thing he did when they were married was get her pregnant, with twins. Then he went back to sea, only to get himself drowned in a stupid accident off the coast of Menton in the South of France, when he had thoughtlessly swum out to sea chasing a football. It happened just a week before Dave and Georgina were born. The plan had been to give up her teaching post, instead it was only maternity leave. She had to go back to work to support her new family. George had lost them all at sea. Both sets of grandparents helped provide a lifeboat of care, but it was she who had to row them safely to shore.

His body had been found on the day the twins were born. Naturally she couldn't go to France, instead George's parents had to go to identify the body and in the circumstances thought it wise to have him interred there. Sara had allowed herself to be convinced it was for the best, she gave her consent, but was unhappy at not being able to say a proper goodbye to him. Mostly though, she was angry and fearful for the future. George had no right to die *now*, and so far from home. She knew it was irrational to blame him for dying, but she did. She blamed him very much, for not being there, and not doing the things they had planned together.

She sighed to herself. It hadn't been easy, but she'd seen the children through. There was little money to spare when they were young and of course, everything came at twice the cost. Life was a delicate balance of making ends meet and being a mother. She had her teaching, and being able to share the same school holidays was good, they'd usually spend them at camp sites in the Dales. The twins loved that when they were young, but in their teenage years they'd grown resentful about friends' exotic trips abroad. However they were suitably aware enough to know that they needed to work at weekend jobs to finance their various wants.

Eventually being made Head of Music (herself, and one part-timer), meant Sara could put some small savings by, but as they were plundered too often by the twins' ambitions, they never amounted to much. She was happy to help them, but shadows of disappointment lodged at the back of her mind, as her own faded dreams stayed in the dusty box where they'd lain since George had died.

Out of necessity rather than nature, she had to develop steely strength to cope with being a single parent and found an ideal source in her rage at George's profligate waste of his life. She would not let the twins down by behaving irresponsibly as their father had and expected the same consideration from them. She encouraged an inner voice of common sense and reason to carefully construct a carapace to protect herself and the twins from further hurt. But growing children, as she found out, have their own ideas as to what constitutes consideration and it usually isn't on a par with their mother's. When they grew too big for Sara's maternal shell, Georgie and Dave secretly, but not without affection, nicknamed their mother's voice of reason her *Agony Angst*.

She remembered with a wry smile the first time she'd heard Dave let slip the sobriquet, he was eighteen, just before he went up to university. He and his best friend Tom were keen to get a bus they knew of, that would take them to Amsterdam for twenty-four hours. All they needed was a passport, a big packed lunch and the fare (which was incredibly cheap). They didn't even have to book, just be at a specified stop at the right time to flag down the bus. He must have seen the surprise and half smile on her lips as he skilfully nagged her into letting him go and so both boys went off on their big adventure, catching the bus at midnight on the Ripon by-pass.

But they were not on the bus when it returned. No one knew where they were, and for eight unbearable hours, Sara imagined Dave floating face down in a canal, drowned just like his father. In fact, what had happened was, when the boys realised the bus had left without them, they'd found a place to stay for the night and slept until mid-afternoon.

They contacted their frantic parents as soon as they woke. With nothing but a few euros between them, it was complicated getting them home, but everything worked out and they made it home late but safe.

She'd run up to Dave and held him tight. She didn't want to let him go for fear he'd disappear again, which for an eighteen year old in the presence of his best mate, she now conceded, was very embarrassing, and probably why he'd adopted such a casual air when he'd said, "Sorry, Mum, we were late getting in and missed the train we should've got. Only just made it for this one." And then he'd smiled George's smile. It was too much, before she could check herself she'd shouted at him.

"You fucking idiot! You are just like your bloody father! I thought there was another one dead!"

Dave had stopped smiling at once. Sara blushed at the memory. He'd never heard her use language like that before, because she never had. He hugged her close, because they both knew in a moment how much it had cost her to let him go. But with the callousness of youth, as all her worst fears had been shown to be unfounded, from then on all Sara's expressions of concern were openly referred to and dismissed as 'mum's *AA* moments'. In the end she adopted the term herself, it made her laugh to see her anxieties personified as a skinny, strict neurotic. Sara liked to laugh but all the same, in the dark hours and when she was alone, she couldn't help but feel that *Agony Angst* must always be accommodated, for fear of calamitous consequences if her directives were wilfully ignored.

***

Dave was now a qualified accountant, married with a child of his own. Georgie had opted to train as an officer in the Royal Navy. 'The nearest,' she said, 'to fulfilling her dad's ambitions', and Sara was justifiably proud of their achievements. But there was another Sara, not the parent in thrall to her tyrannous *AA*, but one nothing and no one could confine. When the children were still in primary school she had been invited to re-join the choir at Ripon Cathedral where she'd sung in her early BC (Before Children) years. Singing revealed Sara's truest nature. Leonard Cohen's eloquence asserts, 'There's a crack in everything, that's where the light gets in...' but the fissure in Sara's armour did not let light *in,* when she sang light poured *out.* Her fine mezzo voice full of passion and commitment, was more exciting and beautiful than she realised. It was no wonder she was a prized first choice soloist.

At Christmas, the two great Northern Cathedral choirs of Ripon and York Minster had combined at Ripon for a performance of Verdi's Requiem where Sara had sung for the first time alongside York's bass-baritone, Harry Martin. It was quite a coup for the smaller cathedral that Mr Martin should have agreed to sing there, and although it was not something Sara was cognizant of, this was largely down to favourable reports he'd heard of her. She did know that he had a reputation of being very demanding as to the quality of his co-performers and sometimes could be 'difficult', if they proved less than totally committed, and she'd been nervous.

When he'd first entered Ripon Cathedral accompanied by the other York choristers, all eyes focused on him. He was a fit looking man of average height, mid to late forties, with a smile that could probably charm a saint into dining with

Satan. But it wasn't just his appearance, although he was certainly very handsome, there was an air about him that gave Sara a sudden sense of déjà vu and made her heart lurch. He'd brought back a memory from her early childhood when her grannie had possessed a Meissen shepherd figurine, which she'd kept in pride of place in the china cabinet. He'd lost his shepherdess many years before, when he'd been salvaged from a deserted, wrecked farmhouse in Germany, at the end of the First War. Sara was fascinated by his delicate beauty and grace. She loved the figurine more than any of her dolls and was devastated when he was accidently broken.

Grannie had already swept up the debris ready to go in the bin, when Sara and her daddy arrived. Sara had stared at the myriad pieces in the dustpan and saw one perfect hand. Unnoticed she reached out and hid it in a tightly clenched little fist. She'd felt no pain, only a sensation of great warmth when blood seeped through her closed fingers and dripped onto the floor. The memory stopped there, but the scar where the razor-sharp shard had embedded itself in her hand was visible to this day.

Whether it was on this account that she found him so disquieting, she didn't know, but it did little to calm her nerves. He was very correct and smiled as they were introduced, but she felt his scrutiny quite sharply. Nevertheless, Sara was not going to be intimidated by him, and returned his look with one of her own that more than equalled his. She saw in his eyes that he recognised the challenge.

The first rehearsal together began, and it was obvious that some alchemy was at work between them. Harry was delighted with Sara's beautiful voice which matched her innate musicianship. His magnificent strong bass-baritone carried her deeper than she thought possible into the glory of Verdi's Requiem. The sound they made together was a precarious blend of opposites and the result, totally thrilling.

In the following weeks, working together was magic. Her only trouble was she knew it would soon come to an end, and her beautiful shepherd would be gone.

'Mr Martin!' She hadn't even allowed herself to be on first name terms with him. It was ridiculous. In all the years since losing George, she had never even thought of entering into a relationship with another man, yet she couldn't deny the excitement she felt at rehearsals when they sang in such intimate proximity.

Agony Angst gatecrashed her thoughts. 'Stop kidding yourself, Sara. He sees you as nothing more than a voice with a person attached. He'll have forgotten your existence two minutes after the concert ends.'

'Do you really think so? We're good together and I would like to work with him again.'

'It's OK if you can just stick to the singing, but you've got to keep a lid on it. I've a feeling he's a dangerous person to get close to. He'd hurt you, Sara.'

She smiled to herself. 'Alright, I promise just to enjoy our moments singing together and then put him firmly out of my mind.'

'Good girl,' *AA* answered. 'Keep safe.'

Unfortunately, a few weeks before Christmas, Sara had learnt that rumours about her school being merged with a big comprehensive in another part of town after the holidays were true. The comprehensive already had a Music Department of three. A new post of Head of Music and Drama was to be created, which Sara knew she had no chance of getting. Basically, she was facing demotion or redundancy. She thought about the Requiem in only a few days, and it felt like it would be a requiem for her own life.

Dave and Georgie were more up-beat when she told them about it. They said she should get in touch with her union rep, who was a close and trusted friend, to see what could be done. As it happened, a good redundancy package was on offer, with a surprisingly generous lump sum, plus an enhanced pension. With the mortgage paid and the option of supply teaching, she reckoned she could live comfortably on that. She might even, after Christmas, make a visit to George's grave, before taking a little holiday in the South of France.

When she confided her thoughts to them, Dave and Georgie who both loved her dearly, had no doubts as to what she should do.

"Go for it, Mum!"

Although perfectly capable of working out how to do it herself, Dave had insisted he would sort out the minefield of booking tickets, boarding pass, apartment, etc. online, and take time off to get her to the airport. She was grateful for the booking arrangements, but hoped he understood that it was important to her to do all of the journey by herself. When he started to protest, Sara made it clear it was partly a kind of pilgrimage she wanted to make to his father, and one she needed to make alone.

***

The Christmas Requiem had been a triumph, performed to a cathedral packed to capacity. Sara had never been in better voice. Mr Martin had been particularly affable and complimentary about Sara's performance and gave all his fellow soloists a hug. At his touch, a tingle went through parts of Sara's body that she'd almost forgotten she had. The effect was electric. He'd offered to take everyone for a drink, and she was sorely tempted to go but *Agony Angst* counselled against it. 'It would not do,' the voice had told her, 'anyway, nothing but disappointment would come of it.' So Sara declined his offer and went straight home with her family instead. He expressed well-mannered regret, but did not press her to change her mind, which *AA* told her, quite clearly showed his indifference. 'Hey ho,' thought Sara. 'You're right, I'm fine as I am.'

Perhaps it was as well she didn't see him turn his head to observe her departure as he shepherded the others away, otherwise she might not have been quite so sanguine.

CHAPTER TWO

With the same presence of mind which she had brought to bringing up her children, Sara had prepared as well as she could for her plunge into the adventure of foreign travel. She would make the journey to Menton at the end of January to be there for the twenty-sixth anniversary of George's death. It was so odd to think he had been dead two years longer than he'd lived, and that his children were older now than he was then. Should she have waited all these years before going to France? *AA* insisted that the time had never been right before, she had to put the children's needs first. There had been no time or money to waste on sentimental trips abroad.

The main problem was going to be coping with a foreign language. Her schoolgirl French was not up to much and although she'd sung a fair number of songs in the language, she doubted that would suffice, so a French phrase book was a 'must-buy'. A trip to the local library yielded a very useful paperback about Menton and its environs, and both were in her hand luggage now.

Dave's advice to his mother had been to travel out from Tees Valley, which was small and less intimidating for a first-time flyer than a busy airport like Newcastle or Manchester. He explained she would fly first to Schiphol in Amsterdam, then after a break of a couple of hours make the connection to Nice. From there she would need to get a taxi to Menton.

Sara's eyes shone with anticipation at the very idea of travelling through Amsterdam and Nice, but she expressed her nervousness at having to change planes.

"It's OK, Mum," Dave said. "They don't make you do it in mid-air."

She laughed, "You know what I mean," and added only half-jokingly "What if I get it wrong and end up in Timbuctoo by mistake?"

"Well," her son answered seriously, "I guess they'll take you out and after shooting you, make you walk barefooted all the way home."

"David!" she said.

"Truly, you'll be fine," he answered with a smile. "There's no chance of you getting it wrong, because you are going in style. Georgie and I think it's 'payback' time and we are upgrading you to Business Class. This means you'll be looked after from the beginning to the end of your journey. I mean, you and the other elite will be first on and first off the plane. You will have the use of a dedicated lounge to wait in until your second flight, where incidentally, all refreshments are included in the price." His smile turned into a big grin as he saw the delight in Sara's eyes.

"Round the world, like a queen," she whispered.

He took her hands in his, then with mounting pride and excitement continued to tell her of the plans he and his sister had made to make their mother's dream come true.

"Your accommodation is all sorted out too, in a first-floor apartment in La Maison Soleil. It's a pretty little place near the town centre and only a minute or two walk from the beach. You know my friend Jack Williams and his wife, they've owned it for years, but seldom use it in winter. They like you and say you can have it for just the running costs, for a couple of weeks.

"What do you think?"

He looked momentarily worried when he saw the blank expression on Sara's face, but broke into smiles again when she opened up her arms to give him the biggest mummy-hug ever.

"Georgie will be in touch later tonight to talk to you about it as well."

"It's all wonderful, Dave. Thank you both so much."

It was all happening now. Sara's driver told her they were only a minute away from the airport, but it was very cold. Other than hauling her luggage out of the car, he didn't offer to help get it into the terminal building. However he did gallantly warn her to be careful because the temperature was below freezing, and she should watch out for ice.

The airport was as Dave promised, very quiet, and she found the check-in desk easily. There was no queue and the lovely girl there was patient and friendly when she explained all about when and where Mrs Middleton was to present her passport and boarding pass. The most difficult thing was getting her rather large suitcase loaded onto the conveyor belt. She managed security control with aplomb, then followed directions to the departure lounge where, seated in a comfy chair, enjoyed hot coffee and a bacon roll, whilst leafing through a glossy magazine (provided).

It was still dark and very cold, as the half dozen business-class passengers stepped out onto the tarmac to board. They were soon settled, but the icy wind was growing wild and snow began to fall in an almost horizontal sheet just as the door closed behind the last tourist-class traveller.

The plane rocked from side to side in a manner that frankly alarmed Sara, and was made worse by the captain's announcement that the weather was making take-off conditions hazardous. The wind grew wilder as the sleet and snow rattled like a machine gun against the sides of the plane.

It was a good half hour before the engines began to roar and the plane jerked into motion. Sara took a deep breath and with a great effort of will not to be terrified, leaned back in her seat and looked fixedly out into the dark outside, as the plane built up speed down the runway until finally lifting itself into the sky, then her heart began to soar with it. 'I'm coming, George,' she thought, 'you've waited a long time, but I'm coming now.' Pin-pricks of lights below faded in the grey dawn and soon thick cloud obscured everything. Sara closed her eyes now and in great contentment let her mind wander indiscriminately between past, present and future, until the captain's voice broke through her reverie, to say that due to the lateness of their departure from Tees Valley, ongoing connections had been missed, so passengers had been rebooked on alternative flights.

This was a development that she was not totally prepared for, but kept calm, until the KLM representative at the airport desk told her that her next flight would not be until 8.00pm. Ten hours away. The suggestion that Mrs Middleton might go out into the city and return later had little appeal for Sara. Looking through the window she could see nothing but a cold grey, mist and drizzling rain. George had always made travel sound so exciting and full of sunshine, but now she realised perhaps she'd been given only the edited highlights.

"Or," the clerk continued, looking kindly at Sara's crest-fallen face "You could go straight to the KLM business lounge. Every comfort is provided."

She smiled as she saw Sara's mood jump up again like a yo-yo. Sara had forgotten about the lounge with all its promised facilities. It would be another exciting new experience. 'Like a queen, George!' she said to herself and taking in directions, happily went off in search of her temporary Shangri-La. It was all she could have hoped for, warm, comfortable and spacious with tea, coffee and even wine on tap, plus as much delicious food as she could want. There was certainly no rush, she had time enough to enjoy this dimension of luxury air travel to the full, and she damn well would make sure she did!

A sign saying Shower Room caught her eye and in just a few minutes she was shown into an elegantly tiled, bigger and better equipped bathroom than her own would ever be. There were piles of soft white towels and expensive looking toiletries. She treated herself to all the creams and potions on offer and eventually emerged looking and feeling pretty good.

After helping herself to a decent-sized lunch, it was time to venture out into the shopping area, where she embarked on and enjoyed a magnificently frivolous, theoretical spending spree in the big shiny mall. Head buzzing with the glitzy thrill of it all, she spent multi-thousands of virtual euros on outrageously expensive clothes, handbags, shoes, jewellery and perfume.

It was amazing how quickly time flew by until it was time to go through the other passport control and visit the next departure lounge for a cup of tea and a rest.

Strangely, her nap made her more tired than she had felt all day and it was a weary Sara who set out to find the departure gate for her flight to Nice. The weather had closed in again with a vengeance and the plane was late. A last-minute change of gate sent the passengers haring off down many corridors and steps to wait for a coach to ferry them to the outer limits of the terminal, to board their flight.

After taxiing for what seemed like miles, at last the engines began to roar and the plane bumpily rose skyward.

In the pitch-black of night, as they approached the landing strip at Nice Airport, the runway lights made it look unnervingly short and narrow, but touchdown was an unerringly smooth and safe experience.

Sara was there. She had done it. She was in France. One last taxi ride away and she would be in Menton.

Once off the plane, she followed the herd through to the baggage hall where she quickly commandeered a trolley and as soon as it appeared, grabbed her luggage off the conveyer belt and hauled it on. Hurrying through the 'nothing to declare' gate she pushed her trolley close to the taxi rank (clearly signposted), caught the eye of the leading cab driver, allowed him to transfer her luggage to the boot of his shiny car, discarded the trolley, stepped into the taxi, handed him a map with the address on it, and drove off to Menton.

The young driver was friendly and garrulous. His *"Comprenez-vous Francais?"* elicited a cautious *"Un peu"* from

Sara, but she understood barely a word he said as she let his chatter flow over her.

Sara gazed in wonder at the twinkling lights of the hill towns and gorgeous long tunnels under the mountains. She didn't care for tunnels as a rule, but these were large and lit like Christmas trees. She felt drunk with tiredness and the strange beauty of it all. It took forty-five minutes before they entered the outskirts of Menton. She caught sight of the sea glinting in the moonlight, and her heart gave a lurch. George had died here. Her euphoria disappeared into the night.

Just short of midnight her taxi drew up outside La Maison Soleil. Almost twenty hours and a world away from Tees Valley. Her driver graciously carried Sara's luggage up to the door and helped her key in the numbers on the door pad. Once inside, he even carried her heavy bags up to her apartment on the first floor. She paid and tipped him well for this kindness and took his proffered card, should she need him for the return trip.

Dave's colleague, who'd lent her the flat had left instructions as to how the central heating worked, she just needed to flip the switch by the door, which she did straight away because it was quite cold. There was dried milk and some teabags in the kitchen cupboard, so she put the kettle on. The apartment itself was plain but clean. It had tiled floors, rugs but no curtains, only blinds and shutters at the windows.

Tomorrow was soon enough to unpack. Feeling not so much a seasoned as a hobnailed traveller, she made and drank the most welcome cup of tea she'd had for years and fell gratefully into her excellent bed where she slept until morning was well broken.

CHAPTER THREE

Sara awoke to the aroma of coffee and croissants wafting up from the floor below, and decided breakfast was a first priority. Showering quickly, she ignored the wretched unpacking and set off to *'mange le petit déjeuner dans un café en Menton'*.

The weather was colder than she'd expected, and she regretted opting for her light travel jacket rather than the Puffa one still lurking by the suitcase. No matter, the sky was blue and Sara was in France. Not surprisingly, it was easy to find a café and she went into *Boulangerie Kayzer,* marvelling at the array of pastries and breads on display. She ordered *café au lait* and a croissant, then chose a seat at the window. Her breakfast was so delicious, she asked for a second helping and, copying a native, happily broke off pieces of croissant to dunk in her coffee.

Looking out, she could see scaffolding and boards going up (or down, she wasn't sure which) around the grassed area in the centre of the main road with a lot of men in hard hats scuttling round like busy beetles. The babble of French being spoken around her was exciting. It all felt odd but good. She let the mood of total ease with the world take hold. Her life up to now had existed in a smaller separate place. Here she felt it was possible to grow her own set of wings and fly anywhere, while *Agony Angst,* exhausted after the previous day's traumas, momentarily held her peace.

But Sara was a Yorkshire lass at heart, and first needed to stock up her food cupboard. It was all very well growing wings, but even free spirits need to feed. She paid her bill and set out to find the Rue de Marins, the morning market would close at noon and it was already going on for 10.45, and needs must.

It turned out not to be too far away and sold all kinds of amazing food. The fish stalls were a revelation, she didn't even recognise half the species laid out so neatly on crushed ice, some of which she definitely didn't like the look of at all. But she did buy fresh vegetables, and other necessities including some very ordinary but very expensive teabags. Nearer her apartment she called back at the *Boulangerie* for a baton of bread. As she had read Menton was famous for its lemons, she also bought *une tarte au citron.*

Laden with bags, she staggered up to the apartment and took delight in arranging her purchases in the copious kitchen cupboards. She answered Dave's message as to whether she had arrived OK, then stepped out onto the balcony, and whilst savouring the quality of Menton's lemon speciality, watched the sea rolling its waves gently on the shore, thinking of George.

Sara devoted most of her afternoon to unpacking, when she'd finished, she put on her warm jacket and took a stroll along the *Promenade du Soleil.* She returned to her apartment before it got dark to prepare and eat a simple supper made from some of the day's purchases.

Settling on the sofa, she studied a map of Menton and checked the exact whereabouts of the *cimetière* in the *Vieille Ville*.

Tomorrow she would buy flowers and visit George. For now, she switched on the TV and began to watch a halfway-through Spaghetti Western, starring Clint Eastwood, dubbed into French. A novel, if not altogether riveting experience and soon fell into a doze, before trundling herself off to bed.

Next morning, wide awake after a good night's sleep, breakfast at 'her' *boulangerie* seemed a good way to start the quest to find her husband's grave. The word 'husband' sounded alien in her head. There was a latent bitterness in her mind because they hadn't been together long enough for him to merit that name, Sara rarely ever thought of him in those terms. She wondered why she should now, it was a bit confusing, so put the conundrum on the back burner, as she licked her fingers free of sticky *pain-au-chocolat*. She sipped her coffee, and gave her full attention to the street map lying in front of her and took a photograph out of her bag.

She had always referred to him as being buried in Menton but this was not strictly true, George had in fact been cremated and his ashes interred in a small plot. There was not enough money to do otherwise. But his parents had arranged with the funeral authorities to have a small plaque placed to his memory. When it was ready and *in situ*, the funeral directors had sent a promised photograph to Sara and his parents. It was the best they could do.

Although it was still far from warm, today she had dressed in the new smart outfit she had brought specially for the occasion. A dark red suit with cream silk blouse, a cashmere scarf, light stockings, and burgundy red shoes with a small elegant heel. She wanted to look good for George. She felt both nervous and excited, as if they were meeting for the first time.

Having already seen a florist in Rue Partouneaux, and made her way there, she looked around carefully, not wanting anything ostentatious, just something 'right', finally deciding on a posy of fourteen freesias. Ten, for the months she had been married plus one each from herself the twins and grandson. Wrapping the warm scarf around her, she began to walk up toward the *Vieille Ville*.

The cemetery was high up, at the top of the old town. Sepia and yellow houses rose like sheer cliffs either side of narrow twisting streets, passages, and flights of steps that seemed like young mountains. She passed the church of St Michel standing high and proud in its piazza, 100 feet above the port, where the wind chilled her to the bone. The climb continued past a primary school situated on the left, clinging on to the steep curve, then she saw the many crosses that towered above the cemetery wall on the opposite side of the road. Up yet further, round a wide swing of road and many steps until, out of the wind at last, she stood in the outer circle of tombstones, where a wall spiralled to the top.

Unlike the jumble of gravestones, she knew at home, these were of uniform shape and size, laid out in formal lines following the walls, set close together with a wide path in the middle to separate the two sides. It was a melancholy experience reading the inscriptions. People from all over

24

the world were buried there. Once, parents, husbands and wives had brought their consumptive loved ones to Menton in belief of a cure. The stones testified the futility of their hope, and so many died unbearably young.

Sara followed the steps up to the top of the mound. This looked more likely, it was more recent. Photographs of the departed were set into the headstones, which were obviously still tended by the living. They were without exception adorned with pretty pot plants; some were even little shrines. But in one respect, they were identical to the gravestones below, they bore the inscription 'Bought in Perpetuity'. Each plot was dedicated to the exclusive use of a particular family. Some headstones showed several photographs of different generations. Sara took out her photograph of George's plaque. There was nothing resembling it. She could find no small plot dedicated to her George.

After a second circuit Sara sat on a bench. She had planned her meeting so carefully, so full of anticipation at the thought of being near him once more and now she felt cheated. He wasn't there. 'Why,' she thought irrationally, 'has he abandoned me again?'

Her tears could not be checked. She had thought herself alone, when she heard a small voice.

"*Grandpapa, la dame, elle est plus triste. Elle a laisser tomber ses fleurs…*"

Little feet ran toward her. A small hand gathered the freesias that were tossing in the wind and gave what it could catch back to Sara.

"*Julie!*" said Grandpa. "*Laisses la dame tranquille…*

Madame." He continued, this time addressing Sara, "*Excusez ma petit fille. Elle se met trop en avant. Pardon.*"

Sara looked up at the gentleman and tried to smile through her tears...

"*Non, non.* She is very kind... *Très gentil. Vous aussi, Monsieur.*"

"You are English, *Madame*?"

"*Oui*, I am looking for my husband's grave. It's not here. I can't find it. *Je ne sais pas que fait.*" She began to weep again. "I'm so sorry. You must think me very foolish. He had an accident and died here in Menton years ago... I was ill and couldn't attend his funeral... I was never able to come before... I only have this photograph." She handed the picture to the gentleman, who called to his granddaughter, "*Julie, trouve ta maman...*"

Julie ran to her mother who had just come into view, looking for her family. The gentleman walked over and spoke to his daughter. She looked at Sara kindly, nodded to her father and walked away with the girl, who skipped off with a cheery *au revoir* to *grandpapa*.

"Now." The gentleman addressed Sara and continued in English. "It is not so strange that your husband is not here. There is another cemetery 100 metres further up the hill, and it is most probable that you will find him there. But it is very large, and if you will permit me, I will guide and help find the place where he is most likely to be."

Sara was most impressed by his kindness and accepted his offer gratefully. They walked in virtual silence out of the old cemetery and further up the steep hill. With the wind whipping round them Sara hugged her scarf close.

The other cemetery was indeed huge, accessed by a

magnificent flight of stone steps, and it was here, she read, that those killed in war were buried. Line after line of young men who died fighting for France. At least, she thought bitterly, they died for something, unlike George who had died for nothing at all... Tears welled again.

The gentleman, affecting not to notice, introduced himself as Jean-Pierre Gascon, and in return Sara gave her name.

He further inquired the name of her husband and she replied, "George, George Middleton. He was a merchant seaman. He drowned here in Menton, but his ship was docked at Marseilles... He was a keen football fan. He and some friends had two days leave and came to see Marseilles play Menton... Marseilles won and maybe they were celebrating by playing football themselves, I'm not sure where exactly... anyway the ball went into the sea... George was a good swimmer, but it was rough... He went out to get the thing back even though it was getting dark. The ball floated ashore, but there was no sign of George. At first everyone thought he had climbed out further down the coast, but after a while they realised something was wrong and alerted the authorities. A cross-current may have caught him... He might have hit his head on the rocks... God knows. But they didn't find his body for a week... I was pregnant at the time... The twins were born on the day we got the news."

Sara fell silent.

"*Madame, Je suis très désolé...* I am so sorry for your loss... We will find your Georges. *Je vous assure. Allez...*"

He led the way to the *Jardin du Souvenir*. There was no sign of George there, nor was his marker amongst other English graves. M. Gascon asked to look at Sara's photograph one more time, and began to retrace their footsteps.

"Your Georges was a *matelot,* a sailor, *n'est pas?* Then, a small plot for him amongst other servicemen may have been thought appropriate. *Alors.* We will see."

Directly opposite the entrance, in a far corner there were two headstones belonging to English servicemen killed in WW1. They walked over, and to the right-hand side, next to the crosses dedicated to the soldiers, they saw a small marble plaque. M. Gascon translated the inscription for her.

"To the memory of George Middleton. Mariner. Born Ripon England 14 August 1967. Died 27 January 1991 Menton. Loving husband of Sara. Beloved son of Kate and Fred. R.I.P."

There he was. The father of her children, the sweet happy-go-lucky boy she had been allowed to love for a meagre total of two years. She remembered his lean muscular body and dark hair that was always falling into his eyes. He was so tall and strong that she, at a mere 5ft 3, weighing in at eight and a half stone, was a feather to him. He would pick her up in his arms and twirl her round and round until she was too dizzy to stand. Then they'd laugh as she wobbled about trying to regain her balance.

She'd forgotten how much fun he'd been, before being melded in her head with the fool, whose early and unnecessary death had sucked the life out of her.

How could he have been so unmindful of her and their babies to let it happen? What did he get for his trouble anyway? A little corner of a foreign field full of dead servicemen. Her resentfulness made her feel sour again. 'He doesn't deserve to lie next to all these heroes' she thought. 'He was just a silly bugger, showing off. He died for no better reason than to get that bloody ball back to please his mates.'

But, that was George, all over and if she was honest with herself, she'd liked his streak of devil-may-care recklessness and once upon a time found it exciting. But they'd both been young and paid so very dearly for his folly.

As she looked round the crosses and wondered how many of the others who shared this field *really* were heroes, or were they just ordinary young men, who like George, had thought themselves immortal and dived just as rashly, not into the sea, but into a current of war that swept them all away without compassion. Ordinary lads who didn't make it because they were unlucky. In essence, George was no different to any of them. It came to her in a moment that she may have been wrong to have judged him so harshly. Maybe, but it was too late to make amends now.

Still, it wasn't a bad place for George's earthly remains to lie, and Sara was glad to have seen it at last. She placed her remaining broken flowers on the plaque, and turned to M. Gascon, who had stepped back to allow her time alone with her husband. *"Merci, Monsieur. Merci beaucoup!"*

The wind lifted the freesias and blew them away.

Sara and M. Gascon left the cemetery and walked down together. After saying goodbye beside the school on the hill, she walked back through the *Vieille Ville* feeling ashamed, hollow inside, and very cold. Back in the new town, she called at the first available café for hot chocolate, which she drank gratefully, but the café was crowded and noisy. She desperately need somewhere quiet to sit.

The chance that led her to choose the nearby Cocteau museum was almost uncanny, it was warm with very few visitors, with upholstered benches running in front of two screens, at either end of a spacious room. The first screen was showing scenes from Cocteau's most famous film *La Belle et La Bête*, which held little fascination for her, but the other was showing clips from his surreal interpretation of the Orpheus and Eurydice legend.

She sat down to watch Orpheus' doomed attempts to bring his wife back from hell to the world of the living. He stepped through a mirror to reach her, but she was in another dimension, much as they wanted to, it was impossible for them to connect. As oil and water will not mix, Death and Life would always be separate.

Yet Sara had experienced something as she stood beside George's memorial. Two and a half decades had passed since she was last near him. She had changed, no longer the ingénue he had known, and as a mature woman, was certain it wasn't a resurgence of first love. It was something stranger and more nebulous, that her normally clear mind could not easily find words for.

Her initial desperate grief at his demise was long gone, but even then, she wasn't as foolish as Orpheus, she had never wanted to steal George back from the dead. She wanted him not to have died in the first place, which was a different thing entirely. He'd left her when she needed him most. She was the one who'd had to cope with the hard reality of bringing up their twin babies alone. She had loved him and mourned his death, but also knew in her heart, that she'd always felt sorrier for herself than for him. After all his promises, she blamed him for not being there for her. But standing by his lonely little memorial, she'd realised herself to be guilty of the same thing. She had, after slamming the door behind him in self-pitying pique, deserted him just as completely, by refusing to visit his grave.

Now, she could forgive him, because she could see there was really nothing to forgive, and wished it was possible for him to forgive her in turn. It came to her like an electric shock, this was what she couldn't express before, the feeling that somehow George was trying to comfort her, to tell her he understood. But it was a silly notion. The technology to communicate between the quick and the dead had yet to be invented. She felt so guilty and the sadness of all those wasted years, was hard to bear.

Agony Angst who had been listening in, said with some compassion, 'Look Sara, George couldn't know anything past the moment he departed this life. His last memory of you was good. Leave it at that.'

The feeling, however, wouldn't leave her and still deep in contemplation, she sat through another half a dozen showings of the same film clip, until the museum began to fill up with more visitors and Sara felt it was time to leave.

Outside it was still cold, but a weak sun was trying its best to warm up the town. The wind was no longer cutting straight through Sara's jacket, but she still needed her scarf wrapped snugly round her shoulders as she walked along the main street back to her apartment.

She was mentally restless and physically tired. The walk to and from the cemetery had been a long one, and her new shoes were causing her feet to ache. She'd had nothing to eat since breakfast, and was also getting hungry. Inviting smells were coming from open restaurant doors. Should she make a dash for home and cook something for herself, or dive into the nearest eating place? Her mind was in turmoil, she needed time alone to adjust and unravel the knots in her thoughts. At the same time she wanted someone to talk to and regretted the kind M. Gascon had left her so soon. She was sure he would have understood.

Feeling very low and alone, she had just made up her mind to enter a bistro, when a rangy youth, who obviously hadn't seen her, charged out of the door and knocked her off her feet. She wasn't much hurt, but the young man, full of pleading apologies, was not only charm itself, but the son of the proprietor. He insisted on seating her inside and poured her a glass of red wine.

The accident was nothing, and it cost her no more than a laddered pair of tights, the trouble was, for a split second she had seen the boy as George. They were the same build and her mind was so full of him, that she was more shaken than she otherwise would have been. The wine she had been given was strong and she quickly became extremely dizzy, which alarmed the proprietor and his son.

She managed to convince them that she was fine just in need something to eat, asked to see the menu and ordered *boeuf bourguignon*, largely because it was the only dish with a name she recognised. Madame Distel, the wife of the proprietor, introduced herself as she bustled out of the kitchen with a basket of bread and olives for Sara.

She spoke a little English, which was about as good as Sara's command of French, "*Pardon, madame. Mon fils…* 'e is a good boy, but 'e have a loss of care. 'E is never looking in front of 'imself. 'E is always is in the 'urry, from 'ere to there," she said, shaking her head.

Sara replied, "*Ça ne fait rien, I am* small, *petite*, and a *grande* man, like your son, would not have seen me coming," she smiled. "I once knew someone, very like him, who would often lose me in a crowd."

Madame Distel returned the smile with some relief and turned back to her kitchen, where she gave her worried son an affectionate hug and sent him out by the back entrance. She called some admonition after him and was rewarded with a cheeky grin.

Madame Distel popped over to Sara's table for a quick word every time she passed when serving bread and olives to other patrons. The good food and the Madame's motherly attention worked wonders on Sara's melancholy mood. She felt better and asked for her bill, but Madame Distel refused to take any payment. After a little wrangling, Sara capitulated and accepted the kind offer.

The day had turned to evening before Sara arrived back at the apartment. She gratefully slipped off her shoes and made some tea before messaging the twins to tell them about finding their father's resting place in a field of heroes, thinking that would please them. She felt that was all they needed or ought to know.

CHAPTER FOUR

By any standards Sara's previous day had been stressful. She had not slept particularly well and was determined not to let herself get into that state again. *AA* had given her a good talking to this morning, telling her George had been gone a long time and it was ridiculous to start having fanciful feelings about him now and to think he could continue to be concerned about the quality of her life from the grave.

Although *AA*'s assessment seemed reasonable enough, Sara still believed she *had* felt his presence and that he was willing her to accept what had happened and rid them both of blame. Being beside him made her remember the forgotten love and good times they'd had together, and see the past, not through the distorting mirror of anger, but as it had been. She wanted to wrap it up carefully, in a box marked 'memories', for safe keeping and start afresh.

If she was ever going to do it, it would have to be now. She'd already made a start by making the journey to France alone, and today she would literally venture a few steps further by going to yet another new country.

She decided to go to Italy, which in itself was no big deal as Menton was very near the Italian border, and she could see her destination from her balcony window, but that was beside the point. It was a symbol of her resolution to destroy the calcifying shell that she had allowed to confine her for too long. It was another country with another language, and the prospect of being able to hop over the border on a whim was a step that pleased her latent sense of adventure enormously.

The station was no more than five minutes' walk from where she was staying. She was very excited. 'Just fancy,' she said to herself, 'Sara Middleton from Ripon, North Yorkshire, swanning round both France *and* Italy in only three days. No wonder George loved his job,' she said to herself unthinkingly, for the first time in decades without a hint of reproach in her remark.

She was at the station for 10.30, where the cashier suggested that if she wanted to travel a lot by train she should purchase a *Zou! Pass,* which would allow her a 50 per cent reduction on all ticket prices. Grand. She intended to visit a lot of places and would quickly be 'ahead', so "yes please." "Did Madame have her passport *s'il vous plait?*" Unfortunately, "*Non.*" It was in a drawer for safe keeping, at the apartment.

She had completely forgotten that she would need her passport and more importantly what Dave had told her about European law that required her to carry it at all times. She went back to her rooms and zipping the bothersome thing securely inside her handbag, rushed out of the door, straight into a man who was coming out of the *Conservatoire Municipal de Musique,* next door.

"*Oh, pardon, monsieur… Pardon moi.*"

"*Madame Middleton,*" said a quizzical voice. "*Ça va. Mais,* what are you doing here?"

"*M. Gascon. Bonjour! Je suis restez dans une appartement, la,*" Sara said in her best Franglais and pointed to the small villa adjacent to the *Conservatoire*. "*Aujourd'hui, Je desirer va à Ventimiglia sur la train et J'oublier mon passport… et Je* had to return to get it!"

M. Gascon smiled broadly at Sara's mangling of his language.

She began to laugh. "I am sorry," she repeated in English. "There was no panic really, I believe the trains are very frequent and it isn't far. I can be a complete idiot at times."

"*Pas du tout!* Not at all," he replied, still smiling.

Sara looked into his face. He was a man a good deal her senior with a kind smile. She liked him.

"I see," she said, "you've come from the *Conservatoire*, are you a teacher there?"

"Not any longer," he replied. "I am retired, but still return from time to time. There is a violin audition later this month and I need to make arrangements. Are you fond of music?"

"Oh yes! I am very fond of music. At home I taught the subject, but mine was only a small school. After Christmas it merged with a much more important one… I was no longer needed. So, like you, I'm afraid I am no longer a teacher… but for the moment, it doesn't matter, because now I have time to come to Menton."

M. Gascon smiled again. He had begun to like this English woman.

"Madame Middleton," he began, "I am an *Ami Des Musees de Menton,* who organise concerts at the Palais Carnolés.

This Saturday we have the Szonyi Quintet playing a varied programme on period instruments. They are very good. If you would care to, I can give you a copy of the programme. I have one here." He dived into his jacket pocket and brought out a sheaf of photocopied sheets.

"I am distributing some today," he said in some embarrassment, when Sara's face registered slight surprise at the number of leaflets in his hand.

"I do not always carry so many," he laughed.

She took one of the proffered papers and expressed her approval of the programme, especially Biber. She was not familiar with the work of Marie Amiot nor Nicola Matteis, but said she rather thought she might like to attend the concert.

"*Bon, Madame! Mais maintenant, votre train vous attendez.* Have a good day in Ventimiglia. Don't forget to visit the old town. It is very singular! *Au revoir, Madame.*"

"*Au revoir, Monsieur,*" Sara repeated. She had taken no more than a few steps away from him when M. Gascon caught up with her.

"I hope you do not think me too forward, Madame, but as you are alone, if you feel you would like to be accompanied to the concert, I would be pleased to escort you." He produced his card. "Please contact me, if you decide you would like me to do so. *Au revoir encore, Madame.*" And he was gone.

'Well,' thought Sara, 'in France just a few days and I've got a date already. These Frenchmen really do live up to their reputations! Good thing you didn't take me to see the world George… a *beau* in every port, *n'est pas?*'

She didn't think she would actually go with him of course,

but it had given an extra lift to her day.

***

Back at the station Sara was initiated into the continental way of *composting* her *billet* before getting on the train. She watched others do it, carefully put her ticket in the machine, then checking it actually printed out the word 'Menton', before going out onto the platform. In minutes the train arrived and she climbed aboard, going upstairs just for the novelty, and smoothly glided off to Italy.

CHAPTER FIVE

Meanwhile Jean-Pierre, a naturally kind man, had a mild attack of nerves. In his enthusiasm for the concert, he may have seemed too forward, and she, a woman alone in a foreign country, may, God forbid, have suspected his perfectly innocent motives. He sincerely hoped not. But of course, when she looked at the address on his card, she would realise there was nothing at all sinister in his invitation to accompany her to the Palais Carnolés.

Jean-Pierre Gascon was seventy-two years old, and like Sara had been widowed. He felt sad that his attractive new acquaintance had been alone for so long. He'd been more fortunate, having had a long and happy marriage, but shortly after celebrating their fortieth wedding anniversary, his wife Marie had been involved in a road accident that caused her to spend the last year of her life as an invalid. It was to care for her that he had taken retirement from the *Conservatoire.*

They had known each other for most of their lives, since the first days at kindergarten when Marie, whose parents owned the best *patisserie* in Menton, gave Jean-Pierre a bite of her tarte au citron at lunch time. Such an act of generosity inevitably led to a great friendship. As they grew up

Jean-Pierre's obvious musical ability earned him a place at the *Conservatoire de Musique*, where he studied violin and cello. He had great success there. His first professional engagement was with the Monaco Opera Orchestra, where he was eventually invited to play first violin. Then he had spent some time guesting with the Northern Sinfonia in England. But he and Marie yearned for home. He also had a vocation to teach, and became a *Professeur de Music* at Menton. With some of his old orchestra colleagues, he formed a quartet, called *La Sage*. For Jean-Pierre and his family, it was the best of all worlds.

There never was a *grande-passion* between Marie and Jean-Pierre but they'd always known that, one day, they would marry and live a very happy life together. Their union was blessed with a single daughter, Monique, who married Bertrand, second officer of a Rhone river cruiser, and they in turn had a little girl of their own, whom they named Julie.

Marie's accident occurred as she crossed the road opposite the Casino de Menton, where traffic was always heavy. Cars were parked on the corner of the pedestrian crossing. It was evening, the light not good. Marie took a step out onto the road to peer round one of the parked cars. It all happened in a second. A cyclist, dressed in black, smashed straight into her. He was going at incredible speed. Unable to stop, he rammed into the low wall round the casino, bounced off it and was killed instantly by an approaching vehicle. Marie was not so lucky, she suffered multiple broken bones. Her right hip and leg were badly fractured, but there were also head injuries. It was days before she recovered consciousness.

A nightmare time followed. So that she might walk again Marie had to undergo numerous operations to rebuild her leg and hip. The head injuries were however much harder to bear. They had prompted a personality change. In place of the sweet loving woman he had known, Jean-Pierre met with a shrewish, angry vixen who nothing and no one could please. Jean-Pierre continued to care for Marie in her new incarnation as best he could, but he desperately grieved the loss of his beloved wife.

Eventually, she had a major stroke from which she never recovered. All night, Jean-Pierre watched by her bed, when he felt a featherlight squeeze from the hand he held in his. Marie's eyes momentarily flickered open, and looked at him with such tenderness and love that he gasped. She died with the shadow of her old smile on her lips. This had all happened three years ago. Jean-Pierre, Monique and Julie had been visiting Marie's memorial at the cemetery when they'd met Sara on Sunday.

After saying *au revoir* to Sara, M. Gascon continued on his mission to distribute programmes for the Saturday concert. He also had a little bit of shopping to do. It was Julie's sixth birthday at the weekend, and he wanted to collect her present from the toy shop on the main street. She had requested, as subtly as a small child can, that if she were to receive a birthday present from her dear grandpapa, of one of the new generation German-made Sasha dolls, it would be most acceptable. Despite the exorbitant cost, grandpapa was willing to comply with her request.

Sara's train journey did not take long and she walked straight off the train into Ventimiglia. She loved the babble of the Italian shoppers in the main street but her real objective was to find the old city that M. Gascon had recommended. It was perched high above the modern conurbation, on the opposite side of the estuary bridge.

It was almost lunchtime and she would eat first. Walking down to the shore she saw a likely restaurant and went inside.

The waiter greeted her with a cheerful *"Buon giorno signora. Tavola per uno?"* Sara sort of understood and replied, *"Bon gerno... er... um... si... er... um... prega."*

Immediately noting her accent, he enquired, *"Inglese? English?"*

"Oh si," she replied gratefully.

The waiter gabbled away in English as he brought a carafe of water, a bowl of olives and some bread to her table. Taking his advice on their quality, she ordered a margarita pizza and a glass of red wine. While she was waiting, she nibbled on the olives and bread, and looked out of the window at the bridge leading to the old city. There were masses of huge seagulls, the kind that looked like they would pick up small dogs for a snack. She thought they were called fulmars but wasn't really sure. All she knew was that their beaks were big and sharp, and they did not look friendly. The wine came and a minute later, the biggest pizza she had ever seen in her life. She gaped at the size and laughingly said, "It's huge, I won't be able to eat all that!"

The waiter smiled and said it was normal size. Sara answered by saying she would get very fat. The waiter's smile broadened as he took a step back and made his tummy stand out.

He patted his exaggerated stomach, saying, "Today!" Bringing his tummy back to normal, he patted it again and said, "Tomorrow is flat! Very good pizza!"

He was right about it being very good. Sara ate and enjoyed every scrap of it. The wine was also excellent. She paid her bill and the waiter wished her *buon giorno* and promised her a warm welcome on her next visit.

She braved the gulls and crossed the bridge to enter the old town. It was a very steep walk up a cobbled street, much too narrow for cars, though there were a few badly parked Vespa scooters. Georgie had wanted one when she was seventeen, but *Agony Angst* had come down heavily against the idea and won the argument. The thought that Georgie and her partner now owned a powerful Yamaha motorbike that frightened the life out of her, was one Sara didn't like to dwell on.

The road seemed to get narrower as ochre and terracotta-coloured houses began to rise on both sides. They looked like they hadn't been touched since the day they were built, sometime in the Middle Ages. Between their lofty walls were narrow arched stairwells, black as night, culminating in a tiny speck of sky. She could barely discern the low doorways lurking in the pitch-black alleys. Part of her wanted to climb the stairs between the buildings to reach their single star of light high in the Stygian darkness. She placed a foot on a bottom step but thought better of it. God only knew what might be up there. She turned back to plodding up the hill where there was a solitary little shop set into one of the walls. Through its grimy window, she could just make out a display of old-fashioned chunks of soap, buckets and brooms. In the gloom of the overshadowing houses, it had a baleful look, like something from Diagon Alley in the Harry Potter books.

As she neared the top of the street the winter sun began to shine, bringing with it the sound of laughter and bells that changed the atmosphere in a moment. A pretty bride and her handsome groom were leaving the church in the square. A crowd of wedding guests poured out after them, half-dancing, half-walking in a happy procession past Sara, down the hill. It was a wonderfully uplifting sight and they exchanged smiles with her as she watched them go by.

There was no doubt in her mind that the old Ventimiglia had a fairy tale quality, part sinister and part delight. Maybe it was just the altitude or the lunchtime wine, but something in the phantasmagorical aura of the city was making her light-headed. From nowhere came a fleeting fancy that she had just witnessed her broken childhood Meissen shepherd made whole again, and joyfully reunited with his shep-herdess, and that it was in the nature of this city of dreams, to make impossible wishes come true.

'Oh my god, George!' she thought, in full consciousness of her desire. 'I'm so sorry. I hardly know the guy. I've no idea why I wished that.'

Because unlike Orpheus, it wasn't her dead spouse she had asked for. With a shock she realised the man she had in mind was the very much alive Mr Harry Martin.

CHAPTER SIX

That night Sara had a vivid dream that she was back in Ventimiglia. She was standing by the estuary bridge between the new and old city. Her children were with her, they were very young and each holding one of her hands.

Suddenly they were in the old quarter. It had turned very dark. The buildings loomed huge and ominous around them, but she knew she had to get the children through the blackness to the patch of moonlight at the top of the steps. She had a lantern to light their way but wasn't able to go with them because the stairs were too narrow. She would only hinder their climb. Although she couldn't get through, it was vital that the children made it to the light. She passed the lantern to Dave, who was the eldest by two minutes. It was important that he should, after leaving hold of his mother's hand to take the light, hold his sister's right hand very tight in his as they ascended the stairs together. She warned them not to let go of one another until they reached the top. She would wait at the bottom until she was sure they were safe.

The children were apprehensive, but Dave held the light steady and they started on their journey. Sara, left in the darkness, watched the lantern light grow smaller and smaller as the children neared the top when they disappeared. She feared for them and called them back. She called and called, but they were too high to hear her now and she was alone. The sensation of abandonment was all embracing and her despair absolute.

She had to find them. She squeezed herself into the narrow gap in the wall, scrambling on hands and knees up sharp, steep, stone steps, scraping her arms on the confining walls on either side. Hardly able to breath, she reached an iron door framed in a narrow ribbon of light. She fumbled at the latch and managed to push it ajar. Inside was her own flower filled garden shining in the sunlight. The children were there, all grown up, beckoning her to enter, but exhausted from her climb, she hadn't enough strength left to push the heavy door open any wider.

'I wish I could, but I can't get in,' she cried, 'I'm not strong enough.'

'Yes, you can,' said a voice she'd never thought to hear again. 'Trust me, you'll get your wish, if you let me help. You were always tougher than you thought and I won't rest 'til I get you through.'

She felt George's strong arm pulling and pulling, as she strained against the unyielding door, until she woke in a sweat to find herself entangled in the sheet and duvet, panting for breath. The dream had been so real that she closed her eyes again, desperate to go back to see if she actually made it, but it had gone.

Having extricated herself from the bedclothes Sara lay still in her bed. This wasn't what she'd expected when she'd envisaged making her long overdue visit to George. This reconnection was not something she had bargained for. It was frighteningly intense. Her life had been narrow, but thanks to the protective shell she'd created, it had been ordered and safe, now her emotions were all over the place. It looked like freedom was coming at a price.

She got out of bed and contrary to normal habit did without her morning shower and breakfast, put on her coat and went out for a brisk walk, not caring overmuch which way. She had to make some sense of that dream.

After he'd died, Sara had never dreamed about George once. She had slammed a door as forbidding as the one in her dream, behind him. Was he telling her when she'd done that, she'd also locked herself out of life in the process? She didn't believe in ghosts qua ghosts, but something had sprung that lock. She'd tasted fresh air again and it felt good. George had said she'd get her wish. She'd made two, one in the dream and one in real life. Which would come true? Probably neither, both were as likely and fantastic as warm snow. In life, George had made many promises that were impossible to keep, one more didn't really signify. It had been her own fault anyway, for wanting too many unobtainable things.

By some circuitous rote Sara found herself in the central park area in town, where she noticed for the first time, how heavy the rain must have been the previous night. Big puddles had formed and the scaffolding which she now knew was in preparation for the Menton Citrus Festival, looked slippery and dangerous.

As she passed along the road there were posters stuck on every other lamp post advertising the event. This year the theme was 'Circus', but nothing prepared her for the sight of huge effigies of a clown and ringmaster, that in the last couple of days had grown ten feet higher than the boards enclosing them. Gangs of men hanging onto the scaffolding, were covering skeletal frameworks of animals with literally thousands of oranges and lemons.

She walked the perimeter of the hoardings, and sometimes was able to get a clear look into the working area. She stopped to admire a particularly fine rendition of a trapeze artist. A man in a hard hat turned to face her. Fearing she was about to be told off for trespassing, she gave a little gasp, so did he. She knew him from York. As she stared at him in disbelief, an iron door seemed to move on its hinges and her heart executed a full somersault.

"Mr Martin, it's you!"

After a moment's silence they both asked the same question in unison, "What are you doing here?"

"We still do harmony well," he laughed, "but I'll let you go solo first."

"I'm here for a few weeks holiday," she replied, "but you are obviously working! Why? What are you doing here?"

"It's the day job. My firm specialises in mechatronics." Sara looked blank. Harry smiled as he explained, "We design and help engineer some of these models. I'm here to oversee the project." He paused. "It's about time for a break, let me take you for a coffee. We can have a chat."

She agreed it would be a nice idea, as she hadn't had breakfast yet.

"Then we must remedy that immediately. *Albert!*"

Harry called to his deputy, *"J'ai besoin d'un café. Vingt minutes, OK?"*

They stepped over the road into the *Boulangerie Kayzer,* he sat Sara by a window seat and ordered coffee with croissants for both of them. They talked about the Requiem concert and how pleasant it was to meet again, then Sara asked how his company got involved in the Menton Festival. He told her they designed stuff for festivals all over the world, including the home-grown one at Notting Hill. This was his third year of coming to Menton and it was a bit tricky, because some of the moving parts were going to be covered in fruit. The extra weight had to be calibrated very carefully as no one wanted a hundred kilos of citruses raining down all over town. But what about her? Why had she come to Menton? Had she come for the Festival?

She had to admit she hadn't and that it was her first real holiday abroad. Then she briefly explained the reasons for her visit and hope of coming to terms at last, with the loss of her husband George.

Harry resisted an unpolitical urge to ask if she had.

She said how much she liked what she'd seen so far, and how the people she'd met were kind and friendly. She glanced out of the window as she spoke and Harry looked warmly at her, thinking how fresh her complexion looked, free from the artifice of cosmetics and so unlike many of the other women he had known. All at once, he remembered he should be working and apologised, saying it was time for him to get back to *Albert* and the 'mechanoids'.

"But look," he said rising to his feet. "Why don't we meet up for supper this evening? We can talk some more, but it must, if you agree, be on the condition that you drop the Mr

Martin thing. If you call me Harry, then I can call you Sara and I'd like that."

Before returning his smile, she blushed a little, guessing he'd seen through her little game at Ripon, before replying, "Yes, I think I'd like that too."

"I can pick you up from your apartment about 7.30. Would that be alright?"

It was an unexpected invitation. *AA* prepared to make reply, but Sara answered first and suffered no qualms as she accepted.

"Thank you, that would be very nice," she said and beamed a smile at him.

"Wonderful," he replied with an equally bright beam. "You said La Maison Soleil, next to the Music Academy? I'll see you then." With a hurried wave he returned to the worksite.

CHAPTER SEVEN

The spring in Harry's step was unmistakable as he returned to the site and it did not go unnoticed by Albert, who casually enquired, "*Ca va, M. Martin*?"

"*Oui, merci,*" Harry replied somewhat coolly, but Albert was not fooled for a minute and rather to Harry's irritation grinned, and began to whistle while he worked. But Harry's mood was a sunny one and his deputy quickly forgiven. After all Albert was a Frenchman, therefore genetically disposed to enjoy a whiff of a romantic liaison in the air.

When Harry had met Sara a few months ago at the first Requiem rehearsal, he was told she was a long-term widow with grown up children. He'd seen nothing particularly special about her, she was such a little scrap of a woman, he frankly doubted whether her voice could be as good as he'd been told. He'd worked with the tenor and soprano before and knew their worth, but Mrs Middleton was as yet, an unknown quantity. In consequence, their first handshake had bordered on the formal rather than the friendly.

Maybe it was in retaliation for his initial frosty manner that she addressed him only as Mr Martin, and continued to do so throughout all the hours they spent together. But as time went by, he was sure it was a deliberate ploy to keep him at arm's length. She was smarter and tougher than she looked, and he rather admired her for that. She was a woman full of surprises and most importantly, well up to meeting his demanding standards.

Her voice and singing technique were excellent, and what's more she worked hard. He had grown to like and admire her, not only for her musical skills but as a person in her own right. He'd enjoyed their chats together while rehearsing and missed her company when the performance was over. He would have liked to keep in touch, but a new relationship with a woman he felt attracted to, required a different set of engineering skills than those used in mecha-tronics. Top of the list was opportunity, and she hadn't seemed that keen to provide one.

He thought for a moment about his marriage. His wife Linda had been a beautiful, clever woman who held a junior partnership with a firm of architects. Her speciality was in the field of 'sympathetic' architecture, the sort that works with, rather than against neighbouring structures. He wanted them to have a child, but the time was never right according to Linda. He was disappointed, but when she did unexpectedly fall pregnant he was delighted. Harry assumed she would be thrilled at the prospect of becoming a parent too. She wasn't. He went on a business trip and by the time he returned the pregnancy had been terminated.

Their marriage could not survive and divorce followed swiftly. All this was nearly ten years ago. Maybe having a baby would not have been good for Linda, but that was no excuse, she had killed his child. He would never be able to forgive her for that. He couldn't imagine Sara Middleton doing such a thing. She had gone to the other extreme and devoted her life to her children. He looked forward to his evening very much.

Sara could hardly believe she had actually seen Harry, and they were to have supper together that very night. The way he'd asked her to call him Harry so he could call her Sara, she mused, was so formal and old-fashioned, but it added extra glamour and made her feel special. *Agony Angst* was quick to point out 'it's all affectation, you know.' Sara had to admit it almost certainly was, but like the theoretical shopping she'd indulged in at the airport, it was a lot of fun. Her mind sailed on, and perfectly at ease with the idea that he had no objections to the meeting, she said, 'thank you' to George. *AA* could find no answer to this further evidence of Sara's madness, except to conclude there was something very foreign in this French air.

It was still only mid-morning and would be hours before meeting him again that evening. She needed a full day's programme to keep her mind occupied and decided a visit to the Villa and Jardins Ephrussi de Rothschild would be perfect.

Taking another train journey would be fun and at the station she picked up a brochure, with an English translation, about the Villa, that had been built during the *Belle Epoque* by Beatrice Ephrussi, who had married into the Rothschild family. Whereas everyone had heard of the Rothschilds, the name 'Ephrussi' had been new to Sara until recently, when she'd read a history of the family and their tragic losses during the war. Although this Ephrussi was not from that unfortunate branch of the family, it still resonated with her, and she wanted to see the Villa that stood in isolated splendour overlooking the bay at Saint-Jean Ferrat.

After leaving the train, trying hard to keep her mind on the Ephrussi and Rothschild families instead of Mr Martin, she soon found herself at the door of the magnificently beautiful Villa. Every aspect of its architecture from the pink stucco of its exterior to the simple elegance of its furnishings was assured and calm. It was a haven of harmony. The views of the bay and manicured gardens framed by tall, wide windows were breathtaking. Beatrice had used her wealth to lavish quality and care on every aspect of its design, despite its undoubted grandeur, first and foremost it felt like a dearly loved home.

Each one of its exquisitely furnished rooms was further enhanced by the incomparable delight of its garden vistas. Sara took more photographs than she could count, everything seemed worthy of record, from the tiny pink cyclamen at the door to the glory of its entrance hall.

If he was interested, she could show Harry some of the better pictures when she saw him that evening and felt a wave of excitement tighten her stomach as she suppressed a little smile of anticipation. *AA* raised an eyebrow, but Sara shrugged her off and stepped out into the garden which, thankfully, was sheltered from the wind. Sara now stood directly in front of the elegant fountains she'd seen from inside the house, to watch the water dance to Tchaikovsky's music from *Sleeping Beauty*. It was delightful. The rest of the garden twined itself around the edges of the mountain. A Japanese area with bamboo water chutes, giant cacti sprouting in another. Garden upon garden of exotic delights with a backdrop of the Mediterranean, lazily resting in the bay far below. Smiling to herself she went on her way, dreaming of a future as pink and rosy as the Villa itself.

'Get real,' said a cynical voice in her head. 'He's only taking you out because he's got nothing better to do.' Sara wished that sometimes *Agony Angst* would take a hike.

On the journey home she mailed her kids to tell them what she'd done today and casually mentioned bumping into Mr Martin, from the Christmas concert, that morning. She said he had been doing some work in Menton. They'd had a quick coffee together as he was going home very soon. She also told them that the Villa she had just seen was lovely and she was enjoying her holiday. What she didn't tell them was she was having supper with Mr Martin in approximately two and a half hours' time.

Sara was back at her apartment just after 5pm and it was cold. After turning up the central heating, she pulled off her boots, made some tea and curled up snuggling into the sofa for extra warmth. It had been quite a day again, this time starting with the dream and then, in a way, her dream turning into reality. Whether it was some remnant of George's spirit or just coincidence that made things happen, she couldn't be sure. Everything was moving so fast. She was like some fledgling, breaking out of its shell and was sure the first fissure had been made at Ripon when she met Harry. The next was coming to Menton, where making her peace with George had given her the will to keep chipping her way out. It was exhilarating and frightening outside, chaotic and full of uncertainties, but for all that, better than the 'stasis in darkness' she'd imposed on herself for the last two decades.

Somehow the clock had reached 6.15 and Sara still had to shower and get herself ready. What to wear was a problem, she'd not anticipated going anywhere smart in the evenings. The only suitable garment she had was the suit she'd worn the day she went to see George. She'd already washed the blouse through as it had picked up some dirt from her encounter with young M. Distel. It just needed running over with an iron. She felt awkward about wearing 'George's suit' for her meeting with Harry, but common sense prevailed. It wasn't being disrespectful to her husband's memory to wear it, she would never be disrespectful to him again, she couldn't anymore, because she'd re-opened the door and as long as she lived, he would always be an integral part of her emotional DNA.

After her shower, she dressed and styled her hair as best she could in the short time left before Harry came. Standing in front of the bedroom mirror, she thought she would 'do' and glanced out of the window in time to see him crossing the road to her apartment.

Taking a deep breath, she said, 'Wish me luck, George', and went downstairs to open the door to Mr Martin.

Harry had arrived at La Maison Soleil just before 7.25pm. His face expressed mild surprise as he was early and hadn't even rung the bell. Sara felt slightly embarrassed and explained she'd caught sight of him through a reflection in her bedroom mirror and thought she must be late. He laughed and apologised confessing he had a tendency to arrive for appointments too early.

As they walked to the Bistro, Sara asked how the work for the Festival was going and how long he would be staying in Menton.

"Anything from a couple of days to a week at the most, then the main task is attaching the rest of the citrus fruits to the frameworks. I'm not involved in that, it's a job for the local men," he replied. She was curious to know how exactly they did the attaching.

"With a lot of elastic bands," he said.

"You're joking!"

"No. Really, that's how they do it... thousands of elastic bands threaded through a metal mesh and each one secures a fruit."

Sara was laughing and Harry laughed too. It was such a simple and practical solution to the problem and so delightfully, ridiculously, prosaic.

The *Bistro d'Oiselet* was quite full when they arrived and Harry was pleased he'd taken the trouble to book. He made some small talk about how popular the place was as the waiter brought the wine menu. Sara let Harry make the choice. He ordered a fine Burgundy with great confidence, gave the waiter the order for their starter and main courses, smiled, and asked Sara how she had spent her day. She told him about the Villa Ephrussi de Rothschild.

He'd heard of it of course, but never been. He was always busy during the day in Menton. Nothing was open in the evening when he'd finished work.

"One day, though, I'd like to see it," he said.

She offered to show him one or two photographs and

while he flicked through them on her mobile, she said, "It's a shame you have no time during the day to enjoy being here. Evenings this time of year are not a good time to wander round the sights, even if they were still open, which they aren't, but then, if it wasn't for the work, you wouldn't be here at all, would you?" Sara, realising she was wittering, went on a little more coherently, "On my travels today, I saw something you might be able to enjoy. A performance of *Tristan and Iseult* from the Paris Opera. It's being screened at the local cinema tomorrow at 5pm. I intend to go. Maybe you might like to see it as well?" She felt awkward at asking him, but to her relief he seemed to be delighted at the prospect of seeing Wagner's most intimate and romantic piece.

Smilingly handing back her phone he said, "The Villa does look very fine. I had no idea about the screening, I certainly would like to go, if you don't mind that is!"

"I'd be really pleased," she replied with simple sincerity. "Have *you* ever tackled any Wagner?"

"Not for public consumption, my German accent is really bad, I just can't get my tongue round the language at all… but I can skat a mean *Erl-King* in the shower."

With that their starter arrived.

"Another thing you might enjoy," Sara ventured as she picked up her fork to taste the *champignons à la crème*, "they hold a series of concerts at The Palais Carnolés, on Saturday afternoons." She outlined how she had met M. Gascon, and his kindness to her. "I think you'd like him," she went on, "and his granddaughter, who picked up my flowers. She's a little poppet… a really sweet little girl…"

"I won't have time to meet her. As I said, I'll be gone by then." Harry interrupted more harshly than he'd intended.

This time he didn't smile, to Sara his tone was like an arctic blast, she fell quiet and felt herself blush. In her excitement she'd got a bit carried away, but he'd put her in her place. *Agony Angst* went into overdrive and Sara in her confusion let fall her final forkful of *champignon* that splashed spectacularly down the front of her blouse. Embarrassment on top of embarrassment. Harry handed her a clean white napkin. Near to tears, head down, she used the napkin to dab away the offending mess.

She looked up, their eyes met, he smiled kindly and apologetically said, "You better get that cleaned off right away or it might stain." She tried to smile back as she rose to her feet. "Be quick, we don't want your main meal to get cold," he added.

When she left he was disappointed with himself, he wasn't usually so crass, dammit. Sara had no idea of his history. In casually praising little Julie she had touched a raw nerve and provoked an angry knee-jerk response from him. He'd tell Sara about his personal loss at the right time, but not yet, it was too soon. He was well aware though, it did not excuse his sharp reaction to her perfectly innocent invitation. It was clear she liked him, as indeed he liked her, but he had made a counterproductive move, it was against his intentions to upset her. No matter, he'd make it right.

Another, and not at all irrelevant factor was a result of feeling slightly redundant. Harry had set himself up as Sir Galahad, rescuing this shy, self-effacing woman from the lonely existence of a single traveller in a foreign land. In reality, she was coping very well without his interference. He was amazed she'd met so many people in less than a week. 'She's made more friends in days than I have in all the years I've been coming here,' he thought. It was true he had the occasional beer with Albert, but that was it. He marvelled at her. Why had he been so dismissive? Of course he could easily stay for the concert there was no great rush, he was a private consultant. His next contract was a month away.

In the ladies' room Sara rubbed hard at the stain and managed to do a reasonable job of cleaning it, then held the soaked part of her blouse under the hot-air hand drier, burning the ends of her fingers on the buttons which quickly became considerably hotter than the drying fabric. She felt a complete fool and wanted to run off home to hide, but her coat and bag were still at the table. *Agony Angst* was unsympathetic and Sara had to go back to Mr Martin.

When she returned, he smiled encouragingly, and looking at the damp patch said, "That's better, it hardly shows. Anyway, you could always boil it up as a bit of mushroom soup for breakfast."

Sara laughed ruefully.

"Better luck next time," he said cheerfully. "Here comes the main course." He beamed such a smile that Sara was once again entirely under his spell.

He didn't mention leaving again and the rest of the evening passed in pleasant equanimity. Yet she couldn't forget or deny being cut through by his sudden coldness. He'd only asked her out for supper, he was in Menton alone and so was she. For goodness' sake, they'd met and worked as colleagues so what was so special about that? Nothing!

'But' she asked herself, 'Why did it matter so much to me?'

The meal was very good and it was close on 9.35pm by the time they left the Bistro. It was no great distance back to Sara's apartment and despite her protestations that it was not necessary, Harry insisted he should walk her home. Glad of his thoughtfulness, she admitted she was nervous about walking alone at night. He could play Sir Galahad after all and maybe redeem himself a little.

She began to feel uncomfortable again by the time they reached her apartment block. She didn't know what to say or do. The only certainty was she was too old to engage in a snog at the front door, as she had done with George, so she offered Harry her hand and thanked him for a very pleasant evening.

He smiled and with eyes twinkling with mischief, he took the proffered hand and like an old-fashioned gallant, gently kissed her fingers and said, "I'll be in touch about the opera. Goodnight, Mrs Middleton."

She knew he was playing at her old game, she also smiled and after reclaiming her fingers answered in kind, "Goodnight, Mr Martin."

She waved *au revoir* and entered La Maison Soleil.

Walking back to his hotel Harry was once more comparing Sara to his ex-wife. She was pretty enough, not as elegant or beautiful as Linda, but she had a sense of humour which Harry felt Linda had lacked. She also possessed a compelling voice which even when just speaking had something melodic in it. They shared a love of music, Linda had little interest in his singing, it was just 'Harry's little hobby' to her.

Sara was a musician. The sound of her voice animated

him. Her attempts to keep him at a distance amused him. The way she blushed so easily, excited him. Yes, he was pleased with Sara. His recent affair with Jen had come to a natural end when her husband had returned from a stint in the Falklands, so the timing could not have been better.

By the time he reached his destination, Harry was happily imagining Sara as a woman who could satisfy all his needs.

Sara on the other hand, despite the butterflies fluttering about her tummy, tried hard to take a pragmatic view of her evening out. She liked Harry very much but his brief dip into moodiness had disturbed her... after all, what did she know about him? She was aware that he was divorced. He had a fine singing voice, but his inability to master the German language was a sad handicap, a baritone's 'bread and butter' work being largely German *lieder*. Maybe that's why he didn't take up singing professionally. She wondered if he had children, he didn't say. Perhaps if it came up, she would ask him tomorrow.

She was looking forward to seeing him again at the cinema... although she'd never thought of herself as that kind of woman, she found herself fantasizing about them having a torrid affair. More shockingly still, she felt a most agreeable ripple of pleasure at the idea. *AA* was there in a flash. 'At your age Sara, you should have more sense!'

'It's only pretend,' she sighed, and made herself a mug of hot milk to clear her head of all her nonsense. 'Anyway, it's all academic. He's going home in a few days.'

She sighed again as she changed into her favourite Snoopy pyjamas, complete with hood and dangling dog ears, and snuggled down on the sofa where Harry walked straight back into her mind.

It's such a shame he has to work and go back home so soon… but that didn't mean they would never meet again, after all York and Ripon weren't that far apart, and they might get a chance to sing together on many more occasions… that would be nice. His voice was incredible, such a range! Probably much safer to think of the voice rather than him, there was a definite hint of a calculating intelligence at work, behind those smiling, baby-blue eyes. She had to admit that old *AA* was right, there was something dangerous about him, but the voice and the man were inseparable and equally delightful to her. The sound of her mobile ringing brought Sara back to planet Earth. It was late and first thoughts were something was wrong with the kids, but then she saw it was from Harry.

"Hello."

"Er… Hi, Sara… Look I've got an apology to make. I can't make it to the opera…"

"Oh… " Her heart sank.

"I feel bad about this, but a chap from the company is flying over… there's a problem. Nothing to do with me really… and it's not actually my job, but he's got it into his head it needs to be sorted out and as I know the guy involved I should be there. We have to do the whole schmoozing thing over dinner. It's a pain in the backside, I was looking forward to seeing you and the broadcast…"

She was glad he had put their meeting and the opera in that order.

"I understand," she said.

"It's rotten and not fair, and just like the self-centred so and so he is. No one's convenience matters more than his," Harry ranted. He was clearly very put out, then in a more hesitant voice asked, "I don't suppose, we could possibly meet up for a while during the day tomorrow instead? That's if you don't mind. We could maybe do lunch and a walk along the promenade."

"That would be lovely, Harry."

"Shall we meet at the *boulangerie* where we had coffee? At about 12.30?"

"OK."

"Great," he replied, "See you then."

"I'll look forward to it." With a grin, she switched off her phone and looking at her ridiculous pyjamas giggled so much she was in danger of spilling her milk all over them.

CHAPTER EIGHT

Sara had slept like a top not waking until 9am, which was much later than usual. 'Lord,' she thought 'I'm turning into a real lazybones,' but found herself not really caring, because she was on the first real holiday of her life and was going to spend some of it with Harry. From now on, or at least for today she was determined to enjoy every second of it. She got dressed, popped on her coat to go to the patisserie over the road for a newly baked *pain-au-chocolat*, and found M. Gascon's leaflet and card still in her pocket. The concert was tomorrow and he had been very kind to her. She felt she ought to let him know if she wanted to take up his offer to take her there. She wanted to go, but didn't want him to get any wrong ideas. It was a big step from accepting help with directions from a stranger, to going to a concert with him.

'Then again' she thought, licking chocolate from her fingers, 'he was at least twenty years older than she, and a very nice man.' The chances of him having designs on her virtue were pretty small. She would message him now and accept his offer. It would take her mind off Harry leaving so soon, but meanwhile she was going to enjoy every minute of the time she had with him as well as the rest of her holiday.

True, she didn't have any sexual fantasies about M. Gascon, but at least she had one more friend in Menton.

Before meeting Harry though, there was another kind of treat awaiting. Today, there was a flea-market being held at the Place aux Herbes. She loved that kind of thing, and it being a foreign market, 'pun intended' she giggled to herself, gave it an extra dimension of delight. What's more she could easily fit it in before her rendezvous.

With an insouciance new to her, she washed her hands, grabbed her bag and made for the market, where she inspected every one of the twenty or so stalls, until a small, rather tatty-looking marquetry box caught her eye. Basically, the carcass housed two deep drawers of a perfect size for storing pens and pencils. The top was meant to slide along on runners to a point where it could be raised to reveal a mirror, but parts of the runners were missing, so the top just flopped helplessly back down, despite the stallholder's heroic attempts to keep it in place. It was the kind of object she adored, a once lovely thing needing only a bit of TLC to bring it back to its former glory. She thought how much she would enjoy the repairing and finding it a place amongst all the other pieces she had restored, back home in Ripon.

She also thought she'd have a go at bargaining and told the vendor, at 15 euro, he was asking too much. But her French was not good and he knew a sucker when he saw one, so charged her the full price. He did, however, give her a free, used, extremely grubby, plastic carrier bag to take it away in. Feeling very pleased with her purchase, and mollified about the price, when she peeled off the 15-euro sticker to reveal one for 20. She took the shabby box and its shabbier bag, back to her apartment for safe keeping and to smarten herself up.

It was a bit of a rush, but she arrived at the patisserie smack on time, to find he was already there. On seeing her, he quickly rose to his feet and they greeted each other in the traditional French manner, with a quick kiss on each cheek. She coloured slightly, but liked it very much.

"I'm sorry about the opera tonight," he began, "it won't stop you going, will it?"

"Not at all," she answered with perfect frankness, "but it would have been nicer if you could have come as well."

He was satisfied with her reply and handing her the menu asked what she would like to eat. They both settled for a simple coffee and quiche. Sara told him all about the flea-market that morning and the interesting little box she had bought.

"I never knew there was a flea-market here, never visited the sights either." He laughed.

Sara said nothing but found it odd that he should affect to know so little about the town where he must have spent weeks at a time.

Then he went on, "I was thinking, if you didn't mind of course, of staying on for a few more days after my project's completed, and maybe catching up with some of the things I've missed… With you."

Sara was taken aback by what he said, but her face registered pleasant surprise.

He waved the idea a little nearer to her nose, by saying, "Only if you wouldn't mind. I promise not to get in your way. If you think it's a bad idea, I understand."

Although not at all convinced by his assertion of ignorance of the area, she thought it a perfectly splendid notion, so she lied. "Goodness, I don't know," before laughing, and asking rhetorically, "Why not?"

"Thank you, this is really exciting. I've been coming here for years and this'll be the first time I've enjoyed it… would you believe I've never stayed for the actual Festival either, shall we go together?" He asked.

Strangely, she thought the last statement had more of a ring of truth about it. Also, she mentally noted that to go to the Festival, meant him staying more than just a few days, it was more than a week away, and said, "What fun, I'd really like that!"

Their walk along the Promenade was necessarily of short duration, Harry had to be back by 2.30. He gallantly held her hand when they crossed the busy road, but forgot to let go again until they said goodbye.

To calm her nerves and take her mind off what was happening she thought it might be the right time to visit the Regional Prehistoric Museum, its very name redolent of dust and dullness. It would be the very thing, an extremely worthy way to spend an afternoon and keep thoughts of Mr Martin at bay.

As it happened, the road to the museum took her closer than she'd imagined to the emerging Festival displays. She didn't want Harry to think she was stalking him, so like a mouse fleeing a sleeping cat, she scuttled past at great speed, almost on tiptoes.

The museum was in fact, rather interesting, with a collection of ceramics from the 17th century, retrieved from shipwrecks in the bay at Villefranche. Feeling quite cosmopolitan, she thought, 'That's not far from here, I could go there, if I wanted to.' But the opera was due to start in less than an hour, so she didn't stay as long as she might have. She also needed to buy something for a half time snack, because the performance was going to be over four hours long!

The cinema was larger than it looked from the outside, with many very comfortable high backed seats, she chose one in the centre with what she hoped would give an unimpeded view of the screen. At 5.00pm she put her mobile on silent and realised her worries about a good view had been groundless, disappointingly there were no more than a score of people dotted around the auditorium. Nevertheless, the broadcast was of a virtuoso performance with a golden cast who sang their hearts out. Sara judged Iseult's final aria to be truly magnificent. How she could produce so powerful a performance at the end of four fraught acts, was miraculous. 'That,' Sara thought, 'is the difference between a good and a great singer.'

Walking home in the dark, she was on a 'high' after her incredibly enjoyable eventful day, and frequently broke into happy smiles. If the occasional passer-by thought she was crazy, maybe they were right.

Back at her apartment, Sara's day got even better. She found a message from Harry on her phone, asking if it was OK for him to call for her around 10.30 tomorrow, so they could spend a day together. He didn't know what time he would be free tonight, so, would she mind just texting him, yea or nay.

With only a slight hesitation, she sent a message back reminding him she had a previous engagement to go to the concert with M. Gascon at 3.00 in the afternoon. But Harry was very welcome to join her for a morning visit to the Madonne Garden. She could tell him about the opera on the way there.

She wasn't too sure about putting him off, but after all, when she'd told him about the concert, he'd said he would be gone by then. She could give him a whole morning instead and that would have to do. Anyway, it was probably best not to seem *too* keen, but she was nervous and hoped she'd done the right thing. By the time she'd put the kettle on he'd messaged back, 'Sounds good see u 10.30 your place. Sleep well. H.' She messaged M. Gascon to thank him again for his offer but she had decided to go spend the morning at the Madonne Gardens tomorrow, and as the Palais Carnolés was on the way back to town, she would see him there.

She ate the roll she had bought for her half-time snack, got into her snuggly pyjamas, and climbed into bed, relieved and very, very happy indeed.

CHAPTER NINE

Next day, the weather kept its promise. The wind had stopped and it wasn't so cold. At 10.20 Harry arrived. Tying her warm scarf in a snug knot around her neck Sara went down to meet him and they set out on the first outing of the day. She asked him how his meeting went. He said simply "Even if the food and wine is good, which it was, it spoils the flavour. Business is business and eating is eating. Why contaminate one with the other, it only leads to indigestion. Never mind it's done. Everything appears to be fine. How was your opera?"

She told him the cinema had been almost empty but the performance and production had been very exciting.

"So it was really worth going," he said. "I wish I'd seen it, but four and a half hours in a cinema seat is pretty marathon. I salute you!"

Sara laughing replied, "Having sat through numerous school plays and concerts, some of which have seemed infinitely longer than the opera, balanced on the hardest of wooden chairs, I have developed great powers of perseverance. At least the seats at the cinema were well upholstered!"

"Well then, which way do we go to see your gardens?" he asked.

"We catch a bus, just round this corner. One's due in five minutes."

It was a funny business catching a bus on the 'wrong' side of the road. Much more disorienting than she'd imagined, but Harry, who was good at knowing his right from his left, managed quite easily to catch the one going in the correct direction. It was an electric vehicle, Sara had never been on one before, it was otherwise empty and she bagged the back seat, but soon found out it had a way of vibrating in a most original manner. Harry thought it was very funny when he saw the expression of surprise on her face. She put on what her twins called her 'schoolmarm' face, and relocated herself, but had to smile as well.

The bus halted exactly outside the entrance to the grandly titled Serre da la Madonne Gardens. There were two means of access available, one up some very steep steps, and the other along a wide path gently curving uphill. She guessed 'steps', he said 'path'. They went with his choice, it was a long walk that led to a large car park. Following the signs round the perimeter, they found the final direction to the gardens at the top of the steps he'd rejected. Sara smirked, snorted and then laughed at him, but he knew it was his turn to be mocked and took it well.

Because they were built into the mountainside, the gardens were terraced like those at Ephrussi de Rothschild, but not quite as manicured. If it was ever to be brought back to the grandeur of its creator's original vision there was still a lot of work to be done. No doubt, even as it was, parts would look beautiful and softer in the spring, but today in late January, for the most part, the gardens looked as sombre as the mountains opposite. Scratchy and bleak with little colour to soften them. It was not what Sara had been hoping for.

After an hour or so, rather than catch the bus, they calculated that if they walked down the hill and called in somewhere for lunch, they could still make it to the Palais Carnolés in good time for the concert.

With more than half an hour to spare, they arrived at the Palais. At the rear of the house was an orchard which, Sara had read, housed one of the most important collections of citrus trees in the world. They were amazed by the sheer number of differently named varieties, but to their untutored eyes, it was impossible to tell one kind of clementine from another, but Sara could easily spot which were lemon trees. So could Harry, as he astutely pointed out the fruit was yellow and pointed at both ends.

Sara felt awful. She'd dragged Harry out on this outing, promising him beautiful gardens in winter sunshine. What they got was a walk round a lot of bare shrubs, and then a game of 'spot the difference' in an orchard of nearly identical citruses. Stricken with guilt, she started to apologise.

"I'm so sorry for wasting your morning like this, but I can explain."

He smiled and waited.

She wouldn't look at him and put her head down, like a child.

"The truth is, M. Gascon had offered to bring me here today. I accepted his offer because I really wanted to hear the concert. But then, I had second thoughts and was worried, because I didn't think it was quite right to accept an invitation from a man I don't know well. I didn't want him to get the wrong idea. So I hatched a plan to visit those particular gardens this morning, as a 'get out without offending him' excuse. I could do that, because it's more or less a straight road from there, here, and my apartment. I would already be at the right end of town for the performance, you see?"

Harry was nodding gravely and answered her, and with the appearance of perfect seriousness said, "You're right, that would never do," but his eyes were full of suppressed merriment.

She looked up suddenly and he tried to keep his face straight as she continued speak. "When you said you were staying at Menton for a few more days and would like to come with me when I visited the sights, I saw no reason to change my plans. I just didn't realise how disappointing the gardens would be."

Briefly, he took her in his arms and said, "Sara, I've had a wonderful morning. It's great fun just being with you."

His smile warmed her through, "You don't mind then?"

"There's nothing *to* mind, except if you don't go soon, you'll disappoint M. Gascon again."

She glanced at her watch, the concert would be starting shortly. Loathe to see him go she wondered if he would not like to come to the concert as well, but he refused on the grounds that he had not been invited.

"Perhaps next time, if your friend has no objections." He took her hand, kissed her cheek and saying *"Au revoir, à demain,"* set off to walk back to town alone.

***

The queue outside the Palais had begun to move and soon she was on a spacious landing at the head of the stairs, requesting a ticket for the performance. It was all very friendly, with that slightly overzealous air one often finds at events organised by enthusiasts. She bought her ticket and then heard M. Gascon talking and laughing with another man. He looked round and caught Sara's eye. Excusing himself for a moment he stepped over to her, still laughing.

"*Bonjour, Madame Middleton*. I am so glad you could make it. Did you enjoy your gardens this morning?"

"I did." She smiled. "You have a good house here today."

"*Oui, c'est toujours la même chose,*" he replied casually. "Let me introduce *mon ami*, Anton Dupo. We will be playing here together with other members of our Quartet at next week's concert. Anton, cello, *et moi, violon.*" Sara shook hands. M. Gascon explained to Anton that he had met *Madame* Middleton some days previously, and as she was a teacher of music, on a few weeks holiday in Menton, he thought she might enjoy today's concert.

"I have," he continued, "taken the liberty of reserving *Madame* a place next to myself and Anton." He showed her into the music room and indicated three chairs on the end of the second row, each with a handwritten *Reservé* sheet carefully placed on the seat. Sara was pleased to accept the courtesy and sat down on the chair indicated by M. Gascon, who along with his friend excused themselves, "*Pour la moment.*"

It was a charming music room, with large floor-to-ceiling windows overlooking part of the park. Two of the ornate windows were mirror glazed and reflected back the box stage that was centred on the long wall. At the right-hand side of the podium, nearest the door to the chamber, stood a full-sized golden harp. On the left was a double door through which she could see the musicians going in and out, like, she thought (the simile being apposite), fiddlers' elbows.

Soon M. Gascon returned and took his seat beside her.

"Anton will introduce the programme in a few minutes," he said. "I am so pleased you managed to come. It is my granddaughter Julie's birthday today; she has six years. She is having a party at my house with a dozen little friends. I love my Julie very much but, *une douzaine petites en fête!... brrrrrr...* is too much for a poor old *grandpère, n'est pas?* She gave me her permission to arrive later after her party, if I promised to ask if you would also like to attend. I couldn't promise you would say 'yes' of course... but as you know from my card, my home is very close to your apartment, in *La Close Des Lucioles...* perhaps you have seen it already from your balcony. It would give Julie, my daughter Monique, and myself much pleasure if you would join us."

Sara was surprised and rather flattered by the invitation. She hadn't actually read the address on M. Gascon's card, which was very remiss. If she had, she would have known it was the most natural thing in the world for him to offer to escort her. All that angst for nothing! She smiled her thanks and nodded 'yes', as Anton was beginning the 'welcome everyone' speech, which he delivered in jolly but rapid colloquial French. Sara caught only part of what he said and realised, not for the first time on this trip, that being familiar with operatic arias of Bizet and Gounod was not a lot of help in such circumstances.

The Quintet and their programme were excellent. It had been a delightful way to spend the afternoon. She thanked

M. Gascon very much for telling her about it. After saying farewell to Anton, it was perfectly natural they should walk home together, to see Julie.

During the twenty-minute stroll, they chatted generally about the joy of good music, the concert they'd just enjoyed and the concert to come next week. Sara learned that many years ago, Jean-Pierre and his friend Anton, had played in the UK with the Northern Sinfonia Orchestra at the Sage in Gateshead. As a regular concert goer, she thought it would have been amazing if she'd actually been there when he'd played. They agreed it was a small world.

Conversation turned on to her musical history. She'd told him she had always loved singing BC, but the opportunity to do much after the twins were born was very limited. Only when they grew up a little could she devote more time to do what she enjoyed so much. She spoke with great enthusiasm about how exciting it had been to sing the mezzo role in Verdi's Requiem next to the brilliant bass-baritone who had been 'loaned' by York Minster. His performance she said, was thrilling. She mentioned that the singer was in Menton now, in his role of consultant engineer helping to construct automatons for the festival. She had been very surprised to see him, as she had no idea that he was involved in such things. M. Gascon asked his name and she replied "Mr Martin."

As they drew nearer to central Menton, Sara expressed a wish to get a little gift for Julie's birthday. Although insisting it was totally unnecessary, Jean-Pierre helped her choose a box of Julie's favourite chocolates, prettily wrapped with a ribbon by the chocolatier.

***

La Close de Lucioles was exactly as described, directly opposite La Maison Soleil. The attractive, orange-painted villa was just visible from the road. Monique and Julie were very welcoming as Jean-Pierre opened the door, Julie, momentarily solemn, formally shook hands and bid *bonjour* to Madame Middleton, before launching herself into her beloved *grandpapa's* waiting arms, babbling away at a fantastic rate about what Sara could only guess.

Monique made coffee and offered Sara birthday cake, told them how the party had gone, and that everyone seemed to have had a good time. The children ate a lot and played games, but, goodness, they were noisy! Julie brought one of her presents over to show Sara.

"Mon grandpapa donné moi cette jolie poupée! Elle est magnifique n'ést pas?"

"Oui, très belle!" Sara breathed. She recognised a Sasha doll, a thing she would have given her eye teeth for herself, forty years ago.

"Elle s'appelle Violetta... J'aime ma poupée, et mon grandpapa, beaucoup!" she added giving Jean-Pierre a big hug and kiss.

"Petite coquette!" he smiled ruefully.

As Julie admired and played with her expensive new Sasha doll, Monique turned the conversation to Sara's impressions of the Cote d'Azur and Menton in particular, then to the concert and music in general. It was clear that Monique, like her father, shared a passion for music. They discussed favourite composers from the Baroque to modern day. Sara had a natural inclination towards choral works, Jean-Pierre and Monique to orchestral pieces. Time flew quickly by, Julie was dressed for bed when just before 7.00pm the door opened to admit Monique's husband Bertrand who, newly

78

returned from his latest trip, had managed to get home for his daughter's birthday.

There was much rejoicing at his unexpected homecoming. Little Julie was very excited, especially when *papa* produced a huge box, which she had no doubt contained an equally large birthday present. After being introduced to Bertrand, Sara saw it was time to leave. She felt awkward and didn't want to intrude, remembering too well times when George had wrangled an early disembarking, to get home a day sooner.

She said her goodbyes and thank you. Monique invited her to come again, as she had enjoyed their talk very much. Jean-Pierre accompanied her to the door and said, supposing Sara was still in Menton, it would be a pleasure to see her in the audience at next week's concert, when his quartet would be playing. She said she would be there, left the villa and crossed the road over to her apartment.

CHAPTER TEN

There was another message from Harry waiting on her mobile 'Where tomorrow? H.' She phoned him back. His voice answered after only a few rings.

"Hi, Sara, how was your concert? Any good?"

"Excellent, very enjoyable," she replied, "and Jean-Pierre invited me back to his place."

There was a moment of silence before he spoke again. "*Jean-Pierre,* um? Did you go?"

"Oh yes, I didn't realise he lives just over the road from me, in fact I can see his house from here. That's why he offered to take me to the Palais. It made sense because he had to walk past my door. I was an idiot to even consider he might have had no sense of propriety," she said, a little facetiously.

"So, despite being a Frenchman, he had no ulterior motives. What's he like?"

"As I told you, a very nice man. It was his granddaughter's birthday today and she had a party at his house. He said at his age a dozen children *en fête* would have been too much for him. Julie agreed he could go to the concert instead, as long as he took me home with him afterwards.

She feels protective towards me because she found me in the first place. You know what kids are like, they get attached to waifs and strays," she said with a little laugh.

"No, I don't really. I was never fortunate enough to have a child," Harry replied with regret.

"Oh, I'm sorry," Sara said and meant it. The disappointment in his voice was so marked.

"I'll tell you about it one day, but not now."

Changing the subject quickly, she asked how he had spent his day after leaving her.

"I had a really exciting time finishing off some paperwork, but it's almost done now and I hope I can devote more of my time to sightseeing with you. I enjoyed our outing to the garden today, and the back seat of the bus certainly provided an unexpected extra dimension of pleasure to the experience."

Although she couldn't see his face, she knew he was grinning. That his sense of propriety was almost certainly questionable, oddly didn't bother her at all, and she smiled too.

"I thought we might try a train next time," she said drily. "I went to the museum yesterday and saw some lovely ceramics they found in the port at Villefranche, I'd quite like to go just to see, and it's not far to the Villa Kerylos. You're more than welcome to join me."

"Now," he said, "I have actually been to Villefranche but it was a long time ago. It's a very old town and has some unexpected features. I won't spoil if for you if you don't know, but I certainly wouldn't mind going again. The Villa I've seen, but only from the outside, so I accept your kind invitation."

Somehow they talked another twenty minutes, before saying goodbye and finally deciding to meet at the station at 10.00 next morning, whatever the weather.

A fierce wind had started again during the night and hadn't quite blown itself out by morning, but the forecast was good. Harry was, as usual, already there when she arrived at the station. She found it very endearing that he should be waiting for her, even though she was five minutes early, and playfully considered should there be another time, turning up even earlier, just to see if he still would be there first. Somehow, she thought he would.

The station at Villefranche was set above the town. It all looked very clean but the walk down was permeated by a hint of eau-de-sewage. Doubtless the smell came from the old pipes that lined the step-wall. Sara was glad of the cool weather, had they arrived in full sun the smell would have been more than a hint. Harry asked if she had heard of the *Chapelle de St Pierre des Pecheurs*, because that was one of the secret highlights of Villefranche. She hadn't. He said it was smaller than its name, tiny in fact, and quite easy to miss, which indeed it was. They must have walked past it twice before seeing the door, with a paper *fermé* notice pinned on the front. According to the timings listed it should have been open, but perhaps they could try on the way back.

He led the way to the old fort that dominated the harbour area. The path was mercifully high enough to avoid the worst of the spray that the wind helped crash against the sea wall. The sound of the angry sea made conversation between them difficult as they walked along hand in hand.

Sara assumed this would be where the artefacts she had seen were found, but in truth, her mind was not altogether on 17th-century ceramics. Being so near to the jagged rocks and lashing waves brought home to her not only how easily a ship might be dashed to pieces here, but how many of its crew caught in the maelstrom would perish, so close to shore and safety. She thought of George. 'It must have been like this when he went in to get that ball.' The waves were like wild beasts, vicious and raging at the confines of a cage. 'Bad enough in daylight. How much worse it must have been in the dark, and the water would have been freezing cold. He couldn't have survived for more than a minute. What had possessed him? Was he not frightened? He can't have been in his right mind. Only a madman or a drunk would do something that foolhardy.' It came to her, not for the first time, he probably *had* been drinking heavily, and as usual left his brains behind at the bar. She wasn't sure if that made it worse or better, and despite herself gave a little snort, a combination of understanding and sorrow. Poor George, he could be so funny when he'd had too much to drink. He'd pretend to be Superman to make her laugh. She'd found his boyishness so lovable and felt a stab of guilt. In the end it was the very quality she had so adored that had been the death of him.

"Are you alright?" Harry asked her. "Are you cold?"

"I am a bit."

He put his arm protectively around her shoulders, "Not far to the port now, or would you like to go back?"

"I'm fine," she said. "I'd like to see the boats." Grateful for the warmth of Harry's arm, she tucked her memories of George safe in a corner of her heart, where they nestled like a bird after an arduous journey, returning home to its nest. No bitterness, no anger, just a shadow of warm young love to wonder at and cherish.

The gale across the harbour tossed the little ships crammed together there, knocking and bobbing them against one another. Protected still from the heavy gusts by Harry's arm, they made their way down to the old ship-building yards, ancient caverns built into the wall only metres away from the sea. A dry dock complete with boat awaiting repair marked the end of the harbour walk and they retraced their footsteps to find the old town, built on a now familiar pattern, of steep hills lined by high narrow houses with multitudinous steps. Harry led them to a particular intersection where there was a choice of going up steps to the right or down to the left. He said, "I think this is it. Follow me." Intrigued, she followed him on the downward side, to be rewarded almost immediately by discovering she was in a spacious, obviously ancient underground street, illuminated by what looked like gas lamps giving out a warm orange glow.

"Wow," she said, spreading her arms out wide to spiral along. "Harry, this is wonderful, I'd never have found it by myself." Her smile was like another light. He grinned back to see such pleasure on her face. The street was very wide, its vaulted roof pierced with patches of light streaming down flights of steps which led up to the surface. House doors appeared in the gloom. Who, she wondered, would live down here? Troglodytes? Coming to the end, which finished literally in a blank stone wall, they mounted the nearest steps to the road above and she saw with astonishment magnificent houses rising from below. Troglodyte dwellings they were not.

The wind had dropped a little but it was still on the cold side as they neared the big strong plastic conservatory extension at the front of a nearby bistro. It looked very inviting and was surprisingly warm inside, so they took a table, ordered lunch and talked happily about what they'd seen and the history of Villefranche. Harry excused himself for a moment. As Sara watched him leave the table she wondered what George would have made of him? They were so different, worlds apart. Sara herself was not the same person, she was older and much wiser. The question she had not dared to ask, formed unwonted in her mind. 'Would she have made George her first choice now?' Reluctantly honest, she thought not. But then it wasn't a fair thing to ask. Harry may have been just as callow in his youth as George, but she doubted it. Then again, George was little more than a boy when he died, and she was a grown woman now, with much more experience of how hard just living can be. He hadn't been able to grow and learn with her. Her tastes and needs were not what they were, just as having had the real thing she didn't want to play with dolls anymore. So was Harry the real thing? Who and what was he? A man of the world certainly, who obviously liked the good things in life, from his elegantly understated Patek Philippe watch to his shiny Penny Loafers, he was handsome, confident, witty and charming. Merely thinking about him gave her forgotten frissons of desire. What, Sara asked herself, he wanted and expected from her she didn't like to think, or then again, maybe she did.

He was back by her side. "Shall we try that Chapelle again on our way out?"

"Yes please," she said, as lunch was brought to them.

85

The Chapel was open by the time they had retraced their steps. As they entered Sara almost squeaked with delight.

"What do you think of this?" Harry asked. "All the paintings are by him, so it's often known just as the Cocteau Chapel."

"Yes. I see. Did you remember how much I told you I admired his work, when I visited his museum in Menton?"

Harry nodded.

"And you kept it as a surprise for me. Thank you so much. I just love it."

It was the tiniest chapel imaginable, only one room covered floor to ceiling in Jean Cocteau's paintings of Biblical stories, modelled by ordinary men and women of Villefranche who, like Saint Peter, were fisherfolk. She liked his way of painting, stripped down to ethereal, single flowing lines and his surreal sense of humour. The profile-painted head of a girl, whose eye was the outline shape of a fish, made her smile. But what intrigued her most of all, was that despite the reduction of form to the pure minimum, every upraised arm, angels and men alike, contained in its pit a vigorously painted crisscross tuft of black hair, as a vivid reminder of what earthy creatures we really are. Cocteau's work graphically showed he knew what chaos lay under our pretentious sublimity. It didn't diminish her attraction to Harry for one moment but she looked at him, and wondered under that urbane exterior he presented to the world, what manner of man lay hidden underneath. She also wondered at herself for finding the desire to know so urgent and compelling. The artist had achieved his objective.

***

It was a pleasant walk along the shoreline to where they could see the Villa Kerylos standing on a promontory overlooking the bay. Sara pointed out the Ephrussi Palace on the opposite side. It looked absolutely gorgeous in the sunlight and Harry thought he would have to visit it too, if not now, then soon.

But today's next treat stood before them now. Theodore Reinach, a Grecophile of the first order, built his dream home between 1902 and 1908. A beautiful oddity where everything was done to an ancient Greek pattern, but with all mod cons of the day hidden within its walls. It was without question a house designed by a man for a man, and was much to Harry's taste, cool and elegant. The entrance contained a wonderful light-filled portico complete with pillars and fountain. Large frescoes adorned the walls, opulent and sensuous but without a hint of vulgarity. The floors were marble and lacking in any fabric carpets, but most of their mosaic designs were edged in a pattern of stylised fringe work, serving as facsimile rugs to create a warm, soft aspect. Marbled panels on the walls and superbly crafted furniture gave harmony to Reinach's ideal, well-loved home. Harry was busy imagining himself inhabiting this exquisite house, when he noticed rather too many images of naked young boys adorning the frescoes and began to have doubts about the nature of the architect. Mr Reinach did have a wife, but with such frescos Harry suspected his marriage may have been on the same ancient Greek lines as his taste in furniture.

Sara liked the shower room best, housed as it was in an arched niche ten feet high, three and a half feet wide and lined with a geometric terracotta mosaic motif. There was a ten-inch shower head, centrally fixed in the marble archi-trave, which had a staggering six different shower settings! 'B&Q,' she thought, 'eat your heart out!'

CHAPTER ELEVEN

When they got back to Menton, Harry went up to Sara's apartment for the first time for coffee. He saw the shabby-looking box she'd bought at the flea market, with which she'd been so pleased, and laughed. She assured him she could restore it, he just smiled and wished her 'good luck'.

'Cheeky bugger' she thought, but still made his coffee and as she handed it to him, he apologised for being less than complimentary about her purchase. His eyes, however, belied his contrition and she had to laugh too. It *was* in a state.

Sadly for Sara, he obviously was going to stay only as long as it took to drink the coffee, but then on approaching the door he turned and suddenly felt reluctant to leave. Taking a step back towards her, he looked fondly into her eyes, and smiling gently gave her the sweetest goodnight kiss she'd ever had. Her heart turned to water. He was sorry, but tomorrow he needed to be back at work, there was a bit of finishing off to do on a couple of exhibits but hoped they could still enjoy one another's company in the evening.

"It's a terrible thing to have to work for one's living, while others go out to play," Sara said. "But I will commiserate as you crawl homeward, tired out from hard toil in the muddy fields but I can, if you would like me to, cook supper for us here," she ended practically.

"That would be very kind," he replied. "If it wouldn't be too much trouble, I'd like that. What will you do with yourself tomorrow whilst I'm doing all this toiling?"

"Don't know, maybe pop over to *Monte* for an hour or so before opening the tin of beans for you."

He kissed her again lightly and said, "Sounds good... About seven, OK?"

She smiled at him and he couldn't resist a final hug before his customary "*à demain.*"

Sara was no master chef but was, as her daughter Georgie had remarked, 'queen of the slow-cooker'. She'd found one in the cupboard and although not sure Georgie was paying her a compliment or not, she was confident enough to think she could use it to make a decent rabbit casserole. Ridiculously excited at the thought of cooking supper for Harry, she decided to go to the market early in the morning, buy everything fresh, pop the lot into the pot and let it simmer to perfection while she was out. She was so ludicrously happy, even *Agony Angst's* voice asserting that he was probably after a damn sight more than rabbit stew didn't faze her, because in all honesty, she rather liked the idea that he might be.

She was at the market by 9am and bought half a fresh rabbit and vegetables. Wine was more difficult, she didn't know which sort to get, and after asking advice of the wine merchant paid rather more than she had anticipated for, what she was assured, was a very good choice to go with rabbit. She took her purchases back to the apartment and within the hour prepared the meat and vegetables, put them in the slow cooker, pushed the automatic button and went for her shower. Clean and dry, she dressed warmly, checked the pot was actually starting to heat up and then plugged it in properly. Ten minutes later everything was working, so she stepped out of her apartment and was on her way to see the legendary Monaco and Monte Carlo.

On arriving, she was overwhelmed by the majesty of Monaco's mountains. They were spectacularly beautiful. With the famous Grimaldi Palace sitting high above the city, grandly dominating the skyline, nothing looked quite real as it all sparkled in the winter sunshine. She sat on a bench and breathed in the wonder of it all, but absolutely at a loss as to which road led where. She wished Harry was with her, when her inner voice brought her up sharp: 'For goodness' sake, Sara, stop mooning over him like an adolescent school-girl. You've coped very well thank you, for years, without some ageing lothario having to hold your hand.'

Sara knew *AA* didn't have a high opinion of Harry but thought 'ageing lothario' a little harsh. Nevertheless, she got the point, smiled a little and had to agree with the principle expressed. She got to her feet, and hoping her casserole would be alright, set off to explore the heart of the Principality so beloved of the uber-rich.

Harry as promised, arrived a few minutes before 7.00pm. Supper went down well and the wine was very good.

He'd had a hard day and suspected tomorrow would be just as fraught. He listened with patience, though not total agreement, to Sara's rather damning assessment of the morally bankrupt, conspicuous worship of wealth, rampant in Monte Carlo and Monaco, lay back on the sofa to enjoy his wine, wrapped an arm round her, closed his eyes and went to sleep. He woke around 5am to find himself lying on the floor where he had fallen off the sofa. Totally disorientated he wondered where he was for a moment before remembering he was at Sara's apartment. Why had she let him go to sleep? She should have woken him. How could he have been so inconsiderate? He picked up the blanket that she had thoughtfully laid over him, feeling a complete heel, tiptoed over to her bedroom and peeked around the door. She was fast asleep. He didn't want to wake her; it was far too early in the morning. He'd just go quietly back to his hotel, it wouldn't be the first time he'd done that to a woman, but this time he would leave a note.

Sara opened her eyes a few hours later, found his note full of apology and smiled. He must have been exhausted last night. He'd continued to sleep soundly and quietly as a baby even when she'd slipped off his shoes and lifted his legs carefully onto the sofa, before tucking the blanket round to make him more comfortable and warm, prior to going alone to her own bed.

Around 10am her phone rang. It was Harry. He apologised profusely and explained, "It should have been an easy day yesterday, but there was a problem. Remember the high winds on Sunday? They blew down a heavy branch from an old tree and it fell across one of the exhibits. It wasn't discovered 'til morning. They got rid of the tree but the damage was done and the electronics were completely shot. It was a case of all hands on deck and we've had a hell of a job getting hold of the components needed to make the repair. It's such short notice, you see. In fact we're waiting for a vital part now, that's how I've time to call you."

"Oh Lord, Harry. No wonder you were tired, and there was me wittering on about the Evil City of Monte Carlo all evening. I'm so sorry."

"The food, wine and company were good and I didn't suffer your wittering for long, if you remember, I went to sleep."

"Which exhibit was damaged?"

"The elephant. Its ears should flap like Dumbo's, the trunk go up and down and its tail whizz round like a propeller. What we've got is one ear jammed to the side of its face, the other pointing to heaven and a trunk sticking out at an angle that would make a rugby player blush, but so far the tail is OK."

Sara laughed. "I'm sorry, really I am."

He laughed too, "I know, I believe you… but it does mean I probably can't see you at all today. God knows how long it's going to take to put right."

"That's a shame. Poor you. Would you like me to make supper again for you tonight?"

He hesitated then said, "I'd love you to, but better not. I honestly don't know what time I might finish, it could go on well into the night, if the components don't come soon, I dare say it will. But it's got to be done. I'll just have to keep on until it's working again."

She could find no answer to this, and saw a correlation between his music and his work. It was clear he would not make do with half-measures in things he really cared about, it had to be right. It was a character trait she admired, even if it meant she wasn't up there with his first priorities.

But Harry went on "Then when it is done, I will permit you to make supper for me every night. You're a very good cook."

Laughingly she answered with the cliché about flattery getting him anywhere and ended with, "My rates are very reasonable too."

"That's good to know," he replied. Although she knew he couldn't see her, she wished she didn't blush so easily. "I'll have to go," he said. "Albert is signalling to me… I'll be in touch. Have a good day." He ended the call and pocketed his mobile.

CHAPTER TWELVE

The next day was as sunny and bright as the one before. Sara had washing and ironing to do, but the day was too good to waste. Sadly there would be no meeting at all with Harry today, but she wasn't going to sit around and mope about it. Her friend Evie had told her that Èze, one of the most lovely hill towns in all of Southern France, was near to Menton. Sara had heard of it in a different context, and had planned to go anyway, but was also eager to see if what Evie had said was true. She had looked at the photo of the town in her guide book, and it did look amazing. She hadn't been certain if she would walk up the mountain or take a bus, and opted for comfortable walking shoes to leave the option open. On arrival, looking up at the height of the mountain from the bus stop outside the train station, she decided unequivocally that the bus was a good idea.

After a steep and twisty journey, Sara was awed by the sight of the old town rising out of an even higher mountain that was accessible only on foot. Ignoring the very busy restaurant at the base, she thought lunch and a cup of tea right at the top might be preferable. She went up through the narrow, ancient arches into Èze.

The high honey-coloured stone walls, and twining narrow passages of the small town were full of light and very fine. Èze was so ancient, it appeared as natural a feature of the landscape as any part of the magnificent panorama below. In comparison Menton's and even Ventimiglia's old towns, looked like new-builds. As it wasn't yet tourist season, she was able to wander around without the crowds that would almost certainly jam the walkways later in the year. Unfortunately, not being tourist season had a downside, there wasn't a single café open. The one she'd initially turned down started to look good. It was still busy, but she didn't have to wait too long for a huge bowl of the best onion soup she'd ever tasted. Sara had picked up a leaflet about Èze as she'd come in the door, that confirmed a story she'd already heard about the original path to the town. It was reputed that the German philosopher Nietzsche had walked there, and it had provided him with inspiration for his major work, the infamous 'will to power', *Thus Spake Zarathustra*.

When she left the café Sara wandered over to the head of the so-called 'Nietzsche Steps' and looked down at the view, without a doubt this was the way she wanted to go. To call the path 'steps' was a slightly optimistic way of describing the series of loose-stoned sloping levels that twisted down the precipitous mountain. Sara was glad of her chosen footwear, there was little evidence of the 'health and safety' precautions so pedantically adhered to in England, but it was grand and a real adventure to tackle those slipping and sliding stones. With only herself to please, she stopped when she found a suitably sized rock and sat down on it to admire the amazing view. Her mobile gave a buzz.

"Hello," said Harry's voice. She couldn't believe how clear he sounded, out in the middle of nowhere.

"Harry! How are things going?"

"Slowly, but not too bad. The stuff we wanted is on its way at last. We've already taken the head apart and all we will need now is to put it all back together again. What are you doing?"

"I'm sitting on a rock halfway down a mountain."

"Where?"

"I've been to Èze, I admit I got the bus up, but I'm walking down the Nietzsche Steps. It's magnificent."

"The Nietzsche Steps? Isn't it a bit wild and woolly up there?"

"Well as I had the opportunity to walk where he was inspired to write his *Magnum Opus*, I thought I might as well take it."

"You're a fan of Nietzsche? Have you read his work?"

"Not a fan exactly, but I know a bit about him. His reputation suffered because of the Nazi's perversion of his ideologies. He's much better respected and understood now. He was a very passionate writer you know, but I think all this business about the '*ubermensch*' or superman is basically just his way of advocating a 'self-help' policy. He thought it was a bad thing to rely on Christian and liberal ethics and wanted to kill off God. Saw no need for him, and thought the idea was positively destructive to mankind. He undoubtedly expressed his ideas in an odd and extreme way, but I think he may have had a point," Sara said, with the air of someone who knows what she is talking about.

Harry was amazed at her erudition. "I had no idea you knew about philosophy," he said.

"Why should you?" she replied lightly. "I was widowed for twenty-six years and spent four of them doing a part-time degree. I did my thesis on Nietzsche. I managed a First, so it can't have been all that bad. Anyway, I bet there are lots of things we don't know about one another."

Harry answered, "Yes, I suppose there are." But he wasn't as keen or open as Sara on saying how he'd spent a lot of his spare time. Much of it certainly had not been furthering his academic qualifications. He could 'see' her bright smile and said, "I wish I was there with you, sitting on my own bit of rock with the wind whistling through my jacket instead of being here in our warm *boulangerie* having to drink fresh hot coffee and chew on a warm *pain-au-chocolat* or two."

'So do I,' she thought but said, "I'm sure you do!" with a sarcastic inflection in her voice.

From the window he could see a van pulling in to the worksite. "It looks like the delivery's arrived. Let's hope everything we need is there," he said. "I'll phone you later this evening… Bye, Sara." The phone went dead.

She stared at a tiny solitary farmhouse precariously perched on the opposite mountainside. A home carved out of a desolate landscape, built by a man who survived its harsh isolation by a will as implacable and sheer as the rock itself. She'd done it once, by sheer will she had made a new life for herself and children after George had died. Was she taking too big a chance letting herself get so fond of Harry? She had been so sure she could keep it all under control, but now could feel figurative as well as real loose stones beneath her feet. She had to tread carefully.

It took well over an hour to come within view of the coast, it had been more exhausting than Sara had thought it would be. She recalled the four elderly ladies who had been climbing up the last few steps as she had started the journey down. They'd been very lively and were chatting happily, without the least sign of being tired. She conjectured she would have been on her knees crawling up by then. Conceding her own lack of fitness, she made a mental note, to take up jogging or something, when she went back to Ripon. She hoped the café opposite the bus stop was still open, she really needed more tea. Thankfully it was. She had her drink and with excellent timing got onto the platform just as the train back to Menton pulled in.

Walking home from the station, she saw Monique and Jean-Pierre waiting at the kindergarten nearby. She stopped to say *Bonjour* and they chatted whilst waiting for Julie to appear. Sara couldn't resist telling them she had spent some time at the weekend with her friend Harry, but today he had to work so she had visited Èze on her own, and thought it a very fine town. She expressed a hope that he might go to the concert with her on the coming Saturday.

"Would this be the Mr Martin with a wonderful bass-baritone voice?" Jean-Pierre enquired.

"Yes, the very man," she said happily, colouring slightly.

"*Alors*," he said graciously. "*Puis*, if you would both care to join us for a glass of wine after the performance, we would be very glad to meet our new friend's *ami*. *Ah, ici Julie…*"

The little girl was in the centre of a group of friends whom she hurriedly left behind, as she made a beeline for her family.

She kissed *mama* and *grandpapa* before shyly smiling at Sara. Then slipping her hand into her grandfather's, quickly began to babble away about her day at 'school'.

Monique and Sara smiled indulgently at Julie's immediate commandeering of his attention.

"It will be good to see you again this Saturday. I enjoyed our last conversation very much. I'm afraid Bertrand had to return to his ship for two days, so we are back 'looking after' *grandpapa* again. He has been so sad since *ma mère* died," she confided, "and I'm afraid Julie looks after her *grandpère* so well, she tires him out! *Mais*, he is very good natured and loves her dearly… I will catch them before she talks off his ears… *Au revoir*, Sara, until Saturday, when we will meet your friend."

"*Au revoir, Monique*, and thank you."

CHAPTER THIRTEEN

Harry didn't contact Sara that night. She was a little bit downhearted about it, but assumed he'd been so busy he'd simply forgotten he said he would. In the morning she saw there was a message from him that had been sent at 2.35am. It said simply 'We're finished. H.'

The message was only slightly ambiguous but *Agony Angst* was onto it right away. 'Aha!' she crowed triumphantly. 'I said so all along. He saw you were getting too keen and gave you the old heave-ho line about having to work, and you fell for it... We're finished... it's over! I don't know how you could have thought it would end any other way. He's just been amusing himself, passing time nothing more... You need to listen to me more, my girl!'

Sara's stomach tightened, she felt nauseous and fell onto the sofa which he had occupied so recently. Such a cold message. That those two brief words should have the power to wound her to the core, made her feel humiliated, devastated and wish for oblivion. They were so curt, so final. Was he tired of her already? Had her comments about Nietzsche's philosophy yesterday somehow offended him? She didn't know. She did know her new-found world was collapsing about her. Just how long she sat there she couldn't tell. Her phone rang and rang before she finally picked up…

"Hello… Hello," said a familiar voice.

"Harry?"

"Yes, it's me. Are you alright? You sound a bit odd."

"Sorry, I've just woken up."

"It's almost noon. I know you're on holiday, but really… you've not got my mail then? We're finished, thank God. That bloody elephant can flap its ears and wag its trunk to the end of time now, providing another tree doesn't fall on it."

She laughed though tears were falling fast.

"I'm free for the rest of the day," he said. "I was going to suggest meeting for lunch at our *patisserie*, but if you are still in your pyjamas…"

"I'll be there," she said. "Just give me half an hour."

AA with well-pursed lips, sulked and disapproved in the background.

Lunch was a perfectly jolly affair. Harry was full of high spirits and he regaled her with funny stories about all manner of things. She delighted in being with him and that evening they went to a local cinema club to see the 1990s cult black-comedy film *Tatie Danielle*, about a thoroughly nasty septuagenarian, whose mission in life is to ruin the lives of her long-suffering friends and family. Sara thought how very like her own *Agony Angst*, and laughed until she cried.

She mailed her children when she got back to the apartment, to keep them up to date with what she'd been doing, and the places she'd visited, but made no reference to the fact that Mr Martin had chosen to extend his stay in Menton.

On Thursday, as Sara explained to Harry, she had something important to do. It was twenty-six years ago to the day, that George's memorial plaque had been erected. Certain in the knowledge that someone at the cemetery would care for it, she was going to take a pot plant for him, as a token of remembrance. Also, most importantly, although she said nothing of this aspect to Harry, she needed to be alone to 'talk' to George, not only about the past but how Harry had so recently impacted on her life.

The first half of her mission was relatively easy. She went into town to the same florist shop where she had bought the freesias for her first visit, but this time bought George a weighty, decorated, emerald green pot in which to place a large, beautiful blood-red cyclamen plant. Although it was very heavy to carry, she chose to walk up to the cemetery through the old town, rather than get a taxi or bus. It was a kind of Via Dolorosa for her. A penance for the years of anger and resentment she'd harboured against him.

It took a long time and a great deal of effort to climb the hill, and she had to take frequent rests. The last one was at the bottom of the cemetery steps, which looked high enough to climb to heaven itself. She found his memorial easily this time and gratefully stood the pot with its plant by the plaque, making sure it stood straight on the ground. The flowers shone bravely, the only living tribute in the field.

Satisfied with her work, Sara stood back. It felt strange, she old enough now to be his mother, bringing flowers to the dead boy who had been her husband for such a short time, so long ago. She remembered how the girl she had been was so pleased and proud when her friend Jilly said George looked like Bryan Ferry from Roxy Music. But despite the Ferry-style military khaki shirt, his heart had always been set on being a seaman. He'd enlisted as soon as he could. She took a teaching degree and they became engaged on her gradua-tion day. They soon married, happy and confidently looking forward to the future. They were young and everything seemed to be within their grasp, nothing could faze them. They were in love and because they had each other they could take on the whole world and win. 'Well,' she thought, 'we got that wrong, didn't we, sweetheart? You died and I had to grow up alone. It was so hard, and I blamed you for everything'. Then she said out loud, "I'm sorry."

She returned to talking to him in her head, 'I hope you don't mind that I've met someone else now, who I really like. I don't know how deeply he feels about me, but I dare say I'll find out, one way or the other. I'll keep you posted on events George, before I go home.' Sara had attached a label to the flowers 'From your loving Sara', she touched it tenderly by way of *au revoir,* and left the cemetery.

At the bottom of the steps she crossed the road and spent some long minutes leaning over the wall watching boats bobbing in the harbour far below, then turned left to make her way back to town by the broad Boulevard de Garavan.

The boulevard followed a long lazy curve down to the port, she saw precipitous steps at intervals going down too, and she thought they may be short-cuts. Feeling a little tired she decided to take a chance and see where the next set led. She unknowingly chose well, as the particular flight she took eventually led to a steep road down past the botanical gardens of Val Rahmeh which she had on her list of places that might be worth a visit. They were closed today, but she could peep through the high railings and it looked beautiful. It was unfortunate they were closed, but tomorrow they would be open. She could, all being well, if he wanted to come, make up to Harry for the rather dull Serre de la Madonne fiasco by bringing him here.

The road continued abruptly down to the coast road. Almost at the bottom there was a secondary school or college. Some adolescent boys were playing football on the road outside. She hurried by them, trying not to think.

It was still a reasonable walk along by the harbour into central Menton but at least it was flat. She passed a little Italian restaurant which looked good, but thought she'd save that until tomorrow too when she would be with *him*.

The light was starting to fade as she approached the town centre. It had taken almost her whole day to make the pilgrimage, but she was in no doubt that it had been worth it. They had both been absolved by the memory of their love. Bitter memories shed, her peace with George felt warm and complete.

As for Harry, that was a different matter. He was an infinitely more complex man than George had ever been. Even as she was being helplessly drawn closer by the magnet of his personality, she felt under his strong attraction and easy charm lived a troubled soul. His sudden cold behaviour on their first evening together still bothered her. She was now convinced it was provoked by something she'd said. Although it had been brief and had not happened again, she knew she hadn't just imagined it.

By the time Sara was opening the door of La Maison Soleil it was getting dark She unzipped her boots, rubbed her aching feet, made supper (she'd had nothing since breakfast), and although it was still early, changed into her pyjamas, made herself comfortable with a cup of tea on the sofa and closed her eyes. Her phone bleeped, it was Harry.

"Hello. I was just thinking about you. Everything alright?"

She answered, "Fine, thank you. You and the elephant OK?"

"He is very lively, but I've been chained to my desk all day coping with the mountain of paperwork his accident dumped on me. I desperately need a holiday, I was hoping you might take me out somewhere tomorrow to get over it."

"I like a man not given to hyperbole, so I'll try to organise a schedule for you. Have you been to the Val Rahmeh Gardens?"

"No," he said, "they've always been closed whenever I've been free to go."

"Well they're open tomorrow. If you like, we can meet at La Place aux Herbes at about ten and we can have a look round the flea market first. It's very small and won't take long."

The idea of spending time at such a market did not excite Harry, but it would be a new experience and he was willing to go along with the suggestion, as long as they could fit lunch in somewhere along the way. Sara told him about the restaurant she had seen, and the itinerary was settled. They talked for another half hour before saying goodnight.

Harry was beginning to occupy too much of her thoughts. It was only 8.00pm and she needed something to take her mind away from him, or she just wouldn't sleep. She looked at the little box she'd bought the previous week that he had been so dismissive of and decided to make a start on it. Basically, it needed a good clean. She went to the kitchen and poured some olive oil into a dish and, with some cotton wool pads, found pacific pleasure in gently rubbing the oil into the wood to remove years of grime. A couple of hours and a shower later, she slipped into bed and slept like a baby.

CHAPTER FOURTEEN

As Harry waited for Sara the next morning, he cast a bemused and cursory glance over the market which was obviously very popular. There were stalls with second-hand books, carpets, handbags, silverware and an amazing amount of old oil lamps. 'So' he thought frankly, 'this is the place to come if you want to sell a lot of useless bits of rubbish to gullible punters.'

In minutes Sara had arrived and excitedly joined him for a wander round. The stallholder from whom she had bought her box last week was there again, with a largely different selection of goods, but this time she resisted the temptation to buy. Harry, who was intrigued rather than thrilled by it, made an effort to appear interested in something which gave Sara such obvious delight. He bore up quite well but soon when she, who was nothing if not perceptive, suggested he might like to order them a hot chocolate at the café, where she would join him in a few minutes, he gladly agreed.

In five minutes exactly, she sat down by Harry at his table outside the café, where he had thoughtfully placed a saucer over her drink to keep it fresh and warm.

"Thank you," she said. "You were very tolerant and kind to come."

Harry gave a quick laugh at having been found out so quickly.

"I admit it," he said with a guilty grin. "It's a fair cop, yo'r 'onour. I can't see the attraction. But I am genuinely looking forward to the Botanical Gardens this afternoon. Shall we finish this chocolate and go now, or would you rather we had something to eat first?"

"Tell you what," said Sara. "If we go along the seafront, I've seen a little Italian place, quite near where we turn off to go up to the gardens. It'll take about forty minutes, so we'll build up an appetite. Would that be OK?"

"Can't think of anything better! Drink up and let's go."

They wandered along by the sea, easy in each other's company. There were some children playing on the pebbly shoreline, they stopped to watch their game.

"My grandson, Billy, he's nearly three, would love this... You said you never had children."

"No. I never had any," he said shortly.

"Oh, I'm sorry, I didn't mean to pry."

"It's OK," he replied, in a voice that was suggestive of just the opposite.

There was silence for a moment then he continued.

"I wanted children, but my ex-wife..." Hesitatingly at first, then more fluently with barely suppressed rancour, he gave her an account of the reason which occasioned his childlessness. She listened dumbstruck. "Poor Harry, that's terrible. I don't know what to say. What a horrible thing to happen. How long ago was this?"

"Ten years, more or less."

"And you never met anyone else, who would give you the child that you wanted?"

"No. Forgive me, it sounds awful, but my faith was shaken. I couldn't trust anyone."

"That does seem a terrible waste, I'm sure you would have made a wonderful father."

He was pleased by her assertion. Actually, he knew very little about children and child-rearing, but believed with all his heart he would have made the best dad in the world. He remained silent for a while, immersed in his memories of that time and what might have been. With an effort, he brought his mind back to the present, and Sara.

"I'm getting hungry," he said. "How far is this little restaurant of yours?"

"Over there. Can you see that awning? That's it. I hope we find it worth the walk."

It was not long before they were seated, ordering lasagne and wine that was as good as they had hoped it would be, but Harry seemed quiet and Sara wished she hadn't asked him about children. She tried to lighten his mood by telling him about the eventful journey she'd undergone in getting to Menton. Harry told her of the delays and cancellations he'd experienced in his life. Once, he said, he'd been stuck at Casablanca airport for seven and a half hours because Air Maroc had 'lost' the crew. She decided her experience maybe wasn't that bad.

When nicely full and relaxed again, they set out to find the Botanical Gardens of Val Rahmeh. 'So that's what it was about,' she thought, as they made their way up the steep path. She remembered now, during their first meeting for supper, it was when she'd mentioned sweet little Julie that his mood had changed. Poor Harry, how devastated he must have been by his loss. No one on this earth she concluded, was free of personal sorrow. But bad as sorrow was, an inability to adapt and overcome was infinitely worse. Harry obviously had not managed to do it yet. Damn it, it had taken her more than twice as many years to fully come to terms with hers. But as to making a judgement as to the rights and wrongs of a situation like Harry's, that involved hearing both sides and Sara had heard only his version. She pushed an obvious niggle to the back of her mind. She would sympathise but it wasn't her place to apportion blame. It was a history in which she had no stake. She had made her peace with George, Harry needed to resolve his anger about the past too.

The sun was quite warm by the time they reached Val Rahmeh, the walk up the hill had been hard going, but what a delight they beheld. It was beautiful, stuffed to the path borders with exotic green planting and, as a bonus, carefully provided with excellent directions, so not a corner would be missed. Up stone steps and down, along twisting paths they zig-zagged along the route, until coming to an unexpected dead end, where in the shade of precipitous rocks a bucolic, miniature waterfall poured itself into a small, dark green pond. Taking advantage of a well-placed bench they sat and listened with unabashed pleasure to the gentle music of the water, and playfully augmented the sound with improvised harmonies of their own. The spell was eventually broken by a group of young students on a guided tour. They were very serious and studious, as their *professeur* declaimed with

111

fervent voice they scribbled copious notes, eager not to forget a single syllable of his learning. Harry and Sara giggled and moved on.

They left the magic gardens and progressed down the hill, diverting into an olive grove garden, which in mid-February and declining light was less than spectacular. But it didn't matter at all. They were content to be with one another.

As they grew nearer to Menton town centre, Harry invited Sara to have coffee at his hotel.

"It's got a great café," he said, keeping it light.

As she smiled, her sleeping butterflies awoke to start fluttering overtime in her stomach.

Over coffee Harry thanked Sara for a lovely day.

"Much more fun than working," he said. "Would you like to do something tomorrow, as well?"

Sara reminded him of the second concert at the Palais Carnolés that she had promised to attend.

"I'm sorry… yes of course. I'd forgotten M. Gaston."

"Yes, Jean-Pierre *Gascon*," she replied archly. "I saw him the other day, as a matter of fact. He was with his daughter. They were meeting Julie after her kindergarten session. I was invited back again for supper and a glass or two of wine with them after the concert. I told them about you being here."

Harry was nodding sagely. Sara decided to stop teasing.

"They said, if you were at the concert with me, I could consider you to be included in their invitation. They really are very nice people. Would you be happy to do that?"

Harry said he would and beamed her a smile.

After coffee, he walked Sara home. They decided to meet at the apartment the next day at about 2.30pm, which would allow sufficient time for a slow meander to the Palais.

After he'd gone, she thought he'd sounded a teeny bit jealous about Jean-Pierre and that pleased her so much that she sang a dozen or so bars of the Brindisi from La Traviata, before remembering there was a tenant living on the floor below, who may not be too pleased to hear a drinking song at that time of the evening.

CHAPTER FIFTEEN

In the morning, thinking of the day ahead filled Sara with nervous excitement. She needed something to occupy her mind until she saw him. Partly for the pleasure it gave her and partly to show Harry that his cynicism had been misplaced, she set to work again on her marquetry box restoration. It wasn't possible to finish it completely without the new slivers of wood she needed to repair the broken runners, but she'd found some beeswax in a cupboard, which she rubbed carefully and sparingly into the cleaned wood and buffed with a soft duster. After repeating the process several times over, the box gleamed. It didn't look so bad, it was a shame she couldn't do more, but she'd used up a good hour. Only four more to go.

She made a cup of tea, but soon thoughts of Harry swamped her mind again, this would never do. Determined to keep herself busy, she put on her coat and went out, to explore a bit more of the town. As luck would have it, set out just behind the station there was a weekly market of the sort she understood, it was so like the one in her home town. Stalls selling all sorts of bargains, from clothing, fruit and vegetables to hardware and second-hand DVDs jostled happily together, in a kind of organised chaos. It was very busy and Sara quickly concluded this was the place where the ordinary Mentonians did a lot of their shopping. There was also a delicious aroma coming from a place selling piping hot sausages, wrapped in a bun. Despite the early hour, she joined the queue and bought one, which she ate straight from the paper wrapper, as she inspected every stall.

Going round the back of one, she saw a broken wooden fruit box, and having a skip-rat mentality, picked up a portion of it. With a nod of permission from the bemused trader, she gleefully popped it into her bag. The search was on, she found a bits-and-bobs stall, bought a tube of what she recognised as UHU glue, and hurried back to the apartment to finish off the repairs to her box.

It took a little time and care, using the kitchen scissors, to cut the thin pieces of salvaged wood to size and to glue them firmly into place. Pulling one of her nail files out of her toilet bag she used the fine side to sand the slivers of wood down and blend them into the remaining original pieces. It was beginning to look pretty good. When she was sure the glue was completely set, using her fingertips she brushed a very light film of oil over the new wood, its colour deepening to one compatible with the rest of the box. After one final polish for luck, she stood back and admired what she had achieved. 'That'll show him,' she thought.

The box was clean and shiny, she was grubby and oily, so she took a long relaxing shower. By the time she was dressed and ready it was just short of 2.15. 'Well sorted' she said to herself, using a phrase she'd picked up from the kids at school.

***

Harry had also been in a state of expectation. He hadn't danced around the room the previous evening, but woke with a heart full of hope. After showering, he shaved with so much care that he managed to cut his chin which bled alarmingly. Allowing himself a colourful expletive or two, he examined the wound and decided, with luck, he might live.

Having no diverting restoration work to see to, he had fallen back on drafting out designs for his next engineering project and that helped the clock tick by, until he could set out for Sara's apartment. As was his custom he arrived a little early, but not so much as to seem presumptive. He prided himself on his timing. A small vanity, but his own. Sara looking pink and pleased was there to meet him. The sun shone just brightly enough to make their walk to the Palais very pleasant. As they strolled along, he politely asked Sara about her twins and grandson. Although not one for using her family as a main subject of her conversation, she provided a few amusing stories that seemed to please him.

They had time to stop for hot chocolate and sat outside a bistro looking at the gentle rippling blue sea. Sara thought how seemingly impossible it was, that such a stretch of water could have claimed George's life. Right now, it looked so calm and innocent.

She realised Harry was saying something and brought herself back to the present with a jerk.

"Sorry," she said. "I was miles away... What did you say?"

"I was only remarking on how pretty you look today."

Accompanied by a slight colouring of her cheeks, she smiled and thanked him.

"You're welcome," he said as he raised his cup to salute her.

She laughed and returned the favour.

There was no sign of Jean-Pierre and his family when they arrived at the Palais, which was not remarkable as the musicians had to arrive far earlier than the audience. They joined the queue for tickets and were surprised, pleased and a little embarrassed to be shown to special seats which Jean-Pierre had reserved for them.

Through the side door to the left of the dais stage, Sara caught sight of young Julie and waved. Julie waved back enthusiastically and turned to tell the rest of her family that Sara had arrived. Moments later Julie, Jean-Pierre, and Monique appeared.

"*Bonjour.* It's very good to see you here Sara," said Monique, as she unashamedly assessed Harry.

"*Bonjour.* Thank you for the excellent seats." She smiled. "This is my friend, Harry Martin."

Harry stood and bowed '*Bonjour*' to M. Gascon and first taking Monique's then Julie's hand, said, "*Enchanté, Madame et... Mademoiselle.*"

Monique's eyes smiled approval of Harry's deference to Julie, who smirked with childish pride.

"I do hope you will enjoy the concert. You have a programme, yes?" asked Jean-Pierre. "We must go back now. Watch out for *la petite surprise* at the end." They smiled and turned back into the rehearsal room.

Harry, whose French was far superior to Sara's, translated, as he read the varied programme to her. The concert included pieces by Haydn, Dvorak, Borodin and Schubert. The surprise was a performance by Mam'selle J. Bequale, 'A fantasy on traditional French tunes, arrangement by J.P. Gascon.'

The usual introductory announcements over, they settled down to enjoy the tasty programme ahead. The Sage Quartet personalities created the same sympathetic and easy atmosphere which Sara had so enjoyed at the previous concert. A mutual respect between artists and audience, equal joy in performing and listening to beautiful music, sensitively and expertly played, was, to her, unalloyed pleasure.

The final introduction was for Mam'selle Bequale. Julie, dressed in a black velvet frock with a white lace collar, white socks, shiny patent-leather black shoes and a big white bow in her hair, walked out onto the stage carrying her violin. This was to be her debut performance.

She was a little overwhelmed and nervous but with *grandpère* beside her she launched into a slightly wobbly Frère Jacques. She was not a child prodigy, but equally not a bad little player and when Jean-Pierre joined her for the duet, her bowing became much more confident. She did very well. The audience loved her and applauded enthusiastically as she bowed prettily with a huge grin on her face.

Harry was delighted and thanked Sara for taking him along. He couldn't praise Julie enough, it must be wonderful to have a daughter like her to be so proud of. He envied the Bequales and inwardly mourned his own lost child.

Jean-Pierre's car was already full of instruments and persons. Harry and Sara were therefore accommodated with his cello in Anton's vehicle, for the ride back to the Gascon villa, to an early cold supper and wine. It was a merry party that arrived there. Sara and Harry were introduced to the other members of the Sage Quartet, Henri (viola) and Paul (violin), who had followed on in Henri's small Citroen, and everyone was soon on first-name terms.

"You must be so proud of your daughter, Madame Bequale," said Harry.

"*Monique, s'il vous plait 'arry,*" she replied. "Yes, she did very well, but must not let it go to her 'ead. She could still practise a little more."

"I'm sure she will be a fine musician, like the rest of her family, one day," Sara said. "And there's nothing like applause to spur one on to greater things."

"*C'est vrai,*" replied Monique with a smile. "But practice makes more perfect, *n'est pas*?"

Meanwhile, Julie basked in the glow of compliments from *grandpapa* and the rest of his quartet.

Supper was to be served around 6.30 so that Julie, now a bona fide musician, might also partake, and did so, with great delight. She was very excited about it all because normally she was in bed by 7.00pm. All went well for the first hour or so, but as any over-stimulated six-year-old will, she began to show off. She felt special and so wanted to be the centre of attention. The adults were tolerant, but Sara, fond as she was of Julie, believed children were like seasoning, enough gave wonderful flavour, too much ruined the dish. Julie executed an unnecessary twirl in the centre of the room, and managed to knock a glass, splashing, thankfully white, wine, across the sleeve of Sara's blouse. Monique, whom she suspected held similar views to herself, was very cross with Julie and apologised for her daughter's behaviour, explaining she was past her bedtime, and was probably tired. Embarrassed and cross herself, Julie flounced. Monique announced time for bed. Julie protested she was not tired and worked up a head of steam which could have culminated in a major tantrum but for Jean-Pierre, whose quiet "Julie," brought a look of shame to the little girl's face, and genuine tears.

"I'll take her up to bed now, *papa*," said Monique. "Say goodnight to our friends, Julie."

Julie momentarily looked mutinous, but *grandpapa* nodded gravely. Gathering her dignity tight around her, Julie shook hands with everyone and whispered *"Bon nuit"*, receiving a smile from each one in return.

"Monique, please tell Julie I think she did very well today," said Sara kindly, "and not to worry about my blouse, not too long ago I spilt something on it myself! *Bon nuit, Julie.*" She also muttered an aside to Harry, about this particular blouse being fated!

Harry was secretly relieved to see Julie go. He had no notion of the reality of having children. His was an idealised view. 'No child of mine would ever behave like that!' he thought, and honestly believed it.

"Come, I'll take you," said Jean-Pierre in French to his granddaughter. "Would you like to hear *grandmama's* favourite tune, to help you dream of sugar plums?"

This, Julie knew, was a real treat. She nodded her head, took *grandpapa's* hand, and as they passed through the door, he picked up his violin. A few minutes later it was just possible to hear soft tones of a passage from Elgar's violin concerto, lulling the child to sleep.

Soon Jean-Pierre returned to his guests.

"She was asleep after only a few bars. It has been a big day for *la petite*," he said, regaining his favourite chair and raising his half-drunk glass of wine to his lips.

"*Papa,* you spoil her…" said Monique.

"That, *ma chérie*, is *grandpapa's* privilege," he replied sententiously. "All the kisses and none of the work!"

***

After the departure of Julie, the wine was flowing freely and the musicians talked music. Jean-Pierre mentioned that both Sara and Harry were soloists with the choristers of Ripon and York Cathedrals, and how much he would like to hear them, one day. The other members of the party good humouredly urged an impromptu performance now, after all they had already played that afternoon, and maybe Sara and Harry would like to sing for their supper too. Harry was willing to give it a try if Sara was. After some consultation, they agreed on Handel's piece, 'Do you not hear my lady?', not an obvious choice, but as the lovely song was not much more than two minutes long, it seemed a good one. Harry asked Monique for an E on her keyboard and they began their totally unrehearsed rendition.

Although they were not yet lovers, in the conventional sense, their voices were, anticipating and responding to every nuance and note the other sang.

As they finished, there was a second's silence, then the praise was genuine and unanimous. Sara blushed of course and surprisingly, so did Harry. He put it down to the wine, but in his heart he knew something more profound had happened.

It wasn't too long before the Sage Quartet were reminiscing about their days in Newcastle. Harry, who seemed to know the city quite well, was able to join in the fun with anecdotes of his own. The evening was passing very pleasantly indeed, when Henri got onto the subject of football. He and

Paul were great fans of the game, and they laughed about the time they left Anton and Jean-Pierre to cover for them, whilst they went off to watch United play an afternoon derby in nearby Sunderland. The game had gone to extra time, and because of the crowds, they were in danger of missing not only the rehearsal but the evening concert too. It had cost a fortune to hire a taxi to get back. Only Jean-Pierre's brilliant handling of the conductor won them time and a reprieve.

"Do you remember also, Henri," Paul chimed in. "The night before we left for Newcastle, seeing those three English guys playing football by the sea wall. We thought of joining them, even though it was late and one was obviously very drunk.

"We hadn't gone very far," he said turning to the other listeners, "when we heard them shouting because the ball had been kicked over the wall into the water. The really drunk one had made the mis-kick and his friends were annoyed, so he started hopping about pulling off his shoes and socks, yelling to the others that he'd go and get it. The very tall one and probably the most sober of the three, told him not to be so stupid because he couldn't swim. The drunk took no notice and tried to climb over the wall, but fell off again."

Sara had begun to listen intently, as Paul continued.

"The tall one and his friend, started to haul the drunk to his feet, but he got quite violent with them. We didn't want to get drawn into their argument and walked away, the last thing we heard was the sober one placating the drunk, by saying he'd go in and get the ball himself. It was a nasty thing to witness."

"Did he go for the ball?" Anton asked.

"I don't know. I hope he didn't, the sea is so treacherous here. But people can get crazy when football and drink are mixed."

"*C'est vrai*," said Henri sadly. "I love the game, but too often it is spoilt by anger."

Jean-Pierre looked over to Sara who had turned very pale.

Monique and her father exchanged anxious glances. The others did not notice for a moment but were alarmed as Sara spoke.

"I'm sorry," she said, "I suddenly don't feel very well. I'm afraid I will have to go." She rose unsteadily to her feet and Harry expressed great concern.

"Are you alright?" he asked needlessly, as she clearly was not. "Do you need a doctor?"

"Not at all. Please, like Julie, I've had too much excitement today. I will be fine." She tried a smile. "I have had a splendid evening. Thank you so much, but I must go now. It was lovely to meet you all. I will be better soon. I hope to see you all again before I go back to England." Sara was speaking automatically now. Only she and Jean-Pierre realised the import of Paul's remembrance of that night. He expiated her exit with a promise (if permitted) to call tomorrow to enquire after her well-being. Sara was grateful for his reticence, and told him she would appreciate that, but really there was no need to worry.

Harry put his arm around her shoulders whilst they crossed the road to her apartment. By now he too had guessed the reason for her 'turn'.

"What you told them wasn't true, was it? You've had a shock. You think it was your husband that Paul and Henri saw, don't you?"

She nodded, as tears fell unchecked down her now burning cheeks.

There was nothing he could say, so he didn't try. He just held her close until the tears subsided, then made hot milk with sugar for her, and asked if she would like him to go or stay.

"I mean, of course," he said quickly, "I could sleep on the sofa. I know it's very comfortable."

She managed a slight laugh, "That's very kind, but I'll be OK. I would prefer to be by myself tonight, if you don't mind."

"OK, if you're sure… Just give me a ring, anytime, if you need me. Will I see you tomorrow?"

"Yes," she said. "Tomorrow."

CHAPTER SIXTEEN

Sara woke late the next morning to the ringing of her phone. She thought it might be Harry but it was Jean-Pierre asking if he might call. She was surprised, but grateful for his continuing concern and told him he would be welcome. He asked if in half an hour would be convenient and she said it would. In exactly fifteen minutes the bell sounded. She admitted a very agitated Jean-Pierre.

"Oh, Madame, I am so sorry about last night. Never before, have I heard Paul or Henri speak about this incident. They know football in any shape or form is boring to me. Not for *tout le monde* would I have wished for this to happen."

He was so upset, Sara had to console him. She made coffee for them both.

"Dear M. Gasco— Jean-Pierre," she began, "please don't distress yourself. I learnt nothing that I hadn't already guessed. It was the shock of actually hearing it from an eyewitness that was all. There's no need for anyone to feel uncomfortable about it... I like you, your family and your friends very much and despite our short acquaintance, know that not one of you could be deliberately unkind."

Handing him a cup, she went on, "It is I who should be

sorry. I placed you in a dreadful position yesterday. Neither you nor Monique would betray a confidence, especially if it should make an innocent friend feel bad. Your quandary was of my making. Please, don't let my behaviour cause you any embarrassment. Let it stand that the English rose wilted a little, after a tiring day. Your friends need never know the truth. Since coming to Menton, I've come to terms with my loss and, thanks to all I have experienced here, am learning to leave George's mistakes, and mine, behind."

"I am so glad that you feel that way Sara. We all make mistakes, the biggest one of all is failing to forgive, especially oneself. It is something I have had to learn too." He told her about his wife and how she died. "The dreadful thing was that she had gone out solely because I was too lazy to do my own errand, she suffered terribly because of me. At the end, when she momentarily returned to herself, I'm sure she forgave me. All I had to do then was forgive myself. I have not always been successful, but that is a fault in my character, not in the theory of forgiveness. I am so old I find it difficult to change, but you, if you will allow my presumption, are young enough to yet find a new life. I wish you well." His old smile returned as he continued, "I hope you and your Harry will come again to see us before you go back home, and that we will all continue to be friends."

He patted Sara's hand as he wished her *au-revoir.*

After Jean-Pierre's departure Sara was disturbed by his reference to 'her' Harry. What did he mean by that? He couldn't possibly realise what she hadn't yet fully admitted to herself… she started a dialogue with *AA,* who finding her advice neglected of late, was bursting to speak: 'Your Harry indeed!' she said. 'You haven't known each other for five minutes.'

Sara sighed and responded rather irrelevantly, 'I like him and he's very good-looking.'

'Prince Charming on toast I'm sure, but he's definitely been round the block more than a few times, you can see it in him! What does he want of you?'

'Don't know.'

'Oh yes you do... Look, I know you've taken a fancy to him, but there's something feral about him. Do you think it's wise? If you want a new man in your life there are plenty of decent ones at home who would jump at the chance. You can't trust this one an inch, he's too smooth by half. All this play-acting the perfect gentleman! He's already turned on you once, what makes you so sure he won't do it again?'

'I'm not, but there was a reason for that, he'd been hurt and was short with me because I had inadvertently reminded him of his pain.'

'That's another thing. Did you really swallow all that guff about his wife terminating her pregnancy with no other motive than to spite him? I'd like to know the real story behind that one! He may play the innocent, but I'd need the full details before I'd credit him with telling anything like the truth.'

Sara knew *AA* had a point there, but chose to side step the issue and countered with a defensive move. 'It's nothing to do with me. I don't have to get involved in what happened in the past.'

'You don't think it's relevant?'

'No.'

127

'Pull the other one, Sara, it's got bells on. You don't care, do you? Have I kept you safe all these years just to see you throw yourself into the arms of a no-good heartbreaker like him?'

'Maybe that's the problem. Don't you see, you've kept me too safe. I'm two years short of fifty, and with your guidance I've lived a decent, sensible life, I have you to thank for that and I'm grateful but, I've had enough. I want to live on the edge for a change. Harry excites me and I want him. Not in spite of his character, but *because* of it. It's like how I respond to the thrill of following his lead as we sing together. We sail close enough to disaster to quicken the audience, but never get shipwrecked. That's why despite your fears, I trust him.'

'For god's sake, stop talking drivel, but if we must, let's stick to your analogy, what happens if your ship *does* land on the rocks. I know you like repairing things, but this kind of thing is way out of your league, it would take a damn sight more than a dab of glue to put back together.'

'I'm sorry,' Sara said, 'but that's the way it is.'

'It's too late for me to change your mind, then. OK, but don't let him take you so far to the edge that you fall. It's razor sharp. Keep whatever is left of your wits about you. Remember, you're going into this with both eyes wide open, and there's no one but yourself to blame this time.'

Sara felt a stab of guilt at this last remark, but said 'One more thing before you go. Do you think he knows?'

'Now you are being silly. Of course he knows. Everyone you meet knows. Just try not to make too big a fool of yourself. God luck, I think you'll need it. You can always call me back when it goes wrong.'

'Goodbye, *AA.* '

***

The old voice with its confining rational constrictions, had been sent into exile. Sara was on her own and felt the exhilaration of freedom. No longer would she see life through a single lens and live within the safe tunnel of its vision. She was a kaleidoscope with elements the same but the capacity to create new patterns at every turn. She knew the risk of trusting Harry, but love falls where it may and should the opportunity arise she was willing to take it. She'd done her duty by her children, now it was her turn. Like Jenny Joseph's alter ego, she would wear purple and 'make up for the sobriety of her youth'.

She retrieved her mobile from the bedroom and there was a message from the man himself, asking if he might meet her for a concert at 2.00pm, it was being held at Sacre Coeur, a church only a short walk from her flat. She thought that would be grand, and merrily scooted off to meet him at ten to the hour.

It was an ebullient Sara who arrived at her rendezvous. Harry was pleased, if a little surprised by her upbeat mood. She told him Jean-Pierre had called that morning and everything was OK. It was purely the shock that had made her react as she did, but now she was fine. He did not think it wise to pursue the matter further for fear of upsetting her again, so they entered the church which was packed with people of all ages looking forward to the programme which included a full version of Haydn's Surprise Symphony.

Love of music was undoubtedly in the soul of Mentonians. The packed audience, consisting largely of families and friends settled and glorious music began. The obvious enjoyment and panache of the musicians pleased Sara and her partner beyond all expectations.

The Surprise Symphony, unsurprisingly, was the finale piece. As the last two violinists played, the conductor hammily threw up his hands in disgust at the gradual disappearance of his orchestra, and finally stalked off stage in high dudgeon. The audience burst into rapturous applause and laughter.

Everyone left the church in very good spirits.

"Would you like to go for an early supper somewhere?" Harry asked Sara.

"Well, I'm not very hungry yet," she replied. "But can we go for a coffee? Then what I would really like to do is walk into Italy, and have something there."

He was a little taken aback by this. "*Walk* to Italy?"

"Why not? It's not far and it would be a fun thing to do."

"OK." He laughed. "If that's what you'd like. I hope there's somewhere to eat though, when we get there."

"Bound to be! It's Italy and they love their food. Anyway," she continued, "if there isn't, we can always turn round and come back. We'll work up a good appetite!"

The border itself was quite impressive, with armed guards checking cars entering into France. But Sara was surprised that there was no border check for them. They just walked straight across without so much as a raised eyebrow.

"We must look really boring," she said.

"Just as well we do," Harry replied, looking at the automatic rifles the soldiers were carrying.

They walked a couple of hundred metres into Italy before spotting a restaurant of sorts. It turned out on close inspection to be a seedy shop with a nasty looking café attached.

After a brief consultation, they said almost in unison "I don't think so" and resignedly, but with good humour, made their way back across the border to Menton. Again not raising an iota of interest from the guardians with machine guns. They were quite hungry after what had been a three-mile walk and the first eating place they saw back in Menton, turned out to be the Italian restaurant where they had eaten a few days earlier. Harry with a twinkle in his eye said, "I know it's very nice here, but next time may we not go by the scenic route?"

Sara blushed and apologised, but they both enjoyed their Italian meal and laughed at the irony of it all.

That evening was spent at Sara's apartment. She showed off the box that she had restored. He was very impressed and to be fair, said so. He watched her as she went into the kitchen to make coffee, thinking not about the day's concert, fine as it was, but about their time at Val Rahmeh, and how they had improvised their own music to match the little fountain. She'd begun it and he joined in. He couldn't remember doing anything as spontaneously and sweetly silly as that before, and felt warm at the memory.

Then there was yesterday evening at Jean-Pierre's house. That was of a different magnitude, the way her voice had curled itself like smoke around his was incredible. He could find no words to describe the effect that voice was having on him. He was beginning to believe he couldn't do without it… or its owner.

Sara brought in the mugs of hot coffee and put them down carefully on the side table. Harry still caught up in thought, patted the sofa seat beside him, inviting her to join him. Then wrapping his arm around her shoulder, pulled her close where they snuggled together until their drinks were forgotten and cold. They drank them anyway, and glancing at his watch he said it was late and he should go. But before he left, Harry sprang a surprise on her.

"Would you like," he asked, "to come with me to Nice tomorrow?"

This wasn't quite what she might have been wishing for, but it was a very pleasant consolation prize, all the same.

"With it being a Monday" – he smiled a little mischievously – "I promise there'll be something there that you'll like enormously."

He refused to tell her any more, except he was absolutely positive she would love it. Greatly intrigued, Sara grinned like the Cheshire Cat and said, "I can hardly wait!" They arranged to meet outside the station at 10.00am.

He let his kiss linger gently on her lips before whispering "good night". She watched from the window until he'd crossed the street, then he turned and waved goodbye. Mrs Middleton could hardly believe that she was going to Nice tomorrow with Mr Martin, Sara, on the other hand, simply rejoiced.

On the way back to his hotel Harry began to smile and hummed the tune 'La ci darem la mano', a favourite aria of his from Mozart's opera *Don Giovanni*, the one the Don sings while seducing Zerlina. He hadn't got more than a few bars in, when for no reason discernible to himself, he found the song distasteful and completed his journey in contemplative silence.

132

CHAPTER SEVENTEEN

Although the forecast had not been too bad, grey overcast weather greeted them when they arrived in Nice. Sara had been expecting something much more beautiful, not the modern concrete buildings she saw on exiting the train station. It was a big busy city with a lot of traffic.

More sensitive to her initial reaction than she'd realised, Harry said, "Don't worry. It's better than it looks. This is the modern part of the city. The rest is truly gorgeous and I'm sure you'll love my surprise."

She felt a little ashamed at her lack of enthusiasm and grinned. "I've been spoilt lately. Menton is such a lovely place. I'm sure you're right, and you've got me really curious about what my surprise might be."

He took her hand and they walked by way of the *Promenade des Anglais,* toward the older part of the city, when they saw a Ferris wheel.

"I've never been on one of those," she remarked.

"No more have I. Would you like to have a go?" he asked.

Sara didn't demur for a moment. "Yes, I would! Yes please, I really would!"

They walked over to the wheel. There were no other

customers. The attendant opened the gate, settled them in an open cradle and locked it. A few moments later they rose sedately into the sky. Up and up, all of Nice open below. Three times round then a slow stop at the zenith, where Harry pointed the location where they were headed to. After three more circuits contrariwise, the wheel came to a final stop and the attendant opened the gate for them. It had been an unexpected little gem of an experience.

It took about ten minutes to arrive at the Old City, which was grand and lovely as promised. Sara's surprise lay just around the corner. There was the most enormous flea-market she had ever seen, with stalls as far as the eye could see. They were laden with junk, bric-a-brac and even some genuine antiques.

Harry laughed as he saw the expression on her face. "Like it?" he asked.

She could only gape in wonder and turned eyes wide with delight towards him.

"Enjoy!" he said, leading her up past the first few stalls. "Have a wander round as long as you like." He pointed to a cosy-looking café. "I know you've guessed it's not really my thing, so I shall read my newspaper, have coffee and wait in peace and contentment until you come to collect me."

"Oh, Mr Rochester!" she quoted from *Jane Eyre* with a barely suppressed giggle. "I will return! (Quote from General McArthur)", and happily began her very own bargain hunt.

For himself, Harry was gratified his surprise had gone down so well. He sat down and waved his newspaper and watched Sara disappear into the crowd. He waited a minute or two until she was out of sight, then set off quickly in the opposite direction. Thirty minutes later he was back, ordered coffee and *socca* to eat, then settling at a table opened his newspaper to await her return.

As for Sara, who adored flea-markets, she was like a kiddie in a sweetshop but only glanced at the expensive things. What she really liked was the quirky, dusty stuff, which had probably been brought out every week since the Creation. Halfway round she found a small framed case of butterflies. It was very dirty, but through the filthy glass, she could just see the beautiful iridescent blue of the largest insect. The frame was in a battered but complete state. She was sure she could restore it to something acceptable once she got home, and it was an appropriate souvenir of the effect Harry was having on her during her holiday in France, so at 10 euros she decided to have it. Glancing at her watch Sara was mortified to see how swiftly time had gone by. She realised that he'd been abandoned for over an hour. Clutching her prize, she hurried back to find Harry still patiently waiting, reading his newspaper.

"There you are!" He smiled as she hurried up to find him. "What treasures have you bought?"

"I'm so sorry, I was much longer than I thought I would be. Can you ever forgive me?" she panted through her laughter.

"Well, maybe. Let me get you a coffee, and your penance will be to help me finish this *socca*. It's a local speciality, chickpea pancake."

She looked at the object on his plate and wasn't at all sure.

"It's delicious… Honest!"

With grave doubts as to his absolute sincerity, she broke off a tiny piece. It was truly the most disgusting thing she had ever tasted. He laughed like a drain.

She desperately needed *pain-au-chocolat* with her *cafe au lait,* to take the nasty taste away, and waiting for her order, proudly showed Harry her not quite glittering prize. Whilst admitting the possible gorgeousness of the butterflies, he could not in all consciousness help but be underwhelmed by the shabby frame housing them.

"It's fine," she asserted. "I'll remove the dirty glass, give it a good clean, sand down the frame and put it back together again. No bother!" This followed by a big confident grin.

Harry wasn't at all certain it could be done without damaging the specimens, or even if it would be worth the effort of trying, but he smiled back encouragingly anyway. Not fooled for a moment, she said, "I can do it you know, maybe not brilliantly, but well enough!" and poked her tongue out at him.

Coffee and *pain-au-chocolat* suitably disposed of and butter-flies returned to her canvas bag, they left the café. It was less sheltered away from the market and the weather looked a little threatening.

"Now then," said Harry, "we have a choice. There are some splendid Roman ruins at the top of that hill. It's quite a walk but worth seeing, I've been there before. Or if you prefer something less strenuous, we could go to the Chagall Museum, which I have not seen, but believe is very good."

Roman ruins in summer sunshine would have been attractive but the weather was definitely still on the cool side, after all it was still early in the year, so they opted for the museum where it would be warm and dry.

Harry obviously knew Nice well and had little trouble finding the place, which was prettily located on a hill, with gardens around it. They had left it a little late with only an hour until it closed. However, the museum was a small one, and the timing could not have been more perfect as most of the crowds had already left, so they had the place almost to themselves, and it was enchanting.

The museum, like the Cocteau in Menton, had been created with a large input from the artist. In the seventeen huge paintings that covered the walls, figures from Old Testament stories floated in yellow and aquamarine skies, their rare beauty and mystic power held Sara transfixed. She gorged on the feast that suited her new freedom. Like a desert dry for many seasons, her recent shower of new encounters caused her to bloom into radiance. She loved turning the kaleidoscope of her mind, looking at new things in a new way, knowing they were hers, however fleetingly, to experience at first hand.

Her eyes shining she turned to Harry and squeezed his hand tightly. Harry grinned back, enjoying her pleasure.

They were back in Menton around 6.00pm and rather than go back out for supper, after what had been quite a long day, they decided to get a couple of ready meals from the *traiteur* near Sara's place, grab a nice bottle of Beaujolais and eat back at the apartment. In the window, Harry noticed a poster advertising a live broadcast of *Il Trovatore,* to be screened at the cinema at Beaulieu the following evening at 7.30. Beaulieu was another little town, a rail journey away, unfortunately the last train back left around the time the performance ended. But Harry said if Sara would like to go, he'd arrange for a taxi to take them back to Menton.

Surprised by his suggestion, she said, "If *you* don't mind going."

"Not at all. I missed *Tristan*, and I feel I owe you," he replied lightly.

The offer was a good one, so she accepted and said she'd love to. It was a favourite piece, although given his personal history, she thought it a little strange that he should be happy to see that particular opera, but he *had* volunteered quite unprompted to take her. 'Perhaps,' she thought, 'I'm being oversensitive.'

The rain that had been threatening all day at last arrived in a huge cold downpour. They stood inside the *traiteur* door for a few minutes hoping it would stop but there were no signs it would. It wasn't far back to Sara's place, Harry was already wearing his raincoat and she had an umbrella so they thought they'd risk it. He buttoned his coat and turned up his collar, Sara's canvas bag, holding the butterfly case, was not particularly waterproof and she didn't want it to get wet, so holding it close, she wrapped her coat around herself and the bag, then held the coat tightly together with one hand. Harry had supper safe inside a polythene bag and they set off. A sudden gust snatched at Sara's umbrella turning it inside out, as she tried to turn it the right way round, her coat flew open. She had to abandon the struggle in order to keep her bag safe and the umbrella shot off down the street like a rocket with Harry chasing after it. He caught up, but it was so hopelessly bent he rammed it straight into a rubbish bin. They ran to the porch outside her apartment, Sara opened the door and they fell inside dripping wet, laughing fit to burst.

Once in the apartment, Sara hung up the dripping coats and dived into the bathroom to get a couple of towels. Harry actually wasn't too bad, his shoes and coat had proved completely impervious to the rain. Sara, on the other hand was soaked to the skin. Her hair hung in soggy ringlets about her face and she was very cold.

"I've got to get changed and dry," she said. "Are you alright?"

After vigorously towelling his hair, Harry was in fact scarcely damp. "Fine," he said with a grin.

While Sara disappeared into the bathroom, he phoned the cinema box office. The screening had been sold out but fortunately there were two returns, so he snapped them up. He heard the shower going followed by the sound of a hair drier in the bedroom. Fifteen minutes later Sara emerged, her hair a mass of curls, wearing an over-size shirt, black leggings (which were very becoming) and a pair of fluffy white socks. Harry was delighted with her. He hadn't realised she had such a glorious mop of hair.

"I hate it, I have to spend ages straightening it every morning," she admitted.

Sara popped the meals into the microwave and poured a decent measure of wine for them both and sat down beside him.

"We were lucky, the cinema was booked solid, but there were a couple of returns. I'll see to the taxi tomorrow," he said, and settled down to enjoy the wine.

Sara rested her head on his shoulder. She looked up into his face, her hair tickling his chin and said, "Thank you." He bent to kiss her, more passionately than before, when the spell was broken by a persistent electronic pinging sound announcing supper was ready. Sara walked to the kitchen and switched off the machine. Harry moved towards her and breathed in her perfume, which smelled of roses on a warm summer evening. He took her hand, led her to the bedroom and closing the door behind them, left supper to slowly congeal in the microwave.

He took each wrist in turn, delicately bestowing kisses as he undid her sleeve cuffs. He reached to unfasten her top button and looking into her eyes, asked permission with an interrogative "Mmm?" She blushed, returned his smile and nodded yes.

He slowly undid her shirt, and without taking his eyes from hers for more than a moment, slipped it off her shoulders and carefully draped it onto the chair by the bed. He folded back the duvet to lay her down, then sat beside her to remove her fluffy socks and leggings with more grace and delicacy than she ever achieved in pulling them on. She thanked God she was wearing the satin and lace undies Georgie had bought her for Christmas, when with a flick of his wrist, the socks and leggings joined her shirt on the chair. 'OMG,' she thought, 'he's good.' He continued with gentle kisses to strip her naked.

He undressed and soon lay beside her. A very experienced lover, Harry fondled and caressed her, before allowing his powerful manhood to penetrate her body where with every thrust, submission and pleasure grew, deeper and deeper inside her, until they climaxed together with an intensity that caused Sara to cry out, leaving her breathless and reeling. He stroked her gently until she slipped into sleep.

Harry didn't sleep, he looked down at her. 'Well,' he thought dispassionately, 'that was interesting. I hadn't expected the… the "innocent" desire to please. Quite a bonus. But I didn't mean that to happen just yet.' From the beginning he had been surprised by his attraction to Sara. He'd had many far more beautiful women, before, between and after his divorce from Linda. He had wanted them and, being fully aware of his skills as a lover, took them. His desire for Sara however felt real, and it puzzled him. Had he merely switched to 'auto-pilot' tonight, continuing the habit of a life time? Somehow he didn't think so.

Her body was not perfect. Her flesh was soft and yielding except for… He traced his finger lightly along the long scar low down on her belly, finding the intimacy of touching its roughness strangely erotic… Her amazing hair like spun gold, was more flighty than coiffured as it shimmered like an uncontrolled nimbus round her head… There was a hint of double chin that she tried to hide… Her… He stopped in mid appraisal. No, her body wasn't perfect but it didn't matter, there was something in Sara that made him want her. He wasn't sure, but knew it wasn't the idealised woman he'd been busily building in his mind as an antidote and balm for Linda's spite. He rather preferred the actual thing that slept beside him now… her scar, the way she laughed, her perfume, her honesty, her love of quirky things, and, my God, that voice which could unwittingly quicken a heart of stone… What was it about her that made him feel like this? He could find no answer, the question was too difficult. Dismissing it from his mind, he closed his eyes in sleep.

An hour or so later Sara woke with a start. The sudden remembrance both shocked and amused her.

'Good god!' she thought. 'I should have gone on holiday to France before. Think of what I've been missing all these years!'

She sat up as carefully as possible, so as not to wake Harry, but of course she did.

"Hello," he said.

"Hello," she smiled back, and then said seriously "May I tell you something very unromantic?"

Illogically believing she had read his last waking thoughts, he gravely nodded.

"I'm absolutely starving!"

He laughed, hugged and kissed her. He really liked Sara a lot.

"Me too," he answered. "Shall we brave the remnants in the microwave, or go out after all?"

The rain had stopped so they dressed and left for Harry's favourite bistro.

CHAPTER EIGHTEEN

Sara and Monique liked one another, and had arranged a day or two ago, to meet for coffee and do a little souvenir shopping that morning. It would be fun, Monique knew the best places to go, it was also a good opportunity to spend some 'girl-time' together and cement their new friendship. She was seeing Harry later in the day, when the plan was to go to eat an early supper at her place, catch the train to Beaulieu around 5.00pm, walk along the promenade, perhaps, call at the casino, then on to the cinema. Monique met her in town.

"Julie is at kindergarten this morning, and regrets not being here to say goodbye, but has drawn a picture for you," she said, handing over an A4 sheet of pink paper. "Pink is Julie's favourite colour, at the moment!"

Sara took the work. It was a family portrait, with *mama, papa, grandpapa* and Julie herself, standing in a row outside *grandpapa's* house. There was also a black cat (which they didn't actually have, but Julie apparently had great hopes of acquiring). Each figure had its title inscribed in blue felt tip, and the cat was simply called '*mon chat*'.

"Please tell Julie I like her present very much, and I shall pin it up on the wall when I get home."

Over coffee and a *tarte au citron* each, Monique, without being the least bit indiscrete, soon had Sara chattering blithely about her relationship with Harry. Sara of course didn't go into any detail, and although it was not her place to say so, Monique thought Sara had been alone too long, and filling in the blanks herself was content with how things appeared to be progressing.

She told Sara that Bertrand would be home again tomorrow. His ship was being refitted and all the crew had two weeks holiday. First, he had a few jobs to do around the house for her father.

"Then," she said, "we are free and will be *en vacance* in Paris, for a whole week. Julie is very happy to be visiting the capital city but insisted that first we must go to the opening of the Festival with *grandpapa*. Will you be going to the Festival, Sara?"

"I think so. Harry said he would like to take me. Would you believe, he has been involved in it for three years and this will be the first time he has stayed to see it?"

"*Non!*" said Monique.

"*Oui!*" Sara replied.

"*Oh, les hommes!*" Monique shook her head.

"This evening we're going to the Opera broadcast at Beaulieu."

"Beaulieu? But that is a long way."

"Not really, we're getting the train."

"But it will finish very late, no? How are you to get back?"

"Well…" Sara couldn't suppress a smile. "He is ordering a limousine, and we will be chauffeured home!"

Monique grinned widely and said, "*Oooh la la, les Anglais… toujours les Romantiques.*"

***

They went together to the shops. It amazed Sara just how many gifts she wanted to take home. Monique took the lead with a more sensible approach, suggesting gifts for family only. There was, after all, the problem of fitting too much into an already pretty full suitcase. For Sara's grandson, a smart and very French sailor suit was chosen. It would be the very thing, and had the advantage of being both small and light.

'Which,' Sara thought, 'was more than could be said for the price tag.'

Speciality garlic, lemon and plain olive oils, unique to the area that came in attractive little tins, were purchased for the rest of the family, and the shopping concluded with great efficiency. Another coffee was needed before parting company, then Sara dived into the florist shop and insisted on buying Monique a charming bouquet of flowers, in thanks for her company and help… and hoped there would be time for a final quick goodbye to everyone, before returning to England. Monique set off to collect Julie, Sara wandered back to her apartment, on the way she looked into the window of a shop selling lingerie, and on impulse, bought herself a rather expensive midnight-blue camisole set, to wear that evening for Harry's benefit.

Thanks to Monique's restrictions she managed to find room in her luggage for the gifts she had bought, which was a blessing to say the least.

Memories of the previous night made her glow with happiness and she broke into frequent smiles as she prepared a simple meats-salad to share with Harry, who against all expectations had become her lover.

***

After their meal, Harry and Sara left the warmth of her apartment to discover the temperature outside had dropped considerably. When they arrived at Beaulieu the weather was tending to icy drizzle and neither relished the idea of a long walk along the promenade.

"There's only one thing for it," suggested Harry. "We go to the casino to wait for the cinema to open, it's only next door and we will stay warm and dry. OK?"

"As long as it's warm, I'm game, no pun intended."

Fighting against a strong headwind they made their way to the casino, which wasn't on the same scale as the Monte Carlo specimen that had so overwhelmed Sara, but its architecture and entrance were certainly impressive. They had their passports checked by two bored-looking young men, and climbed the sweeping staircase to the gaming area where slot machines flashed their lights and promises to virtually empty rooms. Sara was not at all impressed by the sight of the half-dozen glassy-eyed punters pouring coin after coin into the maws of noisy, greedy, mechanical monsters. As far as she could see, there was little at all exciting or romantic about it.

Unaware of her reaction Harry innocently asked, "Would you like to have a go on something, while we're waiting?"

"I'd rather flush my money straight down the lavatory, without the middleman," she replied with rather more truth than grace.

"I'll take that as a 'no' then, shall I?"

"Oh, Lord. I'm sorry, I really didn't mean to be so rude. If my lace got any straighter it would cut me in half. After all I am enjoying the warmth here."

"Probably from the inferno below, burning the sinners in hell."

"You're making fun of me."

"Just a little. Come on, shall we take advantage of those comfy chairs over there, and wait in stony disapproval until it's time for the cinema?"

Straight-lace loosed again, she grinned and followed him. The other comfy chairs soon filled up with people, who like them showed little interest in gambling. At a quarter to seven, everyone started to leave. Sara and Harry realised their idea of using the casino as a waiting room had not been unique.

CHAPTER NINETEEN

The cinema was not large but with every seat taken, it was very busy and crowded.

The opera, *Il Trovatore*, is a big one involving a large cast. Its dark, convoluted plot contains fine dramatic arias as well as the famous, stirring *Anvil Chorus*. Sara could hardly wait for Pappano and cast to finish their pre-performance interviews and the orchestra to strike up the opening chords of Verdi's masterpiece.

It was so different for Harry. Idiotically he'd forgotten, ridiculous as it seemed, that the tragedy revolves around the actions of a cruel man who incited the daughter of his victim to take revenge, by killing his baby. A chill ran through him as he took his seat in the middle of the row, where he was trapped by excited, immovable opera lovers.

It was too close to the bone. Had *his* behaviour justified Linda's revenge? He could not bring himself to answer that question. His heart could disclose the truth but he'd locked that firmly shut. Yet whatever his fault, the retaliation had been so bitter. He tried to concentrate on the music, but it was impossible to tear his mind away from his own horror. He wanted to walk away but was ensnared in his seat. He closed his eyes but that was no better. It was opening up a can of worms, which he had thought safely sealed long ago. He found Sara's innocent, intent face beside him almost too much to bear.

After what to Harry seemed an eternity, the opera drew to a close and the audience burst into spontaneous applause. Harry was keen to leave and urged Sara out of her seat, claiming the taxi would be waiting and they should go. It was hard to get through the crowd, no one but themselves seemed to be in a hurry to leave. They invoked many a baleful glare struggling towards the exit. He detached himself from his partner as they reached the door, and under the pretext of searching for their car, allowed himself a few moments to take deep breaths of cold air to regain some semblance of composure. When he spotted it he returned to collect Sara. Their driver was a pleasant young man who escorted *madame* to his immaculate limousine, and opened the door for her. Harry was then also escorted with ceremony suited to male passengers, into the seat beside her. He was shaking slightly and had to pull himself together.

She noticed Harry seemed disinclined to talk but didn't mind, as silence suited her mood. He put his arm around her, as much to steady himself as anything, and she gently settled her head on his shoulder, then he drew her close, which was exactly how she wanted it to be. The limousine swept luxuriously down the famous Moyenne Corniche, taking its hairpin bends with nonchalant ease. The night was dark, and still cold, but the murkiness of the day had vanished leaving the sky a clear, velvet background for the myriad stars. With the echo of Verdi's music filling her head and Harry's warm body so close, she was up there with them. Harry found her serenity calming and soaked up some of her peace as if by osmosis.

The drive home was all she dreamed it might be. Too soon for her, they arrived at their destination and the young man leapt out to open *madame's* door. In turn he opened Harry's who thanked, paid and tipped him. They wished their driver *"Bon nuit"* and Sara thought it was like some kind of romantic movie as Harry, now more in control of himself, asked how she had enjoyed her evening.

"Just wonderful," she replied contentedly.

"That's good," he said with a smile and escorted her into her apartment.

As they entered the flat, Harry was quiet. Sara wondered if her first suspicions had been correct and the opera had been too much for him. She wouldn't broach the subject herself, but wait for him to speak. With nearly a full bottle of red wine already opened she asked if he would like a glass. He accepted and they snuggled together on the sofa to drink it. Harry looked seriously at Sara and said unexpectedly "Tell me about you and George."

"George? Oh he was a sweet boy. We were only in our teens when we met… He became a junior engineer in the merchant navy. His ship was called *Esperanto*, ironic really. He filled my head with all his dreams. One day he'd be captain of his own ship and promised I would sail the world with him… like a queen, he said… and I believed him." She smiled ruefully as she took a deep drink. "He could take any engine apart and put it back together again, but couldn't navigate his way across the village pond… never mind…

"We were so naive and thrilled when we learned I was pregnant. It was going to be such fun having twins. Everyone said how marvellous it would be, because 'they would bring each other up'.

"But as you know, it didn't happen like that, because he got himself drowned and I was left, literally holding the babies. I was so angry, because I blamed him for leaving me alone. I think I told you, they found his body the day the twins were born. That may have been what brought them on, they were a week premature. I wanted George to be there, and was furious with him because he couldn't be. It was a difficult and long labour, they were born by caesarean section, that's why I have the scar. The saddest thing was, I didn't want even to look at them. You see without him, it was all wrong, I wanted him and his dreams, more than his babies. Mum sorted me out though, she made me hold them, and for an instant there he was, looking out at me from both pairs of eyes, and of course I fell in love with them. But poor George, despite bequeathing me these wonderful gifts, I hated *him* for a long time. I wouldn't visit his grave. Money was always an issue, so Mum and Dad offered to pay the fare for me, but I could always find a reason for not going. I still don't know if Mum understood why. How could she? I was so ashamed of how I felt, I'd told no one that I couldn't forgive him for dying.

"To keep myself sane, I ran my life according to a strict list of priorities, children and work took precedence over everything. I had little time for me... I blamed George for that too. I think the word 'uptight' is a gross understatement of how I was then. The saving grace came one Christmas when the twins were coming up to five. The local nursery school children were invited to take part in a Christingle Service at the Cathedral. Would you believe I'd forgotten the pure joy of singing? And I sang my heart out at that service. After it was over, I heard someone call my name. He came across to me.

"'I'd know that voice anywhere,' he said. 'Where have you been, Sara?'

"It was my old choirmaster. You see, before George had arrived on the scene I had been a chorister. Mr Graham had great hopes for me, but I was in love and saw my life taking a different direction. I told him I had been widowed after less than a year. He expressed his condolences, but why did I not come back to the choir? Of course I said I had children now, and couldn't leave them for practice nights etc. Both sets of grandparents interrupted and said they'd love to have them… The twins looked hopeful, grans and grandads were frankly a soft touch compared to me… We all laughed and I told him I'd think about it, and said goodbye. To cut a long story short, I re-joined the choir. It was a first step in my rehabilitation. I still didn't forgive George for dying in that pointless way, but I didn't dwell on it quite so much anymore. Sometimes I even forgot for a while and became, I think, a better mother and provider. Singing gave me back my soul… Does that sound too dramatic Harry?" She took another deep drink.

"No… Not at all," he said. "Go on."

"Finally, everything went well all round. I was made Head of Department, the twins grew into typical adolescents, but redeemed themselves by doing well in their school exams. Georgie joined the Navy and is now an instructor at Dartmouth. Dave is an accountant, married to Chris and provided me with my lovely grandson.

"When it was announced that my school was to be gobbled up by a larger comprehensive, I took the redundancy package on offer, signed up for supply teaching, and with some of my money decided at last to visit George's grave."

She drained her glass before telling him in detail where Jean-Pierre had found George's memorial plaque for her and how it had felt to see him in a field of heroes.

"D'you know, Harry, I'd forgotten how much I used to love him till then… Why did he let it happen?… We were both so young… I'd been nowhere, done nothing… But after seeing him there and remembering how we were, I couldn't hate him any more… even though he broke his promises to me… Promise you won't make me any promises, will you, Harry?"

"Not if you don't want me to."

"Promise?"

He smiled kindly as he said, "Cross my heart."

She was content with that. The wine had definitely had an effect, normally she would not have said these things out loud in a thousand years. She looked in surprise at her empty glass. Harry longed to find a way to release himself from the past as Sara had.

"I think," he said, as Sara stifled a yawn. "It's time for bed."

"Yup." She replied and sleepily allowed herself to be led off to the bedroom.

After silently admiring, then carefully removing her beautiful new underwear for her, Harry took her in his arms, but Sara was asleep in seconds. He smiled at her golden head laying supine on the pillow beside him, kissed her still smiling lips very gently, and was content to let her slumber peacefully until morning, when they awoke to make glorious love.

Harry may have had his faults, but he had always been a gentleman in the bedroom.

CHAPTER TWENTY

Around 11.30 in the morning, they wandered over to the *boulangerie* for a late breakfast and sat at the same window seat they had occupied when they'd first met for coffee only two weeks ago.

"I have something for you, Sara," Harry said seriously, "you deserve this." He reached into his pocket, and opened his wallet.

'Good Heavens!' she thought, 'He's not going to offer to pay me?'

He took out two tickets and handed them to her. He knew exactly what had passed through her mind and laughed.

"You stinker!" she said. "You're incorrigible." As she took the tickets from his hand, she couldn't help laughing too.

They were VIP tickets for the opening ceremony of the Menton Festival in two days' time.

"I got them from a contact in Nice while you were trawling the market for bargains. I had to pull a string or two, but I got to see the right guy. *Et voila!*" He grinned widely, obviously very proud of his great achievement, which indeed it was. These things were rarer than hen's teeth, especially at such late notice.

"Oh, Harry. Thank you, so much. What a holiday this has been. Thank you."

"Sara," he said, "I hope the end of the holiday won't be the end of our meeting. When we go back home, may we still see each other often?"

"That would be really nice," she said.

After a moment of silence, he went on, "You don't think being our age is too old to begin something new and fresh, is it?" He'd been thinking about this last night after she'd gone to sleep. "We have the advantage of being mature enough to know what we want out of a relationship, don't we?"

Sara nodded.

"If we wanted to, you're even still young enough to have a second family, aren't you?"

She had not expected this. "What do you mean, Harry? I know you missed out on having children but I can't help you with that one." She looked straight into his face, "Even if I wanted to, I really can't."

He didn't seem to take this information in and she went very quiet as he said, "Don't you think it would be wonderful for us to have a future together. I mean make a proper family. It might take a while and be expensive, but that doesn't matter, I can afford it, they can do such marvellous things nowadays with fertility treatment for more mature mothers."

She had hoped he was joking, but could see by his expression he was in earnest, and was not pleased by his proposition.

"No Harry, no," she said. "That maybe something you want, but I don't."

155

She could see the puzzlement in his face and began to feel alarmed.

"Is this what it's all been about… ? Oh, Harry, I liked you so much from the first. During our weeks working together on the Requiem, I had such a schoolgirl crush on you, but never dreamed anything would come of it. I assumed I wouldn't even see you again, but when we met so unexpectedly in Menton, I was so excited and fell for you all over again. You made me truly happy, because I thought you liked me too." Her hurt was swiftly turning to anger… "Only I didn't realise I was only being auditioned to be your… " she searched for the appropriate word, "your… your brood mare! Has nothing I've told you made any impression at all? Do you seriously expect me to go to hell and back, just to spend what's left of my life going through the same child rearing routine again? How could you expect me to do it? I want to be free to be myself. I love my children more than I can ever say, and I'm desperately sorry that you were denied a child of your own. But you know, like most things in this world it's not easy, and children are not an unalloyed pleasure."

"But I do like you, Sara, I like you very much," said Harry. "Don't you see? I'd be there for you, you wouldn't have to do it alone this time. I promise."

Her anger turned to fury. "How dare you promise me such a thing, when you don't really know or understand what you're asking. I fell for it once, when I was young and stupid and I'm not falling for it again. You know *nothing* about how hard it is, Harry. Wanting a child and bringing it up are not the same thing. Children aren't the perfect little bundles of joy you seem to imagine. They make you ill before they're even born, and then tear you to pieces as they push their way into the world. They demand food and attention 24/7. You lose so much sleep that you can't think straight, they don't even register you crying from exhaustion every night. But Mother Nature, in her wisdom, programmed us to love and minister to them anyway, which is just as well, otherwise the human race would have become extinct millennia ago… I've been through it all once… in stereo… and I am certainly not willing to go through it again!"

Sara notched up another gear. Harry sat silent and open-mouthed.

"And what's more, when they grow out of nappies the demands don't stop, they just change. Children are adorable and charming self-centred little egotists, who eventually morph into moody, ungracious adolescents. They take you and your love for granted, and you let them. You give up your time, dreams and ambitions, to make life good for them and because you love them, you do it unreservedly.

"It's true, they give a lot of love back, but they take *your* love for granted and will, if the mood takes them, withhold *theirs* from you. It's a kind of blackmail, they can't help it any more than you can, it's how our brains are programmed. As a by-product whilst they are growing into themselves, *your* role is reduced to facilitator and slave. *You* cease to be a person in your own right. In fact at times they act as if, as yesterday's model, you *have* no rights and it's too easy to believe and accept that it's true. They do eventually grow up and it all seems worthwhile, but it takes more time and effort than I am willing or able to give again. I've just begun to find 'me', and I'm enjoying being my own woman. I'm not giving that up now.

"I could have loved you so much… but you are making me doubt your sincerity. I've got to look out for myself. Have you merely misunderstood what I want and need or… and please, don't let this be true, are you one of those manipulating so and so's, who thinks he knows what women *really* want better than they do themselves? Did you try this with your wife? How *was* it you managed to get her pregnant, when on your own admission you knew she didn't want to be?"

This last, she realised was dangerous ground and a bit below the belt. Harry's expression changed and she caught a sullen, defiant look in his eyes she didn't much care for. So, unabashed, she slammed into overdrive and lost all reserve.

"There's got to be more to that story than you're letting on, there are more holes in it than a colander. Were you as blameless as you pretend? I doubt it… That's why you can't forget for a moment why she acted as she did, isn't it? You knew your wife didn't want to be, but somehow you contrived to get her pregnant anyway. You said she was an intelligent woman, for God's sake… I don't know how you managed it… but you did… *Fait accompli,* no way out? Maybe *you* believed you would get away with it, and everything would be fine in the end… She didn't and it wasn't. Game, Set and Match to Linda! Whatever happened, she must have had a damn good reason for acting as she did, Harry… Women do not do that kind of thing lightly… I feel sorry for both of you."

He listened to this in shocked silence. He couldn't reconcile this Sara with the woman he thought he knew and understood. How many sides were there to her? She was like little Julie, turned termagant in seconds. The Fury opposite him was scrambling to her feet.

"Sara?"

"I can't give you a child," she said, all passion spent. "I'm all that's on offer."

He felt as if he had gone ten rounds with the world heavyweight boxing champion, but the knockout punch was yet to come.

"What about the festival?" he asked weakly, "What shall I do with the tickets?"

Sara gave him a look that would have withered a sequoia tree, snatched them from his hand, and stuffed them in the bin as she stalked out onto the street.

'Oh what a mess.' Sara's eyes were brimmed with tears. She was hurt, felt used and desperately unhappy. But had there really been any need to go off the deep end like that? It was true she had wondered how the sophisticated and highly intelligent woman Harry had described, who repeatedly refused to have children 'until the time was right', could 'accidentally' become pregnant. And if she hadn't told him about the baby before he left for Rio, why did she face him with such news when he came home? It felt all wrong. But she hadn't given him a chance to explain. Thinking of how sweet and kind he had been she felt deeply ashamed of herself and her suspicions.

'Oh shit! shit! shit!'

CHAPTER TWENTY-ONE

Harry, like Sara, was also desperately upset. In his obsession for a child, he'd asked too much and lost sight of what he already had. He was aware he was no angel and had presented only his best side to Sara but what did she think he'd done? Forced his wife into… ? No, he could honestly say he'd never forced any woman to do anything she didn't want to. He had no inclinations that way at all. He always waited until they wanted him and usually they did. That Linda had invited him to her bed that night surprised him a little but not that much, he'd been forgiven so often before, it was nothing new.

His mind filled with images of how Linda had left him after she'd killed his baby, then he thought about the tale he'd told for years… so often that he almost believed it himself, but the agony of losing his child was the only bit of truth in it. He claimed Linda had been prescribed antibiotics for a mild throat infection and the doctor omitted to tell her they reduced the efficacy of the pill and it was an act of pure selfishness on her part to have the resulting unwanted pregnancy terminated. Thus he managed, in a very deft way, to absolve himself from any blame. A ray of hope glimmered, for some reason he'd baulked at the usual fabrication with Sara, he'd told her only what he'd convinced himself was the case, that Linda had the abortion out of selfish spite. He *could* try his fable now, it had worked before with others, but he knew he wouldn't, because he didn't want to lie about it anymore, at least not to her. Sara, needless to say, had been right to doubt him, what he'd told her *was* true, but far and away distant from the whole truth. She was nobody's fool and was certainly not going to be his. Utterly crushed and miserable, he got up mechanically, retrieved the crumpled festival tickets from the bin, and made his way back to his hotel.

He had a lot of thinking to do when he got back to his room. He remembered his time at Imperial where he studied for a degree in electrical engineering. He was a young, good-looking charmer. How he got his 'First' was a minor miracle, considering how much term time he spent having fun with the female students of the college. He went on to do his Doctorate in the field of mechatronics and eventually was offered a teaching post in the subject at the college, where he had met Linda Kafka. With high cheek bones that denoted her East European origins, she was beautiful, clever and ambitious. They were enormously attracted to one another. He'd had an idea of staying in the safe haven of education until he'd accrued enough funds to strike out on his own, but she thought with a little bit of help, he could do it now. She was very well connected with the business world in Switzerland, where she had grown up, and soon acquired a financial partner for him, a sprinkling of clients, and smart if small premises for the new business. They married at Christmas of that year. A perfect match.

All went well for the first couple of years. Linda was rising in the ranks of her profession and Harry's business went international and was booming. With only the occasional pursuits of pleasure, on business trips abroad (which he didn't think really counted), he had been faithful to his wife.

Trouble reared its head when Harry's P.A., Miss Bracey, married a farmer, and went off to live with her new husband in rural, idyllic Wales. Her replacement was not well chosen, she had a flirtatious manner that Harry found hard to resist, so he didn't. But like many before him, Harry soon discovered there's no such thing as a free lunch, and he found himself idiotically embroiled in an affair he did not want. She was a liability, coquettish and demanding in turn. As the boss's secret mistress she felt she could wield power over lesser members of staff, and made life unbearable for them. Harry at last had enough, and asked outright how much it would cost for her to just go away. She said she didn't really want to go, but if she did agree to it, she would need a position of real authority in another office, with a higher salary, or she would dish the dirt to his wife. Harry had a choice. He could tell Linda how stupid he'd been or pay up. On balance he decided to take the easy option.

"Give me a couple of days, to sort something out for you."

"Tomorrow," she said.

"OK. Tomorrow. I'll have a new contract for you then."

In the morning, their next interview was equally brief.

"I will comply with your demands," he said. "I'm willing to make you manager of a team of three. You'll receive a yearly salary in excess of £1,500 p.a. more than you are getting at the moment. The office to which you will be assigned belongs to our Newcastle Distribution Branch. There's a spacious flat adjoining the premises which, as manager, will be yours rent free. The contract is dated. All you need do is sign it."

She read it through then raked his face with a triumphant air.

"Newcastle doesn't really appeal. Make it £2,000," she demanded.

Harry hesitated then nodded and she put her signature to the paper.

"Take whatever time it takes to clear your desk. Goodbye, Miss Millar."

She'd sashayed over to him and kissed him hard on the lips, smirked and left his office. Later that morning a colleague from the accounts department knocked on Harry's door.

"Yes, Alex. What can I do for you?"

"Well," he replied "It's about Miss Millar's new contract at the Newcastle depot. Had you forgotten the premises are being demolished in a council development programme, and we've decided not to renew that particular operation?"

With some satisfaction, Harry said, "No."

What a short-lived triumph that had been. After a wonderful mid-summer's day party a few weeks later, Linda and Harry arrived home, they sat opposite one another, kicked off their shoes, and relaxed sipping their evening claret. Linda raised her glass to him and said, "You're quite a bastard, aren't you?"

Transfixed, he said nothing.

Linda went on, "I've recently received an email from a Miss Millar, telling a wonderful tale of lust and deceit, and

I do believe the gentleman to whom she was alluding was you."

"Linda…" he began.

"Not only," she interrupted, "did you sleep with the little whore, you cheated her out of her prize. Tsk, tsk, Harry, how well matched you are… both cheap."

He remembered how he had mumbled and stuttered his excuses and apologies.

She expressed no interest in his explanations, but sat in silence to finish her drink then, although weary, raised herself to her feet in the elegant manner she could not help but assume, saying, "I'm going to bed now, Harry. Join me later."

After an hour or so he did venture into the bedroom. She was still awake and they made love as never before. She was on fire for him. Every cliché, 'the earth moved', 'stars fell from heaven', even what the French call *la petite mort,* was too inadequate to describe that night. It was beyond words. It was also when Linda conceived their child. In the following weeks, if her passion didn't quite achieve such heights, she never refused him. Harry naively, arrogantly or both, unquestioningly assumed he had been forgiven. Linda did not mention Miss Millar again and life seemed to return to normal.

Three months later his annual business trip to Rio was due and Linda, unusually running late, had rushed off to her office on the morning he was due to fly out, leaving him alone to pack by himself. He went into the bathroom and saw the bin needed emptying. A very neat and tidy man, it was no more than second nature to pick it up. A pregnancy-test-kit box fell out. He scrabbled about among the tissues, and found the test strip which showed a positive result. He was amazed and delighted, it was a dream come true. Why had she not told him straight away? Most likely she wanted to save the news until he came back, then they would have time to celebrate properly. He was elated, but wouldn't mention his find to her, just in case it should spoil her surprise. He carefully replaced the full bin, so she wouldn't guess he'd seen the box, which he thought a very clever move.

The Rio project went well, but he couldn't wait to get back. On his trip he'd bought an exquisite christening robe in fluted white silk brocade, from the collection of the Brazilian designer Coco-Pena, whose exclusive baby clothes were desired all over the world. As a sentimental gesture, he also bought one of Pena's trademark white rabbit soft toys, for Linda.

He was incredibly excited when he got home and opened the door to the flat, where he saw Linda sitting upright on the sofa, so calm and beautiful.

"It's dead," she said.

He couldn't take it in.

"You know, Harry, I always promised when the time was right we would have a child, and *I* keep my promises. The last time you betrayed me, the light went out of my life. I wanted to hurt you as much as you hurt me. I deliberately allowed you to get me pregnant and left the test kit where I knew you would find it. You never could resist a full waste bin. Then I flew to Zurich to have your baby aborted... Revenge, they say is a dish best eaten cold... I am Medea."

The bell rang. Linda picked up her jacket and walked over to the door.

"That's my taxi. I am going back to Zurich. We need never meet again. I have already consulted my solicitor, any correspondence can be conducted through her… It was a little girl, by the way. Goodbye, Harry." She walked out of the door and his life.

He drank the best part of one and a half bottles of whisky before passing out on the floor, where the cleaning lady found him, mid-morning next day.

For the next couple of years, life was not good for Harry. He took to drinking excessively and for the first time was indiscriminate in his sleeping around. The man who had always been so clean and careful contracted chlamydia from a one-night stand he'd picked up in a cheap bar. He was put right and thanked god it had been nothing worse. But even that didn't halt the downward spiral. As his drinking continued, he became too unreliable to run the business properly anymore. His financial advisors persuaded him, if he wanted to ward off bankruptcy, to appoint a management team. He felt he'd lost another baby when he no longer had control, a token seat on the board was little consolation. Then a conviction for drunken driving landed him in deep trouble and a rehabilitation clinic.

He'd hit rock bottom and was at the clinic for almost nine months before getting himself straight. During that time, encouraged by the staff, he took up singing again and even created a little choir with his fellow patients. He eventually regained his confidence and felt able to begin life anew.

First priority on his list was to get out of London. He wanted to make a complete break from the city. Although originally from Derbyshire, Harry had always enjoyed going north to York, so that's where he went. He loved the Minster and if they would have him, he'd join the choir. He still had a more than adequate income from his business interests, so it wasn't vital to find work, but he wanted to keep busy. The old company, it turned out, was more than happy to have the rehabilitated Harry in a consultancy role, and he could operate from the north. Perfect.

He could neither forgive nor forget that Linda had terminated her pregnancy, but in time, to make life bearable, managed to airbrush his part into soft focus. Harry bought a small comfortable house, made new friends and settled into his new life. However his real addiction was not to alcohol, but to women, and he easily slipped back into his old ways. Although he had never thought of it in that sense before, he realised now he had not been averse to telling his carefully fabricated version of the past to create sympathy between himself and a woman he was hoping to bed.

He'd done it to Sara as well, hadn't he? Taking advantage of her trust and vulnerability, eliciting compassion he'd laid all the blame on Linda. It had never failed. His tricks may have worked, but they now seemed tawdry and (Linda had been right) cheap. The thought struck him that if Sara had seen holes in his story, others may have seen them too, not that it would have been of great import to any of them. Was Sara exceptionally perceptive, or did she genuinely care? For that matter, why did he?

Suddenly, the wall he had built between his actions and their consequences collapsed and Harry at last saw himself as the self-deceiving bastard he really was. My god! But Linda knew him through and through. She knew his nature, he would never force himself on her. She simply used his vanity to make him complicit in his own destruction. If his little girl had been allowed to live, she too would have been prey to men like him and the thought repelled him. For the first time he understood, and for a moment almost absolved Linda of her crime.

Reality set in, big time. He sent down for a bottle. When it arrived he thought about the bad choices he'd made in his sorry life. Miss Millar, for goodness' sake! He hadn't even liked her that much, but she was available so he had her, that was all. He should have told Linda at once what an idiot he'd been. She would have been angry but she loved him, and he knew if she'd given him the chance, he could have talked her round, he'd done it so often before, unfortunately she knew that too.

He'd been a fool to become embroiled in an affair. He'd been a coward and double fool to respond to Miss Millar's demands and to let moments of brief triumph turn his life to ashes. He deserved all he'd got. He was a complete shit.

The descent into drunkenness had been just as shameful and stupid. Did he really want to go back into that slough of despond? No. He put the unopened bottle down. For once in his life he would man up, he would go to Sara, and tell her the truth. She said she could have loved him, he prayed she would because he needed her to so much, his life was unravelling again. Before he could change his mind, Harry picked up his mobile.

"Yes," she said.

"Sara, it's me… I'm sorry… Can I talk to you?" The silence

was palpable. "I know you're there. I need to talk, then if you don't want to see me again, I promise I won't bother you. I'll get the next flight home… Please, may I come?"

The silence continued.

"Please, Sara… are you still there? Please."

"Alright, come now," she said and ended the call.

CHAPTER TWENTY-TWO

Harry set out at once for Sara's apartment, it was going to be a painful interview for both of them. Halfway there he badly needed a drink and regretted the unopened bottle sitting in his room so he turned to go back. As he stepped into the road, he didn't see the pick-up truck coming. Some sort of projection on the side smashed into his arm and wrenched his shoulder. It might well have flattened him as well, if a fast-acting tourist hadn't yanked him back onto the pavement. A tirade of Gallic abuse filled the air as the truck sped on. In shock, with his head spinning, Harry managed to mutter, "*Merci, monsieur...*"

"Man, that was close! You OK, buddy?" asked the burly, young American who had been his saviour.

"*Oui... oui... merci beaucoup. C'est rien... merci... merci...*"

Clutching his arm, which felt as if it was broken, Harry turned again towards Sara's apartment as a safe haven. On arrival he pressed the outside bell and Sara was irritated by the time he took to mount the stairs to her rooms, she was not pleased by her wait. He knocked at her door and she took her time to open it. He nearly fell in. At first she thought he was drunk and was ready to throw him straight out again, until she saw the torn sleeve of his jacket and blood dripping onto the floor.

"Oh god! Harry, what's happened?" She half carried him to the sofa and set him down.

"My fault, wasn't looking… Truck caught my arm…" and he fainted.

In the past, she'd dealt with the children's cuts and bruises, but this was something different. She didn't know how to cope. Instinctively she ran across to Jean-Pierre's home for help. Jean-Pierre wasn't there but Monique's Bertrand was, and he came at once. He took one look at Harry and called for an ambulance. Sara got a bowl of water and a flannel to bathe Harry's face. Neither she nor Bertrand dared examine the arm for fear of doing more damage.

"Poor Harry," she said.

His eyes flickered open and looked into hers, but he said nothing before they closed again, and she continued to wipe the road dust from his face. The ambulance arrived much quicker than expected, the professional paramedics soon had him more comfortable and carried him down into the waiting van, Sara at his side.

At the hospital an X-ray showed him to have a complicated fracture. The arm was badly damaged and if they were to save it, an operation needed to be performed as soon as possible. Whilst staff prepared the theatre, before his pre-med, Sara was allowed a brief visit. She anxiously waited to be admitted. He was pleased and keen to see her.

"Sara," he began, "I'm so sorry. What I asked of you was selfish and stupid, but that's not all… I was coming to tell you what a complete bastard I am… I've not been wholly honest with you, but I got scared and turned back… the truck caught me… You were nearest, I came to you."

"Harry, you don't have to tell me all this now. I went off at the deep end and I'm not proud of the way I spoke to you. You've been very good to me."

He winced when she said this, and it wasn't caused merely by the agony in his arm.

"Look," he said, "I've got to tell you everything… You may not want to see me again and I'd understand if you didn't, OK? But if I don't do it now I never will, and that wouldn't be good for either of us. If I didn't care about you it would be different, but I do care… very much, very much indeed."

Painfully, metaphorically and literally, Harry proceeded to narrate the wreck he'd made of his life and marriage. It didn't sound good when it was only in his head, spoken out loud it sounded far worse. Its only virtues were its veracity, and obvious reticence when trying not to hurt Sara any more than he already had.

"You see," he concluded, "I had everything, and it came easy. Everything that is except self-control, self-awareness and the common sense to appreciate it all. It was my fault… all of it."

She looked into his face and laid the hand she had been holding back on his bed, before walking away.

"Please Sara, don't leave me… Sara."

She closed the door softly behind her as the nurse arrived to perform the pre-op. In less than a minute Harry lost consciousness and was wheeled into the theatre.

His surgeon was a slight young woman, but older and more experienced than she looked, and well qualified to tackle what was going to be a tricky job. The break itself, thankfully, had not been a compound fracture, but it took a long time for the skilful fingers to carefully repair torn ligaments and muscle, before stitching the poor battered arm and shoulder back together.

It was half-light in the recovery room when he opened his eyes. He took a moment to remember where he was and why. Sara, his Sara had walked away. Hot tears of misery rolled down his cheeks and he fell back into darkness.

"Alors, Monsieur Martin. 'ow are you this morning?" It was the young surgeon who spoke. She was reading from a chart at the time, and barely registered his weak response.

"Ça va bien, merci, docteur."

"Bon, bon!" she trilled, and spotting a figure at the far side of the door said, *"Vous avez une visiteuse"*, and giving brief instruction to the nurse, smiled brightly at Harry before admitting Sara to a place at his bedside.

"You came back!" he said.

"Of course," Sara replied. "You don't kick a man when he's down where I come from in Yorkshire. You wait till he's up and about, then you kick him."

Seeing the confused expression on his face she laughed. He managed a light guffaw before complaining, "Don't make me laugh… it hurts!"

She pulled her chair closer to his bedside and took his 'good' hand in hers. "Seriously, how do you feel?"

"Honestly?"

"Honestly."

Smiling mournfully, he said, "Like I've been hit by a truck! I thought I'd lost you, Sara. Thank you for coming back to me."

"Don't give me any of your soft soap!" she replied, unexpectedly brisk. "You all behaved badly. No one comes out of your story smelling of roses. Maybe you needed a lorry to knock some sense into you. But it's done now. In telling me the truth, you've made it as right as it can be between us. Life's too short and precious for recriminations. Let's make a pact to be as honest with each other as possible. Starting with, if you squeeze my hand any harder you'll break my fingers, then we will both end up in bed!"

"Not a bad idea!" He grinned, releasing his grip.

"Now then," said Sara, assuming a prim attitude. "We need to discuss practicalities. As you were in no state yesterday to do it for yourself, Bertrand rifled through your wallet to find your insurance and EHIC card when you arrived at the hospital. A bit of a jobsworth receptionist insisted that only your next of kin had the authority to sanction the op. you needed. Bertrand phoned the contact number at the back of your passport. I believe it was your brother, but there was no answer, the situation was urgent so your surgeon, being French, assumed our relationship was close enough and allowed me to sign instead. While this was happening Bertrand, bless him, informed BUPA and answered as many of their questions as he could. You'll have to fill in the blanks yourself… you know, give details of any witnesses etc. The doctors say you must remain here for at least ten to fourteen days, to make sure everything is OK before attempting your journey home." She waited a moment for him to assimilate this information. He nodded and she continued, "Maybe you should contact your hotel? There seems little point in paying for accommodation you're not using. Would you like me to do that for you? I can, if you like, get your stuff over to my place. There's plenty of room… "

"That would be very kind… I bet you were a wonderful teacher," he mused, "nothing left to chance in your classes. Your efforts are not wasted on me. I appreciate and am grateful for the efficiency you have shown. I also love you very much, Mrs Middleton."

She blushed red to the roots of her hair as a busy nurse walked in, pushing a trolley of medication.

"Ah, Monsieur Martin," she said, checking the chart. She thrust a thermometer under his good armpit, took his pulse and blood pressure, handed him a selection of pills to take with a glass of water, smiled and said, "*Merci. Au revoir, Monsieur… Madame.*" And was swiftly gone.

However painful for Harry, they both had to laugh. Any embarrassment was dissipated by the farcical interruption.

"Well," said Sara, "back to practicalities. If you would be so good as to phone and check out of your hotel, then I'll get a taxi, collect your luggage and take it over to the apartment."

"OK boss. Would you mind giving me my phone and getting the number for me? I'm not sure I can manage one-handed."

"Certainly."

But this prosaic action proved incredibly difficult. First, she had to gently lift his thumb onto the screen to unlock it, which cost him a disproportionate amount of pain. She picked the number from 'list' and handed the device to

Harry who confirmed a friend would be collecting his luggage later that morning. To settle the bill, he needed his credit card and Sara found herself violating the privacy of his wallet for the second time in twenty-four hours. Harry was exhausted from his exertions. Beads of sweat stood out on his forehead. She took some tissues from the box by his bed and gently wiped his brow.

"I'll go now," she said, "and get everything sorted. If you're very good, I'll bring you some grapes this evening."

He was already asleep by the time she reached the door.

She went straight to his hotel where reception kindly gave her the key and asked after the health of the *charmant* M. Martin. Sara was able to reassure them that he would probably recover fully in time.

It was strange to enter his room. She felt awkward about the need to go through his personal things. She started in the bathroom, gathered his face cloth, toothbrush and toothpaste together in his sponge bag. The soap on the wash basin was a well-used bar of lemon verbena, she threw it in the bin. She'd get him a fresh one. All his other toiletries, shaving kit, tortoiseshell comb and brushes fitted into a leather case on the shelf by the mirror. He would also need the burgundy slippers by the bed, his paisley dressing gown that was hanging on the back of the door, but there were no pyjamas under either pillow.

'Surely he must have some,' she thought, and found on the middle shelf of the *armoire* a beautiful neatly folded pair in maroon silk, edged with cream satin piping. Feeling the quality, she carefully removed and transferred them to the

176

bed. She thought of her own fleecy, Snoopy set and sighed. Taking a soft canvas holdall, she packed all these items ready to take to the hospital that evening.

Next she got his suitcase, which was remarkably light compared to her own heavy-weight effort, and proceeded to load his shirts, jackets, shoes and other things that he didn't immediately need into it. She wasn't very good at packing but did her best. There was a small amount of washing in the hotel laundry bag, but she considered dealing with that herself a little too intimate, and decided to send it to the hotel laundry. She would pay.

Making a final check of the room, she took a cursory glance inside the tiny drawer of the dressing table, and saw two crumpled festival tickets. She tried to straighten them out, sat on the bed and cried.

Five minutes later she surveyed the blotchy wreck of her face in the mirror. It was not a good look. Fishing the half-used soap out of the (mercifully) clean bin, she gave her face a good wash and dried it vigorously on the hotel towel. Satisfied that she just looked remarkably pink and healthy, she made her way to the lift with Harry's bags. Seeing her struggle out of the door the concierge sent a boy to help.

Under the circumstances the hotel would see to M. Martin's laundry if *Madame* would care to pay now, that would be fine, and of course they would summon a taxi *pour la bonne amie de M. Martin.*

Back at her apartment Sara thought she should hang up Harry's clothes before they were permanently creased beyond salvation. To make room, she folded some of her own things into her suitcase. She was going home in only three days. It seemed she'd been in Menton forever, and was beginning to miss her family, but how much more would she miss Harry, and the, damn it, she would use the word, romance, he'd brought into her life. His silk and her Snoopy pyjamas just didn't go together, they were metaphors for different worlds. She suddenly felt very weary, lay down and fell into a deep sleep.

CHAPTER TWENTY-THREE

Sara was awoken by the apartment bell ringing. Disorientated, she asked who it was.

"*C'est moi, Monique!* I 'ave come to drive you to 'arry in the 'ospital."

"Oh, lord," she said "I was asleep. I'll be down in two seconds." She snatched up her coat, along with Harry's bag, and was almost out of the door when she remembered his soap, so quickly grabbed one of the wrapped ones she'd bought earlier.

"It's really good of you to drive me, Monique," she said, once settled in the car.

"*Pas d' tout!*" Monique replied. "*Dix* minutes… I will say 'ello to 'arry then I will be gone, pouff! I will come back for you in one hour, OK?"

Harry was lying in his bed when they arrived, looking very sorry for himself. He had two black eyes blossoming to match the bruises on his cheek that seemed to have sprung spontaneously from nowhere.

Monique fussed around him for a few moments, gave him all good wishes for a speedy recovery from *papa* and Bertrand, and produced from her bag a get-well card which

Julie, who was prolific in her artwork, had made. He *thought* it might be a picture of himself, in bed with a cartoon-sized plaster on his arm. At the last minute Julie had decided to make it pretty by putting glitter all round the edge, and the glue was still slightly tacky. He had never received a child-made card before, and was genuinely very touched and pleased. He asked Sara to put it on his bedside cabinet. Curled and wobbly, the card eventually (possibly due to the excess of glue) managed to stay in an upright position. Monique delved into her copious bag again, and like a magician, produced a bunch of black grapes and a bottle of wine, which she conspiratorially half-hid behind Julie's gift.

In a whirl of sympathetic sentiments, she said, "I will meet you in the lobby in one hour, Sara. *A bientot*", and with a look of despair turned toward him saying, "*Ah. Adieu, pauvre 'arry!*" She left them alone together.

"She's very kind," Sara said. "How are you?"

"Come sit by my bed and stroke my fevered brow. My arm hurts like hell and every one of my orifices has been violated by the sadistic little imps that pass here for nurses. I will never again have erotic fantasies about females in the medical profession."

She laughed, but not unsympathetically.

"I've brought you some of the things I thought you would need. I hope I've not forgotten anything." She let him inspect the contents of the sponge bag and toiletries case, produced his slippers, dressing gown and the wonderful silk pyjamas… He expressed approval.

"Oh, soap," she exclaimed, and reached into her own bag. "Yours was nearly all gone, so I brought you a new one."

He took the bar in his good hand and sniffed at it.

"Roses?… Very nice."

"Oh, Lord! I must have picked up the wrong one… and I meant to be so efficient. You don't like roses then?"

"Not on me," he replied.

There was silence for a moment. He looked at her intently.

"What have I done to merit having you? I've never spent time in hospital before. Never had time when I've been unable to do anything but think. Think, what a shallow excuse for a man I've been all my life. I don't want to be that person anymore, Sara. I don't like him."

She said quietly, "Can I tell you something, Harry? I've been doing a lot of thinking about things too, about what you told me, and I didn't appreciate what a bad time you've been going through. I've been too caught up in my own problems. I want to say something that's very difficult, because although I can't condone your past behaviour to Linda, I can't see how to blame you for it either. Put it this way, when you sing, you're strong, confident and hit every note." She smiled a little. "It's a combination of raw talent and practice, I guess. But you like to take risks, and that's what makes you a dangerous and exciting singer, and even I, with my frankly limited experience of these things, can tell those self-same qualities…" she blushed a little at this point before going on, "are what make you irresistible as a man. You perform best when living on the edge, it's what makes you, you. Perhaps being married was too constricting and you needed the adrenaline rush of playing with fire. I don't know, but whatever the reason, you got horribly burnt, and you've been suffering for it ever since."

Harry didn't know how to respond to this. It sounded as if she was giving him free rein to do as he pleased. He wasn't sure if this was a good or bad sign.

Seeing his confusion, she smiled again. "No, Harry, I don't mean it was OK to do what you did. I mean it's possible to see how it happened. But there's more, and you would be well within your rights to tell me to stop as it's really none of my business, but I believe it's important. May I tell you?"

"My ego's already hanging by a thread and feeling as battered as my arm. Will it be like medicine and make me feel better?"

"I don't know and I can't deny you've taken quite a battering, but I do doubt the assertion that either your ego or your arm is hanging by a thread. My medicine though, is the kill or cure kind. It might taste nasty, so it's up to you whether you chose to take it or not."

"You're scaring me, Sara. You're not… not going to leave me are you?"

"Oh no, Harry! Not unless you want me to."

He held her hand tightly and said tenderly, "I'll never want that. Go ahead."

Taking a deep breath, she began, "To recap a little, I don't think fidelity has, and possibly ever will, come easily to you. You aren't the only one by a long chalk, but marriage can be a mistake for such men, it takes a particular kind of woman to cope with it. Maybe Linda thought she was one. She probably guessed you would have little escapades on business trips, and was aware they would mean nothing to you, so it was easier for her to pretend they didn't really count for her either. As you know too well, your biggest mistake was to get involved with a woman on home ground and Linda just couldn't pretend any more. You must have broken her heart Harry. People talk, and believe me, she would have guessed what was going on, long before the email arrived. She would have been waiting to see how you got out of the hole you'd dug for yourself and wasn't going to help you this time. I'd say we'd have to agree you disappointed her, and she was right to call you cheap."

Sara wasn't kidding, the medicine tasted bitter and nasty. Harry, listening to her analysis, was wondering where it would all lead. So far it hadn't made him feel any better at all, because he knew everything she had said was true. He felt sick and ashamed.

She went on. "In my opinion, and you must remember it is only my opinion, Linda's behaviour points to a scheme well worked out in advance. This time you had gone too far. She would use your desire for a child to cut you down completely. All the signs point to it being no simple, sudden act of vengeance. It was more like an 'Armageddon' plan if you like, a final solution if it all got too much. You'd crossed the line, and she'd leave you no way back. She might have thought of merely fabricating the entire thing. She could have bought a home pregnancy testing kit and doctored it to show a positive result, let you find it, then at the right time, make a bogus claim that the foetus had been aborted at an anonymous clinic in Zurich. How would you have known otherwise?"

Harry's face was a mask of shock and confusion, which Sara only glanced at with pity in her eyes, as she went on to say " But I believe, from what you have told me, because she really loved you, she did the most part of it for real."

His face had turned as white as the sheets on his bed.

"Do you want me to go on? There's more that I think you need to hear. Or shall I stop?" Sara's voice was shaking.

"No. Go on for god's sake, because I don't understand

183

what you mean by, 'she did it for real, because she loved me.' She can't have done that if she loved me."

"What I meant was, I believe she loved you, so *for the most part* did it for real. Shall I go on with my hypothesis?"

He still didn't understand but nodded his head slightly. With a deep breath and tears threatening to fill her eyes, she continued.

"Linda's refusal to allude further to the Miss Millar affair should have rung warning bells. It was unnatural to carry on as if nothing had happened. That night of love was just the beginning of her revenge. Did you really think you could be forgiven that easily? Oh, bless you Harry, she was a far better deceiver than you. Her actions, otherwise, just don't make sense. You told me how intelligent she was. A woman like her, who was determined not to have a baby until she was ready, would have known her menstrual cycle, and when she was at the height of her fertility taken every precaution to prevent 'accidents' happening. I think she meant you to get her pregnant that night. It's even possible she waited to tell you about Ms Millar's mail, until she was as sure as she could be, she'd got her timing right.

"But," Sara continued, "even if this was the case, I don't believe for one minute, she actually went through with all of her plan. You see, Harry, it's not so simple in real life. Had she left the test kit strip for you to find earlier, I might have thought differently, but she didn't, she waited a full trimester. Three months of feeling ill and hiding her morning sickness from someone who probably didn't notice. A woman who is really planning to abort her baby doesn't suffer that, she gets rid of it as soon as she can.

"If I'm right, I'm certain when she planned her scheme,

she wouldn't have realised how emotionally difficult it would be to carry out. Even if she had got as far as attending an appointment in Zurich, a termination is not something entered into lightly. There're many preliminaries before any surgery is performed. They'll have scanned the foetus, and Linda would have seen her baby's tiny heart beating, on the ultrasound screen. She'd have been told it was a little girl, and fallen in love with the totally innocent little soul. In any case, she was smart, and reasoned she could have her cake and eat it. There was no need to do the deed, she could keep the child, just *tell* you she'd had it aborted, and leave you to stew. In fact, a far sweeter revenge in some ways than the original idea." Sara ended with something like respect in her voice for Linda's ingenuity.

"But." Harry was having trouble with this. "What makes you so sure that's what happened?"

"I can't be *sure,* I'm just a woman who has borne children, I know how they hook themselves round your heart, and," she added practically, "in the highly unlikely event that the baby had been aborted without ceremony, she would never have asked its sex. You know, it could also explain her immediate departure, and insistence that all dealings with you were to be conducted through her solicitor. She couldn't afford to let you see her with your baby still growing inside. Think, Harry, about Linda's character before this happened. Was she always a monster or a woman you'd hurt beyond endurance, then tell me, if you can, that I've got it all wrong."

Sara's silence fell like snow.

Harry knew Linda was not a naturally wicked person. He had treated her badly, but she had paid him back in spades for everything he'd done. Could it be true she'd actually kept the baby? He didn't know if he hated Linda more or less. He felt euphoric and angry at the same time. "You're suggesting that she's kept my child from me all these years," he said bitterly. "Don't you think that's retribution enough? Because I'd say we're pretty even."

"Maybe you are now. It makes sense, Harry, but remember, it's just speculation."

But the more he thought about it, the more likely it seemed. Linda was patient and smart. There was a cool elegance to the plan that fitted more with the Linda he had known than the notion of the base, spiteful murderess his tortured mind had turned her into.

He had been so devastated by events that he never thought for one minute that Linda had lied, and his baby might be alive. She would have guessed how he'd react and no doubt included it in her calculations.

His mind raced. 'How old would his girl be now, about nine? Would she be pretty? Of course… and smart? Naturally. Would she be happy? Did she wonder about her daddy? Maybe she had another daddy and knew nothing about Harry. Maybe she wouldn't want to know about him. Why had Sara opened up this wonderful and terrifying possibility to him?' He looked at the little figure sitting opposite, her head lowered and silent.

"Why did you do it, Sara? Why did you tell me this?" he shouted angrily. "It's blowing my mind!"

Her eyes were wet, and she was shaking. "Because it's tearing me in two, Harry, to let you go on believing your child was aborted, when all my reason and instincts are screaming at me that in all probability, her mother was lying.

I don't think you should have to live with the burden of guilt Linda heaped on your head."

He gazed at her with sudden great affection. "Come here and sit by me," he said gently.

She walked over and sat on the edge of his bed. He lifted his good arm and wiped away her tears.

"Closer," he said. She leaned towards him, and his kiss held more eloquence than a thousand words. They stayed together for a short while in silence, until Harry admitted, "My arm's killing me. Sorry, but I've got to move."

"I'll call a nurse to give you some painkillers."

"Oh no you don't!" he said quickly. "You don't know which end they deliver them in France."

She gave a laugh through her tears, then serious again said, "did I do right to tell you what I thought, Harry?"

He smiled at her and said "Yes, you did right. Thank you, my kind and generous Sara, but I should like to be alone for a while now if that's OK with you. There's a lot I have to think about."

"I'll go now," she said.

He smiled at her again, "but don't forget to come back to me tomorrow morning."

"I won't forget," she replied, and lovingly kissed him goodbye.

She was almost at the door before suddenly remembering the Festival tickets she'd found in his room and asked if rather than waste them she might give them to Jean-Pierre and Julie.

"Of course," he replied. "They must have them this time… but next year… it's you and me." He looked at the clock. "You'd better get down to the lobby quick to meet Monique, or she'll be up like a mother hen to get you. Thank you, for everything. Goodnight, and sleep well, my love."

As she turned to close the door, she saw him ring for the nurse.

CHAPTER TWENTY-FOUR

When they arrived back at her apartment, Sara invited Monique inside for a moment, to give her the Festival tickets. Monique was thrilled. It would make *papa's,* and particularly Julie's, day.

After Monique had left, Sara noticed a message on her phone, from someone she guessed to be Harry's brother. He had left a number and she contacted him right away. James Martin answered and made brusque enquiries as to who she was, and how she had connections with Harry.

She kept her temper, and explained they had met at Ripon Cathedral, when as soloists they had taken part in the Christmas performance of Verdi's Requiem. By pure chance, they came across one another in Menton, where she had gone to visit her husband's grave. James became more conciliatory at this information, and even apologised for his gruffness, putting it down to anxiety about his brother. She also told him, she had just arrived home from visiting Harry in hospital, and that, although far from comfortable, he was doing well. As there was no one else to do so, she had with his permission, transferred his luggage to her apartment to await transport home, as there was little point, she continued, in keeping on an hotel room no longer in use. She heard James huff approval at this. "The hospital will have told you when he will be allowed to travel, Mr Martin," she said, "My flight home is on Saturday, that's right, in two days. I believe you're going to arrange his flight. I've left the keypad number to my apartment block with Harry. I'll leave the key to the flat with Madame Dupont, at No.1. Please see that it's returned to her, after Harry's luggage has been collected on the day he leaves. Is there anything else I can help you with? No? Well goodbye then, Mr Martin."

"Nasty-minded little man," she muttered to herself.

On her last full day in Menton, Sara had a busy morning. The Festival had started when she went for her morning croissants, and the crowds were beginning to build. She thought tomorrow would be as bad, so ordered her taxi for the airport to arrive for 9.00am. Her flight didn't leave until two in the afternoon, but better be an hour or two early than a minute late.

After breakfast she cleaned the apartment, did her packing and popped over to say a last goodbye to Jean-Pierre and his family, who thanked her again for the Festival tickets. She wished the Bequales a good holiday in Paris and Jean-Pierre assured Sara that, if she would like him to, he would keep an eye on Harry's progress for her. It was a fond farewell on all sides.

Everywhere in town seemed to be full, so after calling at the hotel to collect Harry's laundry, she turned back to the apartment and the faithful ready-meal shop across the road, where she bought a takeaway lunch, and just to be sure, something for supper too.

After lunch she went out again, to pay a last visit to

George. She wanted to take a new photograph for Dave and Georgie. As it was a tiring walk up to the cemetery, this time she opted for the bus. It took a long time because of the crowds, and it was almost midday before she got there. She took her picture, gently kissed her fingers, touched them on the marker, and whispered, "Wish me good fortune, George. *Á bientot.*"

It was time to go to the hospital and say goodbye to Harry. He was sitting up in a chair with a clean-shaven face, wearing his splendid pyjamas, dressing gown and slippers. She smiled to see him looking so spruce.

"Hello, Harry, are you feeling alright today?" she asked him gently.

"Hello, Sara, in some ways better than I've felt for a long time thank you. What you told me was a lot to take in at once, but realistically I can do nothing until I'm back on my feet again. I've got to concentrate on getting out of here and back home. If she's out there, I've got to find my little girl."

"What if I have got it wrong, Harry? What will happen then?"

"I don't see how I could be any worse off than I am now, for trying. But let's be positive about the hope you've given me and so I can concentrate on getting well. They sat me up this morning and that's a start. They said I should try every now and again to see if I can move a finger. Watch this."

Although detecting no sign of it herself, when he announced he had managed to move one of his fingers a minute fraction, she loyally said, "Well done." He grinned, and asked "While I have been working hard trying to move a little finger, what leisurely pursuits have you undertaken?" he asked.

"Ooh nothing much," she answered, and told him all she had done.

"Nearly worked as hard as I did, then, so we both deserve a kiss." His action suited his words. "Now you can have a lie down on my bed. Which is more than I am allowed to do for the rest of the day!"

Snuggling as close to him as she could, she told him about Jean-Pierre's offer to visit.

He said he would like that. "Jean-Pierre is a very nice man but a poor substitute for you… I'll miss you very much," he said. "My brother's been in touch, by the way, and told me he'd spoken to you. It was good of you to call him. I expect he gave you the third-degree treatment, but you seemed to have proved yourself up to it. He's a lot older than I am, and has the air of a country squire about him… He sends you his regards and gratitude. Honestly, he was born two centuries too late, but he's a decent old stick and I'm very fond of him. He's made up his mind I need taking care of, and will come in person to collect me, he makes me sound like a parcel. Then I'm to be taken to the farm in Derbyshire, to convalesce properly."

"Farm?"

"Of course, you didn't know I was a farmer's son, did you?" He unexpectedly burst into the old folk song.

"The sun had set beyond the hill, across yon dreary moor,
When through the rain, a poor boy came,
Up to the farmhouse door.
Can you tell to me where ere I be?
And wilt thou not employ oy-oy-oy"

Sara joined in the chorus.

"To reap and sow, to till and mow.
To be a farmers boy-oy
To be a farmer's boy!"

"The staff here will think we are completely mad," she said, laughing.

"I must be." He grimaced. "God that hurt!"

"Tell me about your farm," she said, imagining a baby Harry in wellington boots, collecting hens' eggs for his mummy.

"I'll save it for 'when the nights are lang and mirk', and we're cuddled up together by a roaring fire. It's a nice story. I had a very happy childhood." His smile became melancholy as he reverted to thoughts of his child.

"I know," he said. "It's not 100 per cent certain she's out there, but if she is and is happy, I promise to be content... I won't even try to talk to her..."

"I understand," Sara interrupted, "but my dear man, please, please don't make promises it will be impossible to keep."

"Don't worry, Sara, it'll be fine. You will help me, won't you?"

"God help *me*," she replied. "I haven't an idea how I can. But whatever happens, I'll be there for you, Harry."

"Thank you," he said. In happy mood, smiling broadly he squeezed her hand and kissed it.

She stayed with him until visiting time was over. They talked about how they would meet and sing together often, when they returned back home. He promised to contact her every day when he was with his family at the farm, but the jollity was a little forced. They were unhappy and nervous at having to part, for what might be weeks or even months. When the bell rang for visitors to leave and Sara reluctantly rose to her feet, his parting words struck her to the heart.

"Don't forget me, Sara."

She smiled and bowing down to kiss him, replied simply, "I can't. *Au revoir*, Mr Martin."

He returned her kiss. "*Au revoir*, Mrs Middleton. *Mais seulement pour le moment.*"

She smiled again and nodded, before turning to leave.

Sara's taxi arrived next morning, spot on time. The journey to the airport took only slightly longer than normal. The flights home were smooth, and remarkably uneventful. After clearing immigration, she loaded her luggage onto a trolley, and walked through to the arrivals area where she found her family waiting for her. Tears streaming down her cheeks from happiness, she greeted them.

"Welcome home, Mum! Have you had a good journey?" "You look really well!" "Look, Billy, Gran's back." The little boy ran towards Sara and hugged her knees, and she picked up her grandson and gave him a big kiss.

"We all wanted to meet you, so we had to come up in both cars," Dave said, as he took charge of his mother's luggage and they left the airport, talking twenty to the dozen. Georgie's exclamation of "You've got to tell us *all* about it!" made Sara give herself a secret smile, as she thought, 'No, maybe not quite *all*.'

PART TWO

WHEN THE TIME IS RIGHT

Shichigahama, Tohoku Region of Japan, 11 March 2011

They were sitting near the beach having a drink outside the hotel. Linda Kafka, her daughter and nanny Marta had just checked out and were waiting for the bus to take them to Matsushima Bay. A man at the next table smiled hello. He was drinking daiquiri and wore a spectacularly powerful pair of binoculars slung round his neck. Henni, an inquisitive three-year-old, showed interest and he kindly let her have a look through them. She was delighted and pointed them seaward. She asked him what that funny line was at the top. He told her it was called the horizon and took the glasses back casually, to look for himself.

Suddenly he became very alert and shouted, "My God it's a tsunami! A bloody great wave is coming right at us!"

Henni's mother could make out nothing, but the man urged them to run. In a moment he had grabbed Henni, tucked her firmly under his arm, and yelled at Linda and Marta to follow him. As he was holding the child hostage, the two women chased after. He reached his car and bundled Henni in the back.

"Get in, get in now, both of you! Look!" He was almost screaming. "Look behind you… It's coming!" They could see a line

of something still far off but heading towards shore at speed. He pushed Marta onto the back seat with Henni, and pulled Linda, her mother, into the front with him. As they careered away, they could hear a siren sounding, and through the rear-view mirror of the Toyota, they saw people beginning to race in panic away from the beach.

He drove terrifyingly fast towards the mountains. They were tossed around trying to fasten their seat belts. A tremendous noise was building up all around. Looking behind, Linda could clearly see the huge, black wave roaring like an express train toward the shore, now maybe a mile behind. Eventually, though it had already lost much of its force, the wave caught up with their car, spinning it sickeningly sideways. It took a tremendous effort to regain control. The tide of water began to ebb and tried to suck them back with it. He revved the screeching engine hard again and again, until at last the sea let go its hold and they lurched forward.

They travelled at least another mile through axle-deep, swirling water full of debris. It clattered on the sides of the car. Broken furniture, tree branches, bodies of small domestic animals and more… before finally they were high and clear in the mountains where he brought the car to a halt.

Behind them was an horrific scene of destruction. They sat dumb with shock until Henni began to cry. As Marta comforted her, their rescuer turned and introduced himself as Franz.

CHAPTER ONE

Ripon Cathedral, Rehearsal Night, March 2017

"Well!" she said. "Have you heard about poor Mr Martin?"

"Who?" queried Jean.

"You know, Harry Martin. That rather well preserved, dishy-looking chap from the Minster at York. He sang bass when we did Verdi's Requiem. You must remember him!" said her exasperated friend.

"Oh, *him*…! I do, Freda. Bit tasty!"

"He's only very nearly got himself killed!"

"Go on! When?"

"A few weeks ago."

"How did that happen then?"

Having got exactly the response from Jean she wanted, Freda went on with relish. "It seems," she said, "it happened somewhere in France. He stepped out in front of a lorry, or something, and it nearly took his arm off. Left hanging by no more than a flap of skin, it was. If it hadn't been for some foreigner with reflexes like lightning pulling him back onto the pavement, he'd have been splattered all over the road!"

"Never!" Jean replied. "Poor man. What a waste to womankind that would have been!" They both suppressed a little giggle.

"How do you know this then?" Jean asked reasonably enough.

"My sister-in-law's brother Frank's cousin is a chorister at York, and knows Mr Martin quite well. They're all quite upset about it. They were hoping to do Bach's Mass in E Minor, at Easter."

Sara Middleton's life had undergone a seismic shift since her sojourn at Menton. Not everything had changed, but she felt much more in control. Small domestic things did not consume her anymore and she was flying free from the chains, forged by herself, that had so bound her to the past.

Practicalities were an issue of course. She still had to work. Her severance pay would not last forever. She had, very sensibly, applied for supply work before going away and her first three weeks teaching were at the very Comprehensive School that had been the cause of her redundancy. The new Head of Music had contracted mumps and passed it on to both his colleagues. She couldn't help smiling at the irony.

The great pleasure she took in singing, which nothing could change, meant on the evening of the day she began work at the comprehensive, she had also joyfully returned to rehearsals with her beloved Ripon Cathedral Choir. Hardly had she walked through the door, when Jean and Freda bustled up.

"Hello, Sara," they gushed, "welcome back. Have you heard the news about Harry Martin?"

With ever more embellishments, Freda related the story of his accident.

"Of course, as one of the soloists you knew him better

than most of us lesser beings (deprecating laugh…) but it's an awful pity isn't it…? I understand he spends a bit of time working in France," she continued with self-importance. "I know people who told me so… *You're* not long back from a holiday in France, yourself, are you…?" she added as an afterthought.

"I went there to visit my husband's grave," Sara said by way of answer to this irritating woman.

"So you did… er um… sorry," Freda replied a little abashed.

Walking quickly away, she made an aside to Jean. "Hum… That visit took its time to make… from what I heard, he died more than twenty-five years ago!" she said and scooted off to impart her news to the next available person.

Since returning from holiday, Sara had not mentioned her relationship with Harry to anyone. She didn't want well-meaning family or friends, eager to give advice, taking the bloom off her romance. The only one she let in on her secret was her cat Bob, who seemed pretty cool about the whole thing.

She would certainly say nothing to the likes of Freda about him, especially as what happened was on the way to her apartment. His arm was in a bad way, but never quite as gruesome as Freda had described it. Sara missed him so much. It was almost six weeks since the accident, and four since James had gone to bring him, as Harry had said, like a parcel, home to Derbyshire where he was still convalescing on the family farm. Circumstances since leaving him at Menton meant they had not seen each other since, but he had been in touch every day. The idea of searching for his daughter was still very much on his mind, but he avoided talking about it too much. For one thing, he certainly wasn't fit enough to engage on instigating one just yet, and more importantly, he was afraid it might be a fruitless search. He wasn't ready to have his hopes dashed so soon and he knew Sara would blame herself for his disappointment. Which was something he would not want to happen.

During the previous evening's call, he had reported that his new physio regime was working wonders, and asked Sara, as he was now in a reasonable state of repair, to come down at the weekend to visit. Also, he added, his mother would like to meet her.

She replied she would be delighted, and so she was, at the thought of seeing *him*.

Missing Harry was almost a physical pain. She longed to be with him again, but was nervous of meeting his family. How had he explained her to them? She'd had only one conversation with his brother over the phone from Menton, when she needed to tell him about the arrangements she'd made to hold Harry's luggage at her flat. James had sounded so gruff and disapproving, she wasn't sure she wanted to meet him at all. Now Harry had added his mother to the list. She felt more like fourteen than forty-eight. Taking a deep breath, she phoned her son Dave, to tell him she was going to stay with a friend at the weekend and asked if he'd mind looking after Bob while she was away.

"No bother." He answered, once again marvelling at the change in his mother since her holiday. She had been such a home bird all her life and now she was more vibrant somehow and the thought of her going away *again* was unprecedented. Dave had no idea, but his wife, Christine, had her suspicions. 'Good luck to her!' she thought, smiling to herself.

It was in fear and trepidation that Sara keyed the farm's postcode into her satnav on Friday afternoon to make the drive to Derbyshire. She arrived just before it started to get too dark, for which she was grateful, as the farm entrance was at the bottom of a long unmade road. After making heavy weather of the frequent potholes, her little Kia Picanto at last drew to a halt outside a rambling old manor house. At the sound of her approach, the door was flung open, and there in the light-filled porch stood Harry. He greeted her warmly, dropped her small weekend bag off in the hall and led the way inside to the country kitchen. It was complete with two border collies and a cat toasting themselves in front of an old Aga stove. James and his wife were waiting there.

James was just as Harry had described. Dressed in tweeds, with his ruddy face sporting a white moustache with a head of wispy hair to match. This barrel-chested man looked every inch the country squire. He held out his hand to Sara and said, "Hum, thank you very much for taking care of my brother, Mrs Middleton... hum... we appreciate... your concern... hum... very much."

"Thank you," she replied, realising instantly that what she had taken for gruffness on his part when they had spoken over the phone had probably been no more than shyness. She smiled and said, "It was a pleasure to be able to help. Please, call me Sara." He harrumphed and got slightly redder. "Thank you, er um, Sara."

"Hello, I'm James's wife Pamela or Pam, don't mind which," said the woman standing next to him. Kissing Sara firmly on both cheeks, she went on: "It's good to meet you at last… I don't think Harry's stopped talking about you since he arrived!"

Now it was Harry's turn to blush.

Pamela and James were complete opposite personalities who, with indifference to conventional wisdom over the need for compatibility, had loved each other deeply through more than fifty years of marriage.

They introduced their son Michael and his wife Carrie, who had just come into the kitchen. Pam went on to tell Sara "Harry is Michael's uncle even though he's only eighteen months older. Our daughter Lucy, his niece, is three years older than Harry!"

This convoluted piece of information confused her for a moment until Harry said quietly in her ear, "I'll tell you about it later."

A young boy rushed into the room.

"Mum, Dad, the cat's having her kittens on your bed!"

Michael and Carrie rushed out.

"That," said Pamela, "was my grandson Peter. I'm afraid you missed Luke, the older one. He's on a school trip to Italy. Supper will be ready in about fifteen minutes. Harry, you can take Sara up to her room and show her all the necessaries." She concluded by busying them out of her kitchen.

Harry did as he was told. At the top of the stairs, with one of his most charming smiles he said, "Pam thought you might like a room of your own, but I'm right next door, if you want me."

She gave a laugh. He raised his eyebrows in mock surprise saying, "Really Mrs Middleton, surely you don't think I would have any ulterior motives in my mind."

"I've given up thinking where you're concerned," she replied.

He opened a panelled oak door for her and switched on the soft light. She saw an old tester bed covered with a patchwork quilt of similar antiquity. The floorboards, dark and broad, were covered in large, worn woollen rugs. Walnut furniture gleamed, ceramic vases and bowls of potpourri abounded. She went to the window and peeked behind the chintz curtains. The land outside was almost invisible in the darkness, but a new moon shone in the sky.

"Oh, Harry. It's beautiful!"

"Not bad, is it," and with remarkable dexterity for a man with only one able arm, flung her on the bed.

"Ouch," he said, and laid himself carefully down beside her. Their kisses were long and tender until Pam's voice sounded up the stairs saying supper was ready, now! Feeling like a couple of adolescents, she helped Harry to his feet, and they scrambled to the door. As they left the room, Sara asked him about his mother.

"She's down at the end of the corridor. I'm afraid she's very frail," he said sadly. "And she tires so easily. She was already asleep before you arrived. I'll take you to see her tomorrow. Will that be OK? She wants to meet you very much."

Supper consisted of a huge, delicious meat pie and home-grown vegetables. For pudding Pamela produced a crumble made from their own Bramley apples and wild brambles. She served it with cream, fresh from the dairy. Sara's diet was completely blown, but for the moment she didn't care. 'I'll do the crisp bread and celery, next week,' she said to herself.

They retired to the sitting room for coffee and brandy. Settled comfortably in an old chair, with the log fire burning brightly, Sara relaxed totally and soon the murmur of voices made her feel soporific and her eyes began to close.

"Harry," said Pamela's voice, "I think Sara may be tired after her long journey. Perhaps you should take her bag up to her room?"

"You do look very sleepy," he said. "Would you like to go to bed now?"

She glanced at the mantel clock. It showed 10.00pm which was just late enough.

"If you don't think it too rude of me, I think I should."

"Of course," he said. He collected her bag as she said her 'goodnights' and led her up to her room.

"Thank you for coming, I missed you so much. I hope we can talk about things, you know, tomorrow," he whispered.

Sara smiled in understanding. He kissed her tenderly before turning to re-join the others downstairs.

CHAPTER TWO

Sara woke, not having had any visitor during the night, at around eight in the morning, concluding correctly that he realised how tired she had been and let her sleep. The bedroom was an ensuite, with a genuinely old roll-top iron bath with a push-on rubber shower to fit on the taps. She had all the toiletries she needed in her sponge bag, the water was hot and she drew a good depth in which to soak. When the water started to go chilly, she quickly shampooed and rinsed her hair using the antiquated rubber shower. There was a hairdryer in the drawer and soon, sweet and powdered, she dressed and made her way downstairs.

Pam was in the kitchen preparing breakfast for Harry's mother.

"Hello Sara," she said, "I'm afraid you missed the 'boys'. They went off to a special cattle market a couple of hours ago and won't be back till about lunchtime. Never mind, you and I can have a nice little chat."

Sara suspected that Pamela had engineered the outing so she could have a word with her on her own.

"Would you like to come and meet Maggie? That's Harry's mother. She's longing to see you."

"That would be nice," Sara replied.

"She's in the large bedroom at the end. With Michael, Carrie and the boys in the flat conversion on the top floor we thought it would be the quietest for her. Poor soul spends most of her time in bed nowadays. We brought her here from Gamekeepers Cottage about four months ago when she was diagnosed with stomach cancer. It was very advanced and there was nothing they could do, except make her as comfortable as possible. I look after her during the day but we have a nurse who comes in at night. Just in case. She means a lot to all of us, particularly Harry."

Sara looked questioningly up at Pamela.

"Oh, didn't you know James and Harry are only half-brothers? That's why there's such an age difference. You wouldn't think it, but James is in his seventies, you know. His mother died when he was only sixteen or so. With his dad, Arthur, they ran the farm together. It was always under-stood James would inherit the farm."

Pamela filled the kettle and put it on the Aga.

"I'll make you some tea and toast before we go up," she said. "Now, where was I? Oh yes. Well, when Arthur was about fifty, Maggie, who was studying agriculture, came to work on his farm as part of her course. She was a lot younger than him, but they fell in love and eventually married when she was about thirty-six. Yes, that's right, they didn't rush into it. Arthur was well into his mid-fifties by then. There was something like twenty years between them. They were happy and we were happy for them. But I will confess it was a bit of a shock when a couple of years later young Harry appeared on the scene.

"You see, I, much more than James, was concerned about

the inheritance. After all he had been working on the farm all those years, and we had Lucy. It wouldn't have been fair if the new sprog copped for a share he didn't deserve… But I needn't have worried. Arthur was always a fair-minded man and true to his word, he gave the farm, the whole kit and caboodle to James. Instead of James working for his dad, his dad worked for James. It was still a partnership, but James's name was safely on the deeds. Arthur handed it over when he did partly because he'd promised it to his son and partly to avoid James having to pay inheritance tax. Arthur fully expected (and did by a good margin) to live at least another seven years, so the gift never had nasty strings attached. James has done the same for Michael."

"Did Maggie and her son inherit nothing then?" Sara not unnaturally asked.

"Oh, bless you, no. I said Arthur was fair-minded. He also owned a tenanted farm as well as Gamekeepers Cottage with a couple of acres attached and one or two other farm cottages. He turned the tenanted farm over to Maggie in the same way he gave the farm to James. She was to give it to Harry when he was eighteen. You see Arthur couldn't be sure he would live that long and Maggie would only be in her fifties. Consequently, when the time came, she handed it over to Harry. Maggie inherited the rest after Arthur's demise to do with as she wished. I expect it will all go to Harry in the end… After all it's only right it should.

"We all knew though, that farming wasn't for him. He loved it here as a child. Lucy, Michael and Harry grew up like brothers and sister, but he wanted to go to the big city. He used the money he got in rent from his inheritance to furnish a rich lifestyle as a student… and I say this as one who loves him dearly… he was a clever, good-looking boy who let it all go to his head.

"I know he's told you about his marriage to Linda. She was a beautiful girl. All of us, particularly Maggie, were fond of her and thought that Harry would settle down… but we were wrong. I think, from the way he has talked of you, my dear, you may be his and our last hope…" Her voice trailed off and she unnecessarily re-buttered Sara's toast.

Nurse Forster popped her head round the door.

"I'm off now, Mrs Martin. Maggie's comfortable but asking for someone called Sara. I have a few days off so it will be Nurse Porter tonight, OK? 'Bye for now." She nodded at them both and let herself out by the front door.

Although happy enough to hear the family history, Sara wasn't comfortable with Pamela's last statement. She didn't want that weight of responsibility piled on her shoulders. Without question, she loved Harry, but Pam had made it sound as if she (Sara) would have to 'manage' him, maybe in the same way Pam obviously 'managed' James. No… never… she could and would not do any such thing.

Pamela put the small bowl of porridge and a beaker of fruit-flavoured liquid with a straw onto a tray.

"Would you like to come up, now?" she asked.

She didn't, but said she would. She had been nervous of meeting his mother before, but now she dreaded it. She couldn't take another plea to take on the role of redeemer. At the end of the corridor upstairs, Pam expertly balanced the tray in one hand and knocked on the bedroom door then waited until she was bidden to enter.

Harry's mother was sitting propped up in a properly equipped hospital bed in a room furnished with all the medical equipment that might prove necessary. Maggie herself looked very small and ill, but her face wrinkled into a smile when she saw Sara.

"Good morning, Pamela," she said. "And this would be Sara?"

Pamela put her tray down on the bedside table, kissed her cheek and said to Maggie with a cheery smile, "Yes, Sara is here at last! Now then, would you like some breakfast?"

Maggie permitted Pam to spoon some porridge into her mouth, but after a couple of tastes indicated she'd had enough and accepted a sip of juice instead from the proffered beaker.

"Thank you, Pamela. You are kind and I am very grateful… but I know you are always busy and it takes a lot of time to care for an old woman. Why not take advantage of Sara being here with me, and have a few minutes to yourself. Go down and have a nice cup of tea with your feet up. Read one of your magazines in peace. It would please me greatly if for a change you looked after yourself and had a rest."

"Well," said Pam, very tempted. "I could do with getting the free-range eggs in, those new hens are little beggars and hide them under the sheds. If you are sure, and if Sara doesn't mind… I'll go, but only for fifteen minutes or so, mind…" She gave Sara a list of instructions as to what to do if Maggie had a 'turn', plus the number of her mobile which she always carried with her in case of emergencies and eventually they heard the back door shut behind her.

Maggie turned her head towards Sara with twinkling blue eyes just like Harry's, and said, "Pamela is a good soul, but how she does fuss!"

Sara was amused by Maggie's kind handling of her daughter-in-law.

"Now then," Maggie began, "it's good to meet you Sara. I know I am terminally ill and don't have a lot of time left to beat about the bush. You must be aware of who and what I want to talk about." She indicated she needed a drink and Sara raised the strawed beaker to the old lady's lips.

"Since Harry's been home we have spent a lot of time together, just talking, like in the old days when he was a boy. He told me the truth for the first time, as I believe he told you, about his break-up with Linda. I was glad he did, because I'd always known something was badly wrong with his marriage, and why. I didn't tell him how I knew, there seemed little point."

Sara was stunned by this revelation.

"But I must and will tell *you*… You see, Linda and I were very close. I believe I probably knew her better than Harry ever did. She was orphaned as a baby in Romania and adopted aged about eighteen months by a rich, childless couple who lived in Zurich. From then on she had an idyllic childhood, but an horrific car crash robbed her of her parents when she was in her early twenties. She was studying architecture at the time at Imperial College, where Harry was. She was an extremely beautiful and wealthy young woman who had her pick of many suitors, but it was my Harry she loved," Maggie added with pride.

"Harry revelled in showing off his lovely bride. He delighted in her. He was so proud of possessing this wonderful woman and enjoyed the fact that every man in the room envied him when they walked in together. But it pains me to say it, he was not faithful… She often came to

Derbyshire when he was away, and asked what she was doing wrong. Why he was as he was. I couldn't offer much comfort, except to say my father had treated mother the same way, so I had some idea of what she was going through, if only second hand. The trouble was, Harry could always convince her that his escapades meant nothing and she was always so ready to forgive. She longed to have children but wouldn't commit until the time was right, that is, when Harry gave up his philandering ways.

"The Miss Millar affair was the final straw. Linda told me she would not allow herself to be mollified again, the time was right to leave him and it would be as a broken man. I never saw her again. After she said that, I wasn't sure I wanted to. But true to her word, it's what she did." Maggie needed another sip. "Harry has told me that you don't believe Linda went through with her plan to abort their baby… I don't *think* you are right because I *know* you *are*. Look in the top drawer of the chest over there, you'll find a leather writing case. Would you bring it here please?"

Sara rose and did as she was asked.

"Take the envelope that's inside." Maggie's voice was failing. "Open it and read the letter."

Sara unfolded the thin sheet of paper inside dated October 2016, and her heart missed a beat as she read:

My dearest Maggie,

Forgive me for the heartache I have caused you. Many times I have wanted to tell you the truth, that I couldn't go through with the dreadful plan to abort my pregnancy, to punish Harry.

I did not want to hurt you but was afraid as his mother, you

213

would have had to tell him all you knew. If that had happened, he would have come after me and maybe even tried to take Henni away. I couldn't allow that to happen. It was easier to make him and even you, hate me.

I have been happily remarried for three years to a steady, faithful man who loves me and Henni dearly. We both have grown to love him, just as dearly, in return.

After all these years and the true happiness I have found, I have begun to think that the time may be right to forgive and be forgiven.

Your beautiful granddaughter, as you can see from the photograph, taken at her ninth birthday party with little brother Franz (two), is alive and well.

With deepest affection and regret for many lost years,
Linda

Sara could hardly believe what she had just read. Her head was spinning.

Maggie spoke again. "Because of my illness, James and Pamela thought it better that I moved out of my house to live here, where it would be easier to look after me. You can see from the date and post mark the letter was written some months ago. I was in hospital at the time and it was caught up in the letters and cards Pam had bundled together for my coming home. When I read it I didn't know what to do… I have so little strength left… so I am putting my faith in the wonderful woman Harry never tired of talking to me about… That was you Sara… I asked him to send for you. No one but we two know what the letter contains… You must use it as you see fit… but remember you're the one who gave Harry hope that he might have a living child… Give him the letter if you ever consider the time to be right." She was clearly tiring.

"I think I heard the door, shall I go for Pamela?" Sara asked.

"Please... Good luck Sara. For what it's worth, I truly believe Harry loves you in a way he never did Linda. Take care, both of you... I need to sleep now..." Sara kissed the old lady and, clutching the envelope, went first to her room to put it safe in her coat pocket then hurried downstairs to get Pamela.

Actually, it wasn't Pam that she'd heard but the 'boys', coming back from the sale earlier than expected. Sara told Harry she'd just come down from his mother and liked her very much and they had talked together while Pam had gone to the farmyard searching for eggs. Maggie had said she wanted to sleep, so Sara had come down for Pamela.

Harry squeezed Sara's hand before saying he would go up. He was down again in less than a minute just as Pam came through the door, clucking in the very imitation of a hen.

White faced, Harry said, "She's not asleep."

Pamela dropped her egg basket and took the stairs at a run. Maggie was lying still and serene, all the deep lines caused by the pain of her illness had miraculously disappeared. She was totally at peace. Having completed her final task, she had let go of life and slipped away. Harry sat on the lower stair with his head in his good hand.

James came over and gave him a light brotherly touch on the shoulder. "I'll see to everything," he said. "Phone the um, doctor and um, things. If you like."

Harry nodded, stood and announced his intention of staying with his mother until the doctor arrived. He looked briefly at Sara, slowly mounted the stairs past Pamela, who was tearfully coming down, went into his mother's room and closed the door softly behind him.

It took over an hour for the doctor to arrive to tell everyone what they already knew. He gave his opinion that she appeared to have passed away peacefully, without any apparent pain, and muttered something to James about there being no need for a coroner, he would give the certificate himself. Offering his condolences, the doctor made his exit, leaving the family space to grieve.

As it was a weekend, all James could do was cancel Nurse Porter and get in touch with the local undertaker Sam Holburn. Sam was a personal friend who expressed his regret at Maggie's passing and agreed to remove her body to the Chapel of Rest first thing in the morning. Other official notifications could wait until Monday. Then most difficult of all, he phoned Lucy in Canada to tell her the sad news.

Harry didn't come down when the doctor left, but they heard his footsteps go along the corridor as he made his way to his own room. After a good while, Pamela jumped up saying she couldn't stand it anymore and was going to bring him down. James, with quiet authority said, "No, Pamela. Stay! Sara, you're the one… He needs you to comfort him," and he opened the door for her to go upstairs.

She knocked lightly as she reached his room. There was no answer, but it wasn't locked so she silently turned the knob and entered. He was sitting motionless on the edge of his bed with a well-read little book in his hand. He turned his head towards her and said:

"This was my favourite book. You'll think I'm weird, maybe you'd be right, but I've always kept it near me. It's called 'The Teddy-Bear Coal Man'. It's so old, I think it was Mother's before it was mine. She would read this to me every night when I was very young. We'd count together how many bags of coal he would get down from his cart and how many pennies the ladies would pay him for each bag… Not much to it, but I loved it. Now she's gone and all I've got left of her is this book." He tossed it down beside him on the bed.

"She left you a lot more than that Harry," Sara said.

"But you don't understand! I was not a good son to her. I took her for granted and lied to her, to make myself appear better than I was… I killed her with my selfishness."

"Stop there," she said, but not unkindly. "Maggie died of cancer… People don't die from having selfish children, if they did no one would get past the age of thirty! She was old, ill, tired and ready to go. Even if you had been a saint on Earth, she still would have died. Stop beating yourself up… Believe me I do understand, only too well… By all means grieve, rage at the dying of her light, but don't do this to yourself, it does no good… You can't change what's passed… Just remember, she knew you inside out, and loved you warts and all."

He looked sceptical at this last assertion.

"Trust me, Harry. She knew you better than you ever imagined. It's important I tell you what she spoke to me about before she died… it'll make all the difference. She was a wise soul. She told her story to *me*, so I could tell it to you when the time was right. The right time is now."

"I don't think so, I can't take anymore today, Sara."

"Tomorrow?" she said.

"Tomorrow," he replied, defeated.

She hesitated before speaking again, "Would you like me to stay with you tonight? I could sleep on the chair."

It was so reminiscent of an offer *he* had once made to *her* in Menton that he half smiled and so did she.

"Come down with me now," she said. "Let Pamela make us a cup of tea. Everyone is worried about you and you've got to face them sometime."

CHAPTER THREE

After Sam had taken Maggie's body away the next morning, Harry was unsettled. Pamela's fussing, although kindly meant, was hardly helping. The house was shrouded in sadness.

Nevertheless, despite tragic circumstances, work on a farm still has to be done, Michael needed to see to the stock. He asked Harry to accompany him, and suggested Sara should come too and have a look around the farm.

Desperate to be out, Harry got his and Sara's coats and they followed Michael. The weather was chilly but fine, for a change no rain was expected that day. Michael talked to them generally about the need to keep up with modern farming methods and pointed out with pride new machinery that to Sara looked like medieval instruments of torture.

Soon they saw a pretty thatched house that looked as if it had walked out of a Helen Allingham painting. It was enclosed by a cottage garden with snowdrops and the first spears of crocus peeping through the ground.

"That's where I grew up," Harry said. "Gamekeepers Cottage. When Dad gave James the farm, he had this place done up for us. Mum was still living here until she took ill. We loved it. It'll be all locked up now."

"I've got the keys here," said Michael, taking them off his bunch and offering them to Harry. "It's all yours now, you know."

Harry absently took the keys. "Thanks, Michael." He was going to put them straight in his pocket when Sara said, "I'd love to see your house. Will you take me one day?"

"Of course," he replied. "Would you like to see it now?"

"I would like that, very much."

They left Michael to get on with his stock inspection and walked along the path that led to the cottage. Inside lived up to its promise. Old-fashioned storage heaters had been left on a low heat to prevent damp taking over and it felt warmer than it had outside. Its chintz upholstery and antique furniture echoing that of the Manor House gleamed even through its thin layer of dust. It was not as grand, but very cosy with low ceilings and exposed beams. They wandered through the sitting room, the ample kitchen with its pantry and cold-room, and then upstairs. There were three large bedrooms, plus a bathroom that had been created from what had been a fourth. All possessed views worth a king's ransom. Originally the attic had been boarded out to serve Arthur as an office but later transmogrified into Harry's teenage 'den'. Remnants of Heavy Metal band posters still adorned the walls.

'No wonder Harry spoke of his childhood as being very happy,' Sara thought.

They wandered back downstairs. Harry touched the small, polished table that held what his mother always referred to as her 'shiny things'. They were little items, mostly of silver, she had collected over the years. Nothing of great monetary value, just bits and pieces that held memories for her. Amongst them was a small framed photo of young Harry and the family, his dad's old brass pencil sharpener, a silver thimble that had belonged to her mother and her grandfather's ARP whistle from the war, which Harry now held between his fingers.

"When I was young I liked to blow this as hard as I could. It drove everybody mad. It's very loud, you know. Dad told Mum to hide it, but she said she would let me play with it if I promised only to blow it in the far field, well away from the stock. Needless to say I used it too near and frightened the cows so much they ran off all their milk… I got a good hiding for that," he said with a ruefully reminiscent smile. He replaced the whistle on the table, and they sat down together on the feather-filled sofa. He patted her hand.

"Tomorrow's today now. So if the time's still right, tell me what Mum told you."

The conversation had so impressed itself on Sara's mind that she could repeat it almost verbatim.

He listened in silence. So many revelations had imploded in his mind in the past couple of months that he seriously doubted he'd ever had a perceptive thought in all his life. Finally she handed him the envelope containing the photograph and Linda's letter, explaining that his mother had received it only a few weeks earlier. She let him examine them without comment.

"Mum always kept some brandy in that cupboard. Would you get me some?"

She complied with his request. Harry downed his drink in one before re-reading Linda's letter. He then stared at the photograph of his little girl, with her bright happy face, until tears blinded his eyes and he could see no more.

"Oh, Christ! Sara," he said, and sobbed uncontrollably.

She held him close until the paroxysm was over.

***

Eventually they returned to the Manor House. Pamela, affecting brightness, welcomed them back. They were just in time for lunch. Homemade soup with dumplings was served while James tried to lighten the mood by telling stories from Lucy, Michael and Harry's childhood.

"Remember, Harry," he said, "when your dad and I made you the tree house? Maggie and Pamela would make up special picnics and you'd all spend all day there."

"I do," burst in Michael. "It was great, but Lucy liked playing mother and just because she was the eldest, she was always bossing us about. We got her back for that though, didn't we, Harry?"

"Might have," he said.

Carrie asked, "What did you do?"

"We filled her doll's plastic teapot with slugs," Harry admitted.

Michael hooted with laughter. "That sorted her out! She went ballistic, didn't she? But eventually saw the funny side. Took her twenty years, though," he joked. "But we had some great times. Remember the rope swing in the barn and how we'd climb to the top of the bales and dare each other to let go…"

"I remember," put in James, "the time when all three of them decided to 'help' by painting the floor of the new milking shed with some red gloss they'd found in a barn. They were spotted soon enough to stop any real harm being done but what a mess! We made them clean off what they'd done with turps and yard brooms. Maggie and you, Pamela, almost had to use scrubbing brushes on *them*, they were so covered in paint by the finish."

"I sometimes think I've still got remnants under my finger-nails," said Michael, laughing. "D'you remember, Harry, when Lucy made us all go scrumping for pears in Mr Bowton's garden and he chased us off with the rake? He came round to see you Dad, didn't he? And we thought we were really in for it. Then we heard both of you laughing, and it turned out, you and he had done the same thing years before when you raided Old Jim Green's garden for peaches."

"Harrumph," said James with a twinkle in his eye. "Don't remember that one."

"Harry mentioned something about his great-grandfather's ARP whistle," Sara ventured.

"Oh God, yes!" said Pamela. "Maggie and I thought Arthur was going to skin him!"

"He did," Harry said. "I couldn't sit down for a week!"

"Your dad regretted what he'd done though," she continued seriously. "I think it frightened him because he knew he'd hit you too hard. You were only eight or nine at the time. He'd got in four good belts with all his strength behind them, before your mum could stop him. But he never lifted his hand to you again. Kids are funny things, you never held it against him. If anything it made you closer. You could still be a little handful, but from then on, it was your mum who meted out any punishments, usually in the form of a severe tongue-lashing."

"*I* remember those," Michael interrupted. "I was on the end of a fair few of Auntie Maggie's scoldings myself!"

Everyone had forgotten young Peter was there, taking in the stories with unconcealed pleasure.

"She was always very nice to me. Could she be very fierce, Grannie?" he asked.

"Peter!" said Carrie.

"She could be tough when she needed to be," his grannie answered. "I remember the day when your father was born. There was freezing fog all down the dale. They couldn't get an ambulance up to the farm so there was no doctor or midwife for me. It was Auntie Maggie who helped bring your daddy into the world."

Peter had been present when a calf had been born, but never a human baby. Logically, he reasoned, it must be about the same.

"Do you mean she was the one who tied a rope round his legs to get him out?"

"I don't think that's quite what Grannie meant, darling," said Carrie quickly. "Human babies don't need to be pulled with a rope."

'Poor little Peter,' Sara thought. 'That'll be a show stopper one day.'

So the stories continued until the meal ended.

Michael had to get back to work. Despite it being Sunday he'd called the vet out to look at one of his best milkers. He suspected mastitis and wanted to get onto it straight away. "I'm sorry I have to go. It was good to meet you Sara," he said. "I'm not sure I'll be back before you leave but we'll try to arrange Aunt Maggie's funeral for a time when you're able to come." The others nodded in agreement. He touched her hand briefly and left.

The women thoughtfully stayed in the kitchen to do the washing up, leaving James and Harry to go into the sitting room where they could spend some time together undisturbed. They sat on the chairs either side of the fireplace and James, taking advantage of Pamela's absence, filled and lit his pipe with evident satisfaction. Although he had on the surface joined in with the mood of the table, inside Harry felt as raw as the day his father had beaten him.

"I need to go home," he said. "I want to get my suit and some other stuff. I've already asked Sara to take me up with her. It's no more than a few miles out of her way and she's said she would. I'll get the train back on Tuesday, if you wouldn't mind picking me up from the station."

"No problem, Harry." James tamped down his pipe with his thumb.

"Shall I begin to make arrangements while you are away?" he asked.

"Yes… please… Mum was a good woman, but had no religion as such. I know Dad was a believer so it was right for him to have a church service, but could we manage an humanitarian one for her?"

"I'll ask Sam. I'm sure he can arrange that."

"You see," Harry went on, "I don't want some stranger mouthing platitudes. I just want the family who knew and loved her to give their own benediction. Do you understand James? I would like each of us personally to say what she meant to us."

"Of course… um… sorry, but Sam's going to need to know whether you want burial or cremation, like Dad. We could put her ashes by his, under the cherry tree at Gamekeepers Cottage, if you like."

"I think she would want to be near him."

"She loved to hear you sing, Harry. Will you be able to do that for her?"

"I'll do my best."

"Look, you can tell me to mind my own business if

225

you like, but I'm your brother and am certain in my mind that your past troubles still haven't gone completely. Now you've… we've lost Maggie, I want to say that I'm still here if you need someone to talk to. Can I help?"

Harry smiled gratefully at James. "Thank you. You're right, I should have spoken to you before, instead of trying to pretend things didn't really happen. I can't just now James, but promise when I come back… maybe after Mum's funeral… I'll tell you then what a sorry mess of a brother you have on your hands."

"What about Sara?"

"She already knows."

James cocked his head to one side saying, "And she loves you anyway?"

Harry nodded.

"That sounds very good. Don't let this one go, Harry."

"Not if I can help it," he replied.

"Tea up!" It was Pam's voice. "Do you want it in there or the kitchen?"

James hid his pipe behind his back. "Kitchen's fine!" he answered.

CHAPTER FOUR

When it was explained to Pam that Harry was to go with Sara, because he needed to collect some things from home, she flew into a mild panic.

"But his house will be cold… There'll be no food… How can he manage with his bad arm?"

"I'll be back on Tuesday, Pam. I think I can survive 'til then."

Muttering "I don't know!" several times, she plunged into her pantry and started packing a bag with eggs, milk, butter, bread and anything else she could lay hands on. She gave him enough food to survive the siege of Mafeking.

"There!" she said at last. "It's not much, but you won't go hungry."

"We'll go get our stuff together. I'll only need my toothbrush and comb, I'll leave the rest if I may until next week," Harry said.

Sara went up to the bedroom to collect her bag. Although it had been a traumatic weekend and the next time she came would be a very sad occasion, she couldn't help but look forward to returning. Not only to Harry, but also to his family and childhood home.

It took an effort to squeeze Pamela's hamper of food as well as Sara's small bag into her car. The boot of a Picanto is not large. With many fond farewells and calls to take care, she slipped the car into gear and they were off. The pot-holed drive was easier to negotiate in full light but it was still a bumpier ride than was comfortable for Harry with his sore arm. He was glad when they got out onto the main road.

He hadn't mentioned Linda's letter since reading it the day before, and she would not broach the subject until he did. As much to take his mind off it as anything, she said, "Pam told me a lot of your family history this weekend, but there are still one or two things I'd like to know. Would you care to fill me in on when you first got interested in singing? Were you a boy chorister, and how did a farmer's son get to study engineering of all things?"

"Good questions, Mrs Middleton. I shall tell you, starting with the engineering.

"After Dad had left me unable to sit for a while, I knew he felt bad, but I also knew I'd deserved it. I'd quite deliberately blown the whistle in the cow field to see what would happen. Well, to cut a long story short, by way of a peace offering, he raked out his old Meccano set and as I was no George Washington, I kept my peace and accepted the gift. I loved it and found I was really good at making stuff. I had my Lego of course and enjoyed playing with that, but Meccano was much better. The pieces were made of metal and I could construct things using nuts, bolts and spanners. It was so much more real. So there began my life-long interest in engineering.

"Next question. How did I get into singing? Yes, I was a boy chorister. Dad always insisted on the children accompanying him to church every Sunday. It turned out I had a decent voice and was invited to join the choir. Dad was pleased on two levels. It made him proud but more importantly, Mum, who wasn't religious at all, then willingly went to every choral service, just to hear me sing.

"My voice broke when I was about fourteen and girls suddenly became more attractive than Matins. I dropped out of church. When I got to university, taking my new baritone voice with me and mainly in hope of meeting female company, I joined the choral society. To my amazement I began to find singing even more compelling than the girls on those nights. I started to take lessons from a master and progressed well. He was keen I should turn professional, bass-baritones being quite rare. He had contacts and could have got me a start, but I agonised over my inability to master singing in German. Being young and proud, I wouldn't persevere and if I couldn't sing lieder without German speakers sniggering at my pronunciation, then that was that. I would continue with my engineering degree where I knew I could succeed without the frustration and effort. The music world would have to do without me. Dad said maybe I should take a sabbatical and give it a go, and I know Mum was disappointed, but I wouldn't even try... another choice decision," he ended bitterly.

Sara thought 'That went well, I don't think!'

"How about we stop for a rest at the next service station?" she said. "I could do with some tea."

"OK."

The next five miles were driven in silence. He would have to get out of his self-pitying mood by himself.

They pulled into a Welcome Break and took advantage of

the facilities. Sara stood in front of the mirror in the ladies' washroom and sighed. Her hair was all over the place and her skirt had creased badly. She tried to straighten the creases with a damp paper towel, but it didn't work and left little knots of paper behind on the fabric, which she had to pick off by hand. She combed her hair into a semblance of tidiness and went back into the main hall to meet Harry.

He smiled as he saw her slightly frowning face coming towards him.

"I'm sorry," he said. "Let's forget all our troubles over tea and cake, shall we?"

She beamed with pleasure at seeing his return to self.

"Can it be a big, fat, chocolate cake?" she asked.

"Certainly, if that's what you want, that's what you shall have."

"Naah," she replied. "Cuppa tea would be fine," and kissed him full on the lips.

It was a tiring journey for Harry to the environs of York, but Harry's house was in a smart little terrace off Lord Mayors Walk and very easy to get to. A car park was situated at the back of the terrace and she pulled in there. Pamela's provisions were heavy but his good arm was strong and Harry took care of that bag, while Sara followed on.

"Trouble with my sister-in-law," he panted as he lugged it across his threshold, "is she has never heard of take-aways."

Harry had left the central heating on a frost setting so although not warm, the house wasn't freezing. He switched on the lamps as the light outside was beginning to fade.

"How long can you stay?" he asked. "I want to ask you a favour."

She listened.

"It's about Mum's funeral. I would like to sing for her. I have a piece in mind that I think she would like. It's by David Foster, called 'The Prayer', he wrote it for his little boy. I have the music here because I've sung it before at a Christening service. I think though, it might be equally apt for a commemoration of her life. I… I don't want to break down, I mean I don't think I could get through it alone. Will you accompany me as a duet?"

'"With pleasure," she assured him. "I've come across it before too and think it would be perfect."

"How long have you got before you need to get home, because I'd like to hear how it sounds."

"Well, I told Dave I'd be home no later than 7.00 tonight. But look, I *am* teaching tomorrow, though not until last period in the afternoon. I could call Dave and ask him to look after my cat for one more night and drive back tomorrow. It's not far and the school is this side of Ripon."

"That's wonderful!" he said. "But we must have something to eat before we start." They looked at the bag of provisions on the floor. "Do you feel like cooking or shall we put this lot in the fridge and go for a Chinese instead?"

"Chinese, any day," she replied swiftly.

"Right. I'll put this away, while you phone your son." He smiled. "Alright?"

"Alright."

Sara phoned Dave's mobile.

"Hi, Mum, I'm here at your house feeding Bob now, is everything OK?"

"Yes… yes, nothing to worry about, but there's been a change of plan. Unfortunately, my friend's mother passed away on Saturday. Yes, that's right, when I was there. We are going to sing at her funeral and have to rehearse the piece. I'm in York at the moment and need to stay the night to make time to do that. I'll drive straight to work tomorrow from here and be home by about 5.00."

"Why can't you come home tonight if you're only in York?"

'Not an unreasonable question,' thought Sara.

"Because it's the way it is."

"I don't understand. Why are you in York and not Derbyshire?"

"Because he lives here. It's just his family who live in Derbyshire."

"He?" said Dave. "He? Who's this he?"

"Harry," she replied. "My friend, Harry Martin… I have got to go. See you tomorrow, sweetheart… Bye."

Dave was flabbergasted.

"What! A man! What… ?" But his mother had turned off her phone. He was not at all happy about this and hurried home to his wife with the news.

"It's Mum!" he exploded. "She's staying the night with some bloke called Martin in York!"

"Oh!" Christine exclaimed quietly. "So that's who it is." She addressed Dave. "It's not Martin, that's his surname," she explained. "He's called Harry… How could we have been so slow?" She sighed. "You haven't a clue, have you, Dave. Come sit by me and I'll explain."

After being appraised of both Christine and Georgie's intuitive feelings concerning Sara's change since coming back from Menton, Dave was astounded.

"But," he asked, "why did she have to feed me some cock and bull story about his mother dying, and having to stay to rehearse a song for the funeral?"

"Because, my darling, knowing Sara, it's probably true. She must have had her reasons for not telling us before. As far as I know, there are no grounds for their not having a relationship. They're both free and grown up and they've got music in common."

Dave still assumed a rather disapproving expression.

"Darling, *we* didn't tell *her* all *we* got up to, did we? Why should she tell us? She'll let us know all about it when the time's right. Calm down, trust her, Dave, let her live her life."

Back in York, Sara helped Harry finish stuffing the food into the fridge. They donned their coats and walked out into the city, chose a meal for two and were back within the hour. The house was warm now, and after the food they were feeling dozy.

"We do have most of tomorrow to rehearse. It may be better to work at it when we're fresh," he said. "What do you think, shall we leave it 'til then?" He looked at her sleepy face. "Shall we go to bed now?"

She opened her eyes and smiled. "It's very early, but yes."

Harry knew his art well. They made love in what Sara found a novel but incredibly exciting way, his weakened arm presenting no impediment at all to the enjoyment of the occasion. Sara had laughed as she asked Harry the name of that position, and he'd replied "How about *Variation of a Theme on the Back Seat of an Electric Bus?*" Then they both slept in deep contentment until the morning sun shone through the curtains.

After a breakfast of Pamela's free-range eggs and home cured bacon, which was very good, they set to work. Being the more competent pianist, Sara played the piece through on Harry's keyboard. It was musically quite straightforward.

As there would be no piano they knew of at the crematorium, they agreed a key that would be most comfortable and sang unaccompanied, both individually and together, quite naturally finding harmonies that worked well without too much ornamentation. After some hours Harry was satisfied that they had achieved the best arrangement they could, and a final rehearsal later, they rested.

Over a late lunch Sara was instructed to practise certain areas that could possibly do with a little more polishing. He was a hard task master but she didn't mind, she found his perfectionism on these points endearing and energising. She would work 'til she dropped to do him proud.

Time was getting on; she would have to leave. He accompanied her to her car and tenderly kissed her goodbye.

"Take care. Drive carefully, Mrs Middleton."

"I will, Mr Martin."

She got into her car and, realising the time, drove like a maniac off to school.

Home again, Sara unlocked the front door. Bob sprang out to meet her, complaining loudly at his abandonment. No one had fed him and he was in terminal decline as a result! He was lying of course, his dish was more than half-full of fresh-looking meat. He was a drama queen merely making a point. She scooped him up into her arms, and soon he had forgiven her for leaving him, by purring loudly. When she put him down again, he condescended to have a bite to eat, but kept a watchful eye on her at the same time.

It had been an emotionally exhausting weekend. She slipped off her shoes, and put the kettle on while she changed into a comfortable pair of slacks and pulled on an equally comfy sweatshirt. Cup of tea in hand, she settled on the sofa. Bob leapt up onto her knee and she could relax.

"Well, Bob," she said, thinking about the previous night with a smile, "I'm going to *have* to tell them about him now."

Despite Christine's words, Dave had got himself into a lather about his mother. Immediately after supper that night he'd phoned his sister Georgie down in Dartmouth.

"Mum's spent the weekend with some bloke in Derbyshire, and now instead of coming home, she's in bloody York with him," he'd exclaimed without any introduction.

"What?"

"Mum's got a… a fancy man and Chris told me you two knew all about it. Why did no one tell me? I'm only her son, for God's sake!"

"Hang on a minute there." Georgie was beginning to get cross. "What do you mean *we* knew all about it? It's true we had speculated on the reason for Mum's sudden '*lèvre*' since coming back from France, but that was all."

"Well," he said bringing his voice back to a more acceptable decibel level, "you were right. He's called Harry or Martin or something."

"Oh, him," she replied.

"How come you both seem to know him, when I've never heard of the bugger?"

"Mum did actually mention she came across him again, in one of her mails from Menton, but only the once. Chris and I thought it might have been that Jean-Pierre Gascon she talked so much about. We even teased her about him, until she said he was old as grandpa!"

"That doesn't answer my question," he said peevishly.

"Harry Martin was solo bass when Mum was singing mezzo at the Cathedral just before Christmas. He's from York," she explained as clearly as possible. "You were there, it's not my fault if you took no notice."

"Humph... What's he like then?"

"I'd say a very attractive man. In his mid to late forties maybe? A bit mature for me... but then so's George Clooney. Lucky Mum."

"Georgie!"

"Don't be such a prude, Dave. Listen, what kind of life has Mum had? She's been widowed forever and spent the best part of her life bringing us up... Now she's even lost her job! We on the other hand, both still have good jobs. You've got Christine and Billy, Alan and I have been happy partners for over three years. What has *she* got apart from her cat? Don't you *dare* spoil this for her."

"So why did she just not tell us then?" He sounded sulky now.

"I don't know, but I can think of a reason. She knew Mr Martin before France and maybe thought it was just a holiday thing. You know, two English people in a foreign land and it wouldn't last once they got back home. Or even, and this is perfectly possible, that certain people might not take it too well!"

"I just don't like to think of him taking advantage," he said, running out of steam.

"Dave. How long have we known Mum? Under that soft exterior she's tough as old boots. Nobody could take advantage of her unless she wanted them to."

"That's true," he laughed.

"Now then," she said, "tell me how that lovely nephew of mine is getting on." And the conversation wandered off in a different direction.

Sara had not been home long when she heard her front door open. It was Dave with young Billy.

"Gran'ma!" the little boy shouted and rushed over to give her a big sticky kiss.

"Hello. Nice to have you home, Mum," said Dave. "Bob missed you."

"Yes, I know."

"Sorry if I sounded off a bit, when we spoke yesterday. It was a... a surprise. Chris and Georgie knew who you were talking about, even if I didn't. They're well pleased that you've found someone... and so am I. When the time's right we'd like to meet him."

"Thank you," she said, as she extricated herself from her grandson to give Dave a kiss, which transferred some of the stickiness she'd received from Billy onto Daddy's cheek. They laughed and she went for a cloth to clean them all up.

CHAPTER FIVE

Maggie's funeral had been arranged for the following Saturday. Lucy would be arriving from Canada a couple of days before, Sara was invited on the Friday. Although she had been made most welcome the previous week, this time she felt like an interloper. Everyone was very sweet to her but Lucy was the star attraction for James, Pamela, Michael and even Harry. She understood their excitement, but human nature being what it is, understanding is not the same as liking. She was an outsider and felt uncomfortable. She would, she thought peevishly, come up with an excuse to go home immediately after the funeral and let them get on with it.

However, by morning, the gaiety of the Martin family had completely evaporated. Dressed in mourning black they were sombre and sad. Sara felt terrible when she thought of her jealous moodiness the previous evening. The family had needed that hour or two of joy together before facing the dreadful ordeal of the funeral.

Arrangements had been made as Harry had requested. Mrs Goatham, who was leading the service gave a short address about Maggie and then handed over to James who read, on behalf of Pamela and himself, a brief but moving account of the first meeting they had with their beloved step-mother, who had been more like a big sister to them. Stories from others followed, some funny, some sad, but all speaking of great affection. Harry sat white-faced and still, staring at his mother's flower-laden coffin, hands resting on his knees throughout the service.

After the readings Mrs Goatham gave another short address, then invited everyone to close their eyes for one minute, in remembrance of Maggie. This was the signal for the curtains in front of the coffin to close and Harry to sing. He grasped Sara's hand and they rose in unison.

Harry began *sotto voce*, then his magnificent voice rose soaring like a condor over the Andes. It was clearly not going to be the careful performance they had rehearsed. But Sara was musician enough to know when to let him fly alone, when to follow and when to rein him back into the exquisite harmonies which he transposed effortlessly, *molto sospirando*, into the C sharp minor key. No one in the congregation had ever experienced such heart-rending musicality. Everyone was stunned by its beauty. It was sublime.

There was a moment of silence as profound as death itself after the last echoing notes faded away and the piped crematorium music marked the time for mourners to take their leave.

It was over.

The family gathered outside where the wreaths had been laid. Sara stood a step or two back in respect. Lucy said something in Harry's ear, lightly laid a hand on his arm and walked towards her. With a look of great friendliness and sincerity she said, "Come on, Sara. Join the rest of the family."

Harry took and held Sara's hand tightly as the cars drew up to take them home to Manor Farm, for Maggie's wake.

Naturally, he'd wanted to stay until Lucy returned to Canada, but in a few days Harry was back in York. He was more tired than he could remember. The train from Derbyshire had been slow and due to a points failure somewhere along the line, it had been delayed in the middle of god knows where, for one and three quarter hours. In a couple of weeks, all being well, he would be able to drive again. He could hardly wait.

During the longeur on the train, he exchanged texts with Sara, who had left her next day clear so she could be with him before ten in the morning. The thought of which cheered him greatly because he'd missed her a lot. Right now though, it was well past midnight and his arm throbbed like the toothache. He needed to sleep. Grabbing a glass of water from the kitchen, he took two prescription painkillers, sat on his sofa, closed his eyes for a moment and woke with a start four hours later, thinking he was still on the train.

He came to in a moment and was wide awake, went up to his bedroom, undressed and got into bed and tried to go back to sleep, but it was no good. He had been through an emotional mill and the wheels wouldn't stop turning. As the clock slowly ticked past 5.00am he put on his dressing gown and went downstairs to make himself a hot toddy in hopes that would do the trick. When he was poorly as a child, his mum would make him one. They were 98 per cent hot water and sugar, but they'd comforted him and he would sleep.

The stuff was horribly sweet and thin, but he drank it

down, wondering how he could ever have liked the taste, but the magic ingredient must have been mother love, as it had no effect at all.

He wanted to talk to Sara about the contents of the envelope she'd given him almost two weeks ago. He hadn't dared read it again until he was quite alone. Now, he reached for and opened his wallet. He eased the envelope out and saw how its edges had folded over a little to follow the rectangle of the photograph inside. Linda's letter was lightly clinging to the picture of the child that was his daughter. His own beautiful little girl. He needed a drink, reached for the whisky and poured himself a large unadulterated measure.

He couldn't forget how alluring Linda was. How had it all gone so wrong? The physical side had always been so very good. And, damn it, Linda was aware he had 'needs' when he was away from home for long periods, and other women meant less than nothing to him really... But he had no such excuse for getting involved with Beatrice Millar, had he? He could even see now, why Linda couldn't let him get away with it. Why then didn't she just sue for divorce? God knows she had grounds, and that would have been bad enough. Why instead, did she choose to go through with this terrible charade, calculated to destroy him? It was so cold and cruel. Sara thought it was because she still loved him, but he couldn't believe that part of her analysis. How could love make anyone act that way?

Harry took the photograph and scrutinised it closely. God! She was like her mother. She had inherited Linda's fine cheekbones and firm little chin, but that cheeky grin was definitely his, it reminded him of the photographs his mother had kept of him at about the same age. Because she was smiling so much he couldn't make out the colour of her eyes, he hoped they were blue like his. Her hair looked soft and dark and she wore old-fashioned plaits tied with big, white ribbon bows. She was holding her giggling little brother in a kind of bear hug, presumably to keep him still for the photo. They looked so happy. He wondered who had taken the picture, Linda or maybe Henni's new daddy. He poured another slug of whisky.

It wasn't enough just to see this still image of his child. He wanted to hear her voice, her laugh, to see her run and play. All of this could have been his, if only he hadn't been such a fool. Another drink slipped down his throat almost without his knowing.

Then he started to get angry… *He* should have been there for her birthdays, not some usurping stranger. He'd search to the ends of the earth for his daughter and bring her home where she belonged. He was sure there were people out there who could find her for him. If it cost him every penny he had, he would find her. Another drink.

He had Linda's letter, didn't he? That would be enough proof to show he had a right to see his daughter, and if it wasn't he'd have her DNA tested. He could do that, then take Henni to live with him and Sara. Yes, Sara, she'd make a better mother than that callous bitch-queen Linda, who he'd send down to the hell he'd been in for the last ten years! He laughed harshly at the idea.

Somehow the whisky had all gone, but that was good because he needed to keep himself alert with all his wits about him to sort this out. He cast the empty bottle down onto the rug and opened up his laptop to begin searching the web for private detectives who might take up his case. He would fire off emails to the lot of them if it took all night, but for some reason the computer seemed to have developed a will of its own. He only managed to post a few before it went off on its own trajectory. Damned thing was next to useless. In his frustration he hadn't noticed the sky growing lighter, and was surprised by a bell ringing. Harry looked at the clock and unbelievably it was nearly half past nine. He made his way to the door and opened it to Sara.

His eyes were red and he looked haggard. The empty bottle on the floor showed he'd been drinking. On the mantelshelf stood Henni's photograph. He gabbled excitedly about what he was going to do, then ended plaintively by saying, "I'll bring her home, you see. She'll have everything any little girl could want. Don't you think that's just the best idea ever?"

"Sounds nice, Harry, but I think it might need a bit more work. Why don't you go to bed, have some rest and we'll talk about it later?"

"Umph," he replied. "Maybe that might be a good idea. My computer's playing up something rotten... Yes, now you're here, I can leave you to carry on."

That wasn't what she meant, but he seemed satisfied.

"I'm a bit tired... had a busy night... maybe five minutes... I'll go up now," he said.

She opened the hall door for him and watched as he painfully climbed the stairs, her heart breaking at the pity of it all. She picked up the bottle, hoping it hadn't been full when he'd started drinking.

In the otherwise empty wastebasket Sara saw Linda's letter, which along with its envelope, had been viciously screwed into a tight ball before being thrown in. She straightened them out, re-read them and carefully placed them on the table. Then, picking up Henni's photograph, looked at it closely for the first time. She seemed a very pretty, happy little girl. Sara fancied she could see a trace of Harry in her smile and perhaps a little about the eyes, which she thought might just be blue.

Replacing the picture she went into the kitchen. It's a well-known fact that the average English woman's panacea for every ill is tea, so Sara, true to type, put the kettle on to boil before tiptoeing upstairs to check Harry was OK. He was lying on top of his bed fast asleep and snoring, which she took to be a good sign but the dark circles under his eyes were not. She folded the duvet over him, kissed him gently on the forehead as she had done when saying goodnight to her babies, went back downstairs and made her tea. But as Harry had been away, there was no milk in the fridge.

Realistically there was nothing she could achieve by just sitting there but she didn't like to leave him alone, not even just to pop out for milk, so she drank her tea black. There was a mountain to climb over dangerous ground, and it would take careful planning if they all were to survive. She had some hard thinking to do.

It was obvious to Sara that even if he did manage to find his daughter, Harry couldn't possibly hope to gain custody of her. Henni was clearly well cared for and loved, with an adoptive father who had to be taken into account. Not to mention the emotional trauma such an upheaval would cause. The child did not, and probably never had, lived in this country, it was quite likely she couldn't even speak the language. This was the 21st century, no court in the civilised world would put Harry's claims above the mother's. It would merely cause unspeakable unhappiness for everyone concerned and Henni would hate him for it.

The Apple laptop was lying where he'd left it on the sofa. She picked it up, tapped the touchpad and it opened at Gmail. There were six 'bounced' mails recorded. Sara correctly assumed that these were what he had been busy sending when she had arrived. Feeling only slightly guilty at prying she began to read what he had written, but found so many typos and spell-check howlers that they made very little sense. In any case, it didn't matter as he'd mistakenly read the wrong source page. All the mails were addressed to detectorists rather than detectives. She didn't know whether to laugh or cry, as she closed the laptop shut.

Footsteps sounded upstairs followed by a muffled but unmistakable sound of someone being violently sick. She heard the toilet flush at least three times before shuffling feet bore Harry back to his room. She heaved a heavy sigh of relief at the first stage of his recovery. Although not familiar with the symptoms of a hangover personally, she had sat sentinel over two adolescent children who had to learn the hard way the price of alcoholic overindulgence. She'd give him ten minutes, go up, and if he had gone back to sleep, go for some milk. Sara hated black tea.

In the event, Harry came down to her. He'd obviously scrubbed his face but his normally well-brushed hair was spikey from running wet fingers through it. He looked rough and bleary-eyed. With his head pounding like a jackhammer, he sat heavily at her side and said, "I'm sorry."

"Can I get you something? Have you any Alka-Seltzer?"

He nodded and wished he hadn't because he felt his head might drop off.

245

"Kitchen or bathroom?" she asked.

"Kitchen… wall cupboard."

It took her a minute to find the packet, but she soon returned with a tumbler of water and dropped in the tablets, which sounded to Harry like the roar of Niagara Falls. He drank it down. Sara briskly announced she was just going out for some milk but would be back in five minutes to make them something to eat.

His stomach churned at the very thought of food, but he managed a weak smile as she put on her coat and left. Carefully he laid his head back onto the sofa cushion and looked at the photograph of Henni's laughing face. His anger had blown itself out and left him with a yawning chasm of longing and heartache.

It took Sara longer than she'd thought to get to the shop and back, so it was more like half an hour before she returned. Harry was looking marginally less green, but terribly lost and sad. First, she put her groceries on the worktop in the kitchen and then went to him. In silence, she softly laid her head on his good shoulder and waited for him to speak.

It took a while, but finally he said, "Linda knew what she was doing, she wanted to destroy me and she has… Was it all my fault, did she believe I was so beyond redemption that I threw away the right to be Henni's father?"

There was no kind answer to this question, and it was one Harry had to work out for himself, so she said nothing.

"I feel so wretched. It was one thing to want to hunt down a hypothetical child, but she's so real, isn't she? You see." He touched the image in his hand. "She has a little brother, friends, a life… Can I walk in and take any of it away without harming her? How can she love me when we've never met? I don't know what to do, Sara."

She held him close, hot tears of regret welled in his eyes. He blinked them away.

Sara picked up the crumpled sheet of paper from the table before she spoke, "You know Harry, Linda's letter isn't the gloating kind. She seems to have her regrets too, and look," she pointed to the words on the page, "she says 'the time has come to forgive and be forgiven'. She sent the letter to your mother because she trusted her to judge when the time was right, then she could pass it on to you. You've always said how clever Linda was. From all the evidence she certainly is very smart. She's provided just enough information to make finding her possible. Don't you see, if she had decided to forget you, she would have done nothing. If she wanted to be spiteful and torment you, she could have emailed a photo of Henni directly to *you* at any time, or she could have put it in a blank envelope without even a letter, to be forwarded by contacts all over Europe so you could never trace her. She could have driven you insane."

Harry thought she already had, but stayed silent.

"Yet," Sara went on, "she didn't. I think and believe I'm right, that now she feels it's time to take the risk. She's not being cruel, she's being careful, but because it is a risk she's nervous, and couldn't make it too quick and easy for you. But for all your sakes, I'm sure as I can be, she *wants* you to find them, Harry, so you can make your peace. Without doubt she can't and won't give you Henni, but she can give you back your life."

Harry was still feeling fuddled.

"How? What information?"

"I'm going to make us some tea… with milk," she said. "Look at what Linda sent to you, and by the time I get back you'll see what I'm talking about." A few minutes later she came in with the brew.

"Sara!" he shouted, and his head throbbed painfully. "It's her writing… and on the envelope, the stamp! She's in Prague!"

"That would be my guess," Sara said, and handed him a big mug of proper tea.

He had an absurd sensation of himself hanging upside down on a bungee rope inches from smashing into the ground then being pulled back into the air by spring force. It was dizzying relief, unless the rope was unsound, he'd live. He grabbed and opened his laptop.

"Look, I've made a start already," he exclaimed excitedly. "I've already contacted people who might help." He saw the list of bounced mails, and as Sara had before him, tried to read the gibberish. "This makes no sense," he said unnecessarily. "And what's this? Detectorists? Why would I contact detectorists?" He wore that expression of horrified disbelief a small boy might have when a first big lick sends his ice cream falling irretrievably to the floor.

"You nearly got it right, they do find treasure," she answered, smiling sadly. "But unfortunately not the kind you're looking for."

"Oh Lord, what a state I must have been in."

"I think one could fairly say you were 'tired and emotional' when I arrived."

"I'm so sorry," were all the words he could utter.

"You look wrecked," she said. "Why don't I get you a

couple more Alka-Seltzer. Go and sleep it off properly. I'll see what I can do."

"Good idea, Mrs Middleton." He drank down his second dose and feeling more relaxed than he had for a long time, tumbled back into bed.

CHAPTER SIX

In the time that Harry slept, Sara worked on the computer. She began by looking on Facebook and the like for 'Linda Kafka architect', and found the name and work easily enough, but there was no information on line past 2007, the year she'd disappeared from Harry's life.

A basic, 'best way to locate a missing person?' question on Google, yielded a lot of suggestions, most of which were inappropriate at best. Initially she'd shied away from the idea of private detectives because, fairly or not, they brought to mind visions of seedy little men in raincoats prying into dustbins. What could you know about these people from an advert on line? Could they be trusted? Was it really the only option available to them? She feared it was, and preferring to speak to a person rather than an electronic device, starting at the top of the first page she phoned the contact numbers in turn. The first was 'number no longer available'. The second rang off the wall, nobody answered. The third was sorry, but they only tackled divorce cases, not missing persons, and so on down to the second and third pages.

Had she built up Harry's hopes only to have them dashed again so soon? She rang the last number. An efficient voice answered and asked how she could help. Sara repeated her story that she was searching for a woman and child who had disappeared from the UK some ten years earlier. They were believed to be living somewhere in Europe, possibly Prague. Unfortunately, the woman in question was known to have remarried, and her new surname was not known.

The receptionist was very sympathetic but was afraid they didn't take on many missing person cases, certainly not any out of the UK. As the pair lived abroad plus the fact it happened a long time ago she acknowledged it would be difficult to find them. But she had a suggestion. She told Sara that if both birth date and birth surname of the woman involved were known, then someone with a good knowledge of genealogy might be better equipped to trace them. It was not the kind of thing her agency would tackle, anything that included engaging such an expert and foreign travel would be too time-consuming and expensive. It would take months and months to research. Her agency just didn't have the staff. Sorry she couldn't be more help, she wished Mrs Middleton 'good luck' and set down the phone.

Sara rushed upstairs to Harry. He had been asleep but heard her come into the room.

It was her turn to be excited. "If you're feeling better, come down. I'll warm up some of Pamela's soup and while we eat, I'll tell you what I've just been told."

The sleep and the soup worked wonders. Harry felt slightly less delicate and Sara's news also helped his recovery.

"But we still need to find a genealogist. Are you any good at that kind of thing?"

"No. Are you?"

"I wouldn't know where to start," he admitted. "Then

again, here's an idea. There's a whopping great university in this lovely city. I bet they'll have a genealogy department and if not, they'll know who has. We can ask them for help!"

Harry asked Sara if she wouldn't mind contacting them because although it was only a plea for advice, should they ask for more details, a woman seeking another woman would seem more anodyne. A man, he reasoned, making the same enquiries might raise alarm bells, and they might prove reluctant to offer any help. She thought he was being ultra-cautious but understood why he didn't want to risk falling at the first hurdle.

As it happened York did not have a faculty of genealogy as such, but Professor Marr of the Humanities Department lectured on the subject to graduate students. She asked to speak to him.

"One moment."

A minute later, the voice returned.

"I'm sorry, Professor Marr is not available. Would you like to speak to his secretary?"

"Yes please."

"One moment."

Two full minutes later, the secretary said, "Good afternoon, Professor Marr's secretary speaking. How may I help you?"

Sara told her story.

The secretary was afraid the faculty itself could not offer advice on such matters. But she personally did know of an ex-student who had exactly the kind of qualifications that Mrs Middleton might be looking for.

"He has a First Class degree in Forensics, and is an ex-DI of York's police department who's gone 'private'. To add an extra string to his bow he attended many of the Professor's

252

lectures on genealogy. He was an interesting, and in his field brilliant, young man." She gave Sara his name and phone number, then said goodbye. After a moment, smiling to herself, Professor Marr's secretary messaged the young man. 'Hi, Ollie. Expect a Mrs Middleton to contact you concerning a missing person... Good luck on your first private case! Love, Aunt Connie.'

As she was ending the call, Harry impatiently asked Sara, "What's his name?"

"Oliver Cooper," she said, handing him the paper on which she'd copied down all the information. Harry quickly got the number and throwing caution to the wind phoned for himself. Mr Cooper sounded efficient and polite. They arranged to meet for an interview the following morning at 10.30.

Harry grinned widely. "We have lift off," he said.

Sara was working for the next few days so Harry had to keep the appointment alone. Mr Cooper's office was a small room situated above a fancy goods shop in Gillygate. The walls were painted white and all other paintwork, including an old-fashioned radiator, ancient desk and chairs, was in a satin grey colour. An antique wooden filing cabinet also served as a place to set a tray containing kettle, three mugs, a box of teabags, a jar of instant coffee and a carton of long-life milk. The effect was minimal, but not unpleasant.

Mr Cooper himself was a surprise. He looked younger than expected, in his mid-thirties at most, his manner rather pedantic and professional. He questioned Harry about Linda's personal details and why he believed her to be in

253

the Czech Republic. Harry furnished him with all requested dates and known addresses. As to her present location, although not producing the actual letter, explained one definitely in her handwriting had come into his possession recently, with a date and Prague postmark. Ollie entered all he was told into his MacBook. To his relief, Mr Cooper evidenced no interest as to why Harry was searching for this woman and child.

"Will you take my case?"

"I think I will be able to find Linda for you," he said. "I work for only one client at a time, for a maximum period of three calendar months. As to my fees, for the first month I charge £300 plus expenses per day. If I'm unable to locate them by then, the fee drops to £280 a day, plus expenses. If I have not located her by the beginning of the third month, and you wish me to keep on searching, I charge expenses only until the contract ends, as quite candidly, if I can't find her by then I doubt she will ever be found. Incidentally the charge will be plus VAT. If you accept these arrangements then I will draw up a contract for you."

Harry was taken aback by these terms.

"How can you be so sure you can find them in that time scale and with a diminishing financial reward?"

"Make no mistake Mr Martin. I have no intention of working at a loss. I accept only cases that I believe are solvable. The timescale keeps me on my toes. If you are agreeable, I can begin work for you on the 21st of this month."

"Can't you start now?" asked Harry.

"No," replied Mr Cooper. "I have other important business on hand until after the Easter holidays. Would you like me to proceed?"

Finding something in his dry manner that inspired confidence, Harry answered in the affirmative.

"If you will give me your address, I'll get the agreement to you and perhaps you would be good enough to return it as soon as it is signed. Good morning, Mr Martin."

They said goodbye as Harry apologised for his awkward wrong-handed hand shake. After his client left Ollie rang his aunt.

"Thanks for the recommendation Aunt Connie, but unless Mrs Middleton has had a sex change, she has a friend who wants the search doing. He made no mention of her role in the business and I could hardly ask him yet. But he was upfront about having once been married to the woman he's looking for. Whether the child is a prime motive or an incidental in the search, is a matter of conjecture. He seems alright, but I'm not sure he wants to give me all the sordid details… No, I don't think it will take me too long to locate her… A few weeks maybe… but I'll check out Mr Martin, and see where the mysterious Mrs Middleton fits in, before I pass on any information."

CHAPTER SEVEN

After Harry had texted Sara, telling her he was going to engage Oliver Cooper, his restlessness returned. He wished she could be with him. Not unlike a homing pigeon after a long journey, he sought rest, and gravitated to the greatest place of solace in York, the Minster.

There were the usual flocks of visitors being herded around by vergers. The shuffling feet and low voices were strangely calming. He hadn't been in touch with any of the choristers since his accident. They'd been told of course, even sent a 'get well soon' card, which was nice (he found it among a lot of other mail, when he collected his suit for his mother's funeral). The last couple of months had been traumatic. Like Sara, Harry was not a believer yet he found great consolation in the glorious music dedicated to the incredible non-being called God. It was time to get back to the choir. Looking around he soon saw someone he knew.

"Hello Jim," he said.

"Harry!" his friend exclaimed. "Good to see you again. How are you?" He went to shake his hand.

"Other one, please," said Harry quickly and offered his left hand.

"Oh, of course. Sorry." They shook hands with a grin.

"We're really missing you here. We were hoping to do the 'Bach mass in E Minor' at Easter, but it seems that well may have to go by the board. We only heard this morning, Fred Willington's got appendicitis. Selfish beggar," he joked. "You bass-baritones all seem to be going down like flies!" He paused. "Don't suppose you… No… maybe not, that would be asking too much." But there was a hint of hopefulness in his voice.

"I don't know if I'm fit enough Jim, but I guess if you're that desperate, it wouldn't hurt much to give it a try."

"Attaboy, Harry! Can you make it for seven tonight?"

"Seven it is." Feeling much happier, Harry set off home.

The time until Harry's contract with Mr Cooper began might have stretched before them like a desert. In the event it wasn't too bad. Sara's teaching stint would bring her up nicely to the end of term and the beginning of the Easter school holiday. Ripon Cathedral's choir performance of Carl Jenkins's 'The Armed Man' was scheduled for the evening before Good Friday and was well into rehearsal. It meant less free time in the week to be with Harry, but there was always the weekend.

His decision to tackle the Bach Mass meant a lot of work for him too. The Minster performance was scheduled for Easter Saturday and he had a lot of catching up to do. He wanted to hear Sara's 'Armed Man' on the Thursday and all being well he would be able to drive himself there. She'd said she would like him to meet her family. The neutral ground of the Cathedral would provide a good opportunity for a first encounter.

***

Before leaving York, Oliver Cooper had ordered a police search on his new client, ready to pick up when he returned from his important business spent in the British Library, where he had been researching into cases of 'disappearances,' for his forthcoming treatise on the categorising of different types of missing persons. He read through the search report, which was satisfactory, then after re-reading the information Harry had furnished him with, divided it into computer and leg work. He decided to start at the time when Linda had left her husband and her job. She had been a junior partner at Forbes-Green Architectural Design Agency, located just off Goodrich Road in London, and her departure would have caused a stir. That was the obvious place to go and he booked open tickets (First Class this time) for the capital. He also composed a letter to Forbes-Green describing himself as a PHD student from York whose thesis was on 'sympa-thetic' architecture. He requested an interview concerning the theory behind the concept and would like to talk in particular about the work of Linda Kafka.

Next he had a lot of research to do.

By the end of the week he had received a reply. Mr Foster-Forbes would be pleased to see him, if Mr Cooper would not object to a meeting after office hours and suggested Wednesday of the coming week at about 5.45; if it was convenient, Mr Foster-Forbes could spare an hour then. Ollie emailed a reply saying, 'Thank you that would be perfect.'

To be on the safe side, in case he was asked for proof of his identity, he also contacted his long-suffering aunt asking her to confirm his *bona fides* on college paper. She very properly refused, but eventually agreed to supply a blank sheet. If he chose to tell lies he could do so himself.

On the Wednesday, armed with a file full of facts and print-outs of some of Linda's work, Ollie arrived at Forbes-Green's thirty-five minutes early. His police training had taught him that to get the real story, it's sometimes better to go to the bottom than the top but the girl at reception was obviously too young to have been working there ten years ago. She would barely have been out of primary school.

He gave his name, and offered his proof of identity, she told him there was no need as he was expected. Mr Foster-Forbes would be with him as soon as he could. She offered Ollie a seat, gave him coffee and at 5.15pm precisely, turned off the lights on her desk and left for home.

He saw the cleaning lady pushing her Hoover across the carpet give him a quizzical look. He explained who he was and the story of why he was there. She looked interested and he realised he'd struck gold when she said in a heavy East European accent, "I knew Ms Kafka. I knew her very well."

Ollie encouraged her to talk.

"When I was a young girl," she began, "I joined an agency in Romania that promised to bring me to England for work. I didn't know what kind of work they had in mind for me and I was very upset because they wanted me to do things I didn't. I spoke no English and they kept a close eye on all of us. I managed to get away but had nowhere to go and was frightened, hungry and forced to sleep on the street that night. But I was lucky, Ms Kafka found me, she could speak a little of my language and was kind. She took me for some food at a small café she knew, whose owner was also from Romania. She brought him to me and he asked who I was and why I was alone. I told him my story, he told Ms Kafka, and they were angry with the men who had done this to me.

259

He, his name is Luca, and his wife did what they could to help. They had a tiny room for me to stay in and I could have it for no money, if I would to do washing up in the café.

"Ms Kafka had just got married and was needing a cleaner for her new flat, if I would like the job, it was mine. It sounded too good to be true and I was suspicious until Luca told me that Ms Kafka had been born in my country and had been in an orphanage there, until she'd been adopted and taken away.

"It worked well. I lived in my cupboard with a window, did a lot of washing up, and was paid quite well for cleaning the flat. I meet my John, we married, and I left my cupboard to live with him. Because I was no longer doing washing up, when there was a job here, she asked if I would like it, I said yes, and that was fifteen years now."

"She sounds like a wonderful woman. What was her husband like?"

"Mr Martin? Very handsome, very charming… but he was not a good husband… He went away on business and she would be very sad when he came home, because he had other women. It is hard not to know these things when you do the work I do. But, she loved him, 'til one day I saw the light was no longer in her eyes when she look at him.

"Maybe four months later I arrive for work and when I open the door, the place smells of whisky. I see him lying face down on the floor with empty bottles round him. I check he is still alive. Sadly, he is. I have seen this thing before in the old country, so I open the windows to let out the stink and get cold water to pour over his head. This brings him round. While he pulls himself into a chair I get a plastic bucket and push it under his face… the rug was a good one. I go out slamming the door very hard and never see him again."

A man not dissimilar in age to Ollie opened a door.

"Hello, Mr Cooper. Sorry to keep you waiting. I see you've been chatting to our cleaning lady. She's been here longer than any of us and knew Linda very well, didn't you, Eva?"

Eva let the patronising attitude pass, and with a slight smile pushed her Hoover over to the next room.

"Well, I understand you are doing a PHD thesis including Linda's contribution to what we are pleased to call 'sympathetic' architecture. How can I help you?"

CHAPTER EIGHT

Ollie gave his well-prepared spiel and his special interest in the work of Linda Kafka who up 'til ten years ago had been a junior partner with Forbes-Green. He cited one or two of her designs he particularly admired, and after a general talk about the genre, expressed his regret that after she left this practice he could find no more examples of her work, some very similar in concept but none of hers.

"Ah," said Mr Foster-Forbes. "That's an interesting story. I took over when Father retired, but I do remember Linda. I was a spotty adolescent and madly in love with her. She was an extraordinarily beautiful woman and very tolerant of my puppy crush. I suppose she was used to it. She couldn't walk into a room without every man drooling at her feet. I was invited to her wedding when she married the luckiest man in the world, a guy called Harry Martin. I was so envious and remember thinking up ways to kill him so she would fall into my spindly little arms." He added with a slight laugh, "I was only sixteen, at the time.

"It turned out though, that Mr Martin was a rabbit who couldn't be satisfied with just one woman, even if she was the most perfect one on Earth. After a few years she left him. I'm sorry," he continued, "this is nothing to do with her work, but it does go some way to answering your question. Linda apparently had told my father that she was going to leave Harry and didn't want him to be able to find her. I believe they worked out a plan between themselves that she would publicly resign her partnership here, but continue with her work from somewhere in Europe, in case her husband should try to go after her. But I don't think he ever did. I heard he just fell apart, couldn't tie his shoelaces at one point. Served him right, the bastard!"

"Whereabouts in Europe? Do you know?"

"One of those pretty little medieval towns that suited her style. Tongerin or possibly Leuven. No, that's it, she moved to Tongerin and worked from home, until she finished her portfolio for us, then she moved to Leuven as a consultant to, urm, Herge et Auberge. But what happened to her was tragic. To lose someone as lovely like that…" His voice trailed off.

"What do you mean, tragic?" Ollie asked.

"She'd taken an Easter holiday to the Tohoku region of Japan in 2011, you know when the earthquake and tsunami struck that devastated the power plant at Fukushima? She never returned to Leuven and Dad never heard from her again."

"Did no one try to find her?"

"Of course we did. But the scale of the disaster was too great. A huge area of the East Pacific coast was affected. Many people from all over the world were drowned or missing. It was chaos, no one will ever be sure how many poor souls were lost that day."

"But why isn't it mentioned anywhere?" asked Ollie. "Wikipedia just lists a birth date, there's no mention of her death."

"She was never officially recorded as being dead. She is still only a 'missing person'. The authorities did their best… but she had no relatives, friends are only allowed to press so hard. Besides, to all intents and purposes, as an architect she had ceased to practise two years previously and as her death was not officially recorded, it just wasn't news.

"She was very talented, even brilliant in her chosen discipline, but as you must be aware, architecture that is sensitive to its environs doesn't have a lot of kudos in this world. In fact, after she resigned we lost our head of team, and as you probably know, even we became more mainstream and bowed to the demands of clients to build big and brassy. She was not a Rogers or Christo, she just wasn't outrageous enough to make good headlines.

"That's why I was so pleased to hear from you and your interest Linda's work. The time is right for her to be properly recognised, if only posthumously. She deserves to be remembered. I hope your thesis will help this to happen, Mr Cooper."

"I hope it will," he replied.

Mr Foster-Forbes looked at the office clock and apologised because he was going to have to leave, otherwise he would be late meeting his wife for the theatre. Ollie made heavy weather of gathering his stuff together. Foster-Forbes spotted Eva making her way to the broom cupboard still pushing the Hoover in front of her. Apologising once again to Ollie, he asked her if she would be so kind as to see their visitor out when he'd finished getting his papers back in order. She said she would and with a hasty goodbye Mr Foster-Forbes put on his coat, and left.

Ollie quickly finished stuffing everything into his folder

and found Eva waiting for him. Deciding honesty was the best policy, he admitted to her that although it was none of his business, and not the least bit relevant to his thesis, he was curious to know what happened to Ms Kafka. Did Eva never see her again?

She scrutinised his face for a long moment, but he was patient and knew she was going to tell him.

"After Ms Kafka left her husband, she arrive at my house in a taxi. She tell me about her baby and the dreadful thing she meant to do in the clinic at Zurich, and how she could not. She told Mr Martin a lie, when she said the baby was dead. She hadn't let him speak and said he would never see her again. She knew how much she hurt him, and she hurt too... She asked a favour she once gave me, somewhere to sleep that night. She didn't want to give risk to her baby by flying again, so would get Eurostar next day. She stay with me 'til morning. I watch her onto the train. She ask me to go to her flat to see he was alright. I went... I was sorry he was not dead."

Back in his hotel room Ollie was thinking hard. Mr Martin had said that he was in possession of a letter in Linda's handwriting, posted and written earlier in the year, with a Prague postmark. The conundrum had only two solutions: Harry Martin was not telling the truth, or Mr Foster-Forbes was mistaken and Linda was still alive.

If the first was correct, why was he lying? What had the mysterious Mrs Middleton to do with it? He needed to get back to York for some answers. He would need another interview with Mr Martin.

Next morning Harry found a text from Ollie asking him to call at his office in Gillygate at 2.00 that afternoon. Would he please bring Linda's letter from Prague with him, as it was vital to his continuance of the search.

Harry wasn't happy about this. He had hoped to keep quiet about *his* past and was very reluctant to let a private detective rake through it. After all, it was Linda he was meant to be looking for. He was not being paid to nose into Harry's most painful and shameful memories. It took Sara a fair bit of persuading to get him to agree to take it along. She said detectives would have heard and seen everything before and if Harry wanted to find Henni, he should tell Mr Cooper the whole truth and let him do his job. She even offered to go with him, he was grateful but chose to go alone.

At 2.00pm, feeling as embarrassed and sordid as an adolescent caught pleasuring himself in the school lavatories by the gym teacher, Harry braced himself to tell his story to Ollie.

"Good afternoon Mr Martin. Please take a seat."

Harry sat down.

"You must understand," Ollie said pleasantly, "that in any case that involves, however obliquely, a search that may include a child, I feel it incumbent upon myself to have a police search carried out on my client. I'm pleased to inform you that there is nothing in your record to suggest it might be unwise for me to continue. Except for an unfortunate drunk-driving charge some years ago, your record is quite clear." He smiled.

Harry wasn't sure whether to be pleased or not about being checked by the police. On top of his other misdemeanours was he now a suspected paedophile?

Ollie gave him no chance to voice his thoughts.

"Purely routine," he said. "Nothing in your case to be worried about." Another smile. "But I believe that you may not have given me all the information you might have on the circumstances that preceded your divorce. I have made some enquiries and discovered that your wife was pregnant when she left you and intended, as some kind of revenge for your previous behaviour, to have the child aborted. I believe she told you this immediately before walking out on you. Is this true, Mr Martin?"

Harry was astounded, but nodded in affirmation.

"That's good. I like to get these things right," said Ollie totally without censure. "I do wish you had told me this before, it would have saved me time and you money. However, I hope we can get on the right track now. Please show me the letter you have and then explain how it came into your possession."

Shamefaced, Harry took the letter out of his wallet and handed it to Ollie.

Ollie perused it and he nodded his head.

"This confirms another piece of evidence I received. The Maggie to whom it is addressed is, I presume, your mother?" Harry nodded again. "Your mother then assumed the time was right to give it to you?"

Harry explained that his mother on her death bed had given it to Sara, a trusted and dear friend, the only one he had ever given the whole story to.

"Strangely, when I told her," he said, "Sara intuitively thought Linda hadn't carried out her plan. She said Linda would have had to have a scan before any surgery was carried out, seen her baby and fallen in love with it. It was easy for

Linda to get me to believe the lie because I…" Another wave of self-revelation swept over him, "because… I knew deep down I deserved nothing less."

Ollie was silent for a moment before asking "I take it then that the search for Linda is really a search for your daughter?"

"Yes," admitted Harry. "It is."

"And Sara is happy with this?"

"She was the one who phoned the university to ask advice about who was the best person to help us."

"I'm glad that's all clear then. Would you like me to tell you how far I have got so far with the case?"

Harry was amazed and asked him to proceed.

Ollie outlined what Eva and Mr Foster-Forbes had told him about Linda's movements after leaving Harry. Also, because they knew she was in the Tohoku region of Japan when the earthquake and tsunami struck in 2011, and had not heard from her since, her friends believed Linda must have perished in the catastrophe.

Harry turned white, and Mr Cooper conversationally asked if he would like a coffee, which he declined.

"No? But that speculation appears to be unfounded, does it not, Mr Martin? We have this letter you are positive is in her hand writing, which appears to have been written very recently. I understand there was also a photograph?"

"You believe she is still alive then?" Harry whispered.

"Almost certainly," he answered. "The photograph?"

Harry reached back into his wallet, pulled out the picture of Henni and reluctantly handed it to Ollie.

"Tsk, Mr Martin," he said as Harry's face reddened. "You really must learn to trust me."

"She's a very pretty little thing, isn't she?" Harry said

with a hint of pride. "Sara thought that Linda didn't send it to make me feel wretched at seeing what I'd lost, but because she would like us to make our peace, and that maybe one day I could see Henni for myself."

"Smart lady, your Sara," Ollie admitted. "So that's where I came in, yes? You want me to follow the clues she's laid in the letter?"

"Yes please."

"I'll be back to you in a couple of weeks or so. Goodbye, Mr Martin."

It took Ollie fourteen days to track down Linda's address and a day to write a report for Harry, which he named simply as 'Search for Linda and Henni.'

When written down, it didn't look much for almost a month's work but Ollie was pleased with the result and thought he well deserved his fee. He knew a lot more about all their lives but his interest did not extend beyond the brief to discover two missing persons. He made up and annotated the bill, texted Harry asking him to call at Gillygate next morning at 10.00am, then settled back at his computer to continue work on his 'Categorization of Missing Persons. A Discourse on Methods Concerning the Theory of Voluntary Disappearances of People in Modern Society'.

CHAPTER NINE

Harry was at Ollie's office exactly on time.

"Good morning, Mr Martin," he said. "Please take a seat. I have some news for you." He presented Harry with his bill and an envelope containing his report.

"You mean you've done it. You've found them!"

"Of course," Ollie answered, a little querulously. "I accept MasterCard, Visa or direct payment into my bank account, the number is written at the foot of your bill."

Harry looked at the account, which amounted to just short of £9,860 plus VAT. He blinked a little and then opened the envelope and read:

On March 4th 2007, using her Swiss passport under her professional name, Linda Kafka took Eurostar to Brussels, went on to Tongerin and, as agreed with Forster-Green, continued with her remaining projects, working from home. She had rented a flat in the old city where the concierge, a widow named Marta Beirot, with no family of her own, took a motherly interest in her.

After the birth of her daughter Henrietta Margaret on the 7th of September 2007, Linda moved to Leuven, taking Marta in the role of housekeeper and nanny. After three months, Linda returned to work, this time in a consultancy role for the architects Herge and Auberge. As far as is known, none of her new colleagues was aware she had a child.

The lease on her flat was due to expire at the beginning of March 2011. She decided not to renew, but to take an extended holiday to Japan, then on to Australia and New Zealand. She obtained visas for herself and Henni. Marta Beirot obtained visas for these countries at the same time. It is reasonable to assume they travelled together. In the event, in all cases, only the visas for Japan were presented.

They were booked into an hotel in Shichigahama, near Matsushima Bay from March 9 to March 11. A major earthquake and tsunami occurred on the 11th.

Enquiries have shown that Linda, Henni Kafka and Marta Beirot registered at the Sursuri Hillside hotel the day after, on the 12th. Franz Horbach checked in at the same time. They had travelled from the disaster area in the same car.

The next time Linda, Henni and Marta's passports were used was on a flight to Prague. Mr Horbach was also present on this flight.

Mr Horbach and Linda married October 12th 2013 and live in Prague, in the Czech Republic.

Along with her address, Ollie included a photograph of Linda and Henni entering the house.

"You took this photograph?" asked Harry.

"Certainly. I assumed you would want to see evidence that I have located the correct persons."

Linda looked as beautiful as ever. "Yes," Harry said, "that's my wife," as he fumbled to get his Visa card to pay Mr Cooper's bill.

Harry arrived home, his head and heart full of conflicting emotions. Henni was real. It was happening, he'd found his daughter after years of believing her barely formed little body had been disposed of in a Zurich hospital incinerator. He made himself strong coffee and texted Sara with the good news.

He sat down with his drink and stared at the photograph again, this time at Linda. He was sure he didn't love her any more. But he remembered that beautiful body pressed close to his. Her yielding warmth, her perfume and the soft skin which he longed to taste again on his tongue. He tried to push the memories away, knowing he would lose everything if he continued in this vein. But there was a devil inside that would not let go.

Linda had always forgiven him in the past. Why not now?

Why should Sara need to know? He could lie to her, he was good at that.

If he played his cards right, he could have Sara and Linda. That usurper Horbach could be fitted for a pair of cuckold's horns.

Harry had to stop these crazy ideas filling his head. He was aware of the dangers, so why would these thoughts not go away? He took the new picture of Henni out of his wallet, and the devil disappeared. He was going to see his daughter and nothing could be allowed to get in the way. He put the photograph on the mantelshelf and took himself off for a very cold shower.

Devils however, are not so easily exorcised and Harry's particular demon curled itself round a little corner of his heart to lie in wait.

By the time he had dried off and dressed, there was a reply from Sara.

'Wonderful… Great news… see you here tonight about six. xxx'

A long time to wait. To settle his nerves he took out his diary. His company had been in touch asking how soon he could return. His injured arm was healing nicely and he was fit enough to drive reasonable distances without too much discomfort. In short, the time was right for him to take up his work again. Mr Cooper's bill, although well within Harry's capability to pay, had reminded him of the need to earn a living. His people had been patient but he had been absent nearly four months and they needed him back. The all-consuming search for Henni was over, all he had to do now was find the courage to face Linda and be allowed to meet his little girl.

God help him. He was so scared.

What if they were wrong and Linda was just turning the screw on his misery?

What if Henni didn't know he existed?

What might Linda tell her about him?

What if Henni didn't want to meet him?

What about Henni's stepfather, how would he react to Harry?

What did he know about what kind of husband Harry had been?

Did Franz Horbach think Harry had ulterior motives and intended to steal Linda back as well as Henni?'

The demon in Harry's heart squirmed and nodded. These thoughts were driving him mad. He wanted Sara now, not at six o'clock.

'Damn the woman, why couldn't she be here now? They were all the same, never there when you needed them... She was just like Linda, too busy with her own life to be with him...' He ranted on to himself despite knowing his accusations to be totally unjustified. Becoming more and more unreasonable, he allowed the darkest side of his psyche free rein to vent his fear, frustration and anger. In his rage, misogyny loomed larger and larger. He hated them all. Women were a curse on mankind, they brought nothing but misery and pain. He caught sight of Henni's photograph on the mantelshelf and the manic ravings stopped dead. A wave of pure love washed over him and he held onto the picture like a crucifix.

Harry's demon was definitely shaken but refused to stir.

With an effort of will, he replaced the photo, drew his mind back to his diary and began to sort out the easier side of his life.

Always punctual, Harry arrived at Sara's house just before six. She opened the door to him as the car stopped on the drive. Beaming with pleasure, she welcomed him in. She thought he looked a little drained, but that wasn't surprising, he'd been under a great strain recently and it was bound to have an effect. Having calmed down after his outburst, he gave her a great big hug and was genuinely glad to share his joy at finding Henni with her.

Sara had a little surprise for him. She'd bought a bottle of very decent, if not the most glamorous, champagne, to share in celebration. It took two of them to open it, as Harry's right hand wasn't quite strong enough yet to grip the bottle and pop the cork at the same time, but it was fun doing it together.

With all the giggling and noise Bob the cat thought it must be bonfire night. He took umbrage and hid under the stairs. Sara got him out and soothed him, while Harry poured the drinks. The three of them settled onto the sofa with bottle and glasses on the coffee table. The log-burning stove glowed softly suffusing the chilly, late April evening with warmth. It felt good just to be together.

With the bottle half empty, Sara roused herself to check on the chicken casserole she'd made for supper. 'God bless slow cookers,' she thought. 'Nothing ever spoils.'

She laid the table and called Harry.

"It's ready. Bring my glass with yours please. We can finish the bottle in here."

Not generally a big drinker, wine, especially anything of the fizzy sort, tended to go straight to her head and she felt a little tipsy.

"Funny," she said, attempting to disentangle herself from her apron. "Champagne's a lot stronger than it tastes."

Harry nodded gravely as he helped her undo the pinny which had got its strings tied in an incredibly complicated knot.

She smiled thank you. As she sat down and picked up the serving spoon, Harry kindly took it from her hand and helped them both to a good portion.

Having had nothing since breakfast, he was light-headed too, but the food would soak up the champagne. By the end of the meal he merely felt mellow. Sara felt very mellow indeed.

Washing-up could wait until morning. They retired to the

sofa in the living room, the cat having kept it warm relinquished his spot somewhat reluctantly. But not being one to bear a grudge for long, Bob slinked onto Sara's lap and went back to sleep immediately.

Sara, with her head on Harry's good shoulder, looked up into his face. "What are you going to do next?" she asked.

"I don't know… I guess I can't very well just turn up on the doorstep and say, 'Hi, Henni, I'm your long-lost daddy', can I? She probably wouldn't understand a word I said for a start… Might even think I'm a travelling brush-salesman."

"Do they still have travelling brush-salesmen?" Sara asked.

"Don't know that either… maybe they do in the Czech Republic, it's not somewhere I've ever been. What I do know is I don't speak a word of her language."

"That's got to be a bit of a handicap," she conceded.

"So," Harry went on, "I've got to talk to her through her mother."

"Will you get her phone number through international directory enquiries?"

"No… don't think that's a good idea. Better to write. I'll do that when I get home tomorrow. Has all the champagne gone?"

"Just a drop left. You can have it. I think I might make me some coffee." She had forgotten Bob was on her knee and stood up, the cat clung on to her leg for a second before dropping off onto the floor. Sara said something regrettable about cats in general as she staunched the blood. Harry with the utmost lack of sympathy hooted with laughter, and despite the pain so did she.

***

276

They made love that night, and again in the morning. She was missing him already, even as they were eating breakfast, before leaving the house together, to go in different directions.

CHAPTER TEN

Harry arrived back in York around lunchtime. He had a few business calls to make, and in between dealing with those and meeting with Jim from the choral society at the Minster Arms for a pie and a pint, he would write his letter to Linda. He tore up quite a few, before with the help of his demon getting the letter just as he wanted.

Dear Linda,

I'm sorry to have to tell you that Mother, who had been suffering from cancer, died recently, only days after receiving your letter. She was too ill to deal with it herself.

I have a new friend called Sara and we have become very close. Until I told Mother, in what turned out to be her final days, she was the only one I'd ever told the full story to. Mother consequently wanted to meet Sara and I invited her to the farm. They had only a short time together, but before she died she entrusted Sara with your letter, and left it to her discretion whether or not I should read it.

Strangely, when I first told Sara (who is a widow, with two grown children of her own) what happened between us, she was convinced that you would not have done as you said. She under-stood your pain, but could not see you carrying out your plan when it came to the point because, she said, you would have fallen in love with your baby, and were smart enough to work out how to have both child and revenge. She gave me hope, your letter confirmed her belief.

I on the other hand, believed you were Medea, only because I deserved it to be true.

Thank you for contacting Mother, it meant a lot to her. She handed your letter on to the right person, because it was Sara who convinced me that you had given enough clues to enable me to find you and Henni. I was, as usual, incapable of seeing them for myself.

Henni is very like you, she is a beautiful child and if you would permit it, may I meet her one day?

I hope it's not too late to say how much I regret my past behaviour. Your new husband is a very lucky man.

Kind regards

Harry

He was satisfied with what he'd written. The little devil inside was too. He walked to the post office and sent the letter that very afternoon, believing he couldn't fail to impress Linda with his heart-felt contrition.

When Linda received the letter a week later, she didn't want to open it until she and Franz were together. The biggest secrets they kept from one another were simple ones, such as birthday and Christmas presents. Franz knew what Linda had written to Harry's mother, and that this would be his reply. She wanted her husband there when she read it.

She cast her mind back to Japan where Franz had saved their lives. After his car had finally travelled far enough west into the mountains to outrun the tsunami, he had turned off the engine and introduced himself.

He'd said "Hello, my name's Franz Horbach" and held out his hand in a friendly manner.

"Hello," she replied shaking the proffered hand. "Linda Kafka." Although it was not particularly amusing, he smiled and said, "Ha!… Franz and Kafka!"

She'd known immediately he was referring to the Czech author and they began to laugh slightly hysterically. Henni started crying and Marta gave them sideways censorial looks as she comforted the child. But she felt safe with him, they all did.

"We'd better get going," he said. He tried to restart the engine, but the car spluttered and began to smoke. He turned the ignition off again very quickly, saying, "Sorry, no. Better get out," and helped them safely scramble to their feet. Pacing a few yards ahead he scanned the landscape, returning to say, "Good news, there's a farmhouse not too far off" and smiling encouragingly at Linda.

"Henni, Marta, this is Mr Horbach," she said. "It looks like we need to walk a while. Can you do that, Henni?"

The child shook her head. Franz, with a look at Linda requesting and being given permission, asked Henni if she would like to be carried. She nodded and allowed him to lift her into his arms. She hung on tight to his neck as they continued up the hill to a small ramshackle farmhouse. It was further than it had looked, about a mile and a half.

As they approached a man and woman hurried towards them. They bowed to Franz and he returned their greeting.

The elderly farmer spoke a little English and Franz surprisingly knew a few words of Japanese. But the strangers' presence on the hill was easily explained, inside the house the television was ablaze with news of the tsunami. They could see the terrifying enormity of the wave they had escaped. The destruction it left in its wake all along the east coast, including the nuclear power station at Fukushima, was beyond belief. Marta, who had borne it all in stoic silence at last broke down and cried, and was in turn comforted by Henni.

The Japanese couple were very kind and insisted on feeding their guests. While the farmer's wife prepared some food, the two men went back down the road to look at the car. It was battered and scratched but the principal trouble was that the oil tank had been ruptured. When the engine was running oil had continued to pump round, but when the car stopped, the oil, no longer under pressure, had leaked away, hence the smoke. The farmer indicated that they could get it repaired, but to do it today would not be possible. Franz rooted under the front seat to retrieve his precious binoculars and they walked back.

At the farmhouse rice and vegetables awaited them. They all ate hungrily and after the meal Franz explained the situation to Linda and Marta. The farmer whose name was Mr Yamadori and his wife Mari would put them up for the night. There was not a lot of space so she strung up a couple of large hammocks with mosquito nets on the verandah for them. There were only two hammocks so they would have to share. Franz gallantly offered to sleep on a chair, but this was not a good idea as the mosquitoes would have eaten him alive by morning. So on the first night of their acquaintance Linda and Franz lay together, but not at all in the Biblical sense.

In the morning, with amazing ingenuity and remarkably few tools, Mr Yamadori managed to patch the Toyota's leaking oil tank. He and Franz had taken a can of oil to the car, Mr Yamadori poured it in and started her up. It spluttered and coughed but eventually the engine began to roar. Franz let him drive the car back to the farm in triumph.

When the time came for them to leave, Franz reached for his wallet to give Mr Yamadori some reward. The farmer looked offended, so instead Franz took his beautiful binoculars and hung them round the elderly man's neck. He was delighted with the gift. Linda unfastened the necklace she always wore. It was an exquisite little gold and diamond jewel that Harry had bought her to wear at their wedding. She placed it into Mari's hand, who couldn't believe what a wonderful thing she had been given.

They took their leave, carefully drove back down the hill, found a sign to the tsunami evacuation road and made their way to a surviving hotel, which had too many empty rooms.

Franz notified the authorities that he was not dead and texted his family and friends. He noticed, but didn't comment, that Linda did not.

"Your wife will be pleased to hear you're safe," she said.

"Wife? I don't have one of those."

"You surprise me."

"Once or twice, I got near to marrying. It didn't happen though, somehow the time never seemed right. Now I don't think I ever will. I guess I've yet to meet my perfect woman." He laughed.

"Yes. I thought I'd met the perfect man once, but I was wrong. It's a bad mistake to make. Better to live alone."

When he asked Linda when she would be going home,

she told him that they were only at the start of a supposedly prolonged holiday. She didn't know if or when she was going back. And as she had given up the lease on her flat in Leuven before embarking, she was in a sense homeless.

Franz admitted to her later that when he had asked when she would be going home, he'd already fallen in love with her, and was looking for an excuse to keep her near him. So although he didn't say so, he was thrilled to hear what she'd said. Casually, he suggested, after her holiday, she might like to spend a few days in his home city of Prague.

"I own a couple of boutique hotels there. You could stay in one of them while you arrange a new lease on a flat in… Leuven, you say?… That's Belgium, isn't it… Sorry… wasn't thinking… that explains why Henni and Marta spoke in French… What an idiotic thing to say… it would be a bit of a long commute from Prague… I'm talking nonsense, aren't I?… Sorry…"

She'd laughed at him but accepted his offer. If Marta was agreeable, they would spend some time in the Czech Republic.

She asked Marta for her opinion and was shocked at her reply. Marta was not a native Belgian at all. Her family were activists who had got her out of Czechoslovakia during the Prague Spring of 1968 when she was eleven years old. She stayed with friends in Belgium where her parents meant to join her. But they did not survive the Russian repression. She'd always kept quiet about her roots. Belgians, she thought, were not always tolerant of immigrants. She would like to go home, even for a short time. Perhaps find her parents' graves, and her family if any of them were left.

Also, in all honesty, the booked resort on Bondi Beach was

no longer an attractive proposition. They all had a hankering for land a long way from the sea. So, it was decided. They would holiday in Prague and take it from there.

Franz learned that Linda was an architect who specialised in renovations and extensions to older properties. He had for some time been considering 'upgrading' his hotels and commissioned Linda to do the work. It was, he confessed, a wonderful, perfectly legitimate way of keeping her in Prague.

It was not too long before Linda had fallen as deeply in love with Franz as he was with her. Henni thought he was pretty wonderful too. Marta found long-lost cousins and was very content to stay. When baby Franz arrived the family was complete. Linda was blissfully happy except that her thoughts did sometimes stray to what she had done to Harry, whom she left in such dire straits. She had been viciously cruel, too cruel? 'No,' she thought, 'it was necessary at the time.'

A visit to the Puppet Theatre where she'd seen a gross caricature of what she'd effectively done to Harry, shattered her peace. In hope of finding it again, Linda had turned to the one person who may have understood and wrote to his mother, Maggie.

Now the contact had been made and Harry had found her, she was no longer sure she'd done the right thing. 'The whole idea' she thought 'had been a big mistake… the past was past… hopefully Harry had no more than slight curiosity about his daughter… He may even have other children, that she knew nothing about… but there was no going back… she'd reached the Rubicon and had no choice but to cross to the other side. Soon Franz would be home and they could open the letter.' Marta came in with Henni from school.

"May I to go to play with Anna after tea?" Henni asked as she walked through the door. "She's got a new game for her Xbox."

"If it's alright with her mother, of course you can."

"Thank you, *Máma*," she said planting a kiss on her cheek. "I'll go and eat now, shall I?"

"Is that OK, Marta…? It won't put you out?" Linda asked.

"Certainly not, Mrs Horbach," she replied.

"I do wish you would call me Linda, you know."

"Certainly not, Mrs Horbach," she smiled.

Young Franz toddled up to his mummy and laid sticky fingers on her knee. She picked him up, gave him a mummy hug and was rewarded with a soggy, chocolate-flavoured kiss, before he squirmed away to anoint the furniture with more melting chocolate. Wondering where he'd found it, Linda grabbed some wipes and followed in his wake.

CHAPTER ELEVEN

After dinner, with Henni and baby Franz tucked up snugly in bed, Mr and Mrs Horbach turned to Harry's letter. Linda opened and read it, then handed it over to her husband.

"Sounds all right," he said. "What do you think?"

"I don't know. Harry can be dangerous."

"Do you mean he might hit you?" asked Franz, scandalised.

"Oh no, bless you. Harry is not a violent man, in many ways he can be very gentle. That's what makes it so difficult… What I mean is, he has a silver tongue that can charm the birds out of the trees. He has a way of making you believe every word he says, even if you know it's not true. That's how he could always talk me round. It's why I left him the way I did. I was afraid he would do it again and again until he drove me mad. I can't tell how sincere he is. He appears to be contrite, to accept his share of blame, but I'm not sure I trust him. Maybe I made a mistake letting him back into my life and into Henni's."

"This Sara woman seems to hold some sway with him. Do you think he may be merely using her to get to you and Henni?"

"From my experience, I wouldn't put it past him. For her

sake, I hope she's not as big a fool as I was. But that said, I was very cruel and if he truly is sorry, he should be given the opportunity to meet his daughter at least once in his life."

"I think you're right, but my advice is to invite him here only with his friend Sara. We'll be able to judge the situation better if we meet her. Henni should not be there when they arrive. If we think he is sincere then perhaps we can take her to meet him. If he proves insincere, then *I* will be Golem and knock him back to England in a trice!"

Linda tried to laugh. He kissed her tenderly.

"Nothing will spoil our lives. We are strong because we love and trust each other."

Linda began her letter.

Harry,

My husband Franz and I can raise no objection in principal to you seeing Henni, after all you are her biological father.

But we feel it would be advisable, as she is such a young girl, to meet you and your friend Sara first, to discuss the best way we might approach the introduction. Things will have to be explained very carefully, I have never before spoken to her about you as she has never expressed any interest.

She is aware that Franz did not father her, but he is her daddy in a way you forfeited the right to be, and they love one another very much. You must not disturb that equilibrium.

Please forward the date when you can both come to Prague.

Linda Horbach

It was as cold a letter as anyone could receive. It was like a kick in the stomach.

'The bitch! The bitch! How could the child have expressed any interest in him, when her mother had fucked off before she was even born!' The only way Harry wanted Linda's body right now was dead at his feet. He grabbed Henni's photo that he'd had prettily framed and flung it at the wall. The glass smashed to smithereens, he scrabbled to pick it up, cutting his fingers. There was blood on the picture, as he tried to wipe it off it got worse.

"Jesus!" he bellowed as Sara walked in the door.

There was blood everywhere. She got hold of Harry and pushed him into the kitchen, turned on the tap to run cold water over his hands in an attempt to stop the flow. She flung a tea towel at him.

"Clean yourself up! What the hell have you been doing? You're not safe to be left alone for five minutes!"

She saw Henni's smashed photo on the floor and Linda's letter opened on the table.

Reading the letter, she saw the reason why he was upset but was not going to sympathise.

"What did you expect, Harry? A red carpet strewn with flowers? You've got to prove to her that you've changed, for God's sake! It's not just her life you're messing with, it's Henni's too. If you don't scrub up well, she'll not let you within a mile. You can't just turn up, say 'sorry', and everything will be hunky-dory. You're so nearly there, Harry, don't blow it now! Come 'ere, give me that cloth and I'll try to get the splinters out…"

"I've got blood all over her photograph."

"Yes you have."

"I'm falling apart."

"No you're not. You've had a temper tantrum just because someone said something you didn't like, and if you were forty years younger, I'd tan your backside for you!"

He began to laugh, but yelled 'ouch' as a particularly deep piece of glass was squeezed viciously out of his finger.

Sara was formidable when she was angry.

Half an hour and a lot of sticking-plasters later, a much subdued Harry sat looking at the spoiled photo.

"It's OK," she said. "Get your coat and we'll take it to the photo-repair shop in town. They may be able to salvage it for you."

Surprisingly, he did as he was told. The photo-technician seemed to think it could be done, gave him a receipt, said it would be ready tomorrow and would he like the original back. Harry answered "Yes please" to the techie, and said to Sara, "I'd better get another frame."

Only half joking, she suggested making it Perspex instead of glass this time.

"Let's get some tea and cake before I throw *you* against the wall," he replied.

She gave him a withering look and they both laughed.

When he was alone again he composed a reply to Linda. It was neither as fulsome as his previous effort, nor as cold as hers.

Dear Linda

Thank you for allowing me to visit and bring Sara with me. As well as family commitments she is a schoolteacher so our visit will have to be made out of term time. We could make it early July in just under six weeks. Would around the 9th be OK for you?

That should allow enough time to tell Henni I should like to meet her.

Regards,

Harry

His demon shrugged in disgust at its simplicity and honest sentiment.

Linda was surprised when she read this second letter. His first had put up her defences, this made her confused. She couldn't make up her mind, had Harry changed or become more subtle? She had no way of knowing, what she did know was that Franz would protect his loved ones as surely as he had saved them from the tsunami. Such was her faith in her husband that when he'd said Harry should be allowed an opportunity to prove himself worthy enough to meet his child, she had trusted him to be right.

"And," he'd said sensibly as he read the latest letter, "when we let him know about Henni, we knew he would want to see her sometime. It's better we should be in control and be there when he does."

Harry soon received Linda's reply confirming the date.

CHAPTER TWELVE

Harry had no doubts about his feelings for Sara, he cared, needed and loved to be with her. In return he knew she loved him. He was going to meet his daughter in just a few days now. Life should have felt good and it was, until the moment he stopped working or Sara wasn't there, then his demon inside resurfaced. It was getting worse.

He plotted ways to seduce Linda… 'She used to be such a push over, she'd believe anything he told her… but what of Sara… ? He could keep her in the dark, limit his liaisons to "business trips" abroad, like he used to do… but Sara wasn't a push over, if she suspected what he was doing *she* wouldn't put up with it… she'd leave him too, he didn't want *that* to happen… He'd just have to learn to be more careful, that's all. But, what about his daughter… ? What if she found out what her father had done and was doing… He didn't want *her* to know… maybe her mother had told her already what he was like… Her mother was so beautiful… he had to have her again… She used to be such a push over.' Round and round like a squirrel in a cage.

He'd never experienced conflicting emotions of this sort before. He'd done what he'd done without conscience or thought. Self-awareness was still new to him, had he really no virtue at all? He was ashamed of his thoughts and weaknesses. He needed help. Alone, he was not strong enough to fight the demonic compulsion that relentlessly drove him to put everything he had in jeopardy. What was wrong with him? Had he learnt nothing from the past?

His phone rang, it was Jim.

"Hi Harry. The wife's away. I feel at a bit of a loose end and wondered if you'd like to go for a pint."

"You know Jim, I can't think of anything I'd like better."

They met in the White Rose Inn. Jim had already ordered a couple of Black Sheep ales.

"Best drink in the world," he said, taking a heavy slurp before they spotted a table, and took their drinks over. "You look a bit peaky. You alright?"

"Bit tired." Harry admitted. "It's hard going back to work after such a long time off."

"How's your arm doing?"

"Fine. Get a few twinges every now and again, but basically I'm well on the mend."

They drank in silence for a moment.

"So, where's Carol gone?"

"To see Maisie, you remember my daughter? She's going to have a baby. I'm going to be a grandfather, isn't that amazing?"

"Congratulations! That's wonderful. I still think of Maisie as being at school."

"Time flies," he said, "they aren't children long. You don't have any kids, do you, Harry?"

"Let me get you another pint. Same again?" Harry said.

"Wouldn't drink anything else," Jim replied.

When Harry returned and set the glasses down he said unexpectedly, surprising even himself, "Actually I do, Jim. A little girl. She's nine, and lives with her mother and step-father in Prague."

Jim was astonished at this revelation. He had known Harry for the best part of eight years and in all that time he'd never mentioned having a child at all. Harry smiled wistfully.

"I've just found out recently. My wife was only a few months pregnant when she left me. Can you believe I never knew I had a daughter until a few weeks ago?"

"Bloody Hell, Harry. That's awful."

"Not good," he admitted. "But it was my fault Linda left. Couldn't keep my trousers zipped. I did it once too often and…" he shrugged his shoulders.

"What did you want to do a thing like that for? Was she not so hot?"

"Jim, she was beautiful. Every man in the room almost dropped dead with envy when she walked in with me. I still can't work out why I did it. She wasn't just beautiful either, she was clever and just about perfect. Her only weakness was me. She had rotten taste."

"What about Sara. Does she know?"

"Oh, yes. She's the one who helped me find out about Henni, that's my little girl's name." He smiled. "I think it's a pet name they have for her. Her real name's Henrietta Margaret."

"So she called the baby after you then?"

"What do you mean?"

"Henrietta. It's the female equivalent of 'Henry' and Harry is a version of Henry."

"God. It never occurred to me." He sighed. "Sorry, I didn't intend to load you up with my troubles."

"I'll get us another," Jim said. "You look like you could do with it, and I need one myself."

"Just a half, please."

Jim put Harry's half in front of him and asked if he was ever going to be able to meet Henni. Harry told him that he was going to Prague with Sara at the weekend to do just that. It was all arranged with Linda. He reached into his wallet and pulled out the photograph that Mr Cooper had taken of Henni with her mother.

"There they are," he said, handing it to Jim.

"Bloody hell! You weren't kidding were you? She's gorgeous, the little girl's a bit of a smasher too. What were you thinking about?"

"When I work that out, I'll let you know." Harry prised the photo from his friend's fingers and returned it to his wallet.

"You've been married a long time haven't you, Jim?"

"Twenty six years come September," he answered proudly.

"How do you do it?" Harry asked. "How do you stay faithful to one woman? I saw how you looked at Linda, and that was just a photograph. Given the opportunity, wouldn't you take it?"

"I wouldn't get away with it," he quipped lightly.

"But would you not want to get away with it?" Harry was in earnest.

"No, Harry. I love my wife." He looked at his watch and said, "Time to go."

"I'm sorry," Harry muttered. "I've no business to ask you such questions. I've been a bit on edge lately. Give my regards to Carol and Maisie. No hard feelings?"

"Not at all." Jim tried a smile. "Be careful, Harry. Don't do anything else you may regret. Take care of Sara. I hope all goes well for you in Prague."

"Thanks, Jim." They shook hands.

Friday arrived at last. Harry and Sara were taking a late afternoon plane from Newcastle to Prague. It would be evening when they arrived and that would leave a full day and a morning to settle before the appointed meeting.

Linda had booked them into a boutique hotel near the King Charles Bridge and it was there at half past one on Sunday that they would meet for the first time in ten years.

The flight was full but uneventful and as Harry had taken the precaution of ordering a taxi, it took very little time to clear the airport and drive into the breathtakingly beautiful city. Baroque buildings loomed large, silhouetted against the peach-coloured evening sky. The magnificent illuminated castle had escaped from a fairy tale and formed a fantastic background. Narrow, curving, cobbled streets snaked between ancient houses, but most magical of all to Sara's eyes was their hotel.

It was at the end of one of the wynds, with a tiny entrance that housed a modest desk, manned by the most polite and friendly receptionists she could have imagined. The stairs leading to their third-floor room were a medieval stone spiral. The lifts were gold-leaf inside and out. It should have been bling but it wasn't, it was right. On the landing at the head of the stair was the door to their room, which turned out to be a small suite.

Immediately on entering there was a porch containing a magnificent period wardrobe. The door to the right housed the warm, spacious bathroom with a roll-top bath and power-shower. Ornate double doors to the left led into a magnificently furnished bedroom. A tester bed, not unlike the one at Manor Farm, was dressed in fantastic, deep red fabric and set centrally against one long wall. There were armchairs, a settee and coffee table, as well as an antique mahogany chest with drawers deep enough to hold more than two pairs of socks at a time. On one of the shorter walls, two large windows, framed in the same rich fabric as the bedcover, had white nets waving in the breeze from the open casements. The rugs were luxurious and deep.

In the far corner, a door led to a good-sized, smart fitted kitchen. There was a fridge, a microwave oven, a tray containing four mugs, a kettle, four teabags, four paper tubes of instant coffee granules and four individual tubs of plastic milk, and literally nothing else, not even a spoon, but it was an excellent place to put the suitcases. They were both very pleased with this delightful, quirky hotel.

It wasn't so late that they couldn't go out into the city. They needed to eat. The snack doled out on the plane had been next to inedible. At the desk they were advised they could book either at the in-house Italian restaurant or go out for a Czech meal. They opted Czech, and were given a small street map onto which the receptionist drew excellent directions to a restaurant she could particularly recommend. It was very crowded and a surly waiter came to take their order. When guided by his recommendations they ordered pork and dumplings which seemed to put him in a much sweeter frame of mind and he almost smiled. The food was robust and tasty, and Harry washed it down with a glass of equally robust red wine. Sara went for the safer option of mineral water.

They took a walk across the nearby Charles Bridge which, despite the darkening sky, was full of light and people. They passed at least four bands playing different kinds of music and heard so many different languages it was like the tower of Babel. Sara felt excited and not a little decadent to be part of the crowd, and regretted the small life she'd lived in Ripon. On the other hand, Harry's past excesses had been truly decadent and he didn't find it exciting any more. Feeling both tired and sad he suggested maybe they should return to the hotel.

On Saturday they had a whole day to themselves and spent most of it doing all the touristy things like the Astronomical Clock and Wenceslas Square, which they discovered is not a square at all but a big street. They found an arcade where a full-sized, upside-down stone statue of a man astride a horse was suspended from the ceiling. The horse had horribly rolling eyes and its tongue was lolling out and was really quite gruesome. Then back across the Charles Bridge again for a late lunch, they found a café and sat at an outside table to eat and people-watch. It was the most cosmopolitan city imaginable. Selfishly, no matter what happened, Sara vowed she would have to come back, but Harry's mind was on little except his daughter, and fearful anticipation of what might happen on the morrow.

As they left the café Sara suddenly stopped and exclaimed, "No!"

Coming out of his reverie Harry asked, "What's the matter?"

"That museum over there. When I was still at primary school, my teacher, Mr Bunter, who was mad about Jules Verne, used to read us extracts from the novels on Friday afternoons just before home-time. One day he brought in a film from somewhere to show us, and I'm sure it was that one." She pointed excitedly to some drawings on display by the door. "It was a combination of real people and animation, just in black and white, but it was fantastic. I've never forgotten it. It looks like the chap who made it was called Karel Zeman. Please, Harry, may we go and see inside?"

"That good was is it?" Harry asked.

"Pure magic," she said.

Harry gave a tolerant smile and in they went. It was more of a film set than a museum and sure enough, there showing on a small screen, was a scene from *The World of Jules Verne*. Sara was delighted to see it again. Harry found the whole thing surprisingly fascinating and liked it very much. Spidery but precise drawings of airships and submarines in which M. Verne and his friends travelled, appealed to his engineering instincts. It lifted his mood a little to be there. He bought a DVD of the film as a present for Sara, and said he would look forward to watching it with her, back home.

To round off the day, they attended a short evening concert in one of Prague's great Counter-Reformation churches. Inside, dwarfed by the giant interior, before a sparse audience, a small man performed a dozen pieces on a small wooden cabinet-organ. It wasn't that the instrument was badly played, but the sound was too thin to fill the cavernous building. Huge, heavily shadowed statues of stony-faced bishops, stared down from every corner, seeming to disdain the pathetic offering.

Harry was uneasy. Tomorrow, why should Linda not be as cold and obdurate as the statues, when she knew his defences were as meagre as the music. The awareness made him feel weak and enervated. He had no weapons to fight with, she had them all. It tied him up in knots inside. The need to see his daughter was desperate and the thought of being denied her again, frustrated and angered him. To give him some heart, he longed for the music to put up some sort of a fight. The abreaction would have brought relief. In his head he tried singing the Dies Irae from Verdi's Requiem:

Days of wrath and doom impending
…
When from heaven the Judge descendeth,
On whose sentence all dependeth!

He wanted to hear the soaring sound that he, Sara and the choristers had made when they'd triumphantly raised the rafters, at Ripon Cathedral's Christmas Service. The music was wonderful, but the words terrified him. They were as harsh as the bishops glaring down, damning him with their inhuman eyes, and silencing his cries for mercy. He could only listen to the feeble notes of the little box organ, that made no impression on the implacable statuary. Tomorrow was Harry's Day of Judgement, and it was too late to invoke any god to help him.

CHAPTER THIRTEEN

In his troubled state of mind, that night, Harry needed a woman more than he ever had. Sara, powerless to fight against it, perforce gave him cathartic leave to exhaust all his passion on her. When he'd finished, he flung himself back on his pillow, to achieve his real objective of absolute oblivion. She turned away from him, with hand clasped tight over her mouth to stifle sobs, and rocked herself to sleep.

She was awoken before dawn by a half-dressed Harry sitting by her on the bed, gently stroking her hair, who in guilty consciousness said, "I had no right to take advantage of you like that, Sara... I've never been so... so out of control... I'm sorry... I... I didn't hurt you, did I?"

His distress appeared genuine but she said, "How could you not have hurt me? I saw the devil you live with last night, Harry, and I hope for both our sakes you never let him get the upper hand again. If he does he'll destroy all that's best in you, and I don't want to be around when it happens."

Sara was being no more than honest. Harry could find little to say in his defence except "I'm not a saint."

"I wouldn't want a saint any more than I want that devil, what I want is the unique balance of opposites that I fell in love with… I *know* how much you've suffered… and I *know* you like living on the edge, but last night was well out of bounds. Tell me, I've not been acquainted with you long enough to know, was it *really* just an aberration? Or something I should expect to happen on a regular basis…?"

Harry was mortified by her coldness and fears. "No," he cried, "I may be many things but I'm not a…" He could hardly bring himself to say the word. "…a rapist," he ended very quietly.

She answered just as softly, "You know very well, what you did had nothing to do with making love, or mutual exchange of pleasure. It was no more than a release for all your anger and frustration of the past ten years. I understood and there was no point in trying to resist, but it wasn't fair, Harry, and I hope to God it worked, because it was brutal. I told you once I didn't want you to make me any promises, and I'm not going to ask now, but *I'll* make one you can be sure I'll keep. I will *never* allow you such leeway again."

Harry was chastened by her reply. Of course she was right, and he had no words adequate enough to express his shame and contrition.

She looked up into his face with a sadness of expression he recognised, because he'd seen it before, in Linda's eyes, and his heart began to race, 'O Sweet Jesus. No. Not Sara, don't let me lose Sara,' he prayed in desperation. Forcing down the rising panic he said, "I didn't mean to hurt you. I'm so sorry. What can I do to make it better?"

"I ache all over, I need to take a bath."

"I'll run one for you," he said leaping to his feet, and hurrying to the bathroom turned on the taps. He was back by her side in seconds saying, "Anything you want Sara, anything at all… only tell me it's alright…"

She looked at him very seriously and said, "Tea. I want a cup of tea."

Harry let out a little laugh of relief and went to the kitchen, diverted to the bathroom, turned off the taps and soon returned with two steaming mugs of brew.

She'd pulled on her dressing gown and took the cup from his hand. He sat beside her. "I don't deserve you, Mrs Middleton," he said with a little smile.

"You're quite right Harry. You bloody well don't!" She stood up, took her tea with her to the bathroom and locked the door.

He followed her. "Sara?" He could hear her sobbing. He tried the handle. "Sara, please. Please stop." Sliding to his knees, hands falling uselessly to his sides he pleaded, "Please, open the door… please."

When, after what seemed an eternity, he heard her unlock and turn the handle of the door, he scrabbled to his feet and gathered her body close in his arms. His tears matching hers. He had thought he'd loved her before, but this was on another level. Her pain was indisputably his, and in a moment of almost unbearable intensity, he understood that they shared one heart, one flesh, one soul… "Oh, Sara, I'm so very sorry."

The words were the same but this time wholly sincere, and as such, they both believed them.

As the bath water had gone cool, he turned on the hot tap until the temperature was just right. Sara slipped off her robe and stepped into the bath. Harry, in penitential silence, performed an act of ritual purification by carefully washing her and then, assisting her out of the tub, enfolded her in soft white towels to dry. He reached for the Moroccan rose oil bought for her birthday and took her to their bed where he laid her down. Delicately, circumventing the livid marks so recently made on her flesh by his own hands, Harry lovingly and tenderly massaged her body until she drifted into sleep. He covered her nakedness and lay beside her. They slept until a distant church clock chimed 9am.

When Sara awoke she looked deep into Harry's sleeping face, and as if disturbed by her gaze, he opened his eyes. He gently caressed her cheek, not daring yet to risk a kiss.

"OK?" he asked.

"OK," she replied.

"Tea?"

She gave a sweet forgiving smile and said "That would be kind."

When she too was dressed they went down to breakfast. An excellent buffet was laid out in the dining room but Harry wanted nothing except too many cups of strong black coffee which did little to calm his nerves. He was shaken to the core by the events of the morning. Sara too, seared by the power of so much raw emotion, could eat nothing. They both felt as weak and vulnerable as new-borns, but had to pull themselves together before Linda came. Sara suggested they should take a calming cruise on the river. Keen to do something to please her, he readily agreed.

Within minutes, they'd arrived at a boarding point under the nearby Maritime Museum Bridge, and seated themselves in one of the old wooden barges that lined the narrow quay. There were no other passengers, so the pilot in his white sailor suit, switched on the recorded commentary in English, solely for Harry and Sara's benefit.

Sara's concentration was little more than spasmodic... "Vltava, mere couple of metres deep, only barges with shallow drafts could navigate... so shallow, river used to ice over in winter, citizens enjoyed weeks of skating... to facilitate water-trade, weirs constructed to prevent water freezing, end to the winter sport"... etc.

When the commentary stopped, as the pilot navigated through impossibly narrow channels round the old town, her thoughts were all of Harry. She'd had a right to be upset and angry with him. She couldn't have let him think what he did was alright, because it wasn't. Nevertheless, she felt guilty anyway, 'I should have said nothing until after his meeting with Linda, he has enough to cope with today as it is... I haven't helped... I was to blame. I should have found a way to stop him, poor Harry.'

Then she thought 'No! No, that's not true! I *was* right... there was no way I could have stopped him... it would only have made things worse... the situation he finds himself in is his own fault... Tough love. That's what he needs.' She knew that was what she had to give him, but also knew, because she was so hopelessly in love with the man, it would be difficult, near to impossible. *Agony Angst* had not been wrong when she'd told Sara she was living on a razor edge. Yet she was determined. 'We will survive, because I will not let him think me as easily fooled as Linda... I will *not* let him take me for granted... I will *not* allow *any* weakness in my resolve.' Thus getting her mind in focus, Sara salvaged her equanimity.

But Harry had not. She hadn't yet registered the full effect the episode had had on him. He was deeply shocked to have committed a crime he'd thought himself incapable of, and his victim, to his everlasting shame, was the woman he loved most profoundly. Not doubting for a second how close he had come to losing the love of his life, he tried to resolve why he had acted so maleficently. In his work, he would never jeopardise a project by compromising on time or cheap components. In his singing, he gave and demanded the highest levels of musicianship. Yet he had failed to give Sara commensurate care. It was blindingly obvious. He had only thought he loved her, but he was so wrong. In that moment when he held her in his arms and their very souls melded together, only then he understood what love was, and he inwardly swore what was left of his life was hers as of right. He could never risk losing her again, never knowingly and selfishly hurt her, never give her less of himself than he gave his work and music. She was the fountainhead of the Trinity that was his life. Busy with his thoughts he failed to notice when the barge docked and Sara had to remind him of the need to disembark. He managed a slight smile as he asked courteously if she had enjoyed her boat ride too. She answered in the affirmative, adding she especially enjoyed the invisible parrot fish.

"Good," he replied. "Parrot fish? I saw no parrot fish."

"That's because they're invisible," she said, gently mocking him.

"I'm not paying attention, am I?"

She shook her head. "Let's get some breakfast and start today again. We can take it back to our room if you like. Linda will be there in an hour and we need you to be on top form to meet her. Don't worry, everything is and will be alright."

"I don't deserve everything to be alright."

"As Hamlet said, *use every man after his desert, and who should 'scape whipping?*"

"I certainly don't deserve you, Sara."

"Don't get maudlin, Harry. Let's go feed now, today's not a day you can face on an empty stomach."

CHAPTER FOURTEEN

Back at the hotel at 1.30 precisely, there was a knock at the door. Harry, hyper-ventilating, licked his dry lips, strode over and opened it wide. There was Linda. Sara gasped at how elegant and utterly exquisite she was, and thought Harry must have been mad to ever have even looked at other women.

"Hello, Linda."

"Hello, Harry. This is my husband Franz."

Harry nodded his head and Franz did likewise. "Come in. This is Sara."

Both Linda and Franz shook her hand and smiled at her.

"Where's Henni?" Harry asked.

"At home," Franz answered. "We thought it better for the 'grown-ups' to meet first, don't you think so, Mr Martin?" Harry nodded. "I assume," Franz went on, "you used the services of a Private Detective to find us? I thought so. He was very discreet, or so the gentleman I employed to watch out for him assured me."

After a short pause Franz, who seemed perfectly at ease with the situation, continued to address Harry. "I confess a deep interest in this matter but it is not for me to make things more difficult for either of you, by being here. Might I suggest that I take Mrs Middleton, if she will permit me," smiling again at Sara, "for a short tour of our beautiful city whilst you and my wife discuss the future. Mrs Middleton, would that please you?"

She looked at Harry for confirmation, he nodded, and she said, "Yes thank you. That might be best. I'll get my jacket. How long will we be?"

"Two hours. Would that be long enough, Linda?" Franz enquired.

Linda smiled at him and agreed.

"Take care, Harry," said Sara by way of goodbye.

Mr Horbach's behaviour was very affable and pleasant. He asked Sara to call him Franz and if he may to call her Sara. Such a pretty happy-sounding name, he thought. He asked if she had visited Prague before, she answered no, but for something else to say, mentioned the Jules Verne film at the Zeman museum. Franz said it was one of Henni's favourite places. He told her Henni had a copy of the *Hansel and Gretel* DVD, perhaps they would try her with the *Jules Verne* too.

He suggested having lunch at the Art Deco Municipal House Restaurant. "The jewel in Prague's crown," he said. The municipal restaurants Sara had previously visited were just 'greasy-spoons', and she wasn't the least hungry anyway but she felt unable to refuse the offer. They took a taxi as it was apparently a fair walk.

In the taxi, she was very quiet as Franz chatted politely, then suddenly the oddness of the situation grabbed her. Why should Mr Horbach leave his wife with Harry, alone in an hotel bedroom for two hours, believing him to be a man who in the past had always managed to talk Linda round?

You don't leave a canary with a cat, unless the canary has a loaded gun... Was it some kind of test? Oh God, of course it was! Would Harry be up to it? If he failed, Sara knew with certainty he would never be allowed to even see, never mind meet Henni. What could she do to help him now? He was there on his own.

"Please don't do this to Harry, Mr Horbach," Sara said so quietly that he scarcely heard her.

"Don't do it, please not today. He's suffered so much for his past mistakes and admits his fault. It would destroy his mind if he wasn't allowed to meet Henni."

Franz didn't bother to deny it. "I've got to look after my family. I am willing to let him meet Henni but the terms must be mine. He must prove he is more worthy than in the past."

Sara told him briefly how Harry had, without trying to excuse himself, told her the awful truth of why Linda had left him. "Harry may not be a paragon of virtue, but who is? It's how we deal with our imperfections that matters... It's difficult for him at the moment, but he is trying so hard because he desperately wants and needs to meet his daughter. He's so nearly there. Don't put too much temptation in his way," she said. "Please take me back."

Franz, more for Sara's sake than Harry's, called to the driver to return to the hotel. The traffic was heavy and the driver not pleased, but made the turn.

After Sara and Franz had left, Harry sent down for coffee. Linda sat in elegant silence on the settee.

"It was good of you to write to Mother," he said. "She was very fond of you, you know."

"As I was of her, it broke my heart to leave her without a word."

The coffee came and he poured for her remembering that she liked it black with one sugar.

"Linda. You will let me see Henni won't you?"

"I'm afraid it's not just my decision any more. My husband is her stepfather and of course Henni herself will have to allow it."

"Henni. You called her after me, didn't you? Why did you do that?"

"It was a name, as good as any."

"I don't think so," he said. "Despite everything you still loved me, didn't you?"

"Don't, Harry."

"When we exchanged our wedding vows you meant every word and gladly gave me your heart. I did nothing to deserve it, but it was such a beautiful thing I was greedy and took it anyhow, then abused and didn't treasure the precious gift you gave me. My vows turned out to be nothing but pie-crust promises, easily broken. The fault was mine. You gave me your heart and I was too arrogant and stupid to consider I should have given mine in return. I've said 'sorry' to you too many times for it to have any meaning left. But try to believe this, I am truly happy you have found a man who loves you as he should. Tell me. How did you meet Franz?"

"He saved our lives. We were caught up in the big Japanese tsunami six years ago. He got us out."

"A hero! No wonder you fell for him."

"Yes. He really is my hero and I love him dearly. What about you and Sara?"

"I first met her before Christmas. We were two of the

soloists singing Verdi's Requiem. We met again, by chance in Menton a few weeks later. She was quite alone. She'd gone there to visit her husband's grave. He was a seaman, she was only in her early twenties when he drowned along that coast, leaving her to bring up her twin babies alone. It was her first real holiday abroad and I, God forgive me, thought I could take advantage and walk away... But without being anything other than herself, she's drawn what was left of my miserable little heart and soul into her hands. She's saved *my* life as surely as Franz saved yours. Sara's *my* hero. I have come to realise I love her more honestly and completely than... forgive me, Linda, than I ever loved you."

"It's OK Harry, that's good. You said before Maggie died she handed my letter on to Sara. She must have known she was the one to bring you back from wherever you had lost yourself. I couldn't do it. You see, I never wanted to believe you didn't really love *me,* but I always knew you merely loved the *idea* of loving me, which I learnt, is not the same thing at all. We both made a dreadful mistake when we married... I'm sorry for what I did to you. It was too unkind."

"I hated you for a long time Linda. I didn't understand. When I confided the whole sordid truth to Sara she under- stood very well, and because she's a mother herself, told me you almost certainly would have achieved your ends without harming the baby. She meant to bring me hope, but believing you had lied was agony, it was like losing the child again. I was angry and made her cry, but as you know" – he hung his head like a small boy, before looking up at her again – "I've always been good at that kind of thing. She let me have my moment of self-pity, until I'd summoned up enough wit to work out that it's not impossible to trace missing people, I'd had no reason to look before, now she'd given me one. Then she promised to be there for me whatever happened. Your letter came shortly afterwards and confirmed what she'd only believed. *I* assumed you'd written it only to make my life more miserable and taunt me. She put me right on that too. She made me see that you were offering an olive branch, and I'd be a fool not to take it." He smiled slightly, "But why did you do it now?"

"When Franz asked me to marry him I told *him* the full story. He admitted what I had done was cruel but because he loved me, he, like your Sara, understood. You'll think it trite, but on Henni's ninth birthday treat she wanted to go to the Marionette Theatre to see *Don Giovanni*. It was a much-edited version and mostly very funny. At the end instead of the Commandatore's statue calling on the Don to repent his sins, Golem broke through the walls. He was just a full-sized puppeteer dressed up as a stone man. But we had grown so used to the much smaller marionettes on stage that he looked like a huge monster. He took hold of the Don's strings and thrashed him about until he was nothing but a heap of disjointed wood on the floor. I couldn't laugh anymore. I felt I was Golem when I broke you to pieces ten years ago."

Harry remembered how distressed he had been when he saw *Il Trovatore* in Beaulieu. He didn't think she was being trite at all.

Linda continued, "Franz could see how it had affected me and we decided between us that the time might be right to forgive and seek forgiveness. It was hard to make the decision. We would be risking all that we held dearest. There had to be safeguards in place of course, but we felt you should have the chance to meet Henni, if we were all to find true peace and security."

Harry's head was in his hands. He had fucked up so many lives.

Their coffee had gone cold and Linda walked to the kitchen door and offered to put it in the microwave.

"There's one in there," he said.

"Yes I know," Linda replied. "I'm afraid this was one of the safeguards. Franz owns this hotel. I re-designed it for him." With an unwonted flash of humour she added, "The trap door down to the Vltava is just under that rug."

He couldn't resist the urge to take peek, just in case, whilst she was in the kitchen.

She reheated the coffee and sat down beside him to drink it.

"He is a wise, careful man. A good kind of daddy for Henni to have. Your second choice was better than your first," Harry reflected sadly.

"He is, and from what you tell me, yours is too."

Franz and Sara returned sooner than expected to find them sitting opposite one another, drinking coffee.

Linda rose to her feet and embraced her husband.

Her smile was so dazzling that for a brief moment of all-overishness, Harry regretted his plunge into honesty. His demon opened a hopeful eye but quickly reverted to a dormant state.

"We need to go now," she said. "I'm so sorry we didn't have much time together Sara, but we will meet again this evening. I'll introduce you to the children. We will call at five." They shook hands and left.

After bath time, Linda dried and brushed Henni's long black hair and plaited it into two long braids.

"I'd like to tell you a new story tonight," she said.

They had just finished a book by Josef Capek, who was Henni's favourite author of the moment and she had hoped for another one of his stories.

"I have a different one I'd like to tell you tonight. Tomorrow we will go back to Mr Capek. This one is about you, me and what it was like before we even met your *papa-Franz*."

Henni pricked up her ears. This was something new.

"You know that *papa-Franz* isn't your real father, but why have you never asked me any questions about who your real father was?"

"Because I know about him already," was the unexpected reply.

"What do you mean? How do you know?"

"Marta told me."

"But Marta knows nothing."

"I asked her *ages* ago about my real father. She told me that she had never met him, but knew he had made you very sad, and when I was a tiny baby still in your tummy you ran away so he couldn't find us."

"Is that all she said?"

"Well, yes, except that if I wanted to know more, then I should ask you. But I knew he made you sad, so I didn't… Can you tell me my story now, please?"

"Well," Linda said, "you seem to know a lot."

"You can tell me more, if you like. I just never asked because

314

I didn't want to make you feel unhappy, but although I love *papa-Franz* as much as if he *was*, I would like to know about my 'biologitical'… is that the right word, *Máma*?"

"Biological, darling."

"'Bioloв glogiclickal' father," Henni concluded. "Anna's doing her family tree on her computer and I can't get to do one properly if I don't know anything about him. Not even a half one because you don't know your 'biologiclickal' father either, do you?"

Illogical as it was, it sounded like an accusation of neglect. Linda had never known them, so had no particular feeling towards her real parents. But Henni had made her feel a twinge of guilt because it had never even occurred to her to try to find out their identities.

"I'm afraid I can't help with my side of the family, but I can certainly give you some dates and names of your father's."

"Really, can you do that now?"

"In the morning. I promise. Now, it's a bit late for my story, I'll tell it to you another day."

"Will it make you sad?"

"No, Henni, not anymore."

"Then tell it to me now, please."

Linda took a deep breath and began. She told her they'd first met at university in London.

"Was he English?"

"Yes."

Henni didn't think that it was nearly as exciting as when they met *papa-Franz*, because he had been a hero and rescued them from the giant wave.

Linda told her he was a very clever engineer who designed and made huge moving models to go on carnival floats.

315

Henni thought that was pretty cool. A bit more exciting than owning hotels.

Her mother said he had been brought up on a farm and that *his* mother was called Margaret.

Henni liked this too, because her name was Margaret as well.

Linda then went on to tell her he was not really a bad man, but even though he was married to her, he also liked to have lots of girlfriends as well.

"Ah," said Henni sagely, "that's just what Jitka's father was like. Is that what made you sad, *Máma?*"

"It was, my darling."

Henni took her mother's hand and tried to offer comfort to her by saying, "Jitka's *máma* threw her father out. Jitka *says* her mother hit him with the frying pan first. But she might have made that bit up."

"I wouldn't be so sure about that. She would have been very angry."

"Did you hit my father on the head with a frying pan?" asked Henni, her eyes widening in excitement.

"No my pet, I did something much worse and not nearly so funny."

"What did you do?"

"I knew he wanted me to have a baby very much. I let him get me pregnant, and I deliberately didn't tell him but let him find out 'by accident' for himself. He went away on a business trip thinking he would become a father. When he came back I told him you were dead and left him standing by the door as I walked out."

"That wasn't nice, did he cry?"

"I don't think he's ever stopped."

"Why did you want to tell me this story tonight?"

"Because he knows about you now and would like to come and meet you."

"How does he know?"

"Because I am so happy now, I felt sorry for him. After all the years, I thought it was time he knew the truth."

"Do I have to meet him?"

"Not if you don't want to. We could tell him 'no'."

"Will I have to kiss him, if I do meet him?"

"I don't think so."

"He won't try to take me away will he?"

"You have *papa-Franz* to look after you. He's a hero. No one would dare to try to take you away!"

"Do I look like my real father?"

"Maybe a bit, you have the same blue eyes and your smile is very like his," Linda said a little wistfully.

"Do you still love him?"

"I don't need to Henni, I got all the best of him in you."

"When is he coming?"

"In two weeks. Will you meet him?"

"Do you and *papa-Franz* want me to?"

"We think it would be very kind, if you did."

Henni nipped her brow and thought about it.

"I'll do it for you," she said.

Linda bent over and kissed her goodnight.

"Sleep tight and thank you."

"*Máma*, do I have to call him father?"

"Of course not."

"What shall I call him, then?"

"How about Harry? After all that's his name."

CHAPTER FIFTEEN

After Linda had gone, Harry was like a kid at Christmas. "Thank you, thank you, thank you Sara," he said, joyfully kissing and waltzing her round the room, before laughingly flinging her across the bed and flopping down beside her. His face alight with pure joy.

He closed his eyes. When he opened them he saw Sara had led him out into a garden, where two people were seated at the table. One was Linda and the other was a little girl about nine years old. The little girl with long black plaits stood up and walked to meet him, she gave a sweet little bob as she shook his hand and smiled Harry's own smile. He looked at Linda who said, "Henni was getting tired of waiting for you to come and meet her, so she asked to come and see you instead. We hope you don't mind. Sit down and join us for a moment. We are not allowed to stay long. Henni's brought you a present."

Henni brought out a little box and gave it to him.

"I made this for you, Harr-ee."

He took it, saying "Thank you", and opened the box. Inside was a little beating heart.

Suddenly Harry had stopped laughing and his breathing

became erratic, Sara saw his lips turn blue and in seconds he was unconscious. The words 'cardiac arrest' flashed into her head. She rolled him off the bed onto the floor. He was remarkably heavy, it took all her strength to drag him over onto his back and then begin performing the CPR techniques she had been required to learn for school, never dreaming she might one day need the skill. She was on autopilot screaming for help. One of the staff burst into the room. She yelled for an ambulance and language was no barrier to their understanding. The young man raced back down to reception, grabbed the defibrillator, which was kept behind the desk, and was back within seconds to attach the electrodes to Harry's chest. It fired one shock, Harry still wasn't breathing… it fired another and the heart jumped into an erratic pulse. Between them they kept Harry's heart going until the medics proper arrived. He was rushed to the hospital with sirens blazing, Sara distraught by his side.

This wasn't fair. The sudden release from the strain he'd been under was too great. Please God don't let him die. Not now. Not now.

He was rushed straight into Emergency. Sara paced outside until a doctor came to tell her they had performed a number of preliminary tests. He was a bit confused but conscious now. At the moment they could detect no adverse signs of heart or brain damage, although as they couldn't explain why it had happened, further tests would have to be carried out, as there might be an underlying problem yet to be diagnosed. He would need to remain in hospital for a day or two. But as he had received treatment so quickly, all being well, they were reasonably optimistic about his chances of recovery.

Which in doctor speak means he may or may not be OK. We just need to wait and see.

She sat down in one of the reception chairs with a feeling of déjà-vu. Being with Harry had been a roller coaster ride from the start, she felt totally exhausted. Looking up she saw Linda and Franz coming towards her. The whole thing was getting surreal. How did they know where she was? Franz quickly explained that as the hotel owner he had been contacted when one of his guests had been taken ill.

"How is he?" asked Linda anxiously.

"I don't know. They need to do some more tests," Sara answered through her tears.

Linda left Franz to make more enquiries and put her arm around Sara. She led her to the small café area, sat her down and bought coffee for them both from the machine. Sara found the coffee bitter and strong but she drank it gratefully and felt better.

"He's had a bad time recently," she said to Linda. "I don't know if I'm doing him any good. Ever since he met me, he's lurched from one catastrophe to another."

Linda just sat and listened as Sara talked about what had happened since she'd met Harry again in Menton, a lifetime ago in February.

"Poor Harry," said Linda, "but so many of his troubles have been self-inflicted. Maggie always said he was a bit of a handful, from being a boy. He's not going to change his nature, but that's what makes him Harry. I think maybe now, though, he may be less inclined to act on his… 'impulses.' I know this because he's told me how much you mean to him. He loves you as completely as I love my Franz. You are Harry's hero as Franz is mine."

"I don't understand what you mean by hero," Sara said. "The medical team saved him, not me."

"No. You misunderstand. I didn't mean what happened today, brave as you were. Harry told me you gave him hope when he had none, you gave him back a reason to live. For a long time he had been no more alive than the giant automatons he makes. The word 'hero' was his. As for Franz, he did the same for me."

She told Sara in far more detail than she told Harry, about her 'wilderness' years after she had left him. The planned protracted holiday which started and ended in Japan. How Franz had saved them from certain death, but more importantly the happiness she had found with him.

"So you see, Sara, both Harry and I have heroes who saved us, and everybody worships their heroes."

Franz found them and said to Sara, "They told me to tell you, you can go in and see him now."

It was a worrying couple of days before the hospital team treating Harry told Sara they could find no medical reason for his attack. As Franz arranged for them to stay in ground floor accommodation at his other bijou hotel, Harry was discharged from hospital on the third day. Following medical advice, they were to remain for another couple of nights in the city before attempting the journey home. As he left hospital, a nurse gave him a standard booklet written in Czech, peppered with big diagrams telling him what activities he should and should not undertake in the following few weeks. He was also cautioned against flying home, the train would be a safer option, and once back in England he would be wise to contact his own doctor. Almost as an afterthought, Harry was told as long as he could go upstairs without getting out of breath, then having sexual relations would be fine. With that, the nurse wished him goodbye.

In the taxi taking them to their new hotel, Harry, back to his old self asked Sara, "Do you think Franz is putting us in a ground-floor room so I won't be able to practise going upstairs?"

"Without a doubt," she replied.

"Thought so. Good thing my next contract's not for another few weeks but Hell! My BUPA insurance premiums are going to go through the roof next year. I'll have to send you out scrubbing floors on your days off to help pay them."

"Be a damn sight cheaper if you just took better care of yourself."

"I'll let you do that for me."

Sara gave him her schoolmarm face and he in return gave her his cheekiest grin.

"What time is she coming?"

"You know very well. Linda says they'll be with you for tea at four."

"I know, I know. I just wanted to hear it again."

The other hotel was different, but as lovely in its way as the first. It was still an old building, 18th century not medieval, but it benefited from a small private patio area, a sun-dappled garden with table and chairs half hidden by large pot plants, and purple wisteria twined around the door frame.

They had just under three hours to wait. Time is a very elastic commodity, sometimes a minute can seem like forever and an hour no more than a second. The clock took quantum leaps until 3.30 then dragged into slow motion. Sara had ordered a special tea, with little pastries and cakes, which she hoped would appeal to the child, to be brought up five minutes or so after their guests had arrived. It was not to be a prolonged visit, after all Harry was not fully fit and Henni might well be feeling as nervous as he.

He was sitting in the patio garden trying to keep calm by reading a cheap thriller a former English guest must have left on the bookshelf. At 3.50 when Sara heard footsteps outside, she didn't wait for them to knock but opened the door and there was Henni holding her mother's hand. She beckoned them in and pointed to the patio. Linda nodded in understanding and thanks as they tiptoed over. Harry looked up and saw them. A slow smile mingled with disbelief spread over his face when he looked at his daughter, and his blue eyes shone as bright as any star.

He whispered, "Hello."

The child was clinging tight to Linda's hand, her face registering nothing as she stared at her real daddy. She was assessing him and first impressions were not unfavourable, she didn't find him repulsive, in fact he was rather good-looking. Maybe even as good-looking, but not as big and strong as *papa-Franz*. She heard her mother ask if she was going to say anything. Circumstances had dictated that Henni had grown up tri-lingual, she spoke French, English and Czech with almost equal fluency. Looking at Linda, she asked in Czech what she should say. Linda answered, also in Czech, that maybe she should say 'hello' too.

Henni held out her hand to shake Harry's and said, "Hello, Harr-ee, I am your daughter, Henni Horbach. How are you?"

He took her little fingers and they exchanged a very formal handshake.

"I am very well, thank you. It was good of you to come."

Henni's face broke into a smile and she sat down on the chair next to his.

Sara stood at the door of the patio.

"Have you met my friend Sara, Henni?"

"Oh, yes. She came to my house when you were in hospital. She told me lots of things. She is a teacher and she likes to sing, and that you like to sing, and that you met each other when you went to sing in a cath… cathee-drill, that is the name for a big church. I sing at my school. I too am very good," she said with no attempt at false modesty.

There was a knock at the door and a waiter brought in a tray laden with the most scrumptious pastries, both savoury and sweet. A second waiter's tray held a large tea pot, cups, saucers, milk, sugar, spoons and a bottle of ice-cold, real lemonade for little Miss Horbach.

It was a very jolly tea party. Once she had started, Henni talked almost all of the time. She told him about school, her best friend Anna and the family trees they were making, and that she had a little brother who could sometimes be quite naughty. Harry cherished her every word. Despite her looking so like her mother, it was clear that Henni had inherited her father's easy charm.

She was a delightful, very lovable child who had Harry sitting in the palm of her hand. At 5.30 Linda said they must be going, as daddy and baby Franz would be missing them.

"May we see Harr-ee again tomorrow, please, *Máma?*"

Linda hesitated. "I don't know…"

Henni said something in Czech which neither Harry nor

Sara understood. Linda answered rather sharply in the same language and Henni had a sulky look on her face.

"Say goodbye, Henni," Linda continued, this time in English.

Henni politely shook hands with Sara and Harry and said 'Goodbye.' Then quite suddenly before Linda could stop her she gave Harry a kiss. Linda forced a smile, took Henni's hand and spoke to her quite crossly as they left the hotel room.

Reactions to the visit varied. Henni rather liked her real father and especially enjoyed the fact that she could call him 'Harry'. To call him daddy would be sooo babyish. She looked forward to telling her friends Anna and Jitka all about *Harr-ee*. What *Harr-ee* looked like. What *Harr-ee* did, how she and *Harr-ee* had talked together for *ages*. She hoped he would buy her a present before he left. When she asked to go back tomorrow, *Máma* nearly spoilt it by getting cross, so she gave him a kiss. He'd definitely get her something after that.

Linda was rather less insouciant. She worried that Henni would get too fond of him. She could see he was completely enamoured of his daughter. She didn't want them to get too close, it would create difficulties and upset Franz. Although Harry had been on his best behaviour all through tea, Linda still didn't fully trust him. She was very afraid he might try to steal Henni's affection from them.

Harry was simply enchanted by her. She was everything he had hoped and imagined she would be. He couldn't envisage being without her again. He knew it would be easy to get Henni to love him, then she would make Linda and Franz see him as often as she wanted. Perhaps he could have her visit him in York. He had pretty dreams of taking her round the old city, and casually bumping into Jim just to show her off.

As for Sara, she had a lot of experience dealing with children, her own and hundreds she had taught over the years. Her assessment of Harry's daughter was not altogether as sanguine as his. Sara's mum had an expression she used about such charmers, she'd smile and say, 'That one will break a few hearts one day.' The fear was, that in this case it might just be possible. Henni was an extremely pretty girl full of winning ways, with all the confidence that comes from being a well-loved precious child and, in Sara's opinion, a mercenary streak a mile wide. Not too long ago, she'd heard a similar natured little girl laughingly referred to as 'petite coquette'. In this situation it was not something to joke about, more like a lighted match in a dynamite factory. Henni could quite inadvertently blow everyone's world, including her own, to pieces.

'Well?" Harry asked Sara.

"She's a cute little thing," she answered, and he glowed with pride.

"She is, isn't she?" The smile faded from his lips, "I wonder what it was her mother said to her?"

Sara hadn't realised Harry had heard Linda's obviously short reply.

She looked at him, and her heart melted. All previous 'tough' resolves evaporated as she thought, 'What does it matter? I love him and a little dissembling on small points is neither here nor there.' "I think," she said, "Henni enjoyed her time with you so much she forgot you'd been unwell, so asked to stay a little longer. Linda would've had to remind her they shouldn't tire you." At least the first part of the statement was true.

"Yes, probably that was it," he replied and lapsed back into his rose-tinted dreams.

Actually, Sara had a very good idea of what was going on in Linda's head. There was no doubt Henni wanted to stay, but it wasn't care of Harry's health that caused her sharp words and quick retreat.

Later that evening Harry wanted to go out, so they decided to take a short stroll by the river, no more than 100 metres away. The weather was warm and pleasant, the crowds of the day largely gone and finding a vacant bench, they sat down to watch the swan-shaped pedalos which with no apparent effort glided their occupants smoothly and silently across the water.

After a while Sara remarked, "That looks like fun."

"Have you ever been in one?" he asked.

"Just the once, thank you," she said, half smiling at the memory of a chaotic ride with the twins.

"Then you'll know, they're bloody hard work," he said. "Stone Age engineering. It may look fun and easy but you've got to know how to handle them, they're difficult to steer. Too often you end up on the bank or crashing into another boat. Even if you're lucky and nothing really bad happens, you end up with a wet backside and cramp in your legs."

He waited a moment before asking his question.

"Do you think they will let me see her again? Did it go well? I thought it went well. She was everything I'd dreamed she would be. She was perfect… I thought I'd be satisfied to meet her just once, but that was foolish and naive, wasn't it? I want to take her home… take her and keep her with me… It's my turn, Sara! You know, I could make her want to come, it wouldn't be so difficult. She's such a sparky little thing, she would be great to have around. Her English is very good, she'd have no trouble on that score. Linda should never have stolen her like that. She's my daughter too! I have a right to know her… to take care of her, provide for her, to be a father to her."

There was a long silence before he continued, "But, that's the problem, isn't it? They're frightened. They can't bear the thought of losing her, and I can't blame them. They love her as much as I do, and it's so hard for me to face the fact that I haven't a clue how to look after a child. Oh, I could try to learn, but at best I could only offer Henni nothing more than she's got already or, what's more likely, whilst I'm learning I might wreck her life completely. It's not worth the risk. I want her to, but she doesn't need me."

He looked over to the pedalos. "It's breaking me up, because for everyone's sake, particularly Henni's, I mustn't even try. My 'rights' aren't worth a damn in comparison to the damage they might do. You know only too well from recent experience, Sara, how thoroughly self-centred and thoughtless I can be. In my defence, I honestly didn't know myself. But I do now, and realise that what I want doesn't come into the equation, Henni's already safe and happy with Linda and Franz."

She waited for him to speak again.

"You knew it would be like this, didn't you?" he said. "You tried to warn me. Don't you ever get sick of being right? I'm sick of you being right. No, no I don't mean that, I mean, I'm sick of *me* being so *wrong*. Do you believe I should just go away and let her forget me?"

"She'll never forget you, you're her father, Harry. It's not for me to say what decision you should make. You've already worked out what you think is best for her welfare, it's up to you whether or not you listen to your own advice."

"I don't think I've done a purely selfless act in my entire life. This would be a first. Help me to do the right thing, Sara."

She took his hand in hers and said, "You will, because you're a far better man than you give yourself credit for, Harry Martin," and gently kissed him.

They left Prague without a further visit from Henni, who was more put out at missing a present than anything else. Linda, her husband and Harry met again at the train station. She thanked him from the bottom of her heart because she knew how much it was hurting him to leave. She promised however, that now they had met, Henni should not be allowed to forget him. When she was older and the time was right, Linda would tell her just what a good and loving father he had proved to be.

Linda briefly embraced him and Franz shook his hand when they said goodbye. Sara had not joined him for this meeting. She had waited outside and watching them leave saw a tear steal down Linda's cheek as Franz's comforting arm supported her to the car.

Harry took a few moments to appear. There was nothing to be said. He took her hand and they walked onto the platform to board the train that would take them back. First for an overnight stop at Brussels, on to London and then, instead of going straight home, they went to Manor Farm where, a sadder and wiser man, he showed Henni's photo to his family and told them about his meeting with his daughter.

He left Sara with Pam while he called at Gamekeepers Cottage to collect a few things.

Back home in York, Harry bought Henni a present of a musical box. It was 20cm high, 13cm wide and 6.5cm deep, with a glass front and a drawer at the bottom. The sides and drawer front were covered in red, yellow and blue striped paper with gold stars. The inside of the glass had been painted to depict a set of blue tie-back stage curtains. A flat cut-out Pierrot figure in a red and blue spangled costume was pinned through his heart to the back of the black stage, his waist and knees riveted, to make him move when the music played. Henni could start the melody from Humperdinck's *Hansel and Gretel*, any time she wanted to see her Pierrot dance, just by opening the drawer.

Inside, all wrapped in pink tissue paper, Harry placed his great-grandpa's ARP whistle, his mother's silver thimble that had belonged to her mother before her, the small brass pencil sharpener that had been his father's and a tiny silver-framed photograph of himself as a baby with his parents. He sent it special delivery to Prague, leaving it to Linda to tell their daughter anything she could remember about the stories behind the gifts.

In return, together with a 'thank-you' letter from Henni, he and Sara received an invitation to visit Prague again the following spring.

PART THREE

A BETTER LIFE

When the door of happiness closes, another opens; but often we look so long at the closed door that we do not see the one which has been opened for us.
Helen Keller, 'We Bereaved' (1929)

CHAPTER ONE

Prague

Henni was feeling rather cross because her parents had decided she was too young to be given full access to Twitter and Facebook on her computer. For goodness' sake, she had turned fourteen and would soon be starting secondary school. All of her friends were allowed. The trouble was, her stepfather thought she was still a child, and her mother always agreed with what he said.

She was sure her real father wouldn't be so strict. She'd like to go to visit his home in England one day. Since she was nine, he had visited Prague each year and stayed for a whole week at one of her stepfather's hotels. He'd bring his partner Sara with him, she was nice, but he was lovely.

The musical box that looked like a theatre, which he had sent to her as a present after his first visit, stood on her dressing table. She set the dancer moving by opening the drawer at the bottom. The music was like him, exotic and magical, she loved it. She knew that the little objects inside had belonged to his mother, Maggie, but not the full significance of his choice. The tiny photograph was easy to understand, but the whistle was still a complete mystery. As she was going to sleep sometimes, she would make up stories in her head about them. She'd liked the mystery of not knowing, but now she was older she might ask for the real stories, maybe next time he came.

"Henni," came a voice from downstairs. It was her stepfather, to whom from the age of three she had given the pet name *papa-Franz*. Although they loved each other dearly, she thought he was being very unreasonable about the internet, in consequence her reply was somewhat sulky.

"Yes?"

"Anna's called to see you." Anna was Henni's best friend, so that was good. Forgetting her bad mood, she went downstairs and even managed a civil look at *papa-Franz*.

"Anna wants to know if you would like to go to the cinema then have a sleep over at her house tonight. Apparently she has something special to show you, but she won't tell me what it is." He smiled.

"Cool." Henni said, "May I go, please?"

"I don't see why not," he replied. "Don't forget your toothbrush," he reminded her as they both made off upstairs to collect her pyjamas. For Anna's benefit, Henni rolled her eyes up to heaven, while Anna grimaced in sympathy.

"I'll tell *Máma* then, shall I?" Franz added.

"Yes please," Henni called, and remembering her manners, turned back downstairs to kiss him on the cheek.

"Thank you, *Táta*," she said, using the Czech word for daddy, before hurrying back up.

The import of this slight formality was not lost on Franz. She was right, he did still think of her as the little girl he'd tucked under his arm more than ten years ago, when, being in the right place at the right time, he'd saved Henni and her mother Linda from an on-coming tsunami wave. It had been a dramatic first meeting, but he blessed that wave because he had met the woman whom he adored.

He remembered when Harry first came into his life. He had felt sorry for him. To some extent he even respected him, for although it clearly caused great anguish, Harry had expressed his love by making no claims on his daughter, leaving her happy and secure with her parents in the country she knew. They had been grateful, and in return Linda and Franz had promised not to exclude him from her life, that was why he was invited to Prague, once a year.

At heart though, Franz could quite happily have done without the visits. It had seemed a good idea at the time, but he had reckoned without Harry's charm and allure. Franz very soon resented the ease with which Henni had given him her affection. He was also acutely aware that she found the idea of a foreign father quite exciting. Harry arrived like a summer Santa Claus, what child could resist that?

To be fair, Harry never *actually* overstepped the mark, and gave a show of respecting Franz's role as guardian, but Franz suspected that's all it was, a show. Harry was like chicken pox to him, an itch he didn't dare scratch, and his stoicism made an easy target for Harry's mischievousness. To top it all, they were both jealous of the other's place in Henni's life. They could never be friends.

Linda of course, sensing the underlying tensions between the two men, was careful in her dealings with Harry. Franz appreciated her behaviour, because although he loved and trusted his wife, he liked the reassurance it gave him when she treated Harry with distant formality.

Sara was also always there to help neutralise any potential conflicts. Sometimes it was like walking on eggshells for both women. But as everyone prioritised Henni's welfare, so far, so good.

Harry's quixotic nature revelled at the prospect of visiting his daughter, he found her enchanting and cherished the hours he spent in her company, and, truth to tell, enjoyed seeing Franz squirm at their innocent intimacy. One of his most prized possessions that he always kept in his wallet was a photograph taken by Sara of Henni and himself laughing together.

Life was being very good to him. He had the best of all possible worlds with a bright, beautiful daughter to visit and no mundane aspects of everyday parenting to contend with. All of the kisses and none of the responsibility, a situation that suited him very well. He could cherish his ideal view of Henni without seeing her inevitable feet of clay.

In fact, he couldn't remember being so happy since being a child himself. He had Sara, whom he loved and she loved him just as completely. They were not married. Technically he was still a 'free agent' to play around as he pleased. But like a man having given up a lifetime of cigarettes who smells the delicious aroma of smoke and is sometimes tempted, he refused, out of deep love for her to yield to his own particular addiction.

He was as content as a cat with a seemingly endless saucer of cream. The only fly in the milk was Franz, who couldn't be swatted because it would upset or even break the dish.

Work was going well too. For the previous twelve months, the Victoria and Albert Museum had been planning a major touring exhibition, *'Automata Through The Ages'*. It would run from mid-June until Christmas this year. They intended to include earliest examples to the latest full blown modern-animatronics. Harry, as one of the leading designers of modern carnival automata, had been asked to join the team of designers and consultants in contributing to the project. The exhibition would eventually be going to three other capital cities in Europe, Paris, Copenhagen and, most delightfully Prague.

He had visions of taking Henni and her little brother Fran (a nice kid, despite his father) to see the kind of work he was involved in. He knew she thought what he did was more exciting than her stepfather's ownership of hotels, and that would really piss Franz off.

'Be careful,' Sara had warned. He promised he would, but she knew Harry had a tendency to sail too near the wind at times. 'On his own head be it,' she thought, 'I'm not going to be the one who mops up the blood when Franz dunts him on the nose.'

The Prague exhibition was last on the circuit and wouldn't take place until mid-November. This meant that Harry and Sara would have to make their visit later than usual, but to Harry the delay was worth its compensations.

It was a condition of Harry's limited access that he should not contact Henni directly. Any message, even a birthday card, was to be delivered through her parents and he was given no personal email addresses. He could see the reasoning but hated the implications. Seeing his daughter, however, meant more to him than pride, so he complied. He communicated through work-site pages to Franz or Linda. When he mailed Franz to tell him about the exhibition and that he would like to make his visit to coincide with it, Franz said he would have to consult Linda but thought it would be OK. Privately he was happy enough to postpone the pleasure of Harry's company for a few months.

'As long as the bugger's not thinking of staying on for Christmas,' he thought to himself.

Henni was not pleased to hear the news.

"Why," she asked, "can't he come in the summer as well as November?"

"Because," Franz explained, "it was part of the deal that he should visit only once a year," and he added fatally, "we all agreed it was for the best."

"I didn't agree," Henni muttered under her breath.

"What did you say?"

"Nothing, *Táta*," she replied. "Just it's a shame, that's all."

After Henni had retreated up to her room, Linda came home with young Franz who, known simply as Fran to avoid confusion, ran to his beloved *táta*. He'd played well at his after-school football practice and had been chosen for the team.

"Congratulations. Well done," smiled his father, "will that be for next Saturday's match?"

Fran, grinning widely, nodded his head and breathed a big "yes."

"We'll be there, won't we, *Máma*?" Franz assured him.

"We certainly will," said Linda. "Wouldn't miss it for the world. But right now, sweetheart, I think you should go and have a proper shower, I don't know how you managed it, but you might have missed cleaning your knees in the school bathroom."

Fran looked down at his muddy legs in surprise.

"OK," he said, leaving his even muddier kit for his mother

to cope with. "I'll tell Hen, she can come on Saturday as well!"

Franz kissed Linda and offered to make her coffee.

"That would be lovely," she said gratefully. Linda ran her own architectural practice and had a particularly demanding client to deal with recently. "Thank goodness Mr Brendel has approved the new designs and we can get on with the project at last," she added.

"That's wonderful, darling. Perhaps I should offer congratulations to you too. Would you like something a little stronger?"

"No, not at all. Coffee and a hug'll do."

After the hug they sat down together at the kitchen table to drink their coffee.

"I got a mail from Harry today," he said as casually as he could manage. "He's been working on an exhibition of something or other that's coming to Prague in November, and to keep to our agreement he needs to put off his visit till then. When I told Henni she got quite moody and asked why he couldn't come in the summer as well. I reminded her of what we had agreed and she said something I think I'm glad I didn't quite catch. I don't know what's got into her lately, we used to be such good friends, but now nothing I say or do appears to be right."

Linda had been dreading something like this.

She smiled kindly at him. "I know it's difficult for you having to deal with Henni's adolescent outbursts, particularly with the spectre of Harry looming over your shoulder. It doesn't help much to say it, but we've both just got to ride the storm. Easier said than done though. I was so angry with her the other day I really lost my temper, and it was all over nothing. Thank goodness we still have Marta, she can always pour oil on troubled waters. Even when Henni was a toddler and had a tantrum, it was always Nanny Marta who could calm her down. She and Henni care for each other unreservedly but the difference between Marta's love and ours is that we're the ones who must set the rules, some of which are not amenable to a growing child."

"You're right," he admitted. "But," he continued, going straight to the heart of the matter, "I can't help feeling sometimes, she prefers her real father to me."

"She may have inherited some of Harry's genes but *you're* her real father Franz, and under all her teenage flouncing Henni knows it," Linda replied.

"Thank you," he said and poured his wife a second coffee.

"Maybe we could offer an olive branch," he suggested. "I forget sometimes that she is growing up. She was very put out about my not allowing her full access to the internet. I only want to protect her from anything nasty that's out there. Bit of a waste of time really, because I have a feeling that once round at Anna's house she uses hers. If I warn her of the dangers, maybe it would be alright. What do you think?"

"It may be a better idea than letting her sneak off to use it elsewhere."

"What about Harry coming in November?"

"That's fine, but Henni will be at school most of the time, not that Harry will have thought of that. Sara and I could enjoy the Christmas Markets together, I like her, and it might be fun." Franz's smile was a little broader at the thought of Harry missing out on Henni's company.

"Or," said Linda, "this is something I've been thinking about for a while, and as Harry can't come here in the summer it might be a good time to do it. Do you think we could visit him instead? We could ask Henni her opinion on going to maybe Paris and London, then make our way up to Scotland. We could go through Northumberland – they have some wonderful coastlines up there. An ancient castle sits right on top of the cliffs at Bamburgh, I've seen pictures of it but never been there. Have you?"

"No, I haven't, it is supposed to be quite beautiful. But do you mean we will be seeing him *twice*? Once in England and then when he comes here in November?"

"Would that be so bad for you Franz? It need only be a fleeting visit. She's growing up fast and we can't impose the rules we made when she was nine and not expect her to feel resentful. There are other factors too."

"What other factors?"

"May I tell you later, before we go to bed?"

Linda was also thinking that she herself should make the effort to see Harry's family in Derbyshire again. They had been good to her and she felt bad at having treated them shabbily. She was naturally nervous of meeting again after all that had passed, but they were part of Henni's family and as such Henni had a right to know them. A piece of her wished she hadn't told Harry about his child in the first place, but what was done was done for the best possible reasons. Harry and Henni would have found one another at some point. It was better Franz and Linda had control of the timing. Using the same logic, she thought if they didn't allow him to introduce his daughter to his family soon, Henni might well conclude her parents had not been fair, and acted selfishly deliberately not letting them into her life. Linda felt there would be many more squalls to weather before reaching clear water. However, now was not a good time to voice these thoughts to Franz. He was finding the going heavy enough already.

After a moment's silence he said, "We'll see."

"OK, you decide. Now, I wonder what the wonderful Marta has cooked up for supper. Whatever it is, it smells good and after spending an hour watching the next David Beckham honing his football skills, I'm quite hungry."

There were raised voices upstairs. Fran and Henni were having a disagreement.

"*Máma* said you had to," yelled Fran.

"I've told you, I can't. I'm going out with Anna and Jitka."

"Why can't you *all* come?"

"Because, we don't want to spend the afternoon standing in a cold muddy field watching you showing off. OK?"

Linda had reached the top of the stairs in a single bound."Henni! Fran! Stop this noise at once!"

"*Máma*," said Fran tearfully, "she said she won't come to the match on Saturday and you said she would!"

"No, darling, I said *Táta* and I would be there. If Henni is busy, then she can't come, can she? Maybe she'll be able to go next time. What do you say, Henni?"

"Maybe," she conceded without a smile.

"There you are, Fran, but *we* might have to treat ourselves to an extra big hot chocolate at *Prava's* café afterwards, um? Now supper's nearly ready, have your shower quickly, but try using the soap this time and we'll see you downstairs in a few minutes."

Fran went off to the bathroom. Linda turned to Henni and asked what it was all about.

"He thinks I always have to do what he wants all the time."

"You've got to remember he's only seven. You're his big sister and he just wanted you to share his pride in being selected for the football team. It's OK to have made other arrangements, but you could have been kinder when you told him."

Henni compressed her lips and sighed. "Alright. I'll tell him I'm sorry and I promise to go next time."

"Thank you," said Linda, "come down for supper now."

"I'll just wash my hands," she said. When her mother had gone she sent quick texts to Anna and Jitka, 'What u doing Sat?' knocked perfunctorily at the bathroom door, said "Sorry Fran" loud enough for her mother to hear, and slumped downstairs.

Marta served up a delicious lamb casserole with dumplings. After a frosty start Henni's mood warmed as she ate one of her favourite dishes. When they were sufficiently sated with food Franz raised the question of Harry's deferred visit. Henni's face fell into the now customary frown. He affected to take no notice.

"As Harry's no longer coming this summer," he said brightly, "perhaps we might go away together during the school holidays in July, for a change. I'm sure Tomáš and Novák can manage the hotels without me for a couple of weeks or so. *Máma* has suggested a touring holiday. What do you think, Henni?"

"Don't know," she said miserably, for no good reason visualising driving around in a camper van for weeks, with no one but family. Her idea of a good time. Not.

Linda joined in on cue. "We just wondered if you might enjoy the sights of Paris and London. But it doesn't matter if you don't want to go darling, we can just stay here."

"London!" exclaimed Henni. "You mean England. May we see Harry in York as well?"

"We might be able to fit a visit in," said her father, without any real enthusiasm.

"Oh, that would be wonderful!" Henni momentarily nipped her brow. "He can still come in November can't he?"

"It's part of his job, so I suppose he'll have to."

She leaned over the table and kissed him.

"Thank you, *papa-Franz.* I do love you."

Later that night when they were alone, Linda told Franz her reasons for wanting to go to England.

"Also," she said, "most importantly, at the moment Henni seems to view Harry as a kind of unreal sugar-daddy without fault. He believes her to be perfect too. *We* both know they're living in cloud-cuckoo land. But she's not a little girl anymore and I think our real parenting has only just started. We have to learn to let go a little.

"She needs to see how the mistakes Harry and I made affected so many lives, and how as adults we eventually have to face all of them. She's no idea how hard it was for Harry to leave her with us. How hard it is for you to have to share even a portion of her love with *him*. The trouble is we can't sit down and just tell her these things. She wouldn't listen, she's got to be allowed to work it out for herself."

"I suppose you're right, but it's going to be tough. Here's a happy thought, though, just when Hen is on an even keel, Fran will be approaching adolescence, at least we will have had some practice," her husband said.

Linda replied, "After our daughter, he should be no trouble at all."

Franz laughed and so did she. He took her by the hand.

"Well," he said, "on that principle, let's go to bed and work it out."

To say that the prospect of the July holiday transformed Henni into an angel of light would be an exaggeration. She was still living under the burden of sudden adolescent hormonal attacks but at least she was trying. Her first act of humanity was to talk her friends into going to Fran's first football match with her. It was just as cold and muddy as she thought it would be, but the young boys had older brothers, which was much more interesting. When Fran managed to pull off a good save and the girls loyally cheered, two of the big brothers actually spoke, and told them he was not a bad player, for a little kid. The big brothers went further when after the match they asked if they'd see the girls there again next week. The girls giggled all the way to *Prava's* café and decided maybe football wasn't so boring after all.

CHAPTER TWO

England

It was nearing the end of April. Ripon and York Choristers had joined forces again, this year at the Minster for the Easter Concert. Sara and Harry still had to contend with the day jobs having sung their socks off at rehearsals in the evenings, but the performance of Mozart's Requiem was received to great acclaim. It even rated a paragraph in *BBC Music Magazine* where they both merited special mention, which was very gratifying.

After working so very hard and having exciting news to impart, they took a weekend out to visit James and his family at the farm. They took Sara's grandson, Billy, along with them mainly to allow her son Dave, and his wife Chris, some time with their new, completely unplanned but welcome, baby girl. 'Uncle' Harry was a favourite with the boy because he'd mended Billy's PlayStation and could make paper planes that flew for 'miles.' He was also very excited at the idea of staying on a farm.

Harry liked Billy in the same way he liked Fran. They were nice kids who were fun to be with. They were easily pleased by simple things like kicking a football round and of course his genius for paper plane making. But they didn't tug at his heart strings in the way Henni did. He would make time to amuse them, but he'd do anything in the world for her, his daughter, his little girl, just to see her smile.

Once inside the farmhouse Sara's grandson turned shy.

"Hello, Billy," said James's wife Pamela, offering him a biscuit, after his long journey. He took the biscuit and said thank you.

"How do you do?" asked James, shaking the child's hand in his own great paw.

Billy looked alarmed and Harry laughed, "That's my big brother and he likes to frighten small people."

"Harrumph," said James, and Billy realising it was meant to be a joke, smiled.

"Take no notice of the children, Billy," said Pamela. She addressed Sara. "How are you both? It's good to see you," and kissed her on both cheeks before turning to kiss Harry and pronounced him to be looking sleeker than ever.

"We're very well," Sara replied. "It's great to be here again and thanks for letting Billy come. Dave and Chris need a bit of time together with the new baby."

Pamela's son Michael and his wife Carrie came down from their apartment to welcome them.

"Ah, Peter," said Carrie as her younger son came into the room. He was nearing his eleventh birthday and not too happy at the thought of maybe having to baby-sit Sara's grandson. He had to decide whether Billy was alright or not, so he made his opening gambit.

"You know how to play Assassins Creed Final Solution?"

"You've got Assassins Creed Final Solution? I've only got Origins 2."

"I can show you if you like."

"Yeah! I'd love that."

"Is that OK?" Peter asked his dad.

"Fine with me," Michael replied. He looked round, no one had any objections. "Off you go, then."

They went, with Pamela's voice ringing in their ears, something about lunch being ready in an hour.

"Well, that could be the last we see of them this weekend," Carrie remarked. "Where's Luke, why's he not here to say hello?"

"I hope he's finishing cleaning my quad bike." Michael turned to Harry. "He went joy riding and left the seat as wet and muddy as a fresh cow pat!" Harry laughed.

"How old is he now?" Sara asked.

"Sixteen, going on two and a half. I swear he gets less sense the older he gets."

"Not like us," Harry chipped in, "we wuz perfect."

"Harrumph," said James, who, at many years older than his half-brother, knew better.

After a splendid lunch (no one made a steak and kidney pie to rival Pam's) the boys went back upstairs, Billy confessed to being a bit confused about who was who, and Peter did his best to explain his weird family.

"Grandpa," he said, "is the oldest, then Grandma. Uncle Harry is Grandpa's half-brother, that means," he explained for Billy's benefit, "he had a different mum to Grandpa. Grandpa's mum had died when he was quite young and his dad had married Auntie Maggie and they had Uncle Harry, who is not my uncle because he's really my *great* uncle, OK? So Uncle Harry is my dad's uncle even though he is only two years older, d'you see? I have an Aunt Lucy in Canada who is Uncle Harry's niece even though she's three years older than him. But because they were all kids together, Dad, Aunt

Lucy and Uncle Harry grew up more like brothers and sister. Grandpa and Grandma are old enough to be Uncle Harry's mum and dad."

"Shall we play Final Solutions again?" asked a bemused Billy.

"OK," Peter replied.

In the sitting room downstairs with the children gone, Harry, unable to conceal his excitement any longer, announced "Henni's coming over in a few months." He beamed a smile at the astonished faces of his family.

"No," said Pamela. "You mean we are going to meet her after all these years?"

Harry nodded enthusiastically.

"Well, that's marvellous. But not on her own surely," came as a question rather than a statement from Carrie.

"Her family will be with her." Sara dropped the words into the silence.

Harry took over. "Yes, Linda will be coming. She would like to see you all again… Look, I know it will be awkward for everyone. But" – it was still hard for him to say – "it was my fault she did what she did. Even *I* can see that now. She believes it's time we cleared the whole mess up and introduced you to Henni, and I… I'd like my daughter to know, not just her stepfather's relatives, but my family, and love them as much as I do." He ended by looking pleadingly at them.

Sara had held his hand as he spoke and as he turned to her, she smiled and gave it a reassuring squeeze.

"Well, about time too," harumphed James staunchly.

"When can we expect our niece to visit?"

"They should be here sometime in July. They're taking in Paris and London first. We'll get the dates sorted out soon. Linda wanted to make sure she would be welcome before making any firm bookings... Thanks for being so understanding."

"Uncle Harry!" Peter's voice sounded as he and Billy thundered down the stairs. "Can you make Billy one of your super jets, we want to go out and play. I can make that interceptor plane like you showed me last time you came, and we are going to dive bomb each other."

"Peter!" said Carrie sharply.

"Oh, sorry." He looked from his mother to Harry, and added the magic word "please".

"It's not convenient at the moment Peter, Uncle Harry is telling us something," his father said.

"It's alright, Michael. It'll only take a few minutes. Got some stiff paper, Peter?" Harry asked.

"Yeah, in my room. Shall I get it?"

"No, I'll come," and he leapt up the stairs after the two boys.

"They're about the same age," Pam observed generally, after Harry was out of earshot. "A lot of water's gone under the bridge since we last saw Linda. Maybe *he* can forgive what she did, but I can't. It was shameful what she did to him. What do you think, Sara? You've met them."

"I know it would break his heart if you refused to try."

"I'd do anything for Harry," she replied a little tearfully. "You all know that."

"We do," comforted Michael, "so we must all make an effort to see it does work. OK? Sara, he's clearly keen to be out of the way for the moment, so tell us what we can expect."

Without Harry, they knew she could be a little more frank than she might otherwise have been.

"I'll start with Linda. Obviously I didn't know her before, but she strikes me as a caring and careful mother who bitterly regrets, not leaving Harry, because under the circumstances that was inevitable, but how she did it. I know she still loved him even as she walked out of his life, because she told me so. Do you know how she met her present husband Franz? No? Well, to cut a long story short, she was on holiday with Henni and her nanny in Japan when that huge tsunami hit the Fukushima nuclear power plant, back in 2011. They were staying at an hotel not that far up the coast, a man sitting next to them spotted what was happening and got them all safely away even as the wave was catching up with his car. That was Franz. They fell in love, moved to Franz's home city of Prague, married and would have lived happily ever after, but for Linda's guilt. That's why she wrote to Maggie telling her about Henni. You know the rest.

"Franz, her husband, is a kind and loyal man who adores his wife and loves both his own son and Henni very much. In many ways he's extremely old-fashioned. He likes to be the *Pater Familias*, and will go to great lengths to protect his family from harm. He and Linda have similar natures. Neither likes to take a risk without first weighing up the possible consequences. Why they have decided to risk coming to England now is for Linda to say, not me to guess.

"Franz their son, now known as Fran, is not much older than Billy. He's mad about football and basically a very nice, typical little boy.

"As for Henni herself, for the main part she can be delightful. It's no wonder Harry dotes on her. You've seen her photograph, she's a lovely, exceptionally pretty girl who looks just like her mother. From Harry she's inherited the ability to charm birds from the trees, but as you know very well, part of his charm is his recklessness and I believe she's inherited some of that too. It's a powerful combination that takes careful handling. So far I think Franz and Linda have done a great job. She was thirteen when we last saw her, but growing up fast and getting more and more adept at playing one father off the other. I don't suppose in that she's different to any other child in her situation, possibly just better at it. I've seen her drive poor Franz to the brink of distraction by whispering absolutely nothing into Harry's ear, and Harry loving the joke. She'll be fourteen and a half now and that extra year will have made quite a difference. She certainly won't be a little girl anymore. How she and both fathers cope with that will be interesting. But, if you love Harry, you'll love Henni too," Sara ended with a smile.

"Phew," said Carrie, "that's a lot to cope with. Thank you, Sara."

Obviously happy in each other's company, the boys clattered downstairs again.

"I'm just going outside to test the plane for a minute," Harry called, "not be long." He returned just as the cold coffee was being removed. Pamela went to make a fresh pot as Harry's eyes asked Sara if she had allayed any family fears, she smiled and laid her hand on his in reply. Pam brought the coffee and he happily settled down to talk about what they might do when Henni arrived.

CHAPTER THREE

Playing with Billy outside, Peter assumed the role of 'big brother' for a change and liked it. He impressed his new friend by showing him round the farm, pointing out Gamekeepers Cottage, which was Uncle Harry's house and pulling him up onto the tractor and letting him pretend to drive. His way of enticing his dad's Guernsey cows to come to the fence so he could scratch their ears awed Billy beyond belief. Under instruction he even tried it himself, but the beast tossed its head and he lost his nerve.

"It's alright," said Peter, "she won't hurt you, she was just getting rid of a fly. Try again. It's the bull you've got to watch out for; Dad says he can be one big mean bugger. He keeps it in a special field with the gate locked and a much higher fence than this one."

Billy was very impressed with Peter's knowledge, *and* that he dared use *that* word to describe the bull. With great faith in his mentor's superior knowledge he plucked up his courage and scratched the cow's ear and as he drew his hand away the cow gave it a big, warm wet lick. It was fun and they both laughed.

The weekend was as always, enjoyable, but Pamela had

found it hard to maintain the great effort it took to hide her qualms about meeting Linda again. Harry appreciated how she felt and gave her extra hugs. "It'll be fine," he reassured her, so many times he wondered if it was not just Pam he was trying to convince.

On Sunday afternoon they waved goodbye to the family. Michael and Carrie had work to do on the farm, and Luke kindly put off his revision for an hour or so to play a computer game with the newly abandoned Peter. James and Pamela went into the kitchen and she silently made a pot of tea. From long experience James knew Pam wanted to 'talk', this time, however, there really was something to talk about. They sat at the table and she asked if he would like a biscuit as she'd made a big batch in honour of the visit, but as the meals she'd cooked were so large and filling, no one had much room for snacks and there were a lot left. James dutifully accepted a gingersnap and began to dunk it in his mug of tea.

"Well," said Pamela, "that was a bit of a surprise."

James nodded but said nothing. He knew what was coming.

She continued, "I don't know how she's got the nerve! I don't want her here, James... Henni, yes, she's Harry's girl and of course I want to meet her. But to have to meet the whole brood is too much. I'll go away while they're here. I'll stay with Jenny, she's my sister, she'll understand."

"You must do what you want, Pam, you'll always have my blessing and support. But remember what Sara said, it would break his heart if we didn't try to make this work."

Pamela began to cry. "Oh, James, I don't think I can face it..."

"We'll all find it hard, and I don't just mean our side of the family. Look, I know how much you love Harry. We both do. Let's face it. I'm old enough to be his father and you his mother. The children grew up on this farm together, with so few years between them, it was natural that you and Maggie shared the mothering of all three. Because we already had Lucy when Harry was born, if I remember correctly, you were the one who got the honour of changing his first nappy. Maggie couldn't do it properly, you had to show her how, didn't you?" He smiled as she nodded. "Is it any wonder then that we think of Harry as much as a son as a brother? But as to what Linda did, she had good reason to be angry. Maybe she went too far, but it wouldn't be the first time that Harry pushed someone to the brink, would it?"

Pamela knew what James was talking about. It was the time a young Harry blew his great-grandfather's old ARP whistle too near the cattle and stampeded the herd. She could never forget how his father had thrashed him with a belt. Hearing the child screaming she'd dropped everything to run over to the noise in time to see Maggie forcing herself between Harry and his father. Arthur had dropped the belt at once and walked away, but with such an expression of anger and shame on his face that it chilled her to the bone. Nothing like that ever happened again. Although Harry bore no ill will towards his father, Pamela could not forgive Arthur for beating the child she adored. She felt the same way about Linda.

James knew exactly how her mind was working. "It's easy," he said, "to forgive a child and blame the adult who should know better. But Harry was no longer a child when he behaved so badly to his wife. Linda taught him a lesson just as surely as Father did. But there was no one there for a long time to step in between and stop the hurt. Linda eventually found Franz, and much later Harry met his saviour in Sara. Now Harry and Linda are, metaphorically speaking, looking to us to get out the first aid kit and make it all better."

"It's not the same thing," Pamela protested. "She might have provoked him into being less than… less than faithful." There! She'd actually voiced what she'd secretly convinced herself of for years.

James took her hand. "Pam," he said, "believe me, that just isn't true. Harry was always wild and didn't stop just because he married Linda. Maggie knew, and I could guess what he'd been up to for a long time, but even she didn't know the full story until he told her in the weeks before she died. After her funeral, he told me too. He was so ashamed. Guilt had been eating him up. For all those years trying to deny it, in his heart Harry believed he'd been responsible for the death of his unborn child. No wonder he took to drink."

"Oh, James, the poor boy…"

"The poor boy, yes. That's the problem. He causes chaos and because he's Harry, we forget he's the author of his own misfortune. You know, he wasn't always the adorable little scamp you seem to remember. He was basically a good lad but there was a demon inside him at times. He would push things just to see how far he could go and still get away with it… Let me ask you something. Did you ever consider how Father got to the back field so fast, when Harry spooked the cattle?" She shook her head. "I'll tell you now," he said gently. "We were working quite near by the old barn and saw him sneaking over to the pasture, on tiptoe. We thought he was playing a game and laughed because it looked so funny. But then, Harry stopped and stood square behind the herd, and too late we realised what he was going to do. He looked round and thinking no one could see him, blew that damned whistle of his as loud as he could. When the cows stampeded it frightened him. He stood petrified and if Father hadn't vaulted the wall and scooped him up, Harry would almost certainly have been killed. He was as scared as Harry and that's why he walloped him so hard. I don't know if Harry guessed he'd been seen, to his credit he didn't lie and say it was an accident, neither did he admit the truth, but took his punishment because he knew he had it coming."

"I didn't realise…"

"No, I wouldn't have told you, but he didn't play by the rules then nor did he later with Linda. He hurt her deeply and she retaliated by hurting him just as much. To be honest, Pam, I believe for years he wasn't able to function, because he couldn't face the fact he'd been responsible for the catastrophe. It was like he was still standing in that field, petrified by what he'd done."

"You're being very hard on him James."

"I don't mean to be. But I feel guilty too because I wasn't able to help him get out of the mess he'd made. It was Sara who did that, she brought him back from the brink and gave us back the old Harry we loved. Under that ordinary exterior lives an extraordinary woman. She's not had the easiest of lives herself and that's what must have made her tough enough to pull Harry back together. I'll always be in her debt for that. But he's still scared, and he won't be at peace again unless this meeting with Linda's a success. Without Sara he wouldn't have got this far, now it's our turn to do our part. They say, you know, that everyone holds someone's soul in the palm of their hand, Sara has his in her safekeeping. I've been lucky too, because you picked up mine the first time I met you." He smiled at his wife, patting the hand he still held in his. In fifty years, James had never said anything remotely as romantic to her before, and she blushed like a little girl.

"You're right, James," she said half crying, "we did lose him for a long while and now we have him back we must do all we can. I'll dust down the first aid kit."

"Dust the first aid? Ah, harumph, very good!" He laughed as if it had been her metaphor in the first place.

CHAPTER FOUR

The big exhibition of automata at the V&A Museum was due to open on the May bank holiday continuing until the end of the first week in July. Harry was disappointed that Henni wouldn't be there to see it and ironically it would be moving to Paris on the day she was leaving that city. But it was still on for Prague in mid-November, so he had to be content to wait.

He'd designed a major construction that would hang suspended at the entrance to the gallery, of a fantastic Heath-Robinson-inspired silver-metal stork with a two-metre wing span. Simulating true flight, the primary, secondary and tertiary feathers operated separately in smooth succession. Each feather tip was adorned with silver bells, and as the wings moved lazily up and down they chimed like the Music of the Spheres. The upper tail covert feathers spread into a fan as its long articulated neck bent sinuously towards its nest. The bird's long beak opened and the head swayed from side to side as it picked up a 'baby' wrapped in a silvery blanket, then its eyes blinked shut as it uttered a low rumbling squawk. It was a triumph of his art and was chosen to feature on the exhibition poster. Harry was justifiably pleased with his flight of fancy and could hardly wait to show off the real thing to his family.

He'd been working on the finishing touches since the visit to Derbyshire, and missed Sara a lot. Going home on the train returning from his latest trip to London, he messaged: 'Fancy a dirty weekend together tonight?'

Sara sent her reply a minute later: 'It's only Tuesday.'

'What's in a name? A day by any other name would be as long.'

'OK, Romeo. How in one night?'

'Just have to make the effort.'

'I'm intrigued.'

'Trust me. I can stay on the train till Thirsk, less distance for you to drive. Meet at the station at four?'

'I'll be there.'

Harry accepted the train-steward's offer of coffee and biscuits, paid the extra few pounds to go one stop further to Thirsk, and settled down to enjoy his journey. He closed his eyes just for a moment and woke suddenly as the guard announced the train was approaching his stop. He swiftly gathered his stuff together and made it to the door at the far end of the carriage just as the train pulled up, realising only as he stepped onto the platform, that he must have dropped his jacket in the rush to disembark. Too late to go back, he watched in distress as the train rolled away. Sara was there waiting for him.

"I've left my jacket with my wallet on the train," he wailed.

"Oh dear," she said, sharing his consternation. "Next stop's Northallerton. It's only ten minutes away, but if we hurry and ask in the ticket office, they might be able to phone the guard and get him to drop it off there."

"Right," he said, striding off quickly to the office, where they explained what had happened, to the clerk.

"Sorry, sir," that official said, "I can contact the guard on the train alright, but there's not going to be anyone to give your jacket to. The station's only got one operative, she won't be able to leave the ticket office to collect it. Newcastle's the next stop with a Lost Property Office. I could ask the guard to leave it there."

Harry was agitated so Sara answered for him. "If that's the best you can do, that would be grand, thank you." She turned to Harry as the clerk rang the guard. "It'll be fine," she said, "we can always drive up and get it, don't worry."

The clerk was maddeningly slow in his phone call, but finally turned to them with a smile.

"Well, sir, you're in luck. The guard is off duty at Northallerton, and leaving the train in a couple of minutes. He'd spotted your jacket right away and already has it in his possession. The ticket office at Northallerton closes in half an hour, but, he says, if you can get there by then, he'll beg a cup of tea and wait for you. Would that be alright, sir?"

"More than alright. Thank you."

The clerk spoke into his phone again and confirmed Mr Martin would be there.

"Can we make it, Sara?" Harry asked as they hurried out of the office.

"Yes."

"Where are you parked?"

"Over there."

"Can I drive?"

"No."

***

The roads were blessedly clear and they got to the station with minutes to spare. Sara parked her car as Harry raced to the ticket office where the guard was sipping a mug of tea and gently flirting with the pretty girl behind the desk. He recognised Harry at once, and with a grin handed him his property.

"Thank you very much. I hope I didn't put you to too much trouble," Harry said, as he accepted the jacket.

With a gleam in his eye, the guard at looked the girl, and replied, "No trouble at all, sir."

Harry checked his wallet and breathed again. It was still there, safe inside. He ran his fingers lovingly over the slightly dog-eared photograph of Henni and himself. As an afterthought he checked his visa and credit cards as he walked out to the car park to meet Sara.

He knew full well his panic had been for no other reason than he thought he'd lost Henni's photograph. He also knew it was totally irrational, he could have another print made as easily as he could stop his bank cards, and get replacements, but that wasn't the point, *that* particular print was what he treasured. The panic had been so horribly real, he shook his head and thought 'I've got to get a grip, or next thing, I'll be dancing naked round the maypole making voodoo dolls of Franz and sticking pins in him.' This image cheered him up considerably.

"Now then," he greeted Sara, feeling much better. "Everything's good. As we're in Northallerton shall we eat here before we begin our weekend?"

"Better not," she replied as they got to her car. "I've left my cat locked inside without a litter tray and it could be a dirty night in an entirely different sense."

362

"Why don't you get him a cat-flap?" Harry interrupted, genuinely curious.

"He's too big and well built," she said defensively.

"You mean he's too fat to get through one?" He knew he was skating on thin ice here. Sara was very fond of Bob, so he smiled when he said it.

She assumed her stern 'teacher' expression. "Do you want this weekend or not?"

"Yes please, Mrs Middleton."

"Very well then," she continued primly, suppressing a smile herself. "I've also got a lamb casserole simmering in the slow-cooker. It's not far back and it's not that late. I should remind you though, I'm working tomorrow afternoon. Do you think we can still fit a whole weekend into the sixteen hours we have left?"

"We can but try," sighed Harry. "We can but try." He laughed and kissed her with the quick exaggerated passion of an old movie star, much to the amusement of an elderly matron who happened to be passing by.

After supper at Sara's house the weekend began. They made love three times. Once on the living room rug for Friday, once before a midnight shower for Saturday and once in bed for Sunday. They were falling asleep as the sky grew light, and Sara thought not only was it the shortest, but the most fun weekend she'd ever had.

She awoke to the noise of letters falling through her letterbox and lazily leaned over to glance at her watch to see what time it was.

"Good God!" she said aloud. "It's gone half eleven!" and leapt out of bed.

She flung on her dressing gown and made straight for the

bathroom. There was no time to wash and dry her hair so she pulled an unbecoming plastic cap on to her head as she stepped under the shower. Five minutes later after towelling herself dry she was back in the bedroom trying to open her clean underwear drawer with one hand and the wardrobe with the other. Harry was sitting up by now and taking notice.

"I'm going to be late," she said unnecessarily. "I must bear in mind," she went on, as she fumbled to fasten her bra, "that if I am going to act like a courtesan, then I'll have to give up the day job!"

"Why don't you marry me then? As your husband I could take care of all your pecuniary needs," he said lightly.

She stopped tucking her blouse into her skirt, sat by him on the bed and kissed him hard on the lips. "I don't want a husband," she replied. It was a kind of game they played, he'd ask and she'd refuse.

"Can I say just one thing?" His hands strayed to her breasts.

"Yes."

"Do you really mean to go out with your shirt done up like that?"

She looked down and saw that in her hurry she had missed the top buttonhole and her blouse was completely skew-whiff.

"Bugger!" she said.

He grinned as she straightened herself out. "OK now?" she asked, giving a twirl.

"Just perfect," he replied. "Have a good day, Mrs Middleton, and let me know if you ever change your mind."

***

He heard the front door open and slam in quick succession, followed by the sound of Sara's car engine punctuated by the grinding of a gear or two. The cat appeared in the bedroom, it's urgent meowing making it clear to Harry that *now* was a good time to get up and open the back door to Bob's favourite latrine, located in next-door's flower garden. He complied with Bob's request, then went back upstairs to the bathroom where he showered and tidied away the disorder both he and Sara had left. He made the bed more neatly than she ever managed to do, then went down to the kitchen to pop some bread in the toaster and make himself a Nespresso. After breakfast, Bob was at the door waiting to come back in and be fed. Harry gave the cat some food, removed all evidence of his own presence by washing, drying and putting away the crockery and cutlery he had used. Harry by nature was a fastidious man, and in some ways quite domestic. He made sure he had all his things this time and slammed Sara's door behind him. Then remembered he didn't have his car, and it was his turn to say "Bugger!"

CHAPTER FIVE

Prague

Franz was in his element organising dates and booking the best hotels. After Paris, it was logical to visit London first then travel through Derbyshire for a brief lunchtime visit to the farm before proceeding north to Scotland. He put a night's stay at York on the bottom of the list and chose an hotel on the edge of the city, well out of walking distance of Harry's home. Then, having done his duty by Henni, he could look forward to returning to his own country, and not have to think about Harry for months.

June seemed to last forever for Henni and Fran. Henni was excited at the prospect of seeing Harry, and Fran at the thought of spending two nights at Disneyland Paris, in one of the on-site hotels. His big sister had to admit that might be pretty cool as well. They had both looked on YouTube to select the attractions and rides they liked best. For Fran, the star attractions had to be Buzz Lightyear Laser Blast, and the Ratatouille trackless ride. Henni was more interested in the Thunder Mountain train, with its water-splashes and dark tunnels, not to mention the Rock 'n' Roller Coaster, that had a giant corkscrew twist plus loud music. Franz made them both happy by booking fast track 'speed' tickets in advance for their favoured attraction each day. Not caring for her daughter's choice of high-speed hair-raising rides herself, Linda generously volunteered Franz to accompany Henni on those.

After Disneyland they were to transfer to central Paris and go to the very top of the Eiffel Tower with its magnificent views over the city, then a cruise on the Seine. They would see the Arc de Triomphe and walk the Champs-Élysées, visit the Louvre Palace and more. Every moment before getting the train to London would be filled with sunshine and wonder. Franz had created an action-packed week's programme because he wanted his children to have a wonderful time, but also, far less laudably, he wanted to make the visit to Derbyshire and Harry appear a pedestrian anti-climax.

But fortune did not entirely favour Franz. As the Horbach family arrived at Disneyland, the weather turned unseasonably cold and wet. It was not as bad as the flash flood of 2017 nor did it rival the 1880 deluge, but it did take most of one of their precious days to clear, and standing in drizzling rain that night to watch the fireworks was not quite how Franz had planned it should be. When watery sunshine appeared next morning, the children, wearing kagouls – newly purchased from the gift shop – made the most of it and began to enjoy themselves. But their father still felt decidedly doleful, particularly when Henni joyfully reminded him he'd promised to go on the Thunder Mountain ride with her, the one with the big water-splashes. Dutifully, dressed in his new kagoul, and a smile pasted on his face, he boarded the mountain train that quickly reached breakneck speed. Henni squealed in delight and before he knew it, they were both having a wonderful time. The sun came out in force by the afternoon, Fran had loved Buzz Lightyear and had shot goodness knows how many aliens, with the number getting higher every time he told the tale. The evening fireworks didn't have to contend with the damp and were magnificent. Franz and Linda, catching each other's laughing face in the brightness of their light, felt their love stronger than ever.

On their final day they managed to fit in Fran's Ratatouille attraction while Henni and Franz took the Rock 'n' Roller Coaster ride, both of which had been closed due to the rain on their first day.

The shuttle bus took them to Pont Neuf, near to the hotel where they were staying. After supper they climbed aboard a bus for a night tour of the city. Henni was enthralled but Fran went to sleep on *Máma's* shoulder and didn't wake up once. After the tour *Táta* gently lifted him into his arms and carried him back to the hotel.

The sun continued to shine brightly for them next day as they took their tickets for the Eiffel Tower and river cruise. The tower looked a lot smaller than Henni had expected, but when she got to the second floor it was higher than she thought, then standing right at the top she couldn't believe how very high it was. She drank in the panorama and closed her eyes to enjoy the wind tossing her newly bobbed hair and felt she could have stayed there forever. Franz looked at her and saw as the wind pulled at her clothes, Henni was no longer a little girl but one on the verge of young womanhood. He felt both pride and sadness. Fran held *Táta* and *Máma's* hands very tight, he wasn't sure he liked this, the wind was blowing too fiercely.

"I'll take him down," Franz mouthed to Linda over the gusting noise. "I don't think he's too happy up here. You stay for a bit with Hen, if you want. She seems to love it. I'll get him an ice cream. See you down there."

He took his son to the lift and they squeezed in. When they had reached ground level and safely back on terra firma, Fran said, "I didn't really like that, *Táta*. It was a bit scary."

"That's only because you aren't as tall as me yet. When you are it'll be no problem. I'll show you."

He took Fran a metre or two into the square away from the tower. "Stay there," he said as he took three steps away and positioned himself directly in front of M. Eiffel's creation. "Look," he said, "I bet you can't see the top of the tower any more. So, who's bigger me or it?"

"You, *Táta*," Fran laughed. "Can I try now?"

"Certainly," his father answered. Fran ran to the spot where *Táta* had stood and asked, "Well?"

"Kilometres bigger. Now let's get an ice cream, shall we?"

Linda and Henni came down from the top ten minutes later. They stopped on the first floor so Henni might look down and wave at her brother and *Táta* who were looking up for them. It may have been telepathy because despite the crowd, they quickly spotted one another and both pairs waved their arms vigorously in salute.

"Are you enjoying your holiday, Henni?"

"Oh yes, *Máma*. Thank you."

"It was *Táta* who made it happen," she said. "It's him you must thank. He loves us all very much."

"I know, but I do wish he wouldn't think of me as a child because I'm not."

"You're right, sweetheart, you aren't. But there's more to being grown up than just looking the part."

Henni sighed, she wasn't in the mood for one of *Máma's* 'talks'.

369

Linda took the hint and said, "Come on then, let's get our ice creams before they eat the lot."

Henni managed a weak smile at the weaker still joke, and they went down to join the others.

Later, on the cruise down the Seine the sun felt baking hot through the boat windows. Franz and Linda took her brother out onto the deck to cool down, but Henni wanted to stay inside. She took off her hat and laid her head back on her seat. With eyes half closed she enjoyed the sensation, if only for a short time, of being alone in a foreign city.

As the boat manoeuvred near to its docking point, she opened her eyes fully, and saw her family approaching. A wave of sentimental affection swept over her as she stood up to meet them, but she felt strangely dizzy and flopped back down on the seat.

"Henni," said her mother's voice full of concern, "are you alright?"

"Too much sun. Let's get her off this boat and into some shade," Franz said, and wrapping his arm round her pushed through the disembarking crowd. He turned to Linda. "Have you any water left?" She'd already rummaged in her bag, and was handing him a half-empty bottle as he spoke. He sat Henni down in the nearest shady spot on the quay and urged her to sip. Fran showed his concern by patting her back.

Her head throbbed and she felt sick. "I don't feel very well, *papa-Franz*."

"You'll be alright, Hen, just got a bit too much sun. *Máma's* phoning for a taxi now and we'll get you back to the hotel in no time." Turning to Fran he said, "Will you be a big boy and run over to the drinks machine and get a can of lemonade for your sister, please?" He gave his son a handful of euros.

"Yes, *Táta*." Proud to be of use, he managed his task well and was back in no time. He handed the can to his father to open for Henni. It was ice-cold and she rolled it across her forehead several times before actually drinking. Linda, who had finished her call, sent Fran back to the machine to get something for himself, she didn't want him in the same state.

The traffic was heavy and the taxi slow to arrive. Franz paced the quay keeping a sharp look out for it while Linda comforted Henni. As for Fran, he kept an eye on them all in turn as he quietly drank his lemonade.

CHAPTER SIX

After a couple of hours' sleep in her cool, dark bedroom Henni woke with just the ghost of a headache and a raging thirst. Her mother, who had been watching by the bed saw her stir, fetched a bottle from the hotel fridge and gave it to her.

"Not too quickly," Linda warned, as the girl gulped the ice-cold drink down. "Better?"

"Yes. Thank you. Where's *Táta* and Fran?"

"Fran was tired too and he had a little sleep. He woke up a while ago raring to go, so *Táta* has taken him to Notre Dame Cathedral to look at the gargoyles. Poor man had worked himself into a state because he hadn't made sure you were wearing your hat, leaving you alone in that hot cabin and booking the *bateau* in the first place."

"I'm sorry, it was all my own fault. I should have had more sense."

For a moment she was so like her father with his baby blue eyes, large and pleading. She even used words similar to the ones he had, when he'd been off on his escapades. It wasn't the same thing at all of course, but Linda's stomach gave a lurch and she thought 'Please God, let her mean that.

Don't let her turn out to be like him.' In consequence she said, a little more forcefully than she meant to. "You're right, at your age you should have."

Henni was shocked by her mother's sternness. *She* wasn't the one who had been ill and had a rotten headache, but some guardian angel must have whispered in her ear as she said nothing.

Linda looked at her daughter and suddenly smiled. "Come on. If you're feeling well again we should go out for something to eat. We missed lunch. I'll message *Táta* and tell him you are feeling a lot better and suggest we meet them on Pont Neuf. We'll get the metro to the Boulevard St Germain at Odeon in the Latin Quarter, join the café society for a while and walk back along the Boulevard St Michel. I used to like doing that when I was young." Henni thought she might like that too. Franz soon messaged back, 'Pleased she is OK. Now at Jardine de Tuileries. Will meet you Pont Neuf, Quai Du Louvre side in an hour. X '

While she was getting ready, Henni asked how old her mother was when she first came to Paris.

"Seventeen. It was a birthday present from my parents. They'd kept it as a surprise and had invited my good friend Angelique to come with me. We had a lovely weekend sitting in the cafés, flirting with boys, and trying our first Gitane cigarettes." She smiled as her voice trailed off reminiscently.

"You don't smoke!"

Her mother shrugged her shoulders. "We were young, without a care in the world." She looked at her daughter. "Your time will come, Henni. Enjoy it but be careful, and make it last longer than I did."

"Did you ever come back?"

"Oh yes. I spent a few more summers here. At one time I considered studying at the Sorbonne."

"Sorbonne?"

"That's Paris's great university, we can see it this evening if you like, but I chose to study architecture at Imperial College in London instead. When I lost my wonderful parents during my first year there, I wanted to give it all up and return to Switzerland. I did for a while, but without them there was nothing to hold on to, so I went back to Imperial where I met your father. I thought he was perfect. He became everything to me."

Linda seemed to drift off somewhere and forget she was still talking to her daughter. "We were infatuated with each other and married far too soon, neither taking into account the other's long-term needs. I found out the hard way that some men, however caring and charming they may seem, are not good husbands. I'm sure he never set out to hurt me, but he did, very much. Only this morning I told you being grown up isn't just looking the part. Harry hadn't taken a step into the adult world until the day I left him. He's found it hard going, I'm not certain if he's ever going to make it completely, but…" Linda tailed off a little sadly.

Henni was astounded by her mother opening her heart to her in this way and found it gratifying, if a little disconcerting, to be taken into her confidence.

"But what?"

"But… I hope he does. That's all." Linda managed a little smile.

"What about *papa-Franz?*"

"*Papa-Franz is* a grown up. He's a good man and a good husband. I love him with all my heart for it."

"He doesn't really like Harry though, does he?"

Linda paused for a moment. "No. He doesn't. But do you think Harry likes him any better?"

"No."

"And I think you can guess why. You may be young, but you're not that naive," Linda said with unexpected candour.

"Do *you* like Harry?"

"You can't expect me to answer that, Henni. But I can tell you, I respect him more than I thought I ever could, because he's been a very good father to you."

"How? I hardly ever see him."

"For exactly that reason. You see he knew he had a right to make a claim on you, and could have made life very difficult for all of us. You might have been taken away until a judge decided who you should live with. They almost certainly would have tried to show I wasn't fit to be your mother because I had lied to your father. All kinds of things that don't bear thinking about could have happened. But he cared more about you than himself, and couldn't bear to risk you being hurt or unhappy, so he did the best, and for him, the hardest thing possible. He left you to live out your childhood in peace with us. In return we promised that when you were old enough to understand, we would tell you what he did for love. The yearly visits were our gift to you both."

Henni had fallen silent. Her mother had said so much she wasn't sure she was really ready to hear.

"I'm sorry if I've upset you, sweetheart, there was never going to be a right time to tell you these things and I can't explain why I spoke about them now. Nothing was further from my mind. But now you know what we did, and why Harry has kept at arm's length. It wasn't because we were being mean, it was for both your sakes. A sign of being a grown up is not being able to do what you want, it's being able to do the right thing, even if it's not what you want to do at all."

"I think I understand what you're saying, *Máma*, and it was a good plan when I was a little girl. But now is different, I want to see more of Harry, I like him a lot, he's fun to be with and he *is* my father. I love my *papa-Franz* very much, but they hate each other. I don't want them to do that because of me. I love them both but in different ways, so how can I choose which one to love best?"

"You don't have to. It's something they have to work out for themselves. But a word of warning, don't play one off against the other. It may seem like fun at the time, but it's a dangerous game to play, you could end up losing them both."

Henni hadn't realised her mother had noticed how mercilessly she teased them, especially *Táta*. She decided it was a very childish trick and resolved never, or hardly ever, to do it again. She was, after all, her father's daughter.

"Time's getting on, we should be going or *Táta* will worry. Are you still OK?" Linda asked.

"Yes, I'm fine. Thanks for telling me about things. I'll try not to make it worse for either of them, but will you ask *papa-Franz* not to treat me as if I was still nine years old. I can't help it, but it makes me so cross."

"It's his nature, he only wants to protect you from all the bad things in the world, try to be patient. I'm working on it. Ready? Let's go then."

They reached Pont Neuf in good time to meet Franz and Fran. The metro ride was a bit of a bonus, for some reason it was one of the old carriages, the Art Nouveau kind that were painted dark green and gold. It had old fashioned wooden slat seats, not as comfortable as a modern carriage but much more aesthetic and it was only a short ride to their stop.

Soon they were faced with a street of bistros where students were having earnest conversations across tiny tables. It was one of the few authentic areas left in the Latin Quarter, a little edgy and exciting. They found the Rue Michel le Prince, to look at the *Polidor*, one of the oldest Bistros in Paris, established back in 1845. As it didn't actually open until 7.00pm, they had to opt for a less well-known establishment for supper.

The intersection of the St Germain and St Michel Boulevard was not far from their bistro and when their meal was finished they wandered over to the Museé de Cluny which is set inside the ancient Roman Baths, but decided not to go in as it was getting late and would be too much for Fran at the end of a long day. Henni would have liked to see the *Unicorn and Lady* tapestries inside, that her mother had talked about, but in her new mode of 'understanding adult', she didn't press her suit.

Fran didn't express any opinion about anything, until he got excited by one of the posters displayed by the door. It was very attractive. A midnight blue sky, a sliver of silver moon, seven silver stars and a magic mechanical silver bird flying high across it. The image was stunning.

"Look, *Máma*, *Táta*, look." He pointed at the beautiful poster. "Please, may we go and see that? Please."

Linda looked at the dates and said, "It does look good but I'm sorry it isn't on yet. We'll have left Paris before it opens."

Fran was devastated at not being able to see the beautiful magic bird and began to cry.

"Tell you what," suggested Henni. "Why don't we go in

and I'll ask if they sell the posters in the shop."

Fran looked hopeful.

"They mightn't do that," Linda said, "but it can't hurt to ask."

Henni smiled, took Fran's hand and walked boldly into the museum to make enquiries.

"That was kind," Franz said. "I'd better go and keep an eye on them though."

"No, let her do it herself." She gave him a meaningful look and he smiled.

"OK. She's a big girl now, it was her idea. She can manage."

They stood in the porch waiting for the children to return. Franz went outside to have a second look at the much-desired poster. He hadn't really taken that much notice; whimsy wasn't to his taste. But he hadn't taken much more than a step when he saw a familiar-looking figure coming out of a side door of the museum. The man turned to speak to someone inside, laughed and quickly walked off down the Rue des Écoles away from the Boulevard. Franz could have sworn for a moment it was Harry.

Just then Linda called to him. Henni and Fran were coming out of the museum. Fran was clutching a long cardboard tube. They both had big grins on their faces.

"Well done," Linda was saying, "so they did sell them after all."

"No," said Henni, "but Fran was crying so I explained all about how sad my little brother, who'd been ill, was at missing the exhibition, I even managed to squeeze a tear out myself. The man behind the desk took pity and said he would see if he could find us a spare. He didn't even charge us any money."

"Henni! How could you do such a thing?" Franz asked, half amused.

"Easy," she replied. Linda tried hard not to be amused at all.

They wandered off in the direction of the Sorbonne, and when she saw it Henni was momentarily struck dumb. It was magnificent and she desperately wanted to be part of it.

Finding her voice, she asked, "What do they study there, *Máma?*"

"Lots of things. I once had a fancy for doing Philosophy here. Mainly I can admit now, because it sounded rather grand and clever. But when I looked into it, found it wasn't for me."

"What is Philosophy?"

"In France I'd say, mainly discussions on the bleakness of existence and the pursuit of Universal Truths and Principles."

"Oh," Henni replied.

They crossed over to the Luxembourg Garden to gaze through the railings at the Conseil de la Republique building for a while. But Fran was starting to get fretful because he was tired, so instead of walking back down the Boul. St Michel they took the metro, this time in a modern carriage, back to Pont Neuf and their hotel where Franz helped his son into his pyjamas and tucked him up in bed.

Fran threw his arms round his father's neck, giving him a great big hug.

"I've had a lovely day, *Táta.* I liked you being bigger than the Eiffel Tower, that was funny, and Hen got me my lovely poster. May I have one last look?"

"Of course." Franz pulled it carefully from its cardboard sleeve, unrolled it and held it up for his son to see. "Now off to sleep," he said, but Fran's eyes had already closed.

He turned the poster round to look at it himself. The typography also in silver, ranged right across the bottom edge. At first glance it had looked more like a hedge of bare trees, rather than actual letters. He thought it rather clever and could see why Fran had been so attracted by it. As he looked more closely though, he read the words, *AUTOMATA-THROUGH-THE-AGES*, now shining sharp and bright, against the dark blue background sky. He remembered the man who had looked so like Harry coming out of the museum, and felt physically sick.

CHAPTER SEVEN

'The fucking bastard!' Franz thought viciously. 'They did this on purpose. Henni knew it was *his*. That's why she was so keen to get it for Fran. The manipulative little bitch. She may be his brat, but he's not going to get my son as well...' Never in his entire life had Franz felt such rage. He wanted to tear the poster to pieces and beat the truth out of the pair of them.

He plunged into a chasm of suspicion. Flailing against his descent he held on to the thought that's all it was, suspicion. He had no proof for his belief. How could she have known? How could Harry have known they'd be there? They were walking past, it was Fran who stopped and asked to go in. Fran who wanted the poster. Henni was just being kind to her little brother, as she could be sometimes. It was a coincidence. It probably hadn't been Harry at all, just some French guy who looked like him. Even if it had been, it wouldn't be so odd, the exhibition was opening in a couple of days, and naturally he would have to be there, just as he would when the exhibition arrived in Prague. Harry had grounds for wanting to please his daughter, but Fran meant very little to him. It was Fran who was so enamoured of the wretched poster, and the child didn't even know what it was, he merely liked the pretty picture. Surely none of them had the time or wit to work out so complicated a plot. It just happened, that's all. Rationality was returning to Franz. He realised he was being ridiculously paranoid over nothing. The fall had been frightening, but he was strong, he could get back to solid ground and reality.

Instead, he fell further. What about Linda? What of his wife? She was more than smart enough to arrange it. She was the one who wanted to get in touch with *him* again in the first place. She was the one who suggested this holiday. She was the one who wanted to go to the Latin Quarter tonight. She was the one who walked them to the Museé de Cluny. She was the one who insisted Henni take Fran into the shop alone. She could have told Henni all about her plan, when they were alone together that afternoon... How could he have been so stupid, it was obvious, Linda still loved Harry and wanted to take not only Henni but Fran as well, when she ran back to him.

The adjoining door to the next room opened quietly, Linda's face appeared. She was going to ask if Fran was asleep, but when Franz turned to look at her, she saw the horror in his eyes.

"What's wrong? Is Fran alright?" She ran to the child's bed; he was sound asleep. She looked at her husband and tried to reach for his hand. He snatched it away. Now, she too was distressed. "What is it? Can't I help?"

"Tell Henni to go to bed. I need to talk to you." Linda went back and he heard her urgent voice speak to Henni. A door opened and closed and when she returned he led her back into their room and closed the door carefully on Fran's so as not to wake his sleeping son, then faced her. Alarm was flickering in her eyes. She had never seen him like this, and he frightened her.

"I'm not playing this game anymore, Linda," he hissed.

She was at a loss to understand. "What's happened, Franz? Not an hour ago we were all laughing. We were happy."

"I saw him."

"Saw who?"

"*Him*, Harry. He was coming out of the museum."

"You must be mistaken. Why should *he* be there?"

"Because that damned poster was for his bloody automata exhibition," he said, not bothering to lower his voice any more.

Linda drew her hand up to her mouth and gasped. "I thought his exhibition was going to be in Prague, in November. Are you sure?"

"I'm sure. He told me it was called, '*Automata-through-the-Ages.* Going to four capital cities. London first, then Paris, somewhere else and Prague last. As if I might be interested."

Ignoring his bitterness, she said, "I don't see that written anywhere."

"Neither did I at first, but look." He handed her Fran's poster and after a moment she saw how the 'hedge' at the bottom was made of letters that spelt out the title of the exhibition.

"You can't blame him for that, Franz. He couldn't possibly have known we were there and Fran would want to see the exhibition. Henni got her brother the poster in all innocence, to stop him crying. It's not as if Harry planned it."

"How do we know he didn't?"

Linda was stunned by what he was suggesting. "You

can't mean he deliberately arranged to meet Henni in the museum, and she lied to us about it?"

"She was happy enough to tell us she lied to the curator."

"It's not the same thing, and you know it!"

"How do I *not* know it?" he said, hardly able to control his anger. "I can see through him. He plans not only to ingratiate himself with Henni, but Fran as well."

"How could you believe that?"

He cut across her words. "Because you still love him, don't you?" His words stabbed like ice into her heart. "You're preparing the ground between you. You want to take them with you, when you go scurrying back to him."

Linda stared in shocked silence.

"Deny it then. For the love of God, tell me it's not true!"

"Franz, I don't know what to say, except you're the rock we've built our lives on. You saved my life and Henni's. With no distinction between her and your own son, you fathered them both in equal love. How could we ever want to leave *you*?"

"That's not good enough. I want you to say it! Tell me straight. Do you love Harry?" His face was distorted with fury.

Speaking slowly and quietly she said, "If your heart doesn't know the answer already, how can I convince you in mere words?"

He looked hard into her beautiful face. Full of pity and love she met his gaze frankly. His eyes fell first and he felt shame for doubting her. She reached out her hand to him, he hesitated, then took and held her wrist so tight it hurt her. For a long moment there was silence.

"Help me," he said disconsolately. "Stop this torment. I

believe he's bewitched you, just as he has my daughter, and was about to steal Fran. He's already stolen my reason. It might have been coincidence we were at the museum at the same time, but something inside keeps telling me it was a plot you were all involved in. My nightmares are becoming real to me."

"My poor love," she said, "I knew you didn't find it easy, but I never guessed how much anguish you would suffer when we let him into our lives. You've always been so strong. Thinking too much about Henni's needs I neglected yours… Look, shall we just go home?… Forget about Derbyshire and the rest of it."

He released her hand. "What about Henni? She'd be devastated," he said perversely.

"I'll explain, tell her that circumstances have changed."

"It'll be hard for her."

"Your well-being has to be considered as much as hers. She wants to be grown up. This could be a good first lesson."

"Thank you Linda, but no. You… We can't do that to her because I lost control. It would be cowardly, to punish her for my weakness… I couldn't live with it. Besides, even if you don't, Henni loves Harry…"

The 'if' was another shard of ice. But she answered honestly.

"A child's affection can be bought cheap."

"She loves him best." The acerbity in his voice was palpable.

"I'm sure she doesn't!" Linda even managed a nervous smile. "Henni and I had a little 'heart to heart' this afternoon so I can say that with confidence. The love she has for you is very real and deep-rooted. She may take you for granted but it's because you're her father, tell me any child who doesn't do that. She likes being with Harry a lot, he *can* be good fun, she loves him as a best friend, but even she can sense he lacks the gravitas to be her father."

"She loves me for my gravitas? No wonder she wants to be with him."

"All I'm trying to say is, we know he adores her, she'd only have to ask and he'd give her anything in the world, and that to a child can seem like heaven. But he's not a fool and quite aware Henni needs more than sweets and treats to grow. She needs actual parenting, and he has just enough sense to realise he hasn't a clue. His and Henni's relationship wouldn't last five minutes if he had to cope long term. One of them, without doubt he, would go down. She would end up despising him, as I did. That's why he left her with you and me… He could never discipline himself, never mind a child."

Franz, feeling a little better, but needing more reassurance, said, "Linda, if you despised him why did you want to let him into our lives?"

"I thought I was doing the right thing at the time."

"Do you regret it?"

"At this moment, profoundly."

"Do you still despise him?"

"Since being with you, I've felt sorry for him that's all. I don't even feel that now he's got Sara. She's the one he wants, Franz, not me."

"Ah, Sara. Do you mind he prefers her to you?"

"No," she said wearily, "Harry and I were so wrong for each other. *We,* you and I, my love, have been so right and I've spoiled it. I made you suffer because I neglected to include your feelings in my calculations. You've always been so kind and patient with me. How much you've had to bear. I asked too much of you… Like Henni I took your gravitas for granted," she said, trying to smile. "Please forgive me, forget about my stupidity and let us go home."

"It's too late for that now. It would do more harm than good," he said. "We'll go to Derbyshire and York. We've got to do this for Henni's sake. One more question." Cupping her face in his hands he asked with some tenderness, "Do you love me more than you ever loved him?"

"Please, I can't bear you to doubt me. Believe I love you infinitely more. Loving and being loved by you is a 100-carat diamond. Harry gave me nothing but paste."

He seemed satisfied and held her close. She rocked him in her arms, stroking his hair like a baby, comforting them both, because suspicion is infectious and they were both so afraid she might not have been telling the absolute truth.

CHAPTER EIGHT

Harry had been busy all day getting his exhibit in place at the Museé de Cluny. Tomorrow he would go back for a final check, before the great and the good arrived, for the private view. He had to stay for that, then could fly back to England, Sara and home. It had been a long exhausting day and he was glad to be back at his hotel. Totally unaware of the drama being played out in another hotel a few kilometres away, he took off his shoes and lay full length on the bed. He checked his watch and gauged Sara would be back from the concert by now. He keyed her number on his phone. She answered almost immediately.

"Hello, Harry, how's it going?"

"Fine," he replied.

She had just returned home after taking part in a Festival Concert in her home city. It was in homage to Sir John Barbirolli's EMI recording of Elgar's Cello Concerto, famously played by Jacqueline du Pré, combined on disc with Dame Janet Baker singing the 'Sea Pictures' cycle. The cellist playing tonight was winner of the previous year's 'BBC Young Musician of the Year' contest, and Sara had been invited to perform the songs to complete the programme.

"Tell me about the concert. Were you absolutely brilliant as always?"

"I was very nervous. Baker's a hard act to follow, but I think I did alright. Angela is a brilliant cellist. She was wonderful, and in my opinion was as exciting as du Pré to listen to. She'll achieve great things, I'm sure. We got a standing ovation. How much was for her, and how much for me I don't know. I suspect it was mostly hers, but it was nice anyway."

"It would have been at the least fifty-fifty," he said, loyally and probably truthfully. "I may not have merited a standing ovation like you, but I *have* performed my good deed for the day."

"Have you now? Been helping old ladies across the street again?" she asked, with just a touch of sarcasm in her voice.

"Certainly not! I don't do that kind of thing any more, since the last grannie ran at me with her shopping trolley." She laughed and he went on to tell her, "It was in the museum as a matter of fact. I was in the office just preparing to go, when the curator came in looking for a spare poster to give to a couple of kids. He said the little one had been ill and was very upset because he would miss the exhibition. I had a peek at the two waifs, and one looked so like Henni, much older and taller with shorter hair, but the resemblance was so amazing that I told him to take down the poster on display by the desk and give it to them. I promised to bring another first thing in the morning to replace it. It was near on closing time, no one would ever know."

"That was kind, Saint Harry of the Poster. You'll be seeing the real Henni soon."

"Just over a week. Do you think it'll work out? I'm a bit

worried about Pam, she didn't seem too happy. It's a shame *he's* got to be there as well, but we'll have to make the best of that. He'll just sit in a corner and glower at me as usual."

"He wouldn't glower nearly as much if you and Henni didn't tease him. Try to be nice and get on."

"The only way we get on is on each other's nerves."

This line was going nowhere, so Sara changed the subject. "Oh, I nearly forgot, Monique, Bertrand and Julie from Menton, are going to Paris next week, they're going to her sister-in-law's third wedding, and would you believe, it's the groom's third time as well. A classic case of optimism triumphing over experience, if ever there was one. Anyway, they hope to make time to go to the Museé de Cluny afterwards, to see your automaton in action."

The conversation wandered safely off into reminiscences of the times spent with the friends they'd made during the first weeks of their meeting on the Côte d' Azure, five years ago. Then the two sleepy people continued talking a long while more, before they could bring themselves to say goodnight.

When he woke next morning, Fran, who was the kind of child who could sleep through the Last Trump and had heard nothing of Franz's tirade at Linda, was very excited. Today was the day *Táta* had promised to take him to the Natural History Museum and La Ménagerie, while 'the girls' went shopping on the Champs-Élysées. He didn't notice his parents' restrained mood and Henni seemed to be having trouble getting out of bed. She was never late for breakfast, which they would be if she didn't get a move on. Linda went to Henni's room.

"Come on Sleepy-head, all the *pain-au-chocolat* will have gone if you aren't quick."

"I'm not really hungry, *Máma*. May I miss breakfast this morning?"

"Are you feeling unwell again?"

"A bit," and she began to cry. "I heard *Táta* shouting at you last night."

Linda went cold. "I'll tell them you've got a bit of a headache left over from yesterday. I'll be back in a minute."

She went back and told Franz not to worry. "Girl problem," she said. Franz nodded. Fran had no idea what they were talking about and was pleased when *Táta* finally took him down to breakfast.

This was going to be difficult. Linda could barely cope with it herself. How could she explain to her daughter? Henni's eyes were red with lack of sleep and tears. Linda sat down on her bed and put her arms around her.

"It was horrible, *Máma*. I've never heard anybody say things like that. He was so angry. He scared me."

"He was upset. He'd made a mistake and misunderstood what had happened, so got cross and started saying things he didn't mean."

"But he was sort of right! When Fran and I asked for a poster, at the museum, the curator went to look for one in a room at the back. I heard him and another man talking. When I looked over for a second, I thought I saw Harry. I knew it couldn't have been him really, because he didn't come out to say hello. Then the curator came back and took the display poster down, and gave it to Fran. But if *Táta* saw him as well, he must have been there, hiding from us. Tell *papa-Franz*, honestly I didn't know and I'd never told Harry where we were."

"I'm absolutely certain you didn't, my pet. Tell me, did Fran believe he saw Harry too?"

"I don't think so. He was crying. He doesn't notice anything." Linda breathed again. "You will tell *papa-Franz* I didn't know, won't you?" Henni pleaded.

"It might be better to say nothing at all or he might get upset again. You both might have been mistaken. Sometimes people have doppelgangers."

"What's a doppelganger?"

"Someone who looks very like someone else. Let's leave it at that shall we? Don't talk to anyone else about what you overheard last night, least of all *Táta*." She patted Henni's hand reassuringly. "It's probably better if you keep quiet about it. Do you understand Henni?"

Seeing the bruise her stepfather's fingers had left on her mother's wrist she said, "Yes, *Máma*, I do."

About half an hour later Franz brought his son back.

"*Táta* brought some breakfast for you and Hen," Fran said to Linda, as he held up a plate piled with croissants and pastries.

"How is she?" Franz asked. "Shall I cancel the Natural History thing?" Fran's face fell.

Linda looked down at her son. "I don't think so. We weren't going anyway. If she feels better we can do our shopping later. It wouldn't be fair if Fran missed out on seeing all the giant dinosaur bones," she said, smiling at his eager little face. She turned to her husband and said, "Thank you for bringing us breakfast, it was very kind." As she accepted the plate from the boy, Franz saw the bruise. His face turned pale and he couldn't take his eyes from it.

"*Táta*, can we go now please. Will I need my hat?"

"Er, yes Fran. Go get it now… Brush your teeth first," he called after him, as Fran dived into his room.

"Did I do that?" he asked Linda.

"Not on purpose, you're a strong man who squeezed too hard."

"You forgive too easily." Despite himself, he made it sound like an accusation.

Fran skipped into their room. "I'm ready, *Táta.*"

"I'll just go and see how Henni is before we go," he said to him, "then we're off."

He went to her room and knocked gently. As there was no reply, he quietly eased the door open. She'd heard him coming and was pretending to be asleep, Franz could see the dark shadows under her eyes and tenderly moved a wisp of hair from her pretty face.

"She's asleep," he said to Linda when he went back to their room.

Linda nodded.

"*Táta!* Can we go now? Pleeease!"

Franz kissed Linda on the cheek uncertainly. As their eyes met, her smile was just as tentative.

"Have a lovely time, both of you," she said. "Don't let the dinosaurs gobble you up, Fran."

"Silly *Máma.* Dinosaurs are dead. They don't eat people, do they, *Táta?*"

Franz shrugged his shoulders. "I hope not, but we'll go and find out, shall we?"

"Well, we'll see you later then," Franz said to Linda. "I hope Henni's feeling better soon. Give her a kiss from her *táta.*"

"Yes, I will."

"Bye, *Máma.* Come on, *Táta.*" Fran was eager to be off,

and held the door open for his father who with a glance back at his wife, followed him.

Henni heard her stepfather and Fran leave and went to sleep for real. When she woke she saw her mother resting in the easy chair by the window.

"Hello, Henni." She smiled. "I think you should have some breakfast, it'll make you feel better. Fran brought some up for you." She indicated the large plate of croissants and pastries now looking slightly limp, sitting on the bedside cabinet. "They've gone to the *Jardin de Plants* to see the dinosaurs and wild animals at the zoo."

"I don't want any breakfast and please don't try to pretend everything's alright. It isn't, is it? I heard everything he said. I could tell you were as frightened as me. I was even more scared when it went quiet. I got out of bed and listened at the door to make sure you were still alive." Henni was sobbing so hard, Linda had sprung from her chair to hold her.

"You're right. I shouldn't pretend. He did say unbelievably nasty things about both of us. He did frighten me horribly. I hadn't realised how jealous he felt about sharing us with Harry. He thought we didn't care about him anymore. But believe me, he was even more frightened than we were, he thought he was losing us. Everyone, even the strongest, has a breaking point, and he'd reached his. If you understand, then you'll forgive him as I do."

"What if he does it again – and keeps on doing it whenever I want to see Harry. I'll have to choose which one to love best. You told me I wouldn't have to do that."

'I… We must convince him his fears are unfounded, and in the awful event of his still refusing to believe we love him, then he'll have made the choice. The thing he fears most will happen… We'll lose one another."

"Do you think that it will happen again?"

"I hope not… But I don't know," Linda answered with reluctant honesty.

"Am I not allowed to love Harry anymore?"

"No one can stop you loving someone, only they can do that themselves."

Henni didn't understand what her mother meant and asked her question again. This time Linda answered, "Yes Henni, you're allowed. Now go wash your face and get dressed. We were going to go shopping."

"*Máma*, I can't!" Henni cried. "It wouldn't have happened if it wasn't for me. It's all my fault! And you said he might do it again."

"Don't talk that way. Of course it wasn't all your fault, it wasn't your fault at all… and I didn't say he *would* behave like that again, I said I didn't know, which is not the same thing."

Desperate to try to make Henni understand, Linda remembered something from her daughter's past. "Listen, do you remember when you were about Fran's age and Jitka first came to your school? Anna started playing with her and you got upset because Anna was *your* best friend not hers. You wouldn't speak to her unless it was to say something unkind, then Anna got upset in return. She came with her *máma* to our house with some sweeties as a present. Her *máma* and I went into the kitchen to make coffee, she wanted to talk to me about why the two of you had fallen out. While we were in there we heard you fighting, the sweets were thrown all over the floor and you both were in tears. Then Mrs Vyšna explained Jitka was the daughter of a friend. Knowing the girl would be lonely at a new school she had asked Anna to take care of her and play with her. Mrs Vyšna thought because you and Anna were such good friends you wouldn't mind, but you did, very much."

"It's not the same," Henni insisted.

"Maybe not exactly, but try to remember how hurt and angry you were. You couldn't bear the thought that Anna preferred Jitka and you were very jealous. But as soon as it was all explained, everything was fine. You stopped hating Jitka, Anna and you were best friends again. You even found you actually liked Jitka and now you're *all* friends. None of you have ever fallen out again."

Henni started to get the point her mother was making. "But we were only little kids," she said by way of excuse.

"Children often make the mistake that adults don't feel every hurt as keenly as they do. We just pretend we don't. We bottle it up inside, because we think 'grown ups' shouldn't feel that way. You only spent a few days feeling second best, imagine how *Táta* must have been feeling for the last few years... I know how I felt when I was married to your father," she added quietly. "If it's anyone's fault it's mine. I created the situation in the first place. I could have acted differently but I wanted my revenge on Harry so much. *Táta* understood. He didn't pass judgement but helped me come to terms with what I'd done and took us both to his heart. Then when I wanted to make it right with the past he trusted me to do it, without counting the cost he might have to pay. I... I shouldn't be speaking to you like this. I'm sorry, Henni..."

Now it was Henni's turn to do the comforting. "It's alright, *Máma*, you can tell me if it makes you feel better. I won't say anything... and the more you tell me, the more I understand."

"I've told Franz I'm sorry," she said with tears in her eyes. "There's nothing else I can do."

They sat together in silence until Henni said, "I don't mind going out now, but not shopping. I've seen the Latin Quarter, shall we go somewhere else you liked when you were young in Paris?"

"I'd love to," Linda replied. "Montmartre. Let's go there. No one can be unhappy standing on the marble steps of Sacre Coeur." Within the hour they were on the metro, no longer just mother and daughter, but friends and confidants.

CHAPTER NINE

At the Natural History Museum Franz found it hard to put
the previous evening out of his mind. His reasoning had
been very swift and precise, his argument logically unassail-
able. The only flaw was he'd possibly got his initial premise
wrong. Through a mixture of uncertainty, shame and
embarrassment, he was finding it difficult to keep his mind
focused enough to maintain a father's exaggerated interest
in his son's encyclopaedic knowledge of brontosauruses'
and raptors' eating habits.

Eventually Fran tired of bones and stuffed animals and
was keen to get on to the living specimens of the *Menagerie*.
But before the second half of the day, lunch was in order and
they went to one of the little restaurants dotted about the
jardin. As they were alone together, it would be a good time
to question Fran about that poster. Half of Franz protested at
the idea of quizzing the boy, but the other wanted to know
if the suspicions he'd harboured against Linda and Henni
were valid. It was a tough call. Did he trust his wife or not?
Would it do any harm to ask Fran what had happened in
the Museé de Cluny? Fran saved him the agony of having to
decide by bringing up the subject of posters himself.

"I like my silver bird poster that I got yesterday. *Táta*, may I have another one please, this time of some dinosaurs, *and*," he added, "one from the zoo? I'd like to put them on my bedroom wall when I get home."

"We'll go to the shop before we leave and you can pick which you would like, they'll have lots to choose from. You were very lucky to be given that one at the museum, they weren't for sale, were they?"

"No. The man said they weren't, then Hen made him feel sorry for me so he went through a door behind his desk, to look for a spare one. I thought it was a cupboard, but it can't have been because I heard him talking to someone in there. Then he came out, shut the door again, and took the one they had down, and gave it to us, and we both said 'thank you'. He was very kind."

"You say he was talking to someone in the back room. Did that person come out as well?"

"No. We didn't see him."

"Perhaps it was he who told the man to give you the poster."

"Maybe," Fran said carelessly, clearly having lost interest in his father's conversation. "Can we go now, *Táta*, I've finished my sandwich and I'd like to see the tigers first, please."

Franz paid the bill and took Fran's hand and went out to seek tigers, still with no perfect proof of guilt or innocence, just a vague, uncomfortable feeling of self-disgust.

By teatime they were on the metro heading back to their hotel, Fran was coping manfully with the two long cardboard tubes which held his new posters. One was, surprisingly, of pink flamingos and the other, unsurprisingly, of Tyrannosaurus rex. While the boy prattled happily about his day, Franz sat in silence with a heart as heavy as lead. He'd almost believed Linda last night, why did he doubt again now? Fran suddenly ceased his chatter and his father came out of his reverie.

"*Táta*, why are you crying?"

"Sorry, Fran, speck of dust must have got in my eye," he said quickly, and made a great display of rubbing his eyes. "There we are, that's better." But Fran didn't think it was dust and went as quiet as his father.

They were first back at the hotel. Fran was concerned, *Máma* should have been there. It was too empty without her.

"Where's *Máma* and Hen?" he asked.

"They've been shopping. Shouldn't be long. I thought they'd be back by now." After half an hour Franz said, "I'll give *Máma* a call and find out when they'll be home." Panicking, he put Linda's number up on his iPhone. Immediately there was a 'not available' message. She must have turned it off. Henni's was unobtainable as well. Something was not right. Henni never turned her phone off. Had he frightened and hurt Linda so much last night that at the first opportunity she'd taken her daughter and run not to Harry, but away from *him?* His misery was unbearable. An eyeless beggar could see that he had been acting like a vituperative fool. He had betrayed his innocent wife whom he loved, by jealously doubting her fidelity. His asinine disloyalty had been as crass as Harry's and his punishment just as deserved. He had lost the most perfect woman on earth forever. His life lay in ruins.

When Franz made his calls, Linda and Henni were actually in the hotel elevator which had no signal, so it was only a minute or two later that Linda opened the door to their suite.

Franz's heart turned somersaults when his wife walked in. He ran to embrace her like a long lost prodigal, much to the surprise of young Fran, who whispered to Henni that he thought *Táta* had had too much sun like she'd had the day before, because he was crying on the metro, and now he was acting all funny again.

Henni was just glad, and said, "Come on, little bro', show me what *Táta* bought you at the zoo today," and shepherded Fran into his room along with his new posters.

The day after was their final full day in Paris. As a special treat Franz insisted on taking them to Le 68 Guy Martin Thé Salon, annexed to the original Guerlain Boutique on the Champs-Élysées. He and Fran waited in the salon, nibbling on delicate little cakes, while the two women in his life were invited to choose from the range of perfumes and toiletries, an offer they did their best to enjoy in order to please him. Fran's treat was much less expensive, but he was the most blithe of the family. As he was now a collector of such things, he settled for something he might have had days earlier, a poster of Disneyland Paris.

CHAPTER TEN

Derbyshire

Pamela Martin still didn't feel wholly comfortable at the prospect of the Horbach visit. She would however do her best to make it a success for Harry's sake. As much as anything, to keep her mind off the encounter, she spent twice as much time as usual cleaning and polishing everything to within an inch of its life. Her cooking and baking increased twofold until the freezer was bursting with all kinds of culinary delights. Hams and bacon hanging in the cool pantry were checked daily and stored fruits in the airy shed picked over as if in preparation for the annual agricultural show. James risked an aside to Michael about the need to keep moving, for fear of being plumped up and placed like a cushion at one corner of the kitchen settle.

She engaged Mrs Baines from the village who did the charring, to subject Gamekeepers Cottage (used now only by Sara and Harry for weekend visits) to unnecessary extreme cleaning, until it shone like a newly scrubbed schoolboy.

Mrs Baines had been the regular 'help' at the farm for many years and remembered Harry and his wife from way back. Maintaining absolute secrecy in a small village is rare and it was rumoured that Harry's foreign ex-wife was coming back with a long lost daughter in tow. The Martins were an important family locally, Mr James was a county J.P. They were a well-regarded and respected part of the community, but known to be very close when it came to family matters. Therefore Mrs Baines was in the best position to get any juicy snippets of information out of the conclave and into the pool of general gossip.

When she went up to the main house for her pay, cup of tea and biscuit, Mrs Baines carefully broached the subject.

"Well, Mrs Martin," she said, when seated in the kitchen. "Gamekeepers Cottage is shining now. The Queen herself couldn't wish for better."

Pam was well aware she was fishing.

"Yes, we are expecting visitors. Thank you for coming at such short notice."

Mrs Baines held out her cup for a fill up of tea. "They'll be stopping at Mr Harry's house then?"

"No they aren't staying, it's just a quick visit."

Mrs Baines took a careful slow drink and said, "It's nice to have old friends call."

"They aren't old friends," Pam said too harshly and quickly. She could have bitten her tongue off when she saw a fleeting flash of triumph in Mrs Baines's eyes.

Draining her cup, Mrs Baines said, "Ah," and having gleaned enough information to make two and two make four, or even five, prepared to take her leave. "Will you be wanting me in a couple of weeks then?"

Pam had been indiscrete. She now had to make a quick decision. The cat had somehow got out of the bag. The village obviously had an idea who was coming to Manor Farm and what they didn't know, they would as usual, make up. She could leave it as it stood or tell Mrs Baines an acceptable version of the story and brazen it out.

Admitting defeat she said, "It's Harry's ex-wife and her new family. She's bringing Harry's daughter to meet us. He's visited her in Prague a lot, but it's her first time in England."

Mrs Baines was delighted, this was better than she'd hoped for. So it was true. The bugger did have a kid, they'd kept quiet about that one. Her apron was off and she was out of the door before Pam had gathered up the teacups. Pamela heaved a heavy sigh. It would be all round the village by teatime.

On the way home, Mrs Baines called in at the Black Sheep Inn where her friend was barmaid.

"Hiya, Babs," she said. "Get us a bag of pork scratchings, will you ducks? I've got a bit of news for you."

"Hiya, Sue, how you doing? Here you are. Now then, whatever it is you're busting to tell me, give us one of them scratchings and I'll listen."

"Well, I've just come from Manor Farm," Sue said, offering her bag of scratchings to Babs. "We were right. It *is* Harry's wife that's coming with his kid, it's a girl." She did a quick calculation. "Must be about fourteen at a guess. She's a foreigner like her mother. They're coming over from Prague."

"Prague? I had a weekend there once, for the Christmas Markets," put in Babs.

Slightly irritated by the interruption, Sue continued with her narrative, "*And* – it's not just them, she (meaning Pamela) said, her family's coming with her *as well*. Whatever that might mean. How'd you think of that, then?"

A local man in his mid-fifties had been listening to Sue.

He said sourly, "I'm surprised there aren't more of 'is sprogs coming out of the woodwork. He always put it about a bit."

"Jack, this is his legitimate daughter! He wasn't the only one by a long chalk who sowed a wild oat or two. We were all young once," said Babs.

"Oat or two? He did his best to sow a whole bloody field full."

"You're only jealous. He was… is, very charming and so handsome. Ooh, we fell for him like dominoes."

"You didn't!"

Babs smiled reminiscently and gave a little shrug of her shoulder.

"You dirty devil!" said Jack and they both laughed. "You're right, maybe we were a bit jealous of his successes. And that wife of his, what was her name…? Linda. My God, she was gorgeous, he was always a jammy sod."

"She left him though," Babs said a little sadly.

"Hmm, and it doesn't take a mastermind to guess why either," Jack replied. "Clever as they come but hadn't a clue about certain things that other people take for granted."

"Like her, he's got someone else now," Sue chipped in, eager to re-join the conversation. "She's a school teacher called Sara Middleton. Nothing special to look at compared to the other one, but they seem to suit one another."

"I really hope it works out for him this time. I and a few others I *could*, but *won't* name, Jack, so don't you ask… would like to see him happy. He gave us a good time. He was always so considerate and generous."

"Too bloody generous if you ask me. God! I'm glad I married someone from out of the village," Jack responded. "It sounds like he had a go at the lot of you."

"He certainly didn't have a go at me, Jack Watkins!" Sue, a good five years his senior, was indignant.

"Only joking, Sue, only joking." Although he was laughing, he wasn't joking at all.

CHAPTER ELEVEN

After three days in London doing the sights, Trafalgar Square, The Tower, Planetarium, Greenwich, Soho and Buckingham Palace just to mention a few, the Horbachs could have looked forward to a less frenetic time on a farm if they hadn't been so apprehensive.

On the drive there Franz's remorse still would not leave him. He thought over and over of their last night in the capital city. When as they'd lain in bed, he had said to Linda, "I don't think Henni enjoyed London so much, do you? She's been very quiet. Perhaps all this travelling has tired her out."

"Possibly."

After a few moments he'd articulated the unwanted and unpleasant thought that had actually been preying on his mind.

"She knows, doesn't she? She heard… when we were in Paris."

"She couldn't help it. Unlike Fran, she was wide awake."

"That's why she didn't come out for breakfast next morning. I knew she was only pretending to sleep when I went in. She didn't want to see me, did she?"

"She was upset."

"Does she hate me now?" he'd asked.

"No." Linda had answered kindly, with the touch of a smile just visible in the darkness. "But Henni thought she was to blame. She said it was all her fault."

He had sighed sadly and deeply as Linda continued, "I told her it wasn't at all. That it was just a misunderstanding and the fault was mine for asking too much of you. She said she understood and I believe she did. But she's had no experience of adult anger before and it frightened her, Franz."

"I'd give my soul for it not to have happened," he said. "What can I do to make it better? You've seen a side of me that even I didn't realise existed. I thought I was strong but I'm weak and despicable just like him."

"You *are* strong," she'd told him. "You're like Atlas bearing the weight of our world on your shoulders, but even that giant shrugged at times and sent the stars spinning. You are neither despicable, nor like Harry. You are faithful and truly love me. Harry was not, and did not. He's not a bad person, but if he sees a weak spot he'll exploit it. You both love Henni, and the tighter you hang onto her the harder he will try to prise her away. Half the time I don't think he even knows he's doing it."

Despite Linda's kind response Franz no longer felt so secure about holding the high ground he'd always assumed when dealing with Harry. His latent jealousy had disturbed the equilibrium he'd always taken for granted as being an essential part of his nature and he was so afraid he might lose it again. Also his relationship with Henni was on the edge. She was perfectly sweet and polite but avoided spending time with him on her own… God forbid, was she actually afraid of him? The thought hit him like a hammer. Complete fool that he was, he'd always held the great prizes in his hands and in one invidious moment of madness very nearly thrown them away. No matter what Linda had said, in his own mind he was not that different from the despised Harry, luckier maybe, he still had his wife safe, but he'd lost Henni's trust and had to win it back. Too proud and ashamed to tell her in words, he could only show her he knew how wrong he had been. He had already taken the step of acknowledging her right to love Harry, but that in itself was not enough. He couldn't afford to let Harry get under his skin because if he did, between them they would tear Henni apart. He only hoped it wasn't too late. In order to please her he would have to be magnanimous and allow her father a crust or two from his own munificence, like feeding a duck in a pond. He liked that image, he would hang on to it. It was so ridiculous it might take some of the sting out of what he had to do.

Linda was prey to more worries than she could contain. As soon as the lid was slammed on one, another escaped from the tin. How would Henni react to Harry, now she knew how her stepfather felt when she showed any affection to him? What of the Martin family's feeling towards her and what she'd done? Would they understand? Would they forgive? Would they accept Henni? Would Harry be so emboldened by being with his family to be openly hostile to Franz? How would Franz stand up to the ordeal? Would it all make him angry again? Why had she, even for a moment considered it to be a remotely good or workable idea? She looked at her husband driving steadily towards certain disaster. He turned his head, thinking of Harry as a duck in a pond, and smiled at her, she smiled back just because she loved him.

Henni was wondering if Harry would notice how much

she'd grown since their last meeting; it had been a year where she had changed quite a lot. Would he like her hair, now it was shorter? He'd always said how much he liked her plaits. The nightmare thought came quickly, what if it *had* been Harry in the museum and he just hadn't recognised her with her short hair? He would realise it the moment she got out of the car. Would he tease *Táta* and treat it as a joke? She'd tell Sara, that's what she'd have to do, Sara would help… If only she had her number she could message her now. She knew her mother had it.

"*Máma*," she said, "do you think we should message Sara to tell them what time we will be arriving? I'll do it if you like."

"Good idea Henni, but you don't have her number. I'll do it when we are a little closer," Linda replied.

Henni didn't want to make a big thing of it so just said "OK" as she wondered how to speak to Sara alone before any damage could be done.

Her mind went back to when *Máma* had said it was OK to love Harry, just as long as she didn't forget to love her *papa-Franz* too. She'd told *papa-Franz* from her heart, she could never stop doing that and knew it made him happy to hear it, but she also loved Harry and was now unsure about showing him too much affection. She had never been afraid of Franz before, but could not forget his terrible anger, and the awful violence of his words. She would never dare take him for granted again. His rage had been terrifying enough, but more frightening was the power she now knew she had, to wound them both so deeply. Henni felt more constraint than she'd ever experienced. She had to tread a careful path, not because she'd been told she must, but because she knew it was the only way to avoid strife. If being able to get it right was part of being grown up it was a part she could have done without. Regardless of what *Máma* had said, Henni felt the responsibility keenly; if she didn't get it right her stepfather would get angry again, and her mother, the peacemaker in the middle, would be hurt. She couldn't let that happen.

The only one who wasn't nervous was Fran. He was looking forward to seeing the farm, Harry and Sara would be there and they were always nice to him. Since going to school, his English had improved, it wasn't as good as Hen's, but she was older. He wondered if Sara had remembered some of the Czech words he'd taught her last time they met.

The satnav on their hire car flashed two miles to their destination. Franz drove through the village, a mile out he made the left turn that led to Manor Farm. There was no turning back now. The porch was open but the front door shut as the car drew to a halt. They sat for a moment to compose themselves before Franz turned off the engine and they climbed out. Fran, to whom the influx of honking geese seemed to take a liking, wanted his father to carry him. Franz obliged, but it was mainly to put a barrier between himself and Harry's family that he did it.

The door opened before they had progressed more than a few paces. There was his nemesis, with his arm resting affectionately on Sara's shoulder. Harry was smiling broadly. 'Like a duck,' Franz forced himself to think, 'who had to be content with the crumbs I chose to spare him from my bounty.' This image of Harry, tenaciously held in his mind, blotted out the Machiavellian schemer his fevered imagination had conjured up so recently. He could even turn to Henni with a slight smile to give a little nod of consent, and watch as she shot forward into Harry's now outstretched arms. Henni had hugged *him* like that a thousand times and he felt sad to see her holding fast to Harry, but now he had command of himself again, he could remember those thousand hugs, think of the thousands more to come and found less hardship in sparing just a few for Harry. He put Fran back onto the ground as Sara approached.

Harry had immediately noticed the difference in his daughter the moment he saw her getting out of the car. This was no longer a little child but someone on the verge of young adulthood. He also recognised her as the girl he had seen at the Museé de Cluny, bobbed hair and all.

He'd known they'd be in Paris, but thought it politic not to mention he too would be in the city at the same time. That they might meet seemed highly unlikely, it's a big place. It was indeed unfortunate that they turned up at the museum when Harry was there. Henni obviously hadn't seen him which probably, given what he knew of Franz, had been a good thing. Franz would have jumped to conclusions and made a big thing of nothing. He'd better warn Sara not to mention the girl in the museum he'd told her about. Then again, she was usually miles ahead of him in these matters. She'd probably work it out for herself.

His girl was little no more. He'd missed so much of her childhood and now look at her. He thought about how he had preyed on pretty girls when he was young, and despite his beautiful wife, on pretty women when he was old enough to know better. The thought didn't fill him with delight. He hated to admit it, but Henni needed a solid respectable moral father like Franz, as much now as when she was a child, maybe even more. He needed Franz to protect his daughter from men like him. All this had flashed into Harry's mind, in the time it took for Henni to leave Franz's side and run to him.

Sara greeted Linda with a kiss, and said to Fran as she shook his hand, "*Haló, jak se máte?* Did I get that right?"

Fran grinned widely, "Very near good. Yes. I am well thank you." As they finished the handshake she kissed him too.

Linda smiled. "You must have been practising hard, to remember that," she said.

"Google," Sara whispered, and turned to say hello, this time in English, to Franz. They shook hands and he felt a twinge of disappointment that Sara didn't feel comfortable enough to kiss him as well. He walked up to Harry, whose arm was now firmly clamped around his daughter. Despite his newly munificent mood, all he could manage was "Hello, Harry."

"Hello, Franz." No handshake was forthcoming. Henni's eyes flashed concern, but Harry's hold on her was tight.

Linda, Fran and Sara came up as a trio. Harry dropped his arm from round Henni's shoulder to shake Fran's hand with the ceremony denied his father, bobbed his head slightly, and said, "Hello, Fran, what a big boy you are now. Are you well?"

"Sara ask me that in Czech," he said.

"That's because Sara is very clever, and learns things a lot quicker than I do."

Franz wondered what he meant by that but Fran grinned, and with one hand Harry gently ruffled the boy's hair, before turning to his mother.

"Hello, Linda." He didn't dare risk even an air kiss, but lightly and briefly took her hand. With a slightly nervous smile he said, "I hope you've had a good holiday so far. Did you get to see everything you wanted?"

"*Táta* take us to Disneyland in Paris. There is good," contributed Fran.

"Thank you, Harry. We have had an exciting time," Linda said.

They could delay it no longer. "Come in," Harry said, opening the front door wide "and see James and Pamela. She's been preparing lunch for days, so I hope you're hungry."

Linda's laugh was genuine, as she remembered how fond Pamela was of feeding her family to capacity.

A final intake of oxygen and they allowed Harry to lead them into the farmhouse kitchen that Linda remembered so well.

CHAPTER TWELVE

Despite the warm weather, Pamela and James stood in their usual spot in front of the Aga. The dogs can't have been, but looked the same, as the ones she used to know, and the cat was still asleep on the old rug.

Tears pricking at her eyes, she felt the loss of this timeless setting as keenly as a lost childhood. James, much older than she remembered, still had his County Squire air. Pam's eyes were quite dry as she watched them come into her home. Linda and she had been such good friends and regardless of her good intentions, Pam found it hard to feel any warmth towards her. Linda missed the presence of Harry's mother Maggie, a devoted comforter who never apportioned blame even during the bad times.

James was the first to move. "Good to see you again Linda," he said, putting his hands on her shoulders.

"And this would be your husband Franz?"

She nodded and introduced them. They shook hands.

Pam was staring at Henni and Harry's proud face. "Pretty nice, isn't she?" Harry beamed. "They've not done a bad job on her have they?" He gave his daughter an extra hug.

Franz couldn't believe the compliment. Was Harry trying

a new tack to discomfort him? He searched for some irony or sarcasm in the remark but didn't find any. Could it be the 'duck' he was throwing crumbs to, was actually throwing something 'ducky' back to him in return? The image was getting too confusing, too bizarre, it had to be abandoned.

Pam looked from Linda to Henni, then Franz to Fran, before embracing Linda lightly, and then hugging Henni half to death. She paused for a moment before giving her hand to Franz. Turning to the boy who was hiding behind his daddy's legs she felt more comfortable and said, "You'll be Fran. Would you like a biscuit?"

The atmosphere was cool and tense, with the ice showing little sign of cracking.

Looking at James and Pamela, Sara said, "Why don't I take Fran out to the farm yard to collect the free-range eggs, while you get to know your niece and her stepfather." Then, principally to Pam continued with, "building bridges means saying things that parvenus like me don't need to hear."

"No, no, not at all," Pam protested. She felt so awkward about the situation and had rather counted on Sara to act as a kind of buffer between them.

"Really Pam, I'd rather not intrude. This is too private."

Linda saw exactly where Sara was coming from. She asked Fran if he would like to go with her and he said "Yes, please!"

Pam thought that Henni might like to go too, and she said she would, thinking it a perfect opportunity to have her words with Sara. But her parents insisted she was old enough to stay, after all, whatever they said would concern her as much as anyone. She had hoped *Táta* would object on the grounds she was still a child, but he'd just smiled at her, acknowledging her right as a young adult to be included. No one made any demur. Henni felt the full force of Lowell's remark 'granting our wish is fate's saddest joke.' Sara took Fran's hand, led him to the back door, gave him a basket to carry and they went off together on an egg hunt.

The rest sat round the old scrubbed kitchen table in silence. James then tried to make conversation about the weather.

"It's been very wet lately here, today's the first sunshine we've had all week. But at least it hasn't been cold. Was it dry in London?"

"Yes the weather was very clement," Franz answered.

"Was it good in Paris?"

"The first day rained, then it was very hot," was the reply.

Harry announced Henni used to have long plaits and asked her when she'd had them cut off.

"On my birthday, when I was fourteen," she answered with a sinking heart and little smile. But took the conversation no further.

Harry had never known her to be so shy and quiet before, he wondered if this meeting was going to be too much for her. For all of them.

"You look very pretty," he said. She smiled at him again.

The discomfiture in the room was growing palpable. Pamela took refuge in fussing about making tea or coffee, and asked Henni what she would like to drink.

"Milk please," Henni requested.

Just as a plate of homemade biscuits was placed on the table, James's mobile rang.

"Who's that?" Pam asked, grateful for the distraction.

James didn't reply to her. He simply said, "Right!" His face had gone ashen.

"Harry, quick! Get them back in! The bull's out and heading for the yard. I'll get my gun." James strode away to his gun cabinet and Harry was already gone by the time what James had said registered with the Horbachs.

Franz leapt to his feet. His son was out there. "It's better to let Harry do it. He knows how these beasts' minds work," James said with authority that could not be ignored. "I'll be out there. I'll shoot it dead if he can't handle it." So saying he made for the door, carrying what looked like a high-powered rifle.

Harry scanned the yard and spotted Sara about 50 yards away in front of the hay barn where he'd played as a child. Fran was scrabbling about under one of the sheds and held up an egg for her to see.

"Sara! Sara!" Harry yelled. "Get him in the barn! High as you can! The bull's got out! Coming this way!" He was running towards them as the bull skidded round the corner of the milking shed.

Sara grabbed Fran and helped him climb high on top of the bales. The bull, attracted by the noise Harry was making, turned its full malevolent attention on him. It pawed the ground, head down ready to charge. Harry stopped dead then made a sudden dive for the open shed door, the bull followed, smashing its head into the posts. James was levelling his rifle as the massively enraged beast shook itself and charged again. There was nowhere to hide, the bull would be through in nano-seconds. Harry had seen enough action movies to know that if he put his back to the wall the beast was charging at he might stand a chance. The momentum of the charge would carry it forward, hopefully far enough to give him time to back out of the broken door, allowing that the bull didn't smash the bit of wall he was hiding behind, then of course he would be crushed. The plan worked, the bull propelled in and skittering on the milking shed tiles fell to its knees.

Michael and Luke were bombing up the yard on quadbikes, a stockman was not far behind armed with bull poles and a halter. They leapt to the ground and roughly pulled Harry well clear, before corralling the cantankerous beast, which was having trouble getting to its feet. The cattle crush was trailed in on the tractor and eventually the bull safely contained.

James with his rifle now safely deactivated, said, "Well done lads. I'm glad I didn't have to shoot the bugger… Harumph… It would have made for a very expensive pile of beef burgers, to be sure. But how in hell did it get out in the first place?"

"Don't know yet, Dad," Michael said grimly. "The gate was secure. I triple-locked and checked it myself last night. The bull was still there this morning, we saw it in the field."

"OK, son, don't worry about it. We'll get to the bottom of the matter."

Franz had gone over to the hay barn to help Fran and Sara safely back down. Pam, Linda and Henni had watched in terrified silence from the kitchen window. Harry had disappeared into the old outside privy to quietly throw up.

Back in the kitchen Sara asked, "Where's Harry?" as in walked a dirty, dishevelled-looking figure.

"Sorry, Pam. I'm dripping slurry all over your clean floor, and I don't smell too good," it said.

Sara didn't care what it smelt like, she hurried over to hug and kiss it anyway. "You were so brave," she said, but could feel him shaking.

"That was remarkable," said Franz. "Thank you," and gave Harry's filthy hand a firm shake. Linda kissed her fingers to lay them on the least muddy part of his cheek, and Henni, back to her old self, said, "Wow! What a family I belong to. Two superhero fathers. How cool is that!"

Harry smiled, he'd never heard her refer to him as 'father' before, and his eyes shone when he said, in a mock American accent, "Yeah well, sometimes a man's godda do what a man's godda do, and we superheroes" – with a glance at Franz – "will do anything to impress a pretty girl. Ain't that so, pardna?" They, even Franz, smiled.

Pam, proud of him but ever practical, affirmed his opinion that he didn't smell too good and suggested a shower might be in order. Sara too, having picked up a fair amount of mud herself was also dispatched to wash and change before lunch.

Fran said to James, "That was *vzrušující*!" James looked to Franz.

"Exciting," he translated. "Fran thought it was very exciting."

James had to agree. It certainly had been. But he needed to know how such an inexplicable thing could have happened. He was sure it could not have been an accident. He would see what Michael came up with and contact the police.

As they held hands walking back to their cottage to obey Pam's orders, Sara could feel Harry still shaking.

"You were incredible. Just like a movie."

"I don't know," he said candidly, "just how much of the shit on me is slurry and how much self-generated. I was bloody scared, Sara."

"I know. That's what makes you such a hero."

She let him sluice off the slurry before joining him in the shower, where she sponged him down vigorously with verbena soap to remove all lingering odours. Shampooed and clean they towelled each other dry. He had scrapes and bruises on his forehead, knees and elbows which were dutifully kissed better. She lay naked, face down on the bed, resting her chin in cupped hands, watching him, a white towel tucked round his waist, paring his nails before he dressed. The old scars on his arm and shoulder and the memory of how he gained them, thrilled her. She found him totally beautiful. How meticulously neat he was, she mused. His immaculate shirts were always hung well spaced out in his wardrobe, never crammed in as hers often were. The trousers he wore, except when he'd rolled about in slurry, perfectly pressed. She could look smart enough when the occasion demanded, but as a rule, to put it kindly, favoured comfort over style. 'How can he put up with someone like me?' she wondered.

He caught a glance of her in the dressing-table mirror, and as if answering her thoughts, looking through it said, "It wasn't just the bull that scared me. If anything had happened to you today, I would have wanted to die. I'd do anything in the world for Henni, but without you, Sara, I'd have no world."

Her face burned red. He came over to her. "For one thing, who else would buy me rose-scented soap?" he asked, laughing at her embarrassment. She remembered once, years ago, giving him a bar of hers by mistake. She giggled, "You turned it down, though."

"I have my standards," he replied sententiously.

***

They arrived back at the Manor House by 1.30, by which time everyone else had gathered for lunch. The errant bull safely stowed in an alternative pen, Michael and Luke were no longer in grubby overalls but clean and smart. Carrie and young Peter, having missed the morning drama due to hair-dressing appointments, were concerned and keen to hear all about it.

"You should have seen Uncle Harry," said Luke in admiration, "he was like Rambo."

Harry, who wasn't immune from blushing as red as Sara, said, "But I bet Rambo never got to smell as bad as I did"– a grin spreading over his face.

They all had to laugh, because the smell had been pretty unforgettable.

Michael asked for a word with his dad before sitting down at table. He could tell Harry after his guests had gone, that two of the locks on the gate had been cut right through. The vet had come *pronto* to check the beast was OK. Also, Michael had contacted the police who would call later in the day. His father nodded in understanding and agreement as they processed into the best dining room to act as sommeliers and eat the fruits of Pamela's labour, which were many and varied. Pies of steak, ham and veal, chicken and mushroom, fresh seasonable vegetables from her garden, homemade sauces and condiments were placed in front of the hungry ensemble who devoured them all steadily and completely. Then there were the puddings. Raspberry Pavlova, homemade sorbet in three different flavours, and apple pie with lashings of cream. Then came the cheeses with homemade chutney and Pamela's speciality cheese-straw biscuits, crisp and light as a summer breeze. Franz, Henni and Fran had no idea they could eat so much delicious food in one sitting, everyone else had experience of Pam's culinary skills and knew that it was quite easy to stuff themselves to capacity and still have room for coffee, homemade chocolates and possibly a fine brandy if required, although that was usually reserved for after dinner.

The drama of the morning provided a good launching point of lively conversation for all of them. The men were soon apprising Franz of the amount of rustling that still went on, that led on to a more general discussion on the state of the world today and how things had or had not progressed. They asked if things were different in the Czech Republic etc. etc. The women, without apology, chose to discuss the best way to prepare children for life, and learning how education differed between their two countries. Henni and Fran attended the International School, where lessons were taught in English. As English was now the new *lingua franca,* everyone thought that was a good idea. There were occasional crossovers in conversation, but each sex stuck largely to its particular field of interest, gathering knowledge of each other that could be pooled later to create a fuller picture. It wasn't because either was excluded or uninterested in the other's chosen topics, merely 'division of labour' in action. It was a natural device for getting to know people from different perspectives, which for millennia had worked rather well.

Peter and Fran had a quiet start but soon discovered a shared admiration for Manchester United and their new striker. Fran taught him how to say *Tri nožní klaun,* meaning 'three footed clown', which was a favoured term of abuse for a player who missed an easy pass. "I also have a more good one, but *Táta* is here. I tell you later?" Peter nodded his head. He could grow to like Fran.

423

For Henni and Luke, who sat opposite each other, it was puppy love at first sight.

The clock showed just after three by the time they repaired to the sitting room. Pamela and Carrie insisted they could manage and soon the table was equipped with two large *cafetières* full of steaming coffee and a pot of tea for Sara. The chocolates were irresistibly arranged in a china dish and placed by the best matching china cups and saucers, from the set that had belonged to James's mother. Pam had pulled out all the stops for this reunion. Afternoon sun still warmed them, relaxed and soporific they were content, while the boys went off to play. Luke not caring for coffee, asked if he may show Henni the farm and take her to see Gamekeepers Cottage, where Uncle Harry grew up. That was deemed to be a nice idea, the house wasn't locked.

Thanks undoubtedly to the bull, it had all gone much better than anyone dared hope. Franz realised why Linda had wanted Henni to enjoy being part of this family, it was as close and caring as his own. Harry was clearly the maverick member, but they accepted him for what he was and loved him none the less. He felt mean for thinking so badly of him and in doing so, unwittingly hovered on the threshold of those who forgave him, just because he was Harry.

He looked over to Linda, who sensing his gaze smiled back radiantly at him. He sipped his coffee and helping himself to a chocolate, enjoyed the knowledge that beyond all shadow of doubt she loved him, Henni and Fran loved him, Harry loved Sara and Sara loved Harry. There was nothing to worry about. His world appeared perfect.

CHAPTER THIRTEEN

Luke walked Henni round the farm and pointed out the cottage.

"Would you like to go in? I don't think Uncle Harry would mind. You're his daughter anyway, and I reckon you have the right to go into your own dad's house."

It felt strange to Henni to hear Harry being referred to so casually as her 'dad'. She wasn't sure how comfortable she was about it. The word sounded much more intimate and warmer than 'father'. She wondered if she would ever dare use it herself.

He opened the door and Henni entered. It was quite lovely, like a smaller, less grand version of the Manor. She found it enchanting. Luke pointed out the old beams where the smoke of centuries had blackened them. She picked up a silver frame from the collection of items set on what her grandmother Maggie had called her 'shiny things table'. On it was a larger version of the tiny photograph Harry had sent her years ago. She could see her grandparents very clearly now. Maggie was young and fresh-faced whilst her grandfather was much older than she'd realised, who despite his smile looked rather stern.

"Did you know my grandparents?" she asked.

"I remember Aunt Maggie. She had cancer. I liked her a lot, she was really kind. We were all very sad when she died."

"Was that a long time ago?"

"About five years, now. I remember her funeral. Uncle Harry and Sara sang at the end of the service, and I still get goose pimples when I think about it. God they were amazing, I'm sure I felt her there with us listening. It was weird, but kind of nice.

"She was really my step-great grandmother, but only about ten years older than my gran. We're a funny family that way. But I never knew your grandfather 'cos he was miles older than Aunt Maggie, and died before I was born."

She replaced the photograph carefully on the table. "I've never heard Harry sing."

"Oh," said Luke, "I didn't know. He's bloody good, and so's Sara, if you like that sort of stuff. They go for the heavier kind as a rule, requiems and things. We'll get them to sing something lighter for us before you go if you like. They sometimes do if we ask nicely. Gran's good on the piano and can accompany them."

"I think I'd like that very much," she said. "Will you ask for me?"

"OK. Let's see the rest of the place." They went upstairs and were suitably reluctant to venture into the room Harry and Sara were sharing, so got no further than a quick glance before closing the door. Other rooms they felt free to explore and Henni loved them all. She thought the wide beautiful views from every window were straight out of a storybook. The sight of unalloyed joy on her beautiful face turned Luke's knees to jelly and before it could have too much of an unfortunate effect on another part of his anatomy, he said, "We'd better go."

On the landing Henni spotted another stair. "Where does that go?" she asked not unreasonably.

"That's the attic."

Henni wanted to try it, so they did.

"There's not much in it now," Luke said, as they gazed round the old loft conversion. "It was your grandad's office before he retired then Uncle Harry used it to hang out in with his mates, before going to uni. Look, it's still got some Heavy Metal posters on the wall. They say he was a bit of a tearaway in his youth."

"What's *tearaway*?" Henni asked. It wasn't a word she'd come across before.

"Sorry, your English is so good I forgot you were a foreigner," he replied somewhat crassly. Searching for another word that would fit, only *scallywag*, which he knew was even more obscure, would come to mind. She liked the sound, but was none the wiser as to what he meant. She smiled quizzically at his discomfiture.

He wasn't going to give up and came out with "he was a bit naughty."

She burst into delightful laughter. His heart pounded and he found relief in joining in her merriment.

"*Tearaway* is *scallywag*, is 'a bit naughty'." She continued to laugh. "I like *scallywag* best."

He could resist no longer and kissed her on the mouth.

She nipped her brow and said, "You are a *scallywag*, like your uncle!"

His ardour cooled, they made their way downstairs. When they were outside again she looked at his hangdog expression and said, "*Scallywag!*"

He scratched his forehead, which was a habit of his when embarrassed and muttered, "Sorry."

To show she had forgiven him she lightly brushed her lips against his cheek and said, "There."

He made a mental note not to wash his face for the rest of the day, maybe not for the rest of his life.

She allowed him to take her hand as they walked back, but was careful to let go when they approached the main house. They entered the sitting room as Fran was telling Harry that he had a poster just like the one Peter had on his bedroom wall. Henni froze in her tracks and stood quite still by the door, the colour drained from her face. Franz's stony eyes flicked from her to Harry.

"It is from your ex… exbilitition… *vŷstava,* that I will see in Prague!" Fran was saying.

"My exhibition?" Noticing everything and thinking very quickly, Harry put two and two together, and said, "No, that's not possible. They aren't on sale anywhere. Where did you get it?"

"I get mine in from a museum in Paris."

"How?"

"The man give it to me, because I could not go to the *vŷstava.*"

"Were you the boy the curator told me was ill?" Harry asked with just a soupçon of surprise and accusation in his voice.

"It is Henni who say that," Fran muttered defensively.

"She was with you?" he said looking at her white face. "I didn't know it was you and Henni, or I would have come to say hello. I was going home after my work there. He told me there was a sick boy who wanted a poster, so I said to take down the one he had and give it to him, and it was you all the time! Why didn't you just ask me for one?"

"I not know what it for." Fran's command of English was breaking up under the pressure. "Is a nice picture, I like."

Harry felt he'd done enough. "Ah, well thank you, I'm very glad you like it. I hope you like the real thing as much, when you see the exhibition er, *výstava,* when it goes to Prague in November." He gave the boy one of his best and most comforting smiles, and Fran happily hurried back upstairs to Peter.

Franz had been watching and listening intently. "So, it *was* you I saw coming out of the Museé de Cluny."

Harry's quizzical look was a mirror of that which Henni had given Luke.

"It might well have been. The exhibition certainly was there, and I was staying in an hotel not far away. If you thought you saw me, why didn't you give me a shout?"

'Don't overdo it, Harry,' thought Sara.

"I couldn't be sure it was you," Franz replied.

"Yes, I see. It could have been very embarrassing, for both of you."

'That's it, Harry. Leave it now!' Sara silently pleaded.

Franz thought, 'This man's like quicksilver. Just when you think you've got a hold on him, he slips right out of your hands.' He was no longer clear anymore if he admired or hated him for it. He looked at Henni and saw relief in her eyes as she nervously smiled. His sad returning smile with the slight nod of his head expressed as much shame and apology as a thousand words could. Nervousness vanished and her face beamed with happiness.

429

The doorbell rang. Luke who was nearest went to answer it. Inspector Alec Collins and his sergeant had arrived to take statements. He invited them into the hall.

"Afternoon, Luke. Dad and Grandad at home?" the Inspector asked. James and Michael got to their feet and excused themselves from the company. They closed the door behind them and Luke. "Bloody rustlers, James," boomed the inspector's voice.

The men went into the office. Luke emerged after five minutes and returned to the sitting room with the verdict.

"Two bolts had been sawn right through, but they didn't manage to get more than halfway into the third so they must have run out of time. The inspector reckons because the last bolt was bent and torn apart, the bull must have finished the job off for them later this morning by scratching his backsi— himself, against the gate," he said.

"They must have been damned tough bolts," Harry commented.

"Yeah, they are. Dad bought the new titanium-core kind. The ones with the integral lock and guard plate. There's no old-fashioned padlock on a chain that you can just snap off with bolt cutters. Dad's flabbergasted they got as far as they did."

'Flabbergasted,' thought Henni in glee. 'Another lovely Luke-word,' which she correctly guessed meant 'bewildered'. It also dawned on her that Luke must have been one of the guys on quadbikes who rode to Harry's rescue like Indiana Jones. She hadn't equated the grubby youth with the smart good-looking boy she'd met at lunch. Yet *another* hero. She couldn't wait to tell Anna and Jitka.

It can't have been more than a couple of minutes later that

Michael and James were saying goodbye to the policemen and came back to join the others. If anyone had noticed the secret look between Luke and Henni when he casually sat next to her they didn't pass comment. They were all too busy discussing the attempted theft.

The mantel clock chimed four thirty and Franz, realising time was getting on, announced that they should be leaving. They hadn't planned on staying so late and it was a lengthy drive up to Edinburgh. Henni's face expressed dismay.

"But, *Táta*," she said forgetting herself, "may we not stay a bit longer? Luke was going to ask Harry and Sara to sing for us before we go. I've never heard them sing and if it's alright, I'd should like to very much." She looked over at Harry who tried, but couldn't quite conceal his pleasure at her request, and back to her stepfather, with an expression neither man could deny.

"If they don't mind, but it will mean that we will be very late getting there."

Harry asked Sara, who said she'd be more than happy to sing with him.

Pamela, drawing a bow at a venture, suggested a little timidly, "If you would like to, you can stay here at the Manor for the night. There's plenty of room, we can easily make up the beds. It would be no bother. It's been an exhausting day for you, what with the bull escaping and everything, especially for little Fran. And you've already had one long drive this morning from London… and" – she looked round the assembly – "we would like you to stay."

Franz looked directly at Harry, who raised his eyebrows and smiled a little as he shrugged his shoulders lightly, as if to say why not?

Linda asked, "What do you think, Franz? It's up to you. You're the head of our family."

He looked at his wife and daughter, whose expressions were ones of complete compliance, and quite aware he had been led into giving the desired response said, "If Pamela and James will have us for guests tonight, we would be pleased to accept the invitation." There were broad smiles all round, Franz's big kiss and cuddle from Henni came as a relief and a bonus.

Luke thought, 'I wish she'd do that to me.'

While Franz phoned the Astoria in Edinburgh to explain they had been delayed and would have to cancel their rooms for that night, but would certainly need them for the next, Carrie and Linda went up to the apartment to tell their sons the new arrangements; they were deeply involved playing Assassins Creed Final Solution, which was new to Fran but he was a fast and impressive learner. Fran, like Bill before him, opted to sleep in Peter's spare bed, it would take only a little time to make up and Carrie said she would get on with it, while Linda went to help Henni with her room. Meanwhile the boys continued to concentrate on the far more important issue of the 'Final Solution'.

Pam had given Henni a choice of two of the smaller bedrooms. Linda and Franz were offered what had been Maggie's room when she had been forced through illness to leave Gamekeepers Cottage. It had been kitted out like a hospital for her then, but all signs of that incarnation had been removed and it had reverted back to the old polished dark furniture and chintz character so prevalent in the rest of the house. While Henni dashed about deciding which room to choose, Pamela and Linda were left alone.

"Maggie spent her last few months of life in this room," Pam told Linda.

There were already tears in Linda's eyes when she said, "I'm sorry for all the pain I caused her, you and all your family. Harry and I... we loved one another once, but the marriage was a mistake, we were totally mismatched. It broke my heart to leave him, but I had to sever the bond completely. The way I did it was very harsh and I spent many times regretting... too ashamed and proud to admit just how cruel I had been, until I met Franz."

"You've got the right man now?" asked Pam.

"Yes, Franz and I are good together, we see things the same way, we are very happy. Now Harry also is happy with the correct woman. We are like jigsaw puzzles, we've found the pieces that go together."

"I believe you're right," Pam replied.

Henni came in. "May I have the room with pink roses, please?"

"You certainly may. Whenever you stay with us, it will always be your room."

"Thank you, Auntie Pamela. I hope I get to stay lots of times."

"So do I, my dear," she replied, much touched by the appellation.

Downstairs, Michael and James continued to talk about the rustlers and the advisability of purchasing similar bolts for all the fields. James wanted to see the damage for himself and they invited Franz as well as Harry to accompany them.

The four of them went out to inspect the gate. The vet after his emergency call, had judged the bull to be nothing worse than bruised and shaken, and had given it a sedative before it was transferred into its new pen. The beast looked placid as they walked by, much to Franz's relief, who thought it looked the size of a camper van on legs. The others, even Harry, being much more focused on the ruined bolts, didn't afford it more than a glance.

After they had taken a good look themselves, Franz was given an opportunity to inspect the damage. He was genuinely taken aback by the power of an animal who could snap that bolt, even though it had been cut part way through. The insouciance of the farmers whose lives had been put at risk dumbfounded him, his respect was enormous.

He walked back with Harry and asked, "Does this sort of thing happen often on a farm? Your brother and his son seem to take the danger more lightly than the broken bolts."

Surprised at Franz actually entering into conversation with him voluntarily, Harry replied, "It's all part of the job. Animals can be unpredictable, but if you treat them properly and with respect, they're usually OK. It's not the first time rustlers have had a go and I know from experience how cows are when they stampede. It's people that are the problem, not the beasts. If you are going to keep a bull then you've got to protect it from people. The animal isn't to blame if the protection isn't secure."

"I see. Have you ever had to deal with a bull like that before? Your brother was sure you would manage."

Harry gave a snort of laughter. "James always had more faith in me than I do. That was my first and I sincerely hope the last time I ever have to do anything like that. I was scared

434

stiff... Be honest, were you not scared when you got Henni and Linda out from that tsunami?"

Franz took a moment to answer. "Yes I was, but I didn't have to run towards it first."

Harry smiled. "Look," he said. "We've never really got on, have we? But I do appreciate how you have cared for Henni. She is a credit to you both. As Sara has put it to me on numerous occasions, I get all the lollipops and none of the work, but I'm not completely without sensibility. I won't ask what, but there was definitely something going on between you, Henni and that poster. If it helps, I admit it probably was me you saw leaving the museum, because I left just after the curator took it down for her. She couldn't have seen me, I was in the back office, but I did glance out when the curator came in, and saw a girl who struck me as being remarkably like Henni, who had been asking for a poster for her little brother. That's why I said to give it to her, but I swear to God I didn't know it *was* her, until this morning. I recognised her the second she got out of the car. She's so grown up now, I was still expecting a little girl with long plaits and ribbons... I'm surprised you let Fran have the damned thing in the first place, as it's a picture of my bird. Why did you?"

"I didn't read it properly," Franz confessed, "the lettering at the bottom looked so like trees. And I didn't know until now it was your bloody bird."

"It seems we're both going round with our eyes shut."

"You may be right."

"Bury the hatchet?"

"Just so long as it's not in my head," Franz replied. They shook hands and broke into smiles.

435

CHAPTER FOURTEEN

Back at the house Pamela had pulled out a couple of old photograph albums for Henni to look at. Luke soon joined her as his gran pointed out who was who. As children of the digital age, where numerous images are constantly available and shared, these precious scraps of shiny paper, carefully mounted in albums, held a fascination in themselves. People growing older in stops and starts over intervals of months or even years.

The first album contained some very old monochrome photos, including a little James with his mother and father Arthur. Wedding pictures of Pamela standing arm in arm with her proud new husband. A particularly sweet one of Arthur and James with Pamela seated in front holding a tiny baby Lucy. Also one of Arthur and Maggie standing in front of the Manor porch, which Pam said was taken the day of their marriage. It was the only one they had taken for the occasion. Arthur said they didn't want any fuss. Pam thought Maggie might have appreciated a bit more, not that it was Pam's place to criticise and say so. This led them on to the next album.

Black and white 'snaps' of baby Michael with his sister

Lucy and Harry grinned out at them, then over a series of not much more than a couple of dozen photos they had grown into sturdy children in school uniform and transformed into full colour. There was one of Harry aged about ten standing outside the church porch in full chorister regalia, proudly showing off his soloist medal. There was Lucy, Harry and Michael holding a First Prize rosette for a miniature garden they'd made to exhibit in the local Agricultural Show. Another picture of all three together, dressed this time as The Three Supremes for a fancy-dress party, caused hoots of laughter. Separate graduation photos were mounted on the last pages. Pamela had jibbed at bringing out the next album, the one with Linda and Harry together, best save that for a much later date.

The boys upstairs were expressing a need to be fed again. Glancing at the clock, Pamela agreed it was probably time to bring out something to pick at. A full supper was out of the question after such a large lunch, so she opted for quiche, cold cuts of ham, potato and celery salad, green salad with avocado, what was left of the cheese, plus fresh crusty homemade bread and butter. Because she believed they were best fresh from the oven, she quickly made a batch of scones to be eaten with her own strawberry jam and thick dairy cream. If that wasn't sufficient then there was always the apple pie in the larder that could be popped in the oven, it wouldn't take more than a few minutes to heat up.

Another marathon session of eating followed. After coffee, port, brandy and sparkling non-alcoholic wine were on offer. Pamela and the singers prepared the music for the evening entertainment. It was a wonderful experience for Henni, with Fran on one side and *Táta* with his arm around

Máma on the other, sitting together on the big feather-filled sofa waiting to hear her father and Sara sing for her, for the very first time.

After only a little discussion they decided on a small selection from Lehar's operetta *The Merry Widow*. Not originally written for baritone and mezzo, but pretty tunes, which Harry had transcribed into a lower key so Pam might play accompaniment for him years ago, when he had sung for his mother's pleasure. Pamela began and Harry sang Danilo's famous aria 'Then I go to Maxim's', its light-hearted sentiments suiting the singer very well. Sara's solo was the equally well known 'Vilja, oh Vilja' and their finale was the lyrical love duet 'Love Unspoken'. Their audience was entranced and called for an encore, which Sara insisted Harry should take. Effortlessly changing the tenor aria into a suitable key, he gave an unaccompanied rendition of the 'Flower Song' from *Carmen*. Knowing it to be one of Sara's favourite arias, this time he sang for no one but her.

Franz and Linda were astonished by the brilliance of the performance. Not being particularly musical, Linda hadn't taken Harry's singing seriously, she knew he had a 'voice', but never dreamed he possessed such a talent, and felt not a little ashamed of her ignorance.

Henni just about burst with pride as Luke gave her a sideways look that said 'I told you so.'

The young boys were taken off for baths and bed by Carrie and Linda who came back down within half an hour.

The evening was warm, the darkening sky bright with stars, Luke was known to be keen on astrology and had a telescope.

He asked Henni if she would like to star watch with him. Both Franz and Harry's faces expressed an interest in joining them, but both their women caught their eye and a tiny shake of the head indicated that they might not be wanted. Henni said, "That would be very nice" and looked at both fathers in turn for permission. Like Tweedledum and Tweedledee, looking glum they nodded assent together. After the pair left, "You don't suppose…?" Harry asked for both of them. The women all nodded 'Yes'. "Bloody hell," was all he could think to say.

Outside, alone again at last, Luke sat beside Henni on the garden bench, he pointed out the Plough, Orion's Belt and the Pole Star.

"And look," he said. "There, you see that big bright one, that's called the Evening star. It's not a really a star though, it's the planet Venus. Beautiful isn't it?" She thought it was.

They sat in silence staring up at the sky. He reached out and held her hand, she turned her dazzling smile on him and then returned her gaze to the heavens.

"It's my school prom in just over a week. If you're still here in England, would you come to it with me?" he said.

"What is a prom?"

"It's a kind of special party, where we dress up really smart and dance a lot. It should be good."

"You will have to ask *Táta*. If he says I may, then I should like to."

"What about your mother?"

"She'll agree, if he does."

"Do I have to ask Uncle Harry, as well?"

"I think so."

"Will they let you?"

"We'll see."

Henni thought going to the prom was a lovely idea. It was the first time a boy had asked her out on a date and she really wanted to go, but wasn't at all certain of how they, especially her stepfather, might react. She would much rather let Luke take any flak that might be forthcoming.

"Will you call me a scallywag if I was to kiss you again?"

"Not if you ask me first."

"May I kiss you?"

"If you would really like to." Unsure of what to do, she half smiled and he took his gentle innocent kiss.

"Thank you," he said.

Suddenly feeling shy, Henni said, "I think we ought to go back."

"OK. I'll ask them now, shall I?"

She nodded her head in answer and held his hand as they made their way back through the garden to the house. They kissed once more by mutual consent, before opening the door to the sitting room.

Silence fell as they walked in.

"Well, that didn't take long," said Harry with a slight edge in his voice which Sara hoped she was the only one to catch. "Clouded over a bit, did it?"

"No. But I didn't want Henni to get too cold," Luke replied. Whether Luke picked up on what she supposed was Harry's meaning and answered in kind, Sara couldn't be certain, but she felt uncomfortable.

"*Are* you cold darling?" Linda asked.

"Maybe just a bit, but it is beautiful outside. Luke showed me the Evening star. It's not really a star at all, it's the planet Venus. It's the same one we can see at dawn, then it's called the Morning star."

Linda had heard that one before. It was one of Harry's lines when she first knew him. It could just have been coincidence... it was hardly classified information, but she issued a coded warning to Harry that she was on her guard, and he had better keep his nephew in check, by glancing at him first before saying, "It is lovely to look at the stars, darling, but you must be careful and wrap up against the night. We don't want anything to happen to you."

"I will, *Máma*."

Luke chose this moment to ask about the prom.

He began formally, "Mr Horbach, Mrs Horbach and Uncle Harry. I was wondering if I might take Henni to my school summer prom. It's a week on Saturday."

Silence.

Sophistication blown to the winds, he gabbled on to the Horbachs, "That's if you'll still be in the country and can get back here for then. I know you'll be leaving soon, but it would be really nice if I could take her. She can meet my friends, I'm sure she'll like them and I bet they'll like her. I promise to bring her home before it's too late and look after her really well."

Her stepfather asked Henni how she felt about going to a dance where she would know no one but Luke. Harry was pretty certain that Franz wasn't too keen on the idea and would say no.

"Luke says he will look after me."

"Well in that case, if *Máma* says it's alright, and if you would like to, you may."

Linda who knew her daughter's character well, said, "Yes, of course. Harry?"

It was his first invitation to join in a parental decision

441

concerning his daughter, Harry should have felt pleased, but wasn't at all, it was harder than he'd imagined. He wanted her to be happy, but he wanted her to be safe. Could he trust Luke? Possibly not. What about Henni? Had she sense enough to not let things get out of hand? He thought on balance she probably had. But great-nephew or not, he'd slaughter the little bastard if he laid a finger on his girl.

Harry nodded and Henni's smile delighted them all. Sara breathed a sigh of relief. Harry could be an awkward bugger at times and she could see he wasn't totally convinced about Luke's intentions. Michael and Carrie too noticed the cool look he was giving their son.

Although it wasn't very late, around 10.00pm Michael and Carrie went up to their apartment, Luke was still talking animatedly to Henni about how wonderful the prom would be. "We even get a limo to take us. We can share with Brendon and his date, if he gets one," Luke added. "What time will you be leaving in the morning? Message me. I'll be helping Dad but I'm sure we can take a bit of time to wave you off. You'll keep in touch, won't you? You won't forget me when you're up North will you?"

Henni assured him she would not forget. She would message him every day.

At 10.30 Linda and Franz intimated it was time for them to go to bed too. As Pamela had said earlier, it had been a long day and they were tired. Henni said goodnight to everyone, and gave Harry a big hug. His smile held a sigh, as he held her face in his hands and kissed her forehead. "Goodnight, Henni, sleep well."

After they'd gone, James said, "It's been one hell of a day, but all in all a good one."

"Would you like us to lock up, as we go?" Harry asked.

"Yes. Thanks. I think Pam and I are getting too old for fraught days and late nights. We'll see you in the morning then. Goodnight." With that they left Harry and Sara to see to the dogs, feed the cats, check the locks and close the front door securely behind them, before making their own way to the cottage for the night.

CHAPTER FIFTEEN

Harry was thoughtful as he opened the door to the cottage. Sara admitted to feeling exhausted and said she would like to go straight to bed. He said he would be up soon and poured himself a drink.

"I'll leave the door open for you, shall I?" she asked.

"Yeah, I won't be long."

Sara stood behind his chair and stooped to kiss the top of his head. He squeezed her hand and smiled. She said goodnight, went upstairs and was soon asleep. She woke with a start, it was still dark. He wasn't there. Putting on her dressing gown she went downstairs. He hadn't moved, the whisky glass was empty but thankfully the bottle was still quite full. As if she'd been with him all the time he said, "I had so little time with her and just as Franz is turning human I'm losing her again, to… to my bloody great-nephew."

Sara settled herself on the rug, and put her hand on his knee. "She's just growing up."

"I don't want her to. When I was Luke's age, no even halfway pretty girl was safe. I thought I had a right to have what I wanted and got my way more often than I should. They meant nothing to me. Oh I might have liked them, and they were fun but it never was much more than that. I should have stopped when I married Linda but… What if Henni gets involved with a complete bastard like me? I don't want someone… defiling her for his own gratification."

"I've told you before you can't change the past Harry, learn from it," Sara said as kindly as she could. "Your daughter has a fair idea of what it would be like to be tied to a man like you were. Her mother's history is quite a lesson in reasons to be careful, and Henni's smart enough to take that on board. She might and probably will make mistakes, but she's a tough little cookie and will survive." Then Sara began to sound angry, "Also, do you think your father 'defiled' your mother? James 'defiles' Pamela? Michael 'defiles' Carrie?"

"No!"

"Do you think you 'defile' me?"

"Of course not. I love you, Sara! But once…" he said softly, "the night before we met Henni for the first time… You can't have forgotten… I haven't."

"No, I haven't forgotten," she replied very gently. "But you've proved in so many ways since, that the defiling agent was never you. It was the wretched bitterness and guilt you'd been battling with for years. I'm sure you didn't enjoy it any more than I did. It hurt me and nearly killed you. But the next morning, Harry, that precious moment when you held me so close, the evil thing was exorcised. It couldn't compete any more. Our love did that."

"I never intended to hurt you, Sara."

"I know." She held his face in her hands, smiled and kissed him. "Finding love can be a hazardous, traumatic business. Some have a harder time of it than others but it's a risk we all need to take because, as we both can testify, life

445

has no meaning without it. Soon but not quite yet, it's going to be Henni's turn to try. You can't and mustn't attempt to stop her. You'd be doing her no favours and she certainly wouldn't thank you for it.

"Stop assuming Luke's a budding Don Juan. After all, he's only asked her to go to the school prom. If he tries anything, which I think is very unlikely, she's sufficiently her father's daughter to slap him down. And would it be so bad if she and Luke really fell in love? He's a grand lad and you know it. Anyway, it's just not going to happen. Work it out. The relationship can't go very far, they live hundreds of miles apart and she's going home soon. It sounds counter-intuitive, but to keep her you've got to let her go. Let her grow up. Franz and Linda know it's inevitable and you've got to accept that fact too."

"I lost her once. I don't want to do it again."

"You won't lose her, any more than when you chose to entrust her to Franz and Linda's care. Do you think *they* would stand by and watch her throw herself away?"

"Her mother did."

"Oh Harry, stop it. Marriage is a leap of faith. Neither partner can be certain they've made the right choice. If you need me to say it, I will, Linda's parents were dead, she was alone when she had to make her decisions. Henni has *three* loving parents with a world of experience between them, to advise, and much more importantly, pick up the pieces should it all go wrong."

"It's all so difficult and uncertain."

"It is, I've been there, done it and got the T shirt. There's no definitive handbook for being a parent, that's for sure. Let her have her brief romance, don't spoil it for them."

"I'd be completely lost without you. Why do you bother to love me?"

"Because I really don't believe you are, or ever were, the irredeemable character you claim. Certainly you have a dark side, but as any philosopher will tell you Harry, without dark there can be no light and I know from experience, you have infinitely more good qualities than bad." She gave a slight shrug and a smile. "Incidentally you are also a very brave man, who not only rescued me from a rampaging bull today, but one who has made my life a joy, and whom I wouldn't swap for one, or even two, of Pam's big cream buns with extra jam. Now will that satisfy you, and will you come to bed?"

"Well," he said with a smile, "there's a testimonial. If it wasn't all true I might even blush." He lifted her up saying, "Me, Rambo" and carried her to the foot of the stairs. "I think you'd be safer walking up yourself," he said, and lowered her to her feet.

"Good idea, Mr Martin."

"Probably, Mrs Middleton." And they walked up together.

CHAPTER SIXTEEN

Not surprisingly Harry and Sara were last up in the morning. Pamela had to ask Peter to run over and knock on the door at 7.30 or they would not only miss breakfast, but Henni and family, who were planning to go by nine at the latest. In fifteen minutes they were at the house and ready at the table. Not long after, Luke and Michael called in to say goodbye. As Harry and Sara were leaving later that day too, it was goodbyes all round. To make up for his surliness the previous evening he said, with a sideways look for confirmation at Franz, "Go on, Henni, you can give Luke a goodbye kiss too." She smiled and pecked Luke on the cheek. They ate a hearty breakfast then Franz and the children went up to their rooms to get their overnight bags.

"Linda," said Harry. "Just to put your mind at rest. Luke's spiel about the stars was his own, he really does know about the subject, my knowledge was only skin deep. What I'm saying is, he didn't learn it from me. He's a good lad."

Linda smiled at him. "You improve with age."

"No really," he said earnestly, "it's true."

"I believe you, Harry. How could you possibly think I meant anything other than what I said?"

He wasn't certain how to take that remark, so gave a weak smile.

"We're ready, *Máma*," Fran said in Czech, as he came clattering down the stairs.

They gathered round the porch.

"See you in a few days in York then. Let me know what time you will be there," Harry said to Franz.

James and Pam waved their goodbyes.

Henni hugged Sara, then turning to Harry kissed him and said something in his ear.

The Horbach family climbed into their car and started off. The children all waved until it disappeared over the crest of the drive.

"OK, Harry?" his brother asked. "You look a bit shaken."

"She called me 'Dad', James. She whispered it in my ear. She said it to *me*. She said goodbye and thank you, *Dad*."

James smiled rather sadly at him. "First time?"

Harry nodded.

"Good feeling?"

"The best." With an effort he brought himself down and asked what he hoped was a rhetorical question. "Do you think the visit as a whole was a success?"

"Fair to middling," he replied. "Thank God for that bloody bull though, that broke the ice with a smash." He smiled as he put his arm round his young brother's shoulders and led him back into the house. Pamela had already put the kettle on the Aga and was ready to pronounce the official verdict.

She turned round slowly as they entered and in silence put a large plate of biscuits on the table. In turn, she presented James, Harry and Sara with a mug of tea each. Holding her own mug, she took her place beside them, cocked her head to one side and looked unsmilingly at Harry, whose equilibrium was wavering badly.

"Now then, Harry," she said, in exactly the same manner she'd adopted when he was a child in need of chastising. Looking away from him to James, she lifted her tea to take a sip. "Now then... even though it took you fourteen years to get her here, we're so happy to have met our new niece at last... Henni's delightful. You do well to be proud of her. It'll be a real treat to have you all home again next week for the prom." With that she simultaneously broke into tears and big smiles.

Harry leapt to his feet to give Pamela such a hug that she spilt half her tea. He turned to Sara, took her hands gently, raised them to his lips and tenderly kissed her fingers. His voice, husky with emotion, whispered, "Thank you."

James strode over to give his brother a manly clap on the shoulder.

"I know it's far too early, but I need a drink," he said. "Pam, tip this damned tea down the plug-hole and get out the Château Lafite!"

L H Smith studied graphic design then worked for a time in advertising before becoming a freelance artist who ran a successful gallery in the Yorkshire Dales. She has shown and sold work in the Royal Academy Summer Exhibition. She also has a degree in Humanities (Philosophy and Literature) and turned her hand to writing in 2013. This is her first novel.

Lightning Source UK Ltd.
Milton Keynes UK
UKHW022245080121
376547UK00006B/105